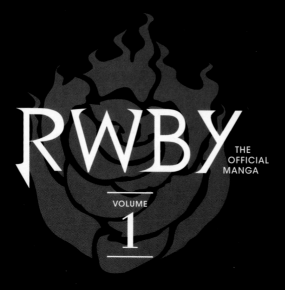

RWBY

THE OFFICIAL MANGA

VOLUME

1

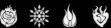

STORY AND ART

BUNTA KINAMI

BASED ON THE ROOSTER TEETH SERIES CREATED BY MONTY OUM

CONTENTS

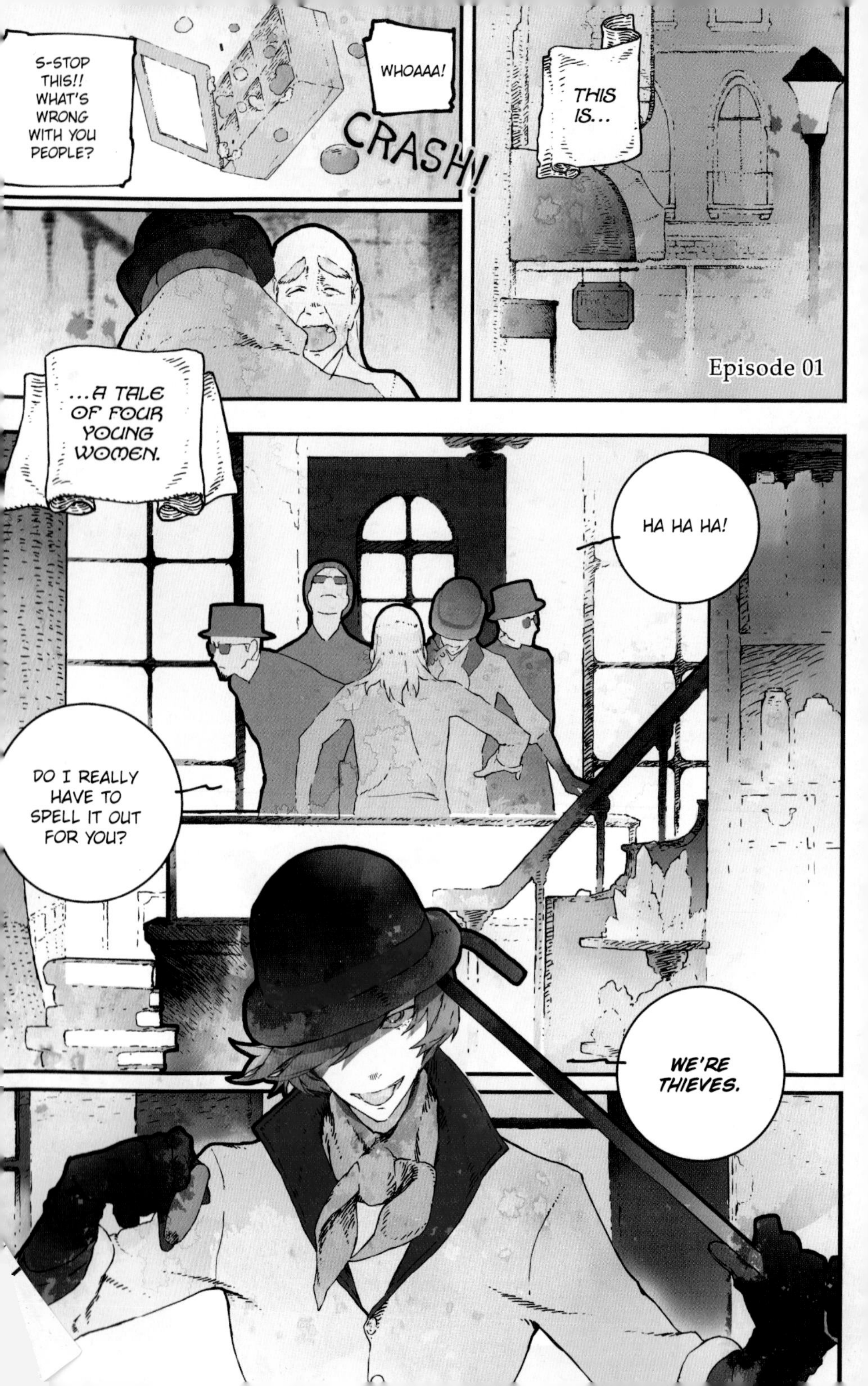
THIS IS...
Episode 01
WHOAAA!
CRASH!
S-STOP THIS!! WHAT'S WRONG WITH YOU PEOPLE?
...A TALE OF FOUR YOUNG WOMEN.
HA HA HA!
DO I REALLY HAVE TO SPELL IT OUT FOR YOU?
WE'RE THIEVES.

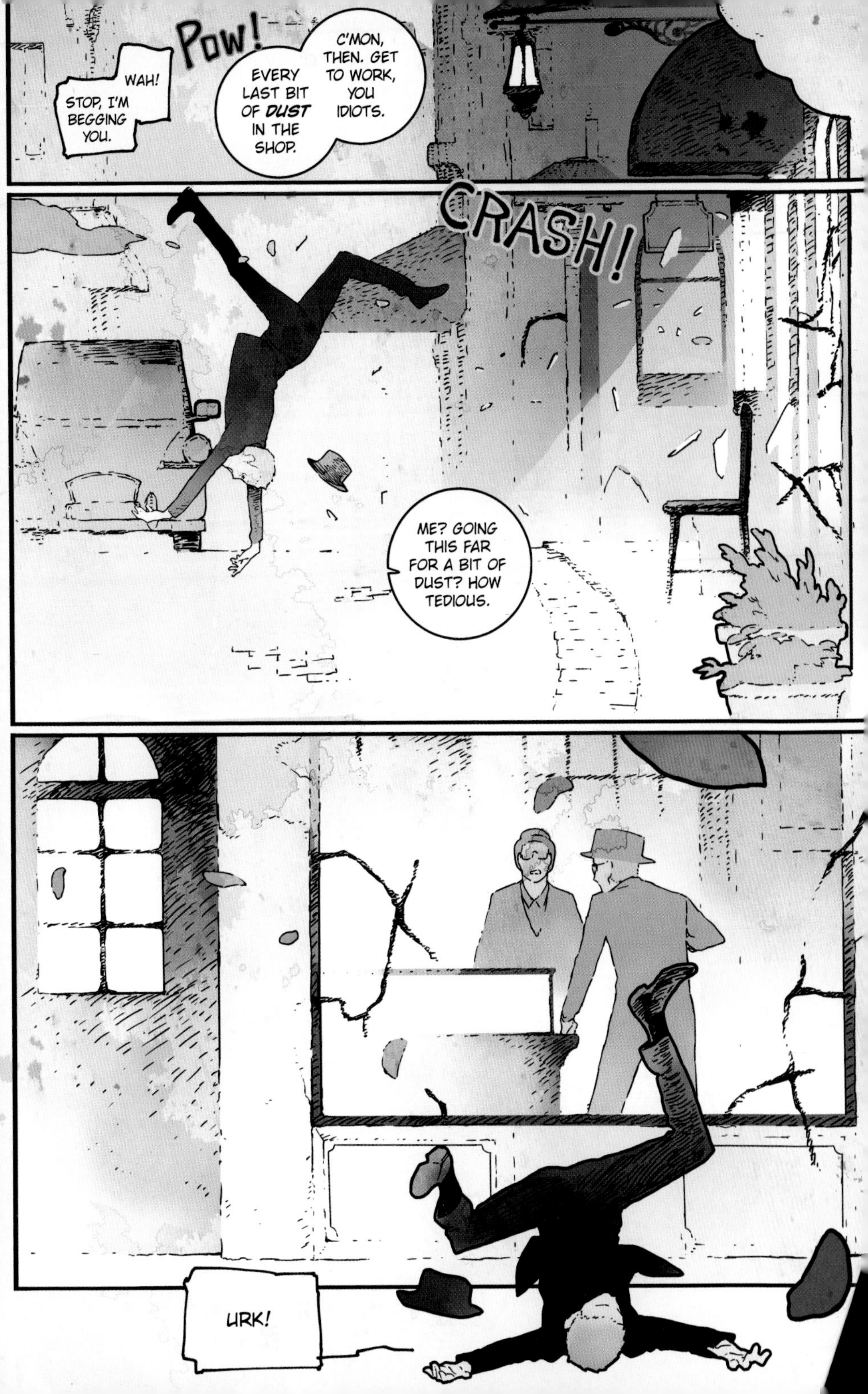
C'MON, THEN. GET TO WORK, YOU IDIOTS.
EVERY LAST BIT OF ***DUST*** IN THE SHOP.
POW!
WAH! STOP, I'M BEGGING YOU.
CRASH!
ME? GOING THIS FAR FOR A BIT OF DUST? HOW TEDIOUS.
URK!

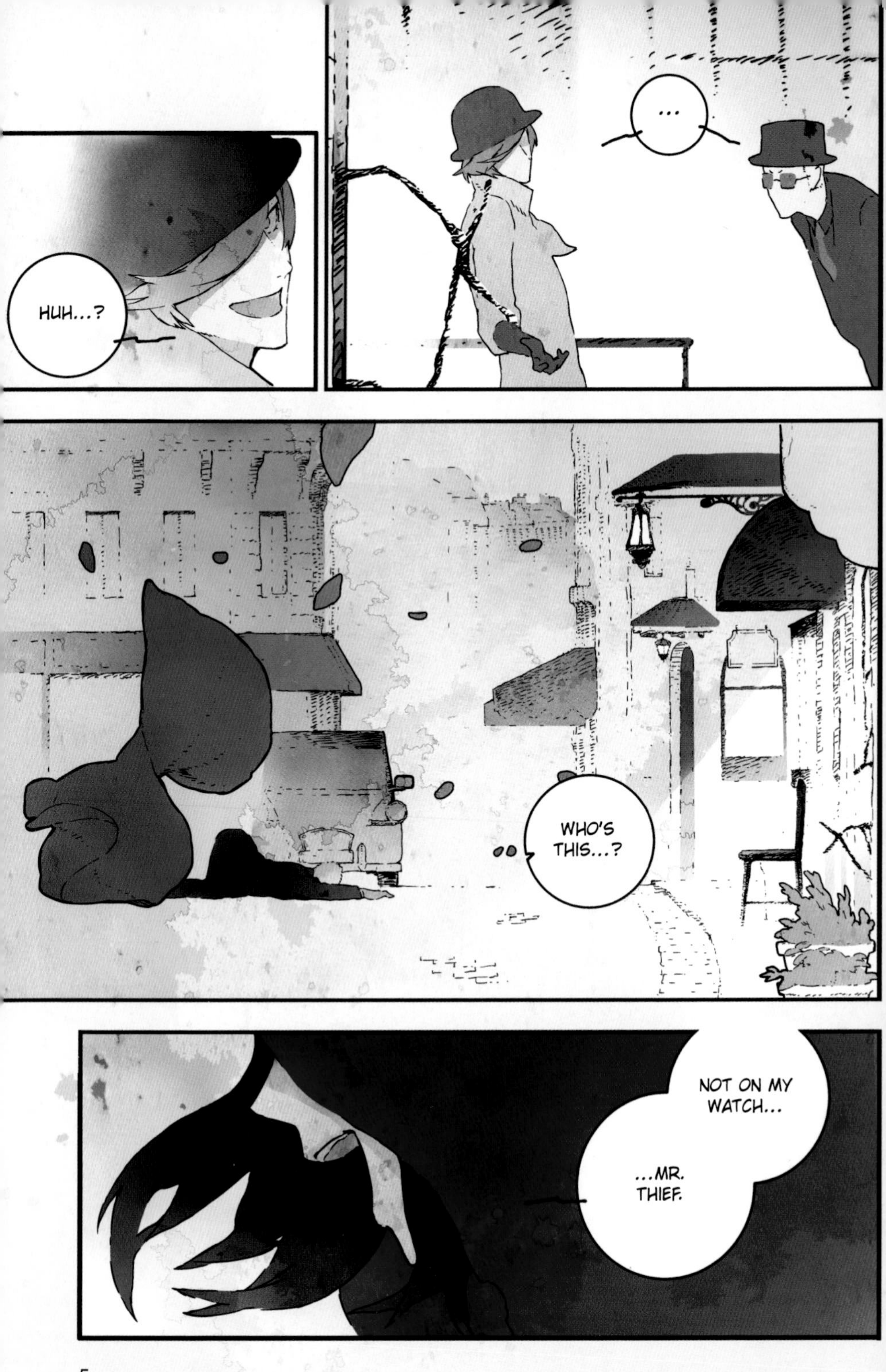
...
HUH...?
WHO'S THIS...?
NOT ON MY WATCH...
...MR. THIEF.

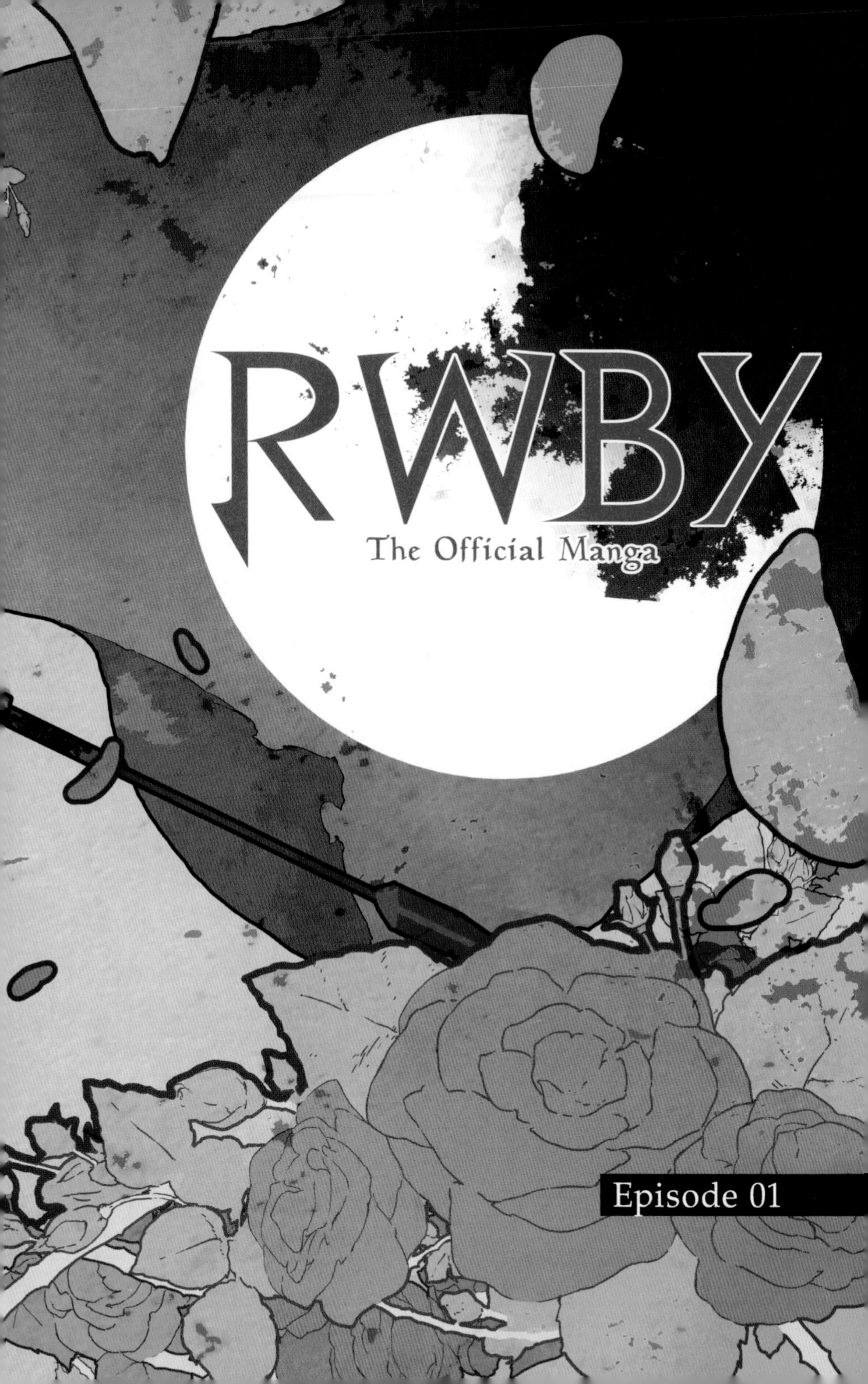
RWBY
The Official Manga
Episode 01

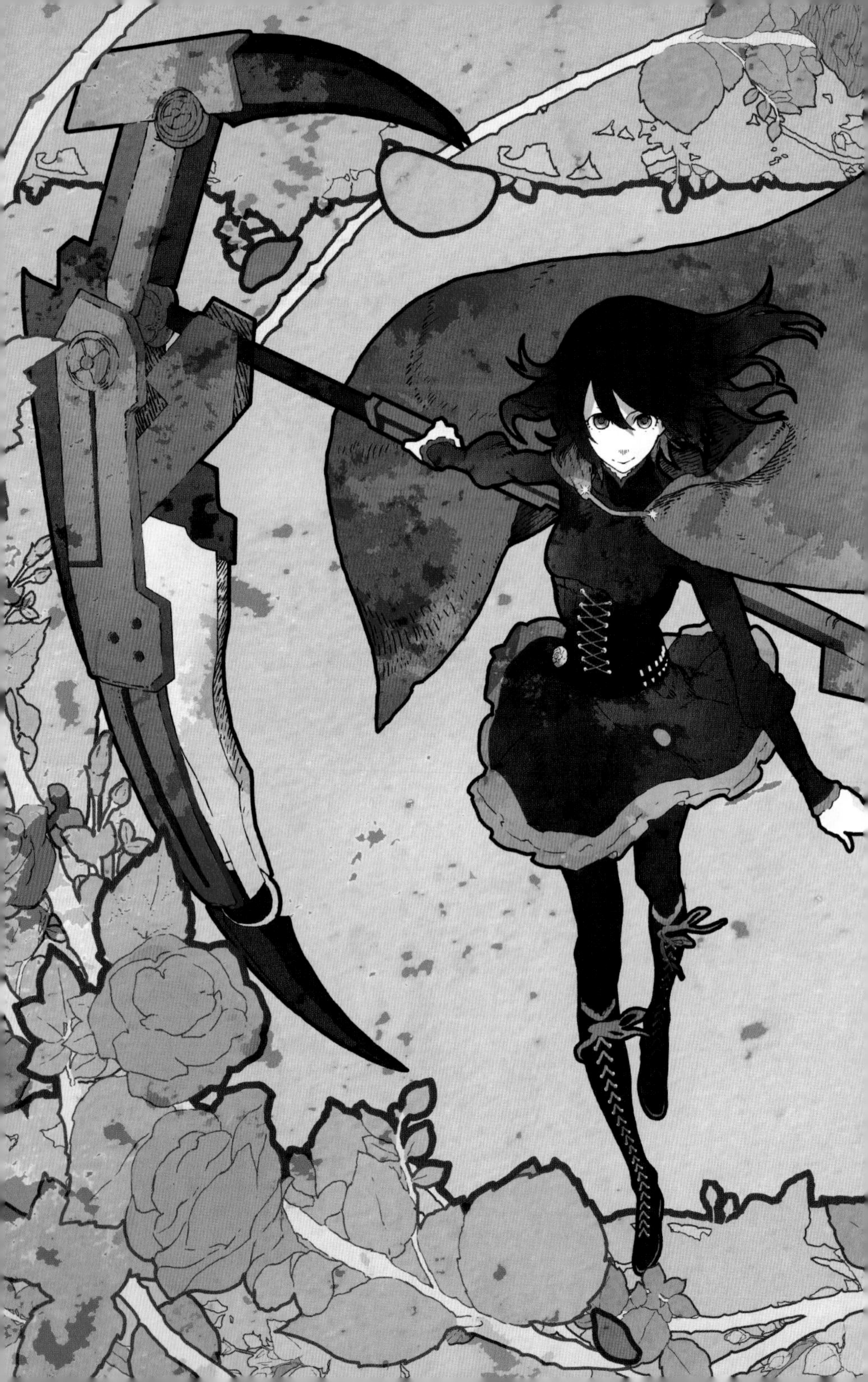

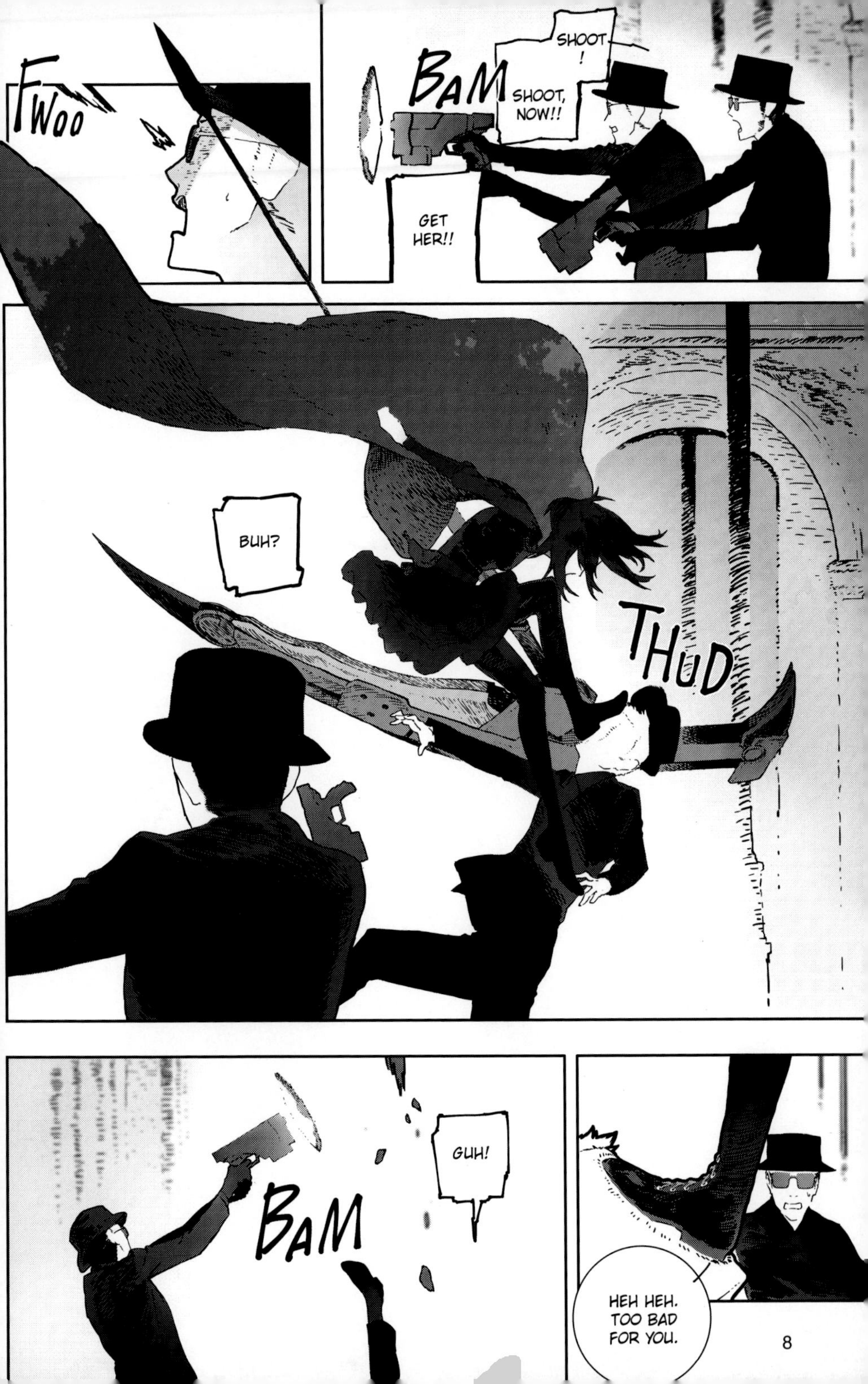
SHOOT!
SHOOT, NOW!!
BAM
GET HER!!
FWOO
BUH?
THUD
HEH HEH. TOO BAD FOR YOU.
GUH!
BAM

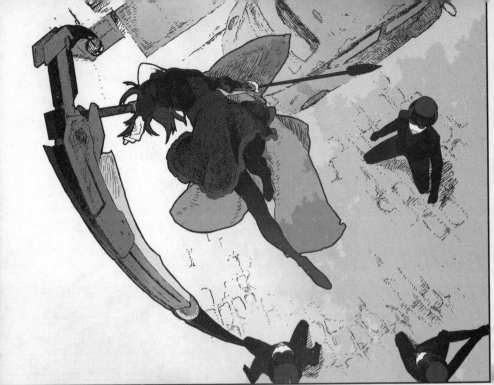

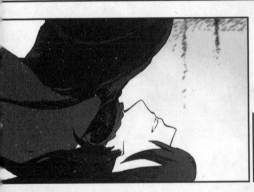

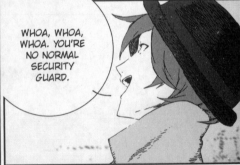

WHOA, WHOA, WHOA. YOU'RE NO NORMAL SECURITY GUARD.

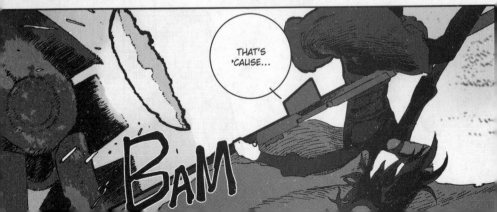

THAT'S 'CAUSE...

BAM

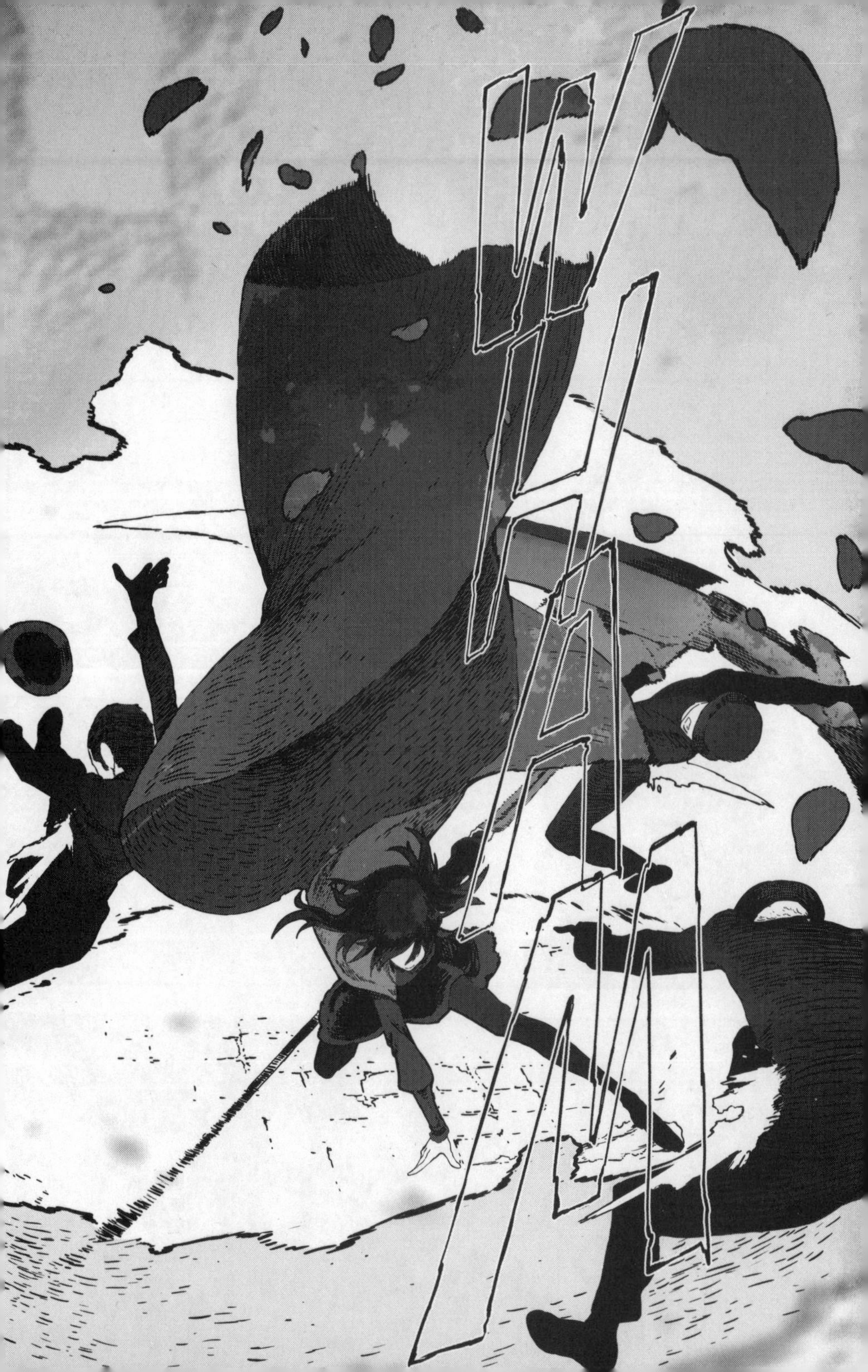

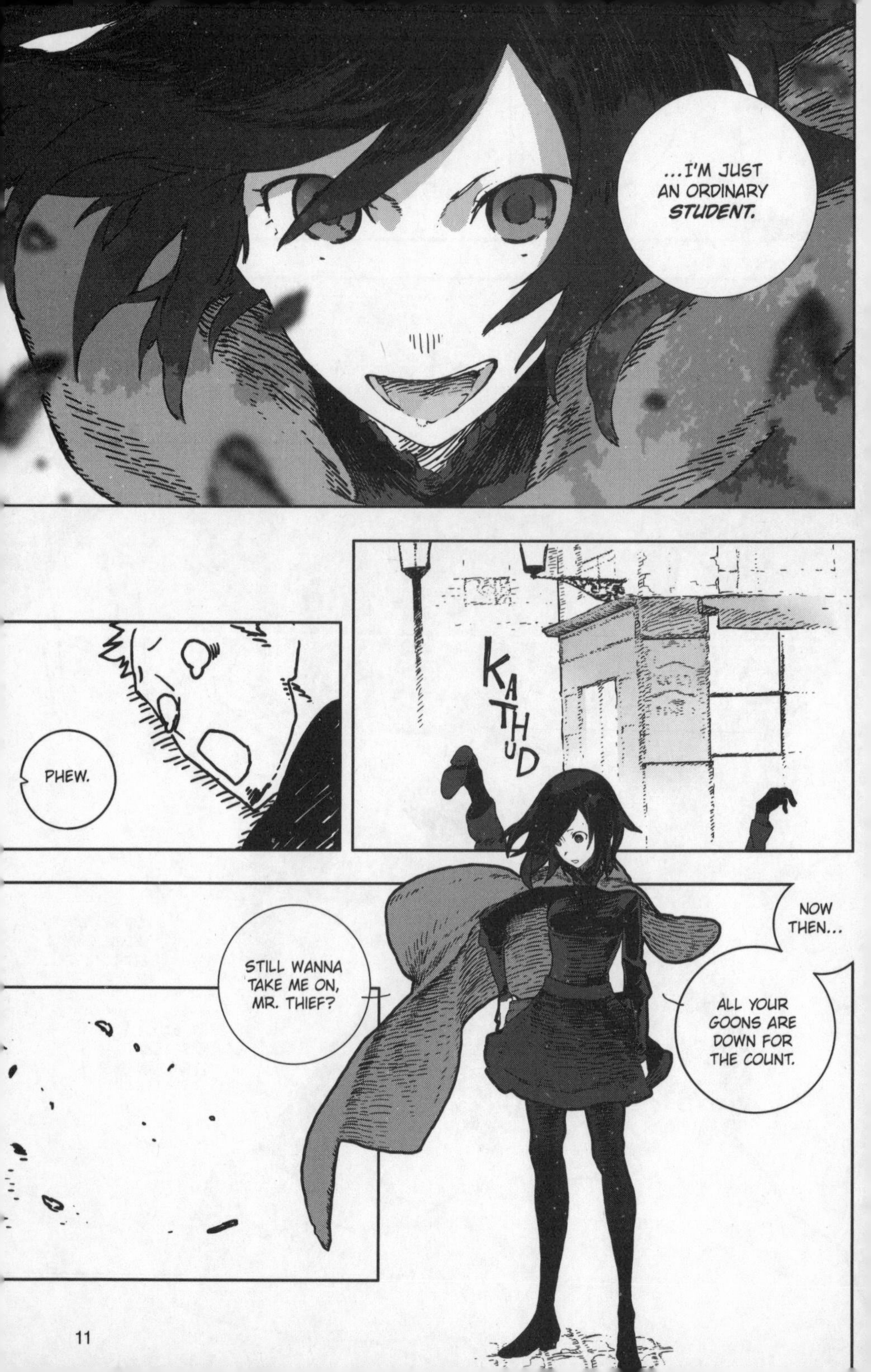
...I'M JUST AN ORDINARY *STUDENT.*
KATHUD
PHEW.
NOW THEN...
ALL YOUR GOONS ARE DOWN FOR THE COUNT.
STILL WANNA TAKE ME ON, MR. THIEF?

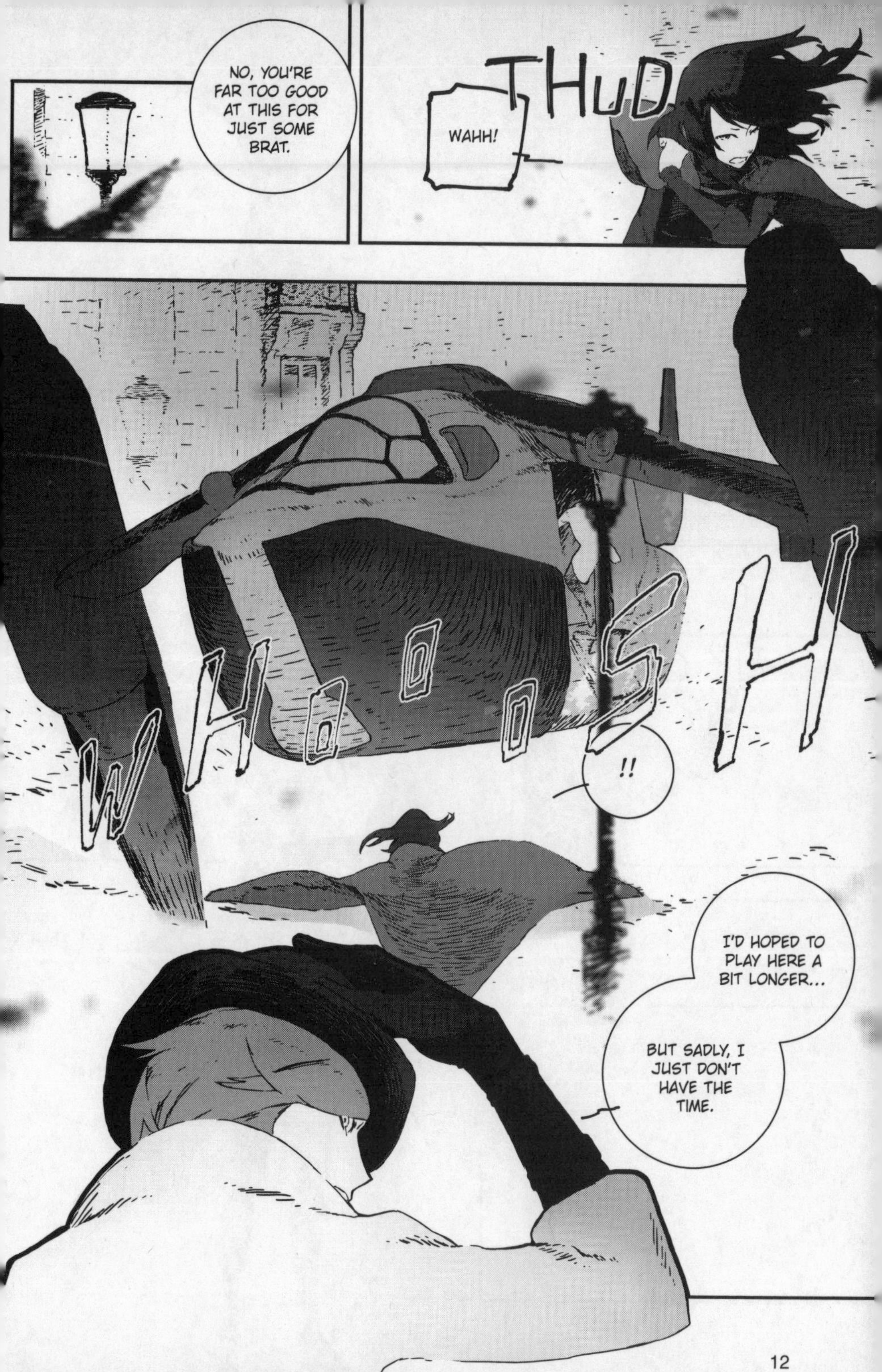
THUD
WAHH!
NO, YOU'RE FAR TOO GOOD AT THIS FOR JUST SOME BRAT.
WHOOOSH
!!
I'D HOPED TO PLAY HERE A BIT LONGER...
BUT SADLY, I JUST DON'T HAVE THE TIME.

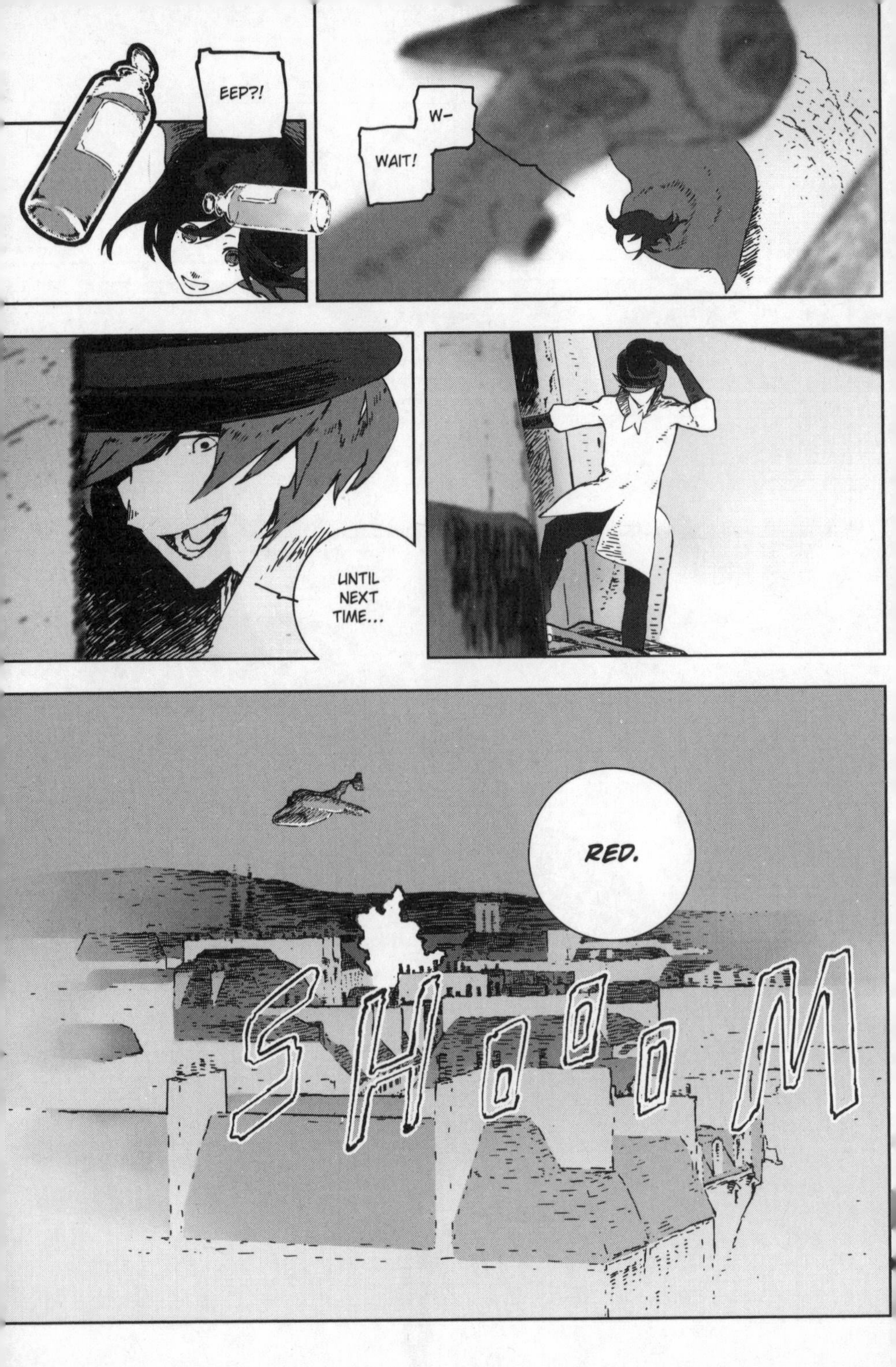
W-
WAIT!
EEP?!
UNTIL NEXT TIME...
RED.
SHOOOM

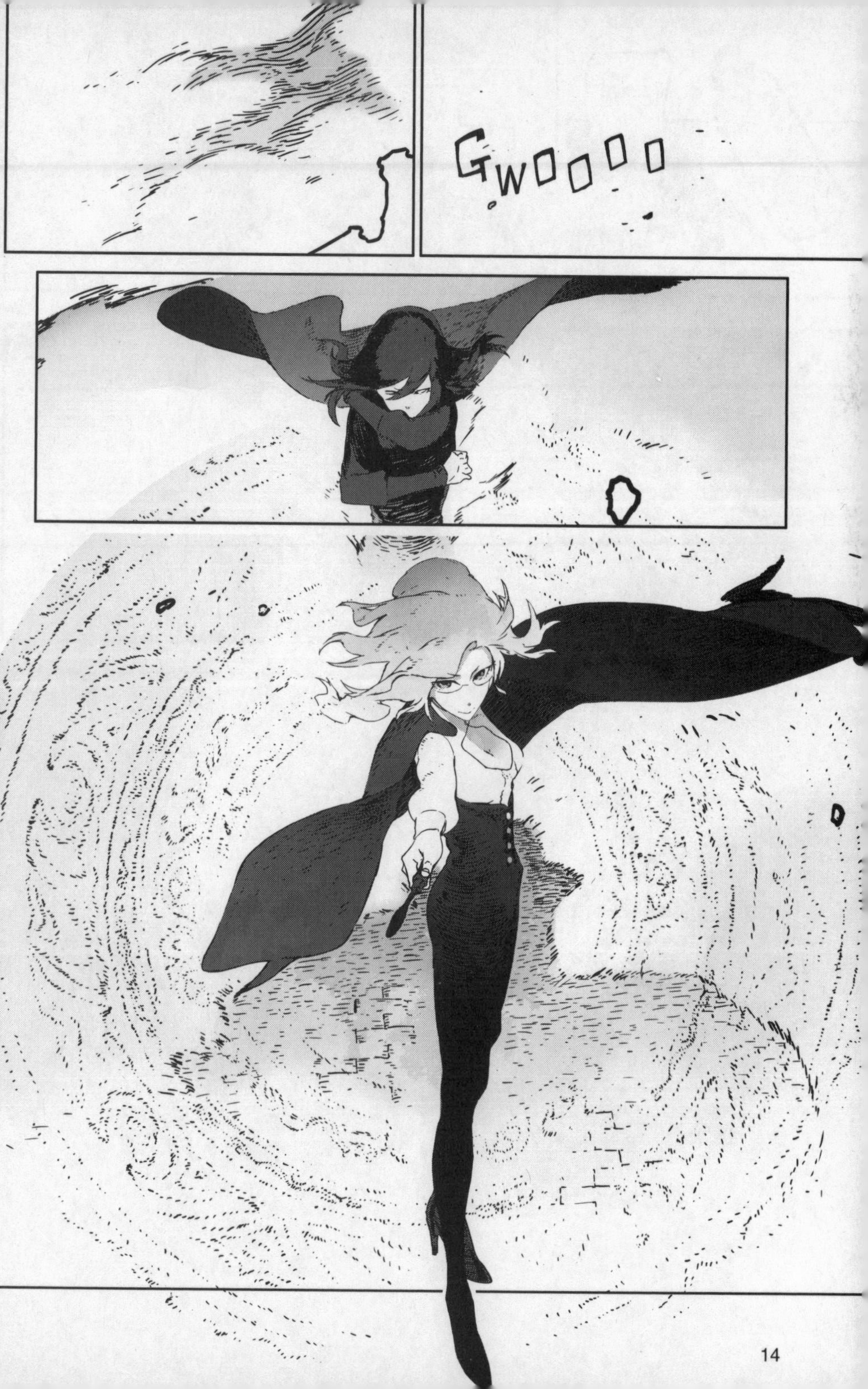
GWOOOO

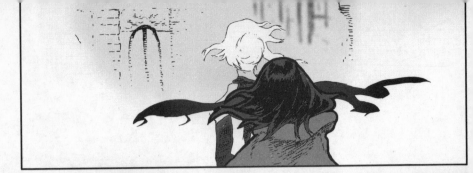

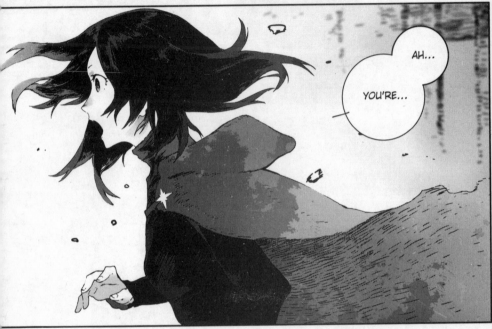

AH...

YOU'RE...

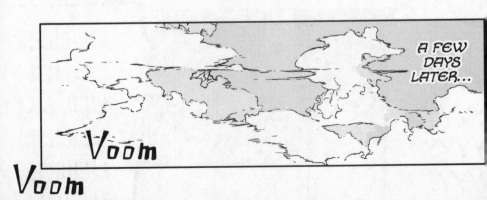

A FEW
DAYS
LATER...

Voom

Voom

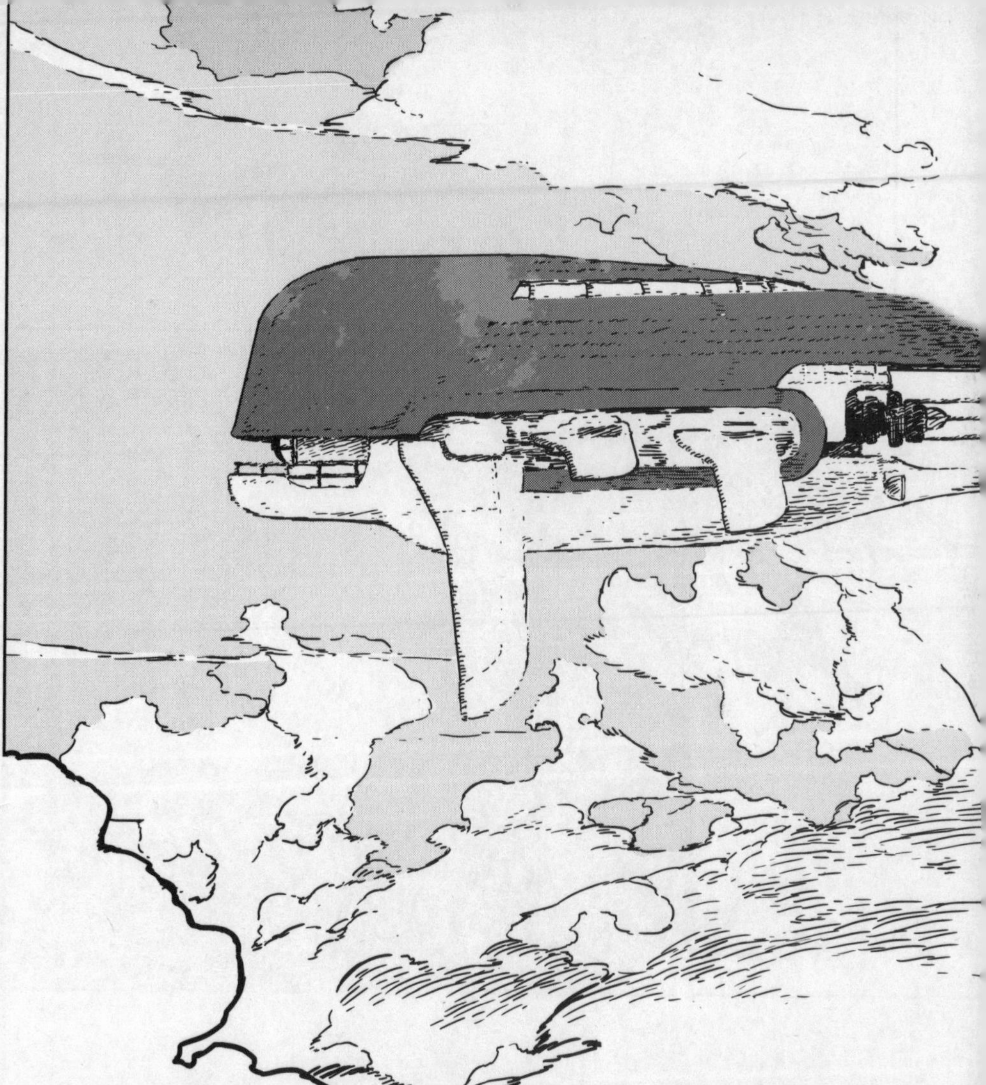

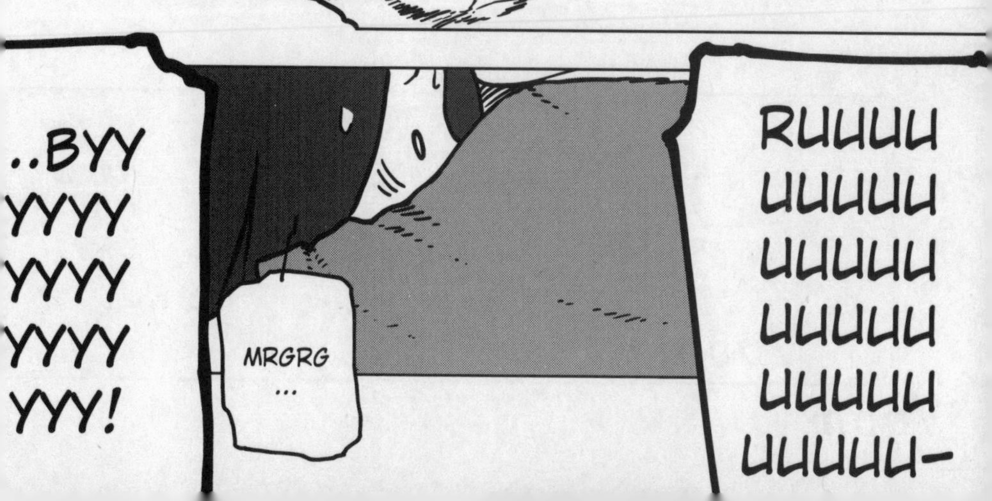
RUUUU
UUUUU
UUUUU
UUUUU
UUUUU
UUUUU-
MRGRG ...
..BYY
YYYY
YYYY
YYYY
YYY!

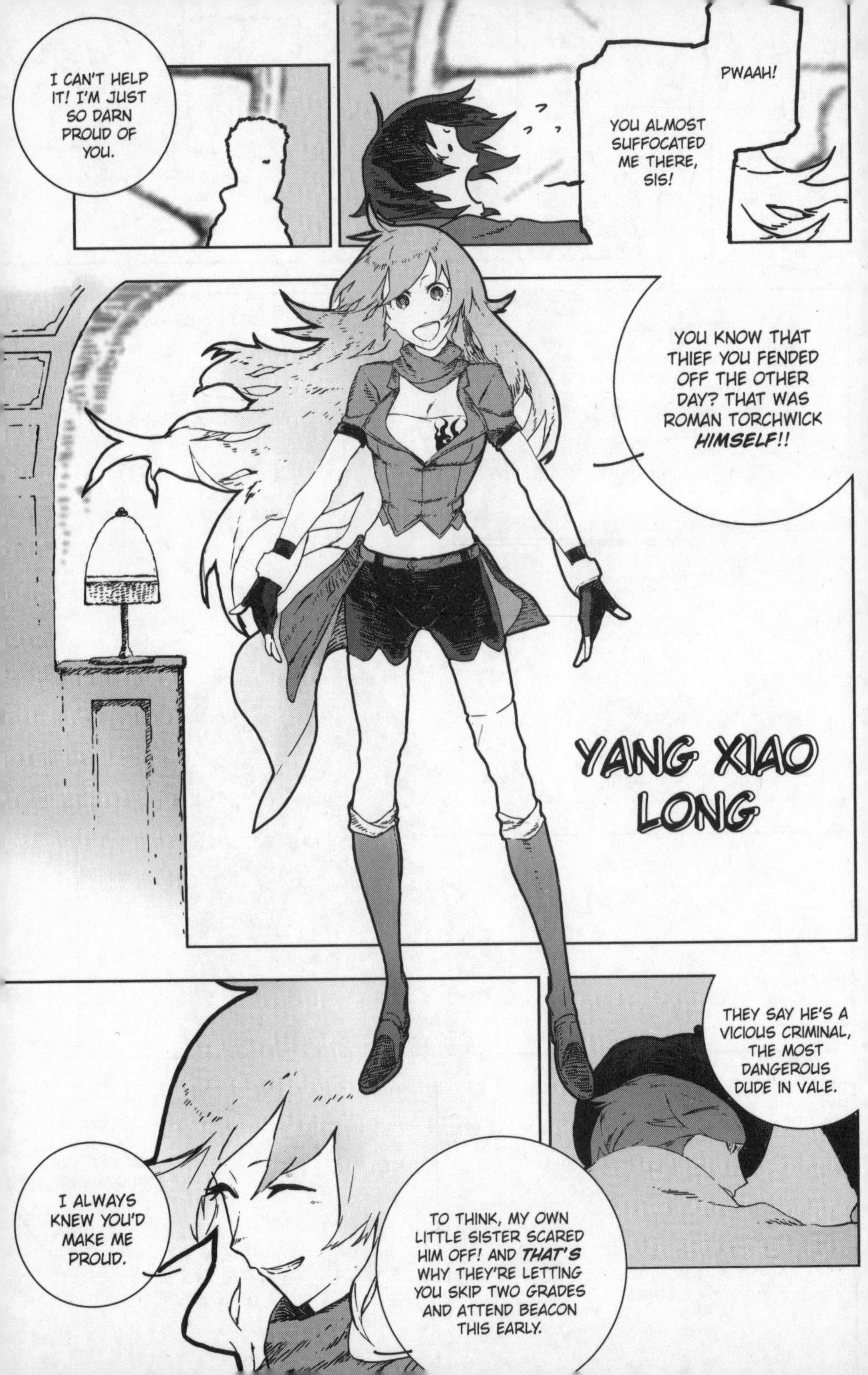

PWAAH!
YOU ALMOST SUFFOCATED ME THERE, SIS!
I CAN'T HELP IT! I'M JUST SO DARN PROUD OF YOU.
YOU KNOW THAT THIEF YOU FENDED OFF THE OTHER DAY? THAT WAS ROMAN TORCHWICK *HIMSELF*!!
YANG XIAO LONG
THEY SAY HE'S A VICIOUS CRIMINAL, THE MOST DANGEROUS DUDE IN VALE.
TO THINK, MY OWN LITTLE SISTER SCARED HIM OFF! AND *THAT'S* WHY THEY'RE LETTING YOU SKIP TWO GRADES AND ATTEND BEACON THIS EARLY.
I ALWAYS KNEW YOU'D MAKE ME PROUD.

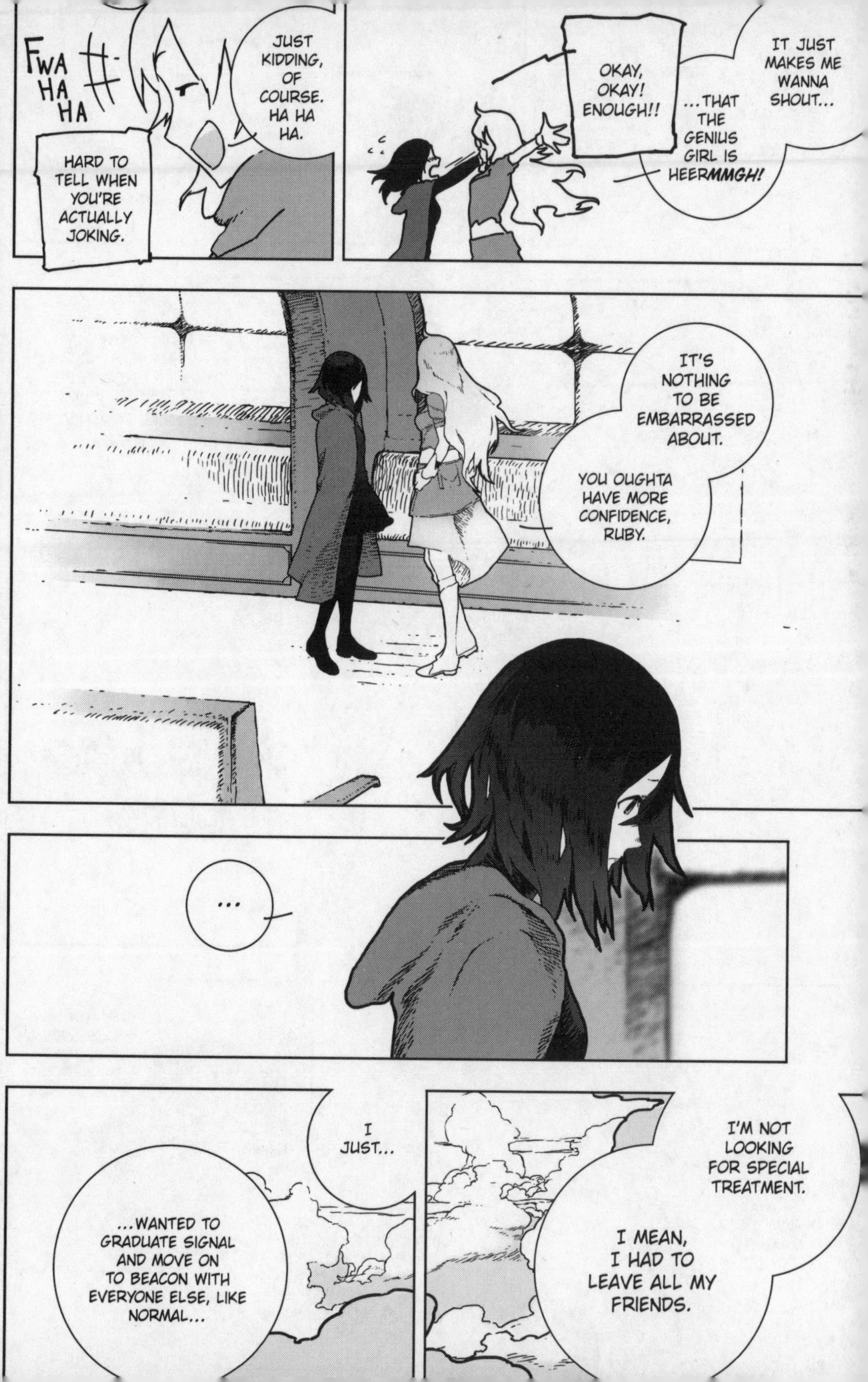
IT JUST MAKES ME WANNA SHOUT...
...THAT THE GENIUS GIRL IS HEERMMGH!
OKAY, OKAY! ENOUGH!!
JUST KIDDING, OF COURSE. HA HA HA.
FWA HA HA
HARD TO TELL WHEN YOU'RE ACTUALLY JOKING.
IT'S NOTHING TO BE EMBARRASSED ABOUT.
YOU OUGHTA HAVE MORE CONFIDENCE, RUBY.
...
I'M NOT LOOKING FOR SPECIAL TREATMENT.
I MEAN, I HAD TO LEAVE ALL MY FRIENDS.
I JUST...
...WANTED TO GRADUATE SIGNAL AND MOVE ON TO BEACON WITH EVERYONE ELSE, LIKE NORMAL...

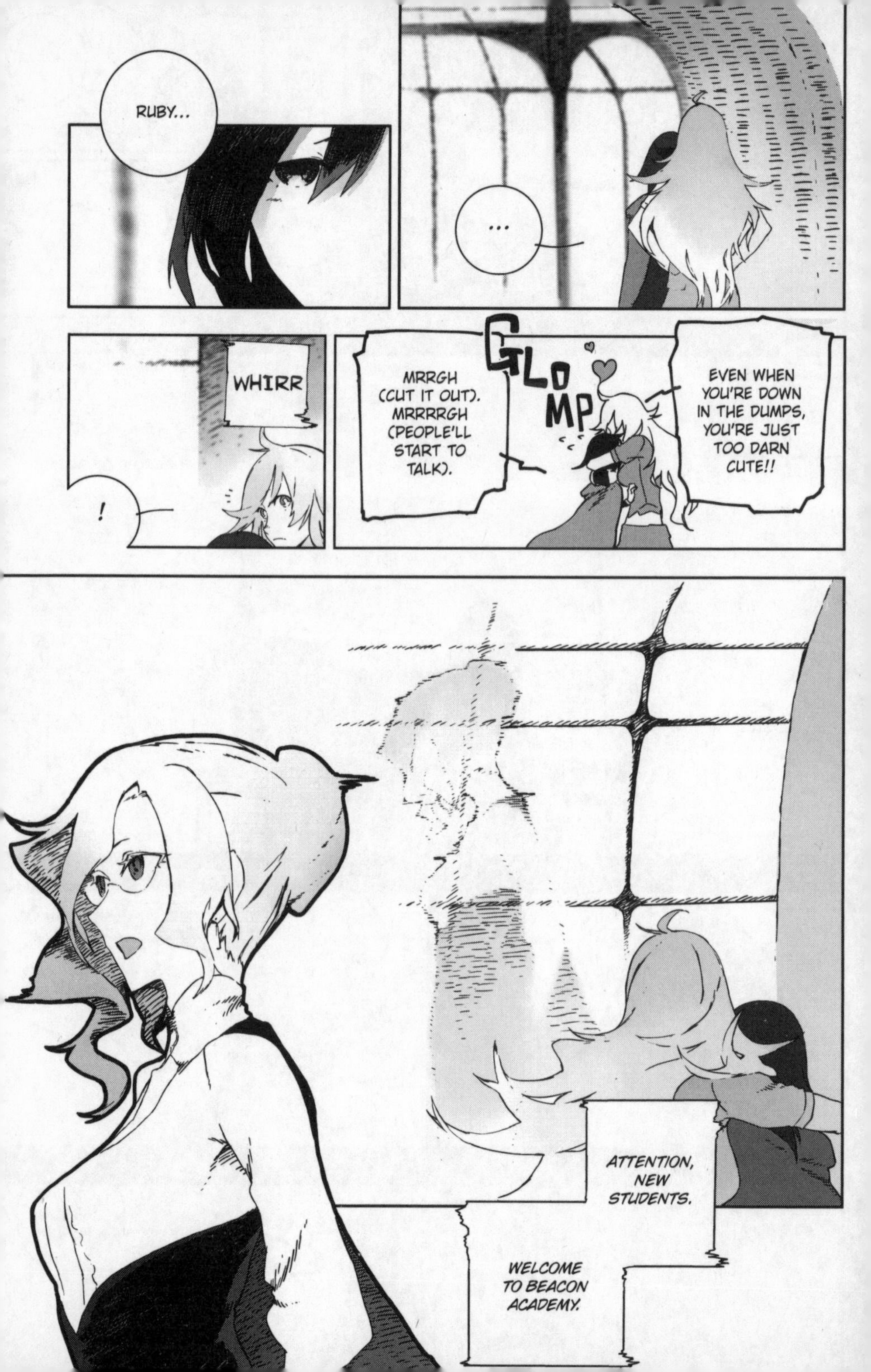
...
RUBY...
EVEN WHEN YOU'RE DOWN IN THE DUMPS, YOU'RE JUST TOO DARN CUTE!!
GLOMP
MRRGH (CUT IT OUT). MRRRRGH (PEOPLE'LL START TO TALK).
WHIRR
!
ATTENTION, NEW STUDENTS.
WELCOME TO BEACON ACADEMY.

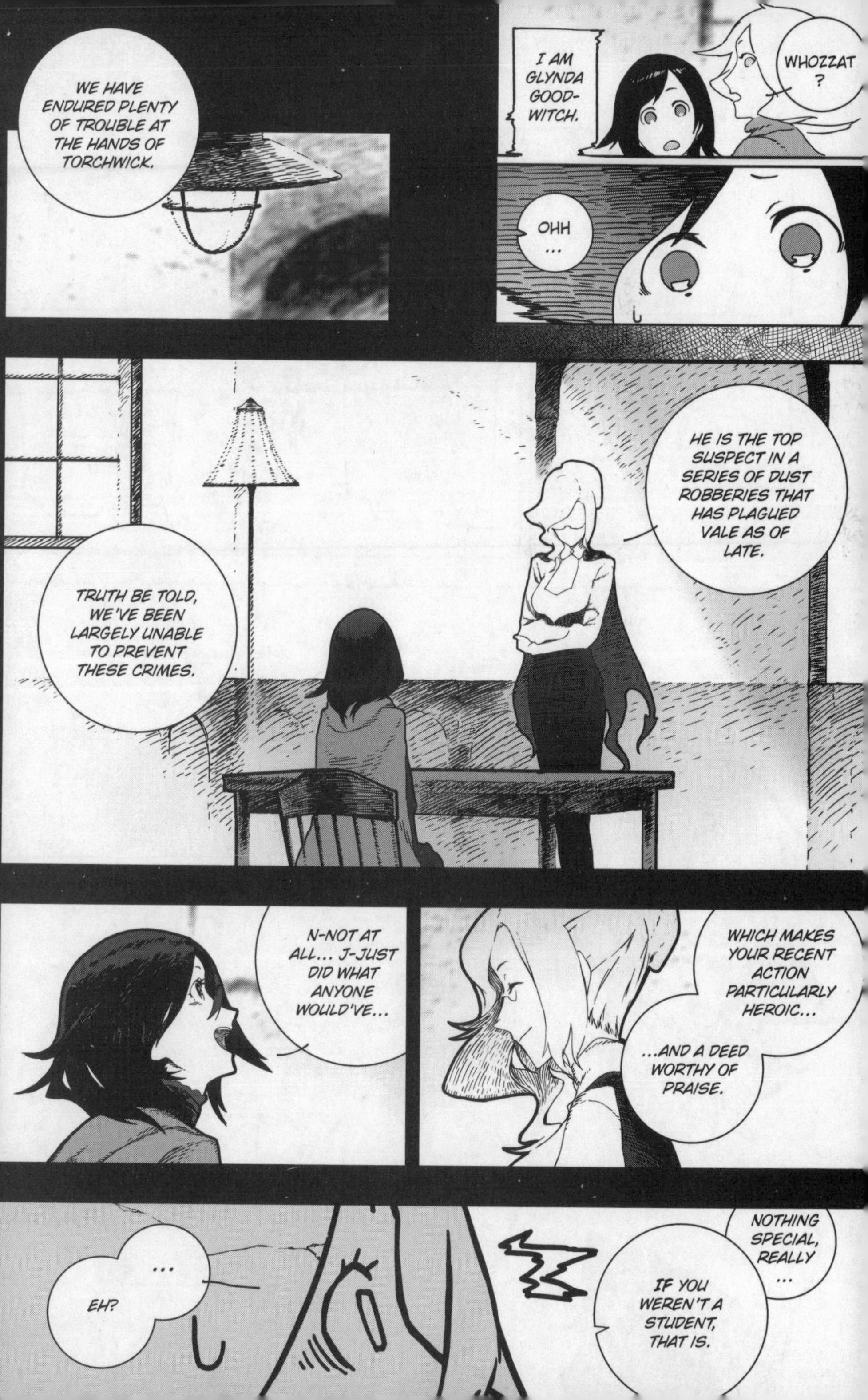
WHOZZAT?
I AM GLYNDA GOODWITCH.
OHH...
WE HAVE ENDURED PLENTY OF TROUBLE AT THE HANDS OF TORCHWICK.
HE IS THE TOP SUSPECT IN A SERIES OF DUST ROBBERIES THAT HAS PLAGUED VALE AS OF LATE.
TRUTH BE TOLD, WE'VE BEEN LARGELY UNABLE TO PREVENT THESE CRIMES.
WHICH MAKES YOUR RECENT ACTION PARTICULARLY HEROIC...
...AND A DEED WORTHY OF PRAISE.
N-NOT AT ALL... J-JUST DID WHAT ANYONE WOULD'VE...
NOTHING SPECIAL, REALLY...
IF YOU WEREN'T A STUDENT, THAT IS.
...
EH?

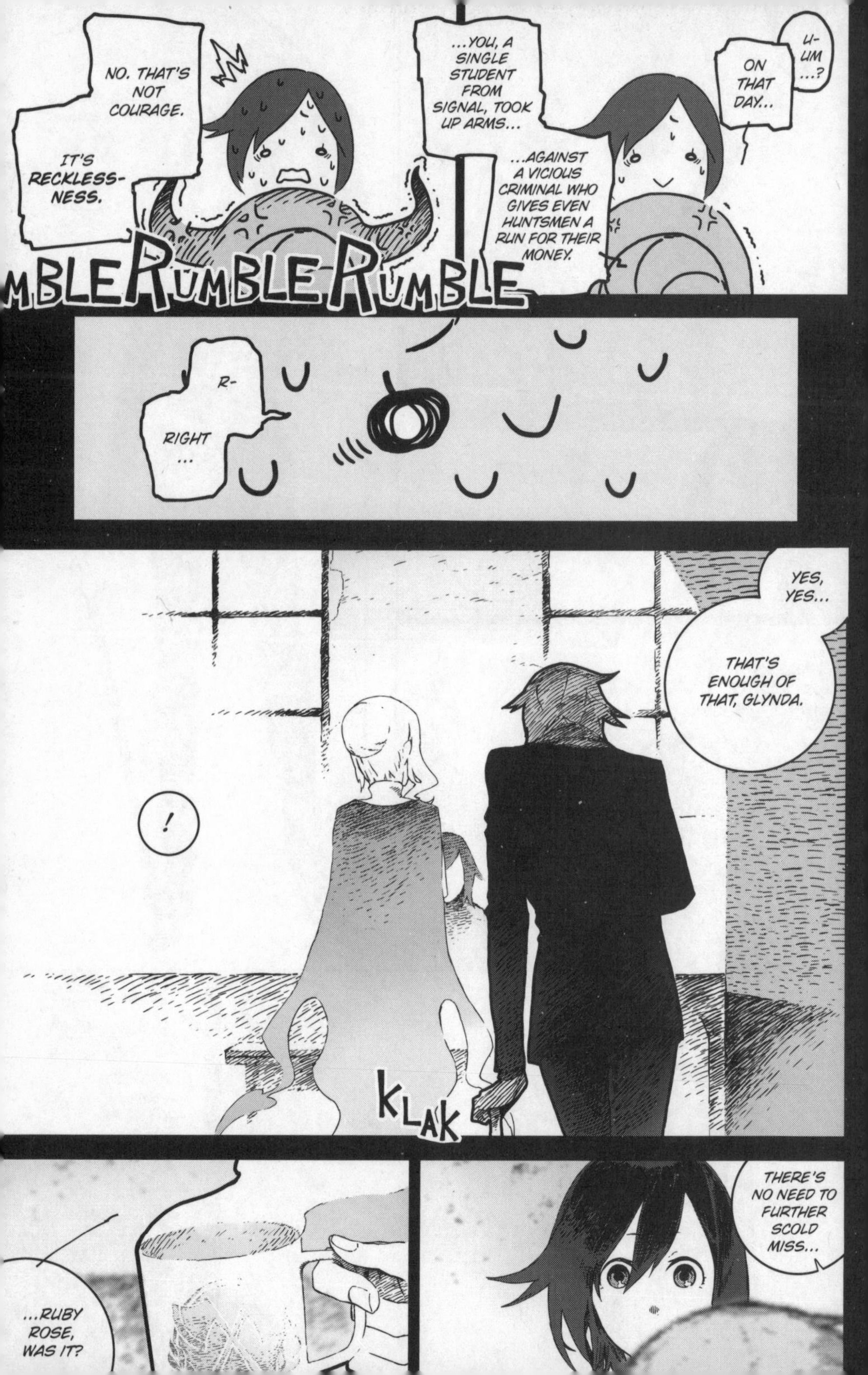
U-UM ...?
ON THAT DAY...
...YOU, A SINGLE STUDENT FROM SIGNAL, TOOK UP ARMS...
...AGAINST A VICIOUS CRIMINAL WHO GIVES EVEN HUNTSMEN A RUN FOR THEIR MONEY.
NO. THAT'S NOT COURAGE.
IT'S RECKLESS-NESS.
MBLERUMBLERUMBLE
R- RIGHT ...
YES, YES...
THAT'S ENOUGH OF THAT, GLYNDA.
!
KLAK
THERE'S NO NEED TO FURTHER SCOLD MISS...
...RUBY ROSE, WAS IT?

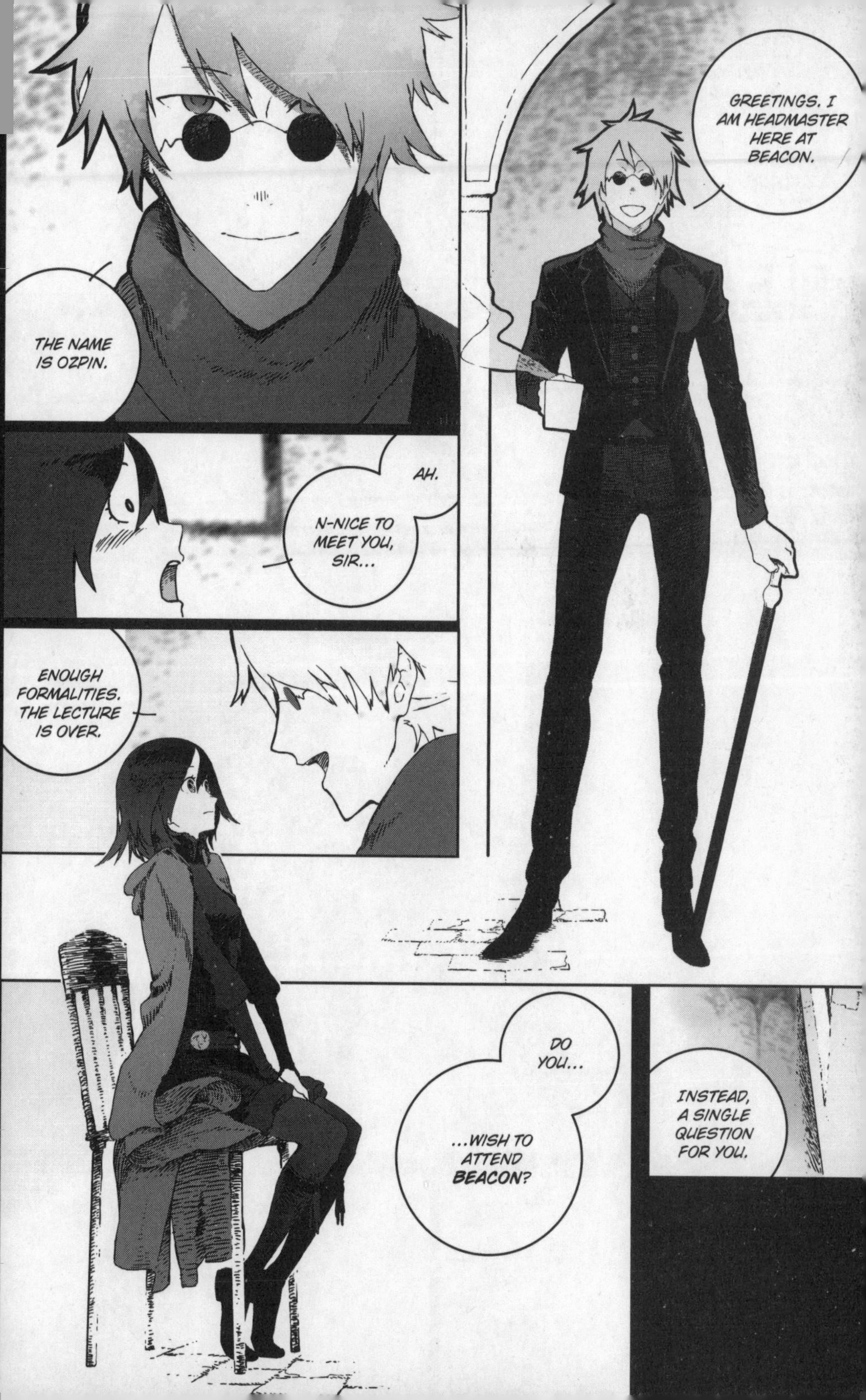
GREETINGS. I AM HEADMASTER HERE AT BEACON.
THE NAME IS OZPIN.
AH.
N-NICE TO MEET YOU, SIR...
ENOUGH FORMALITIES. THE LECTURE IS OVER.
INSTEAD, A SINGLE QUESTION FOR YOU.
DO YOU...
...WISH TO ATTEND BEACON?

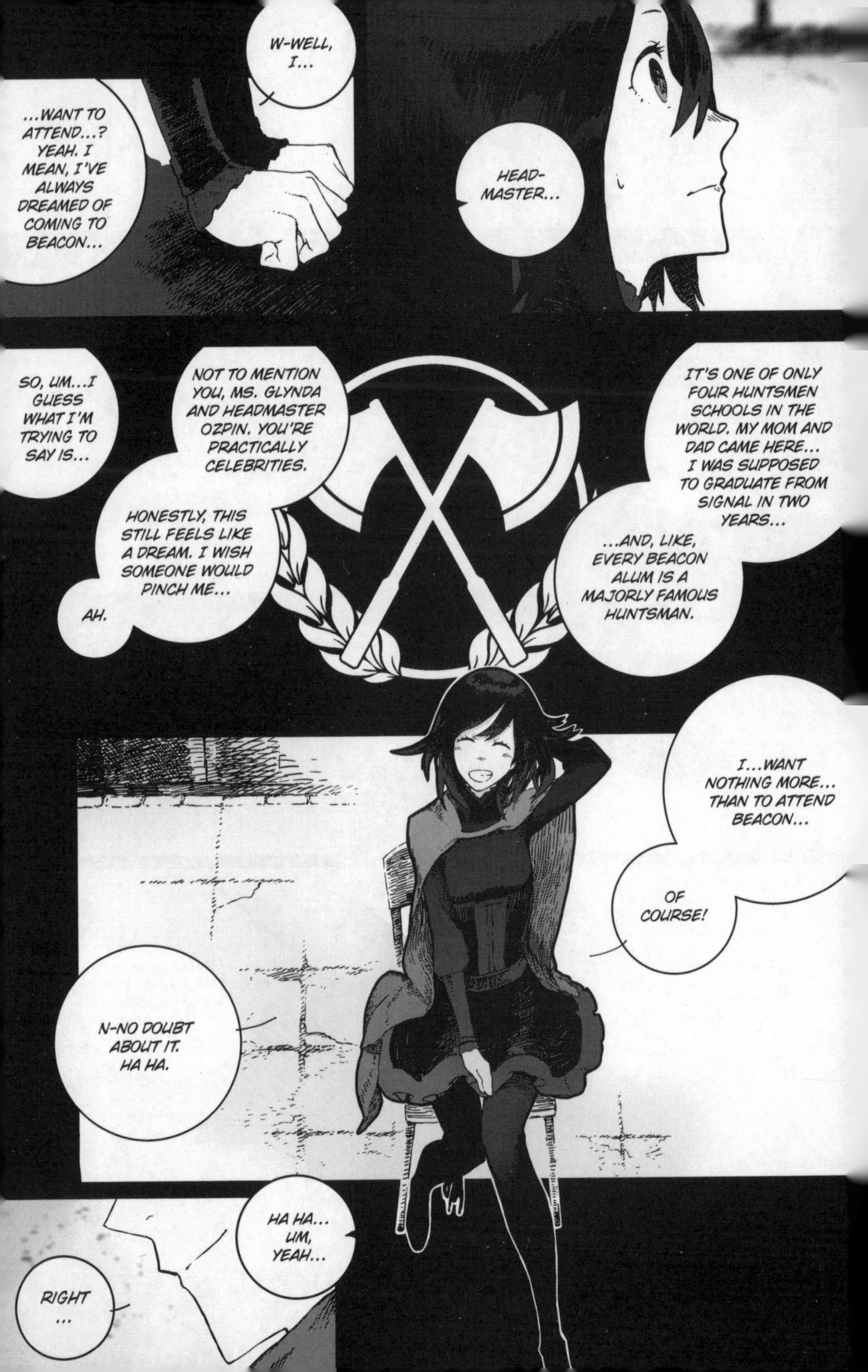
HEAD-MASTER…
W-WELL, I…
…WANT TO ATTEND…? YEAH. I MEAN, I'VE ALWAYS DREAMED OF COMING TO BEACON…
IT'S ONE OF ONLY FOUR HUNTSMEN SCHOOLS IN THE WORLD. MY MOM AND DAD CAME HERE… I WAS SUPPOSED TO GRADUATE FROM SIGNAL IN TWO YEARS…
…AND, LIKE, EVERY BEACON ALUM IS A MAJORLY FAMOUS HUNTSMAN.
NOT TO MENTION YOU, MS. GLYNDA AND HEADMASTER OZPIN. YOU'RE PRACTICALLY CELEBRITIES.
HONESTLY, THIS STILL FEELS LIKE A DREAM. I WISH SOMEONE WOULD PINCH ME…
AH.
SO, UM…I GUESS WHAT I'M TRYING TO SAY IS…
I…WANT NOTHING MORE… THAN TO ATTEND BEACON…
OF COURSE!
N-NO DOUBT ABOUT IT. HA HA.
HA HA… UM, YEAH…
RIGHT …

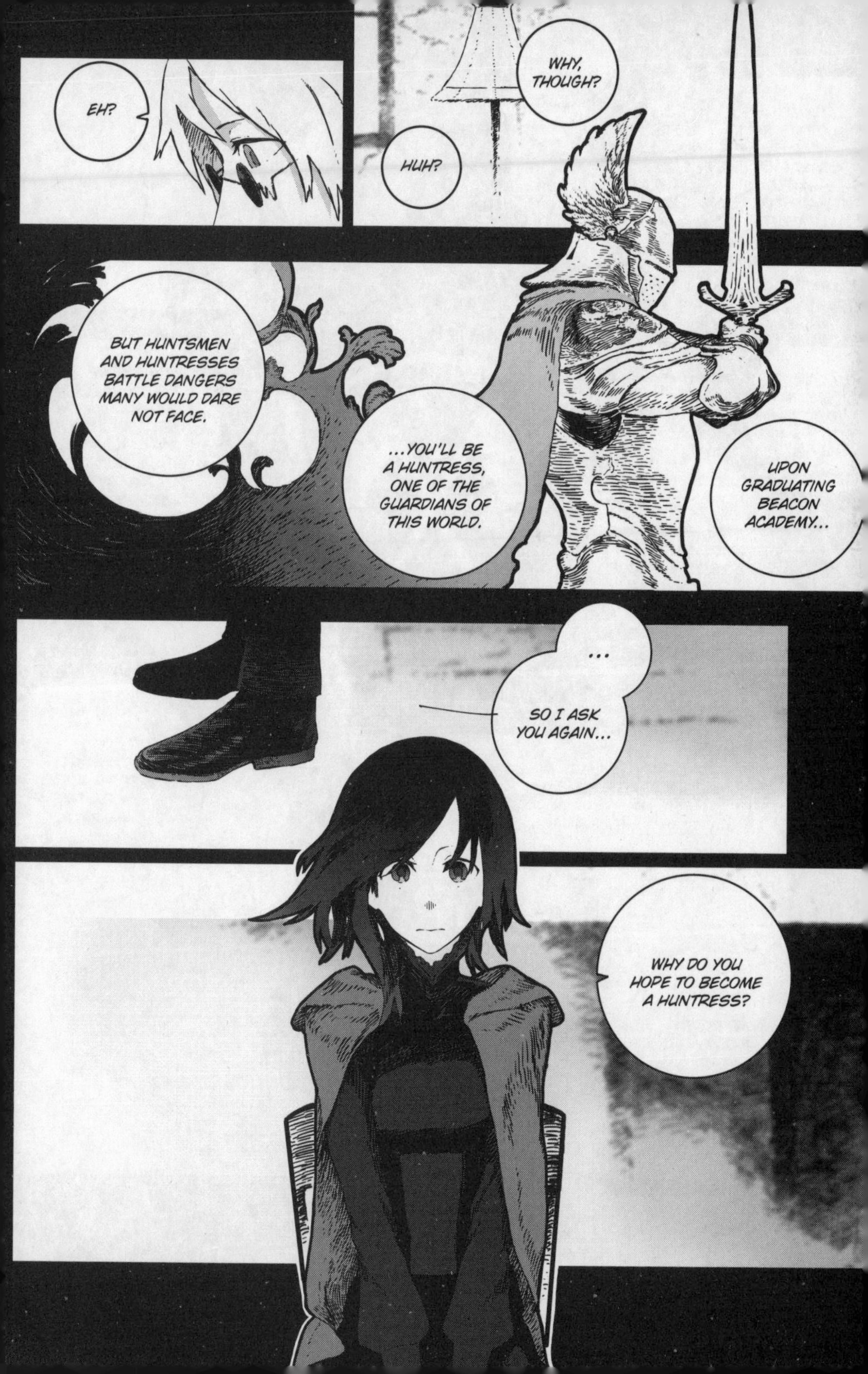
WHY, THOUGH?
HUH?
EH?
UPON GRADUATING BEACON ACADEMY...
...YOU'LL BE A HUNTRESS, ONE OF THE GUARDIANS OF THIS WORLD.
BUT HUNTSMEN AND HUNTRESSES BATTLE DANGERS MANY WOULD DARE NOT FACE.
...
SO I ASK YOU AGAIN...
WHY DO YOU HOPE TO BECOME A HUNTRESS?

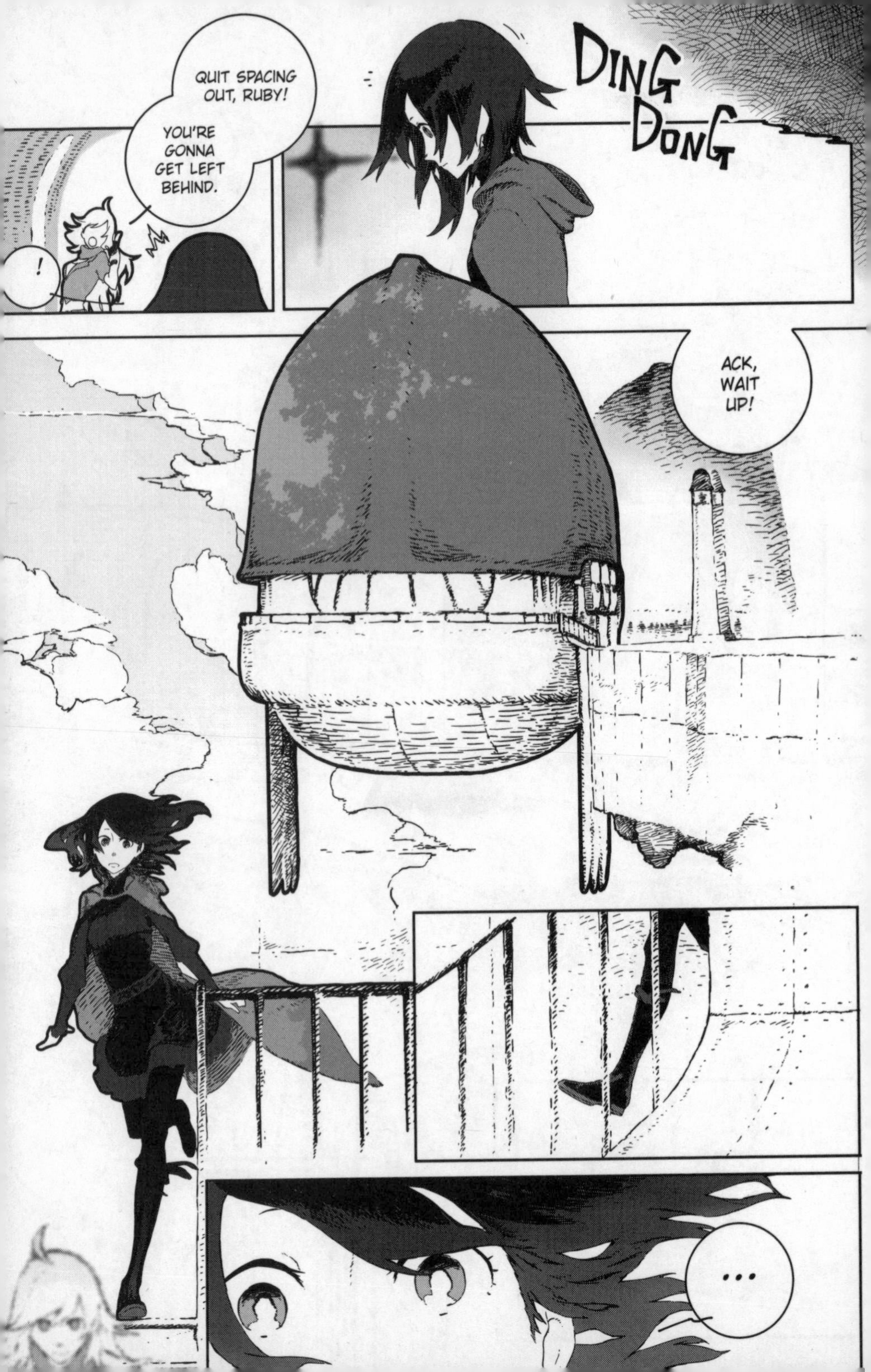
DING DONG
QUIT SPACING OUT, RUBY!
YOU'RE GONNA GET LEFT BEHIND.
!
ACK, WAIT UP!
...

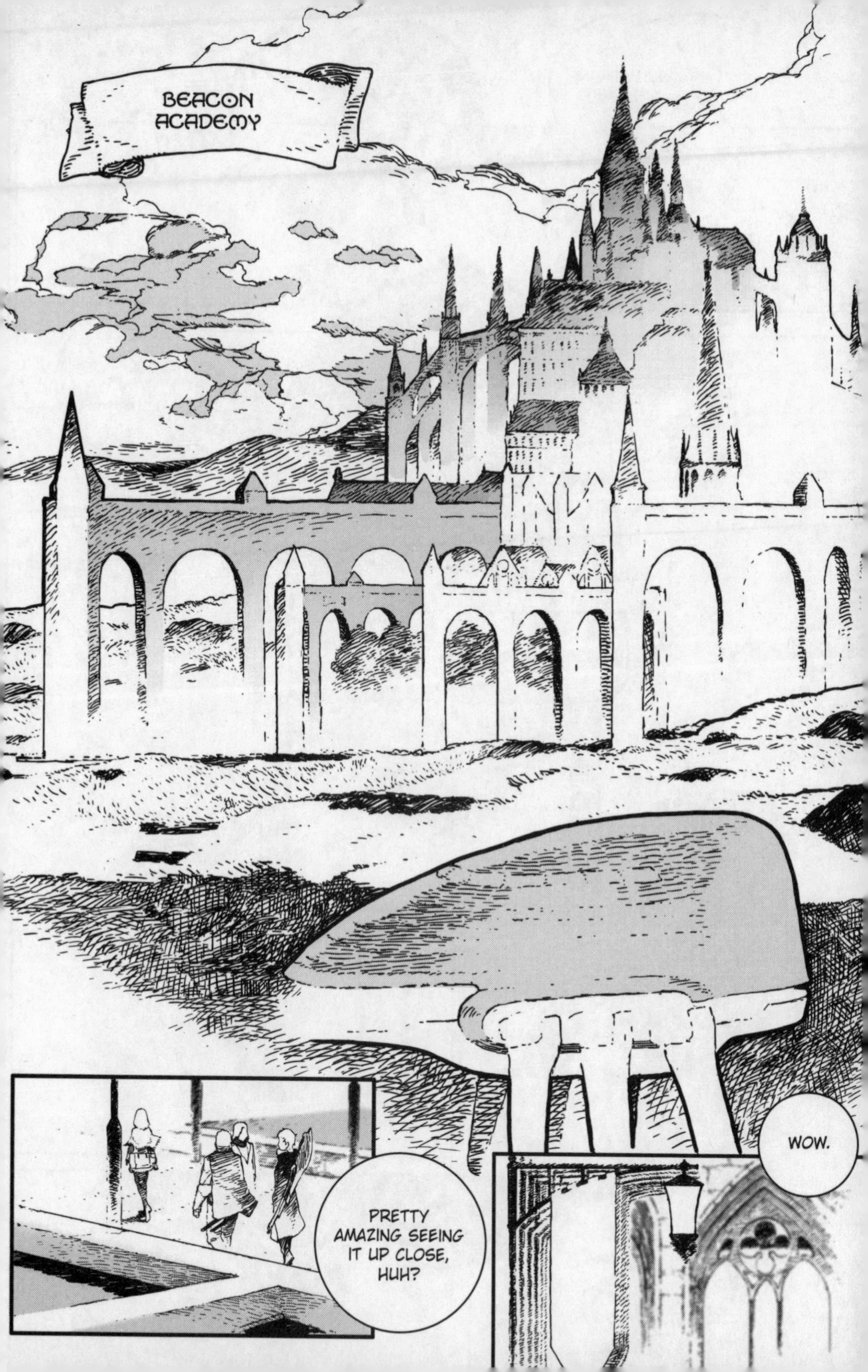
BEACON ACADEMY
WOW.
PRETTY AMAZING SEEING IT UP CLOSE, HUH?

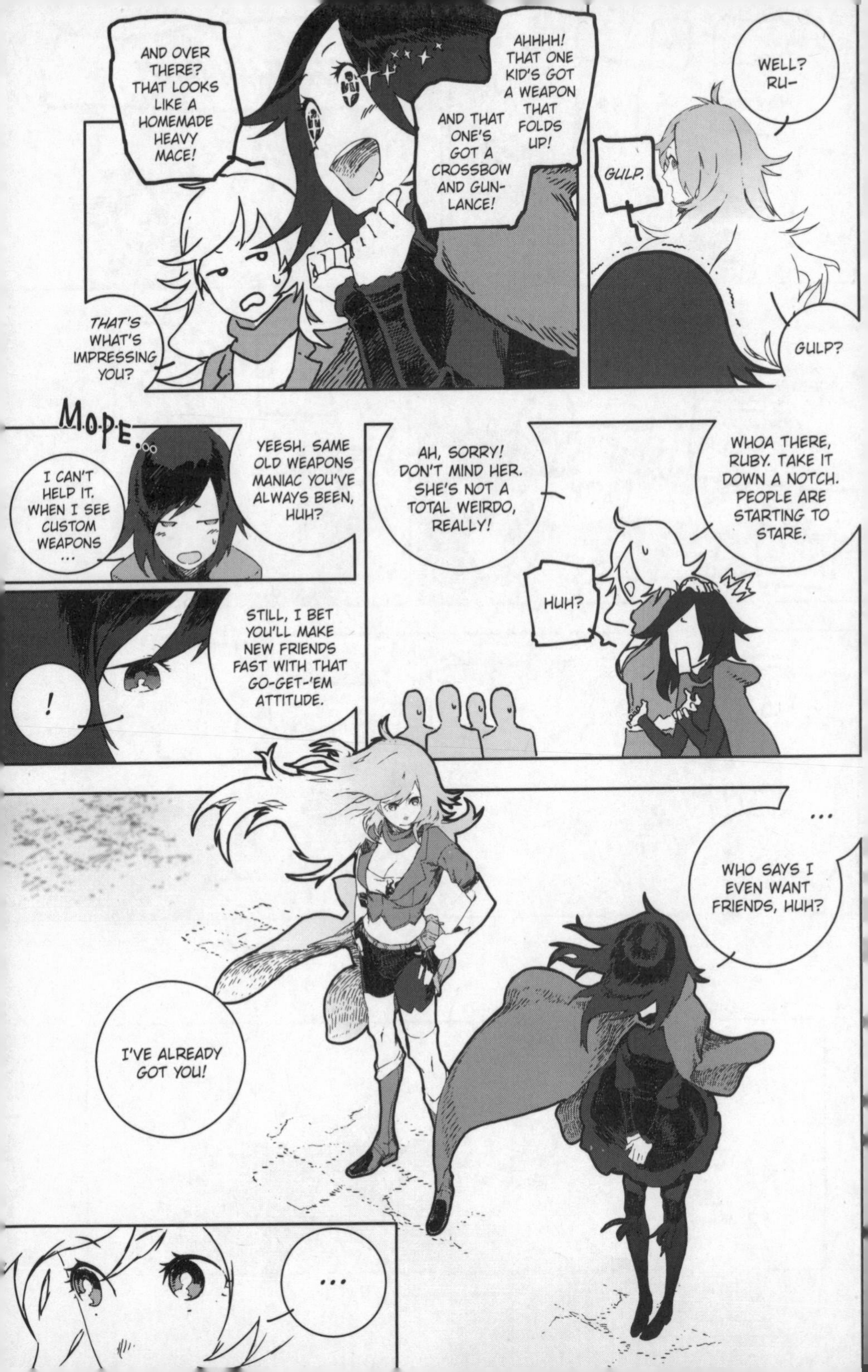
WELL? RU-
GULP.
GULP?
AHHHH! THAT ONE KID'S GOT A WEAPON THAT FOLDS UP!
AND THAT ONE'S GOT A CROSSBOW AND GUN-LANCE!
AND OVER THERE? THAT LOOKS LIKE A HOMEMADE HEAVY MACE!
THAT'S WHAT'S IMPRESSING YOU?
WHOA THERE, RUBY. TAKE IT DOWN A NOTCH. PEOPLE ARE STARTING TO STARE.
HUH?
AH, SORRY! DON'T MIND HER. SHE'S NOT A TOTAL WEIRDO, REALLY!
MOPE...
YEESH. SAME OLD WEAPONS MANIAC YOU'VE ALWAYS BEEN, HUH?
I CAN'T HELP IT. WHEN I SEE CUSTOM WEAPONS ...
STILL, I BET YOU'LL MAKE NEW FRIENDS FAST WITH THAT GO-GET-'EM ATTITUDE.
!
...
WHO SAYS I EVEN WANT FRIENDS, HUH?
I'VE ALREADY GOT YOU!
...

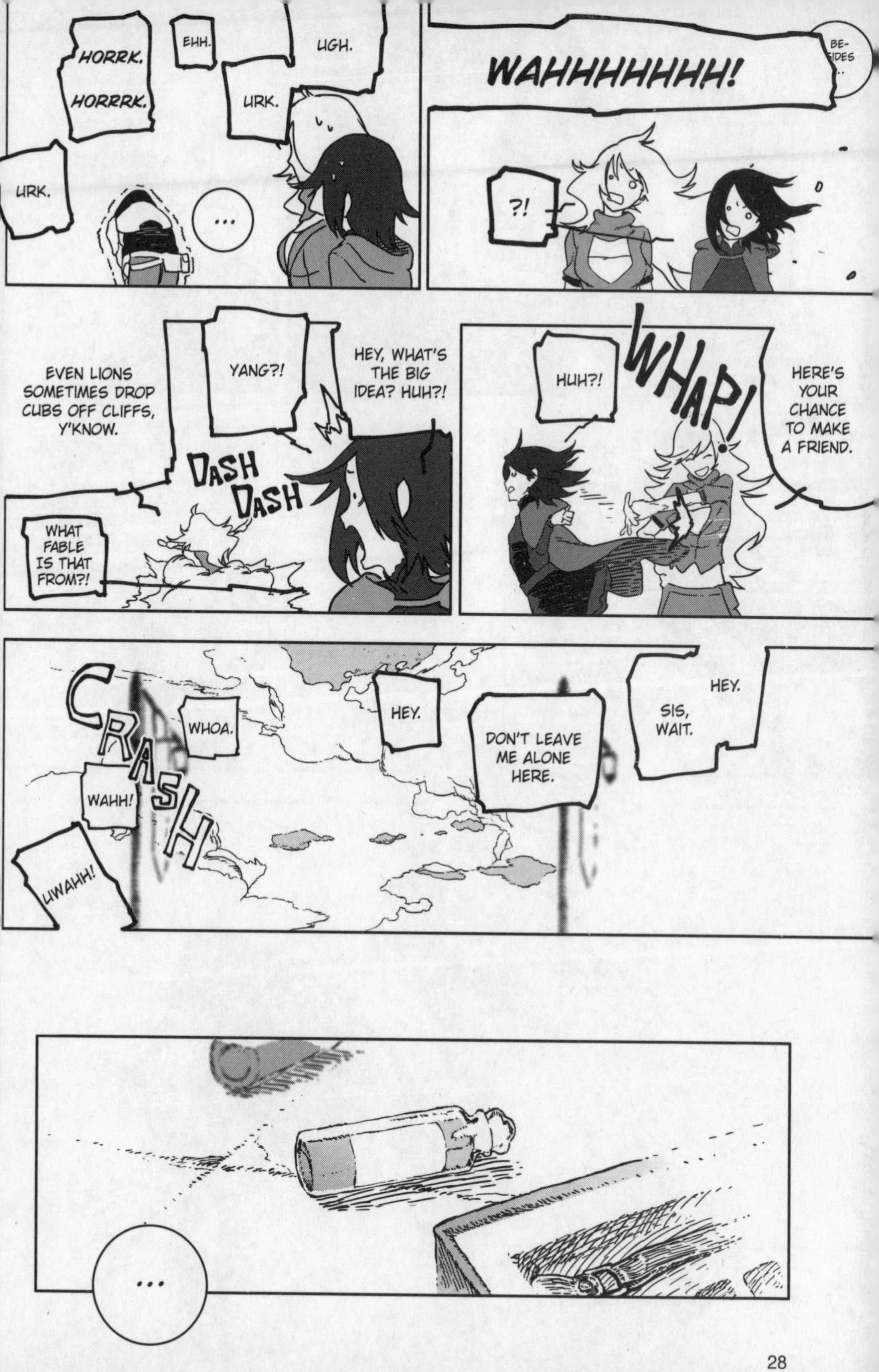
BE-
SIDES...
WAHHHHHHH!
?!
UGH.
EHH.
HORRK.
HORRRK.
URK.
URK.
...
HERE'S YOUR CHANCE TO MAKE A FRIEND.
WHAP!
HUH?!
HEY, WHAT'S THE BIG IDEA? HUH?!
YANG?!
EVEN LIONS SOMETIMES DROP CUBS OFF CLIFFS, Y'KNOW.
DASH DASH
WHAT FABLE IS THAT FROM?!
HEY.
SIS, WAIT.
DON'T LEAVE ME ALONE HERE.
HEY.
WHOA.
CRASH
WAHH!
UWAHH!
...

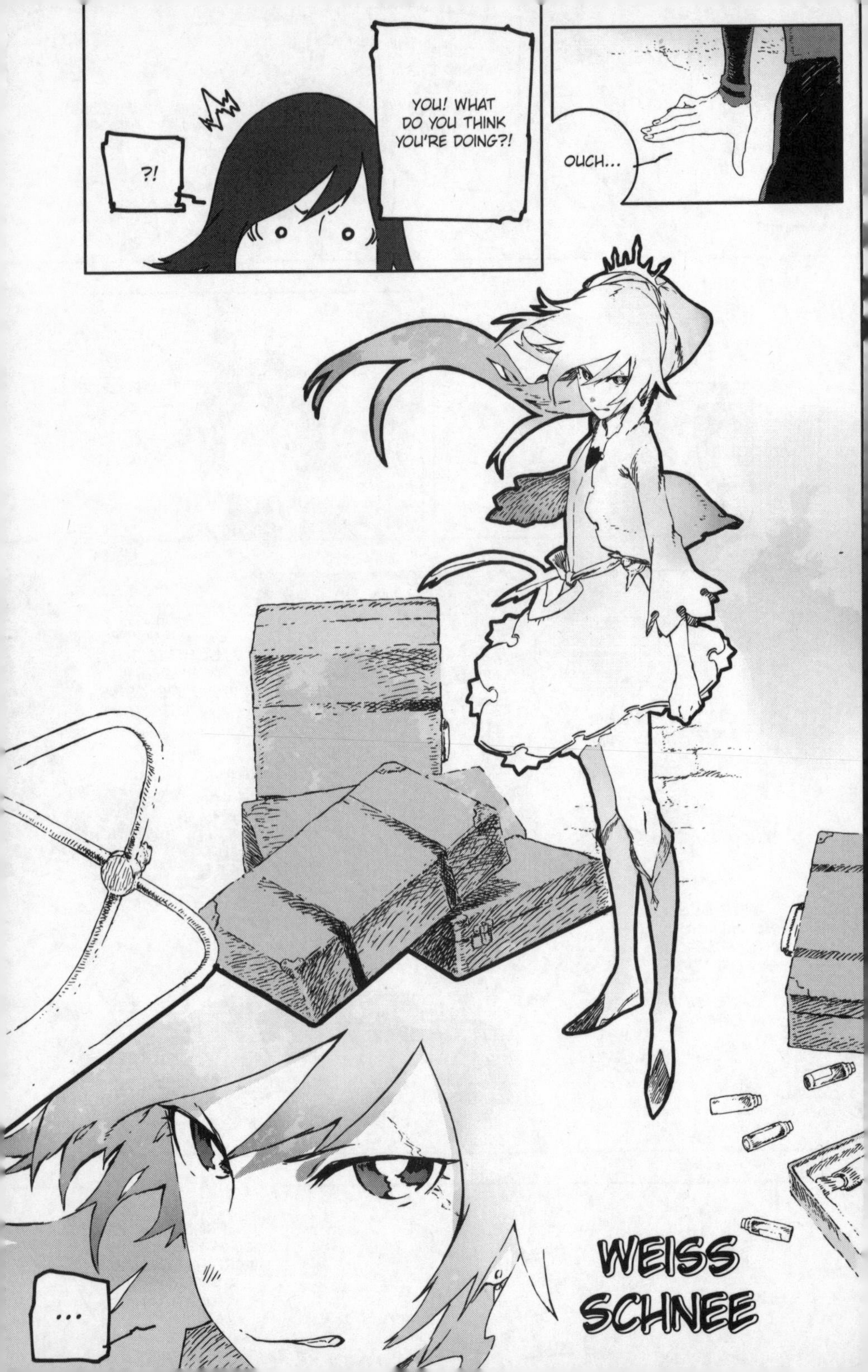
OUCH...
YOU! WHAT DO YOU THINK YOU'RE DOING?!
?!
WEISS SCHNEE
...

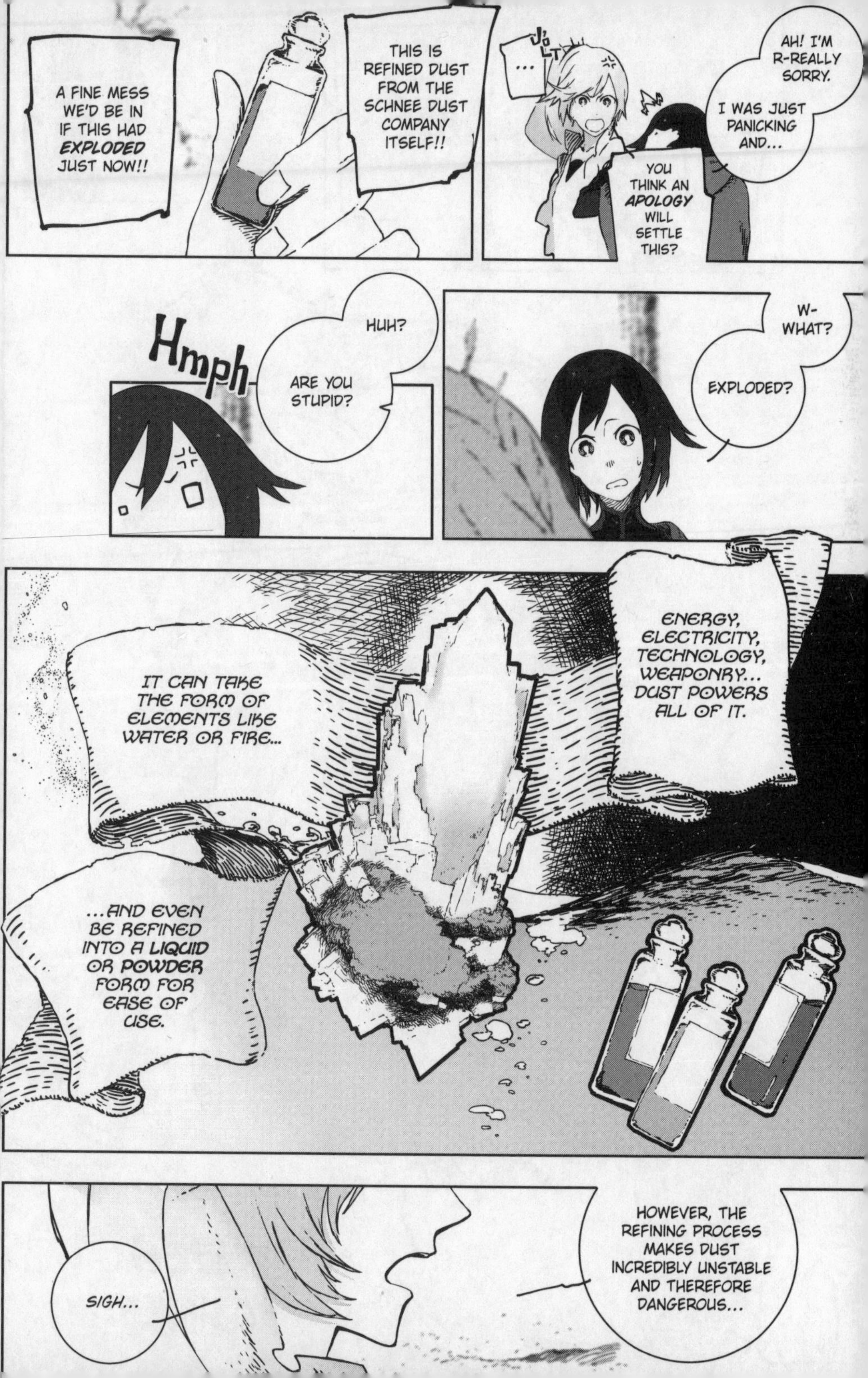
AH! I'M R-REALLY SORRY.
I WAS JUST PANICKING AND...
JOLT
...
YOU THINK AN **APOLOGY** WILL SETTLE THIS?
THIS IS REFINED DUST FROM THE SCHNEE DUST COMPANY ITSELF!!
A FINE MESS WE'D BE IN IF THIS HAD **EXPLODED** JUST NOW!!
W- WHAT?
EXPLODED?
HUH?
ARE YOU STUPID?
Hmph
ENERGY, ELECTRICITY, TECHNOLOGY, WEAPONRY... DUST POWERS ALL OF IT.
IT CAN TAKE THE FORM OF ELEMENTS LIKE WATER OR FIRE...
...AND EVEN BE REFINED INTO A **LIQUID** OR **POWDER** FORM FOR EASE OF USE.
HOWEVER, THE REFINING PROCESS MAKES DUST INCREDIBLY UNSTABLE AND THEREFORE DANGEROUS...
SIGH...

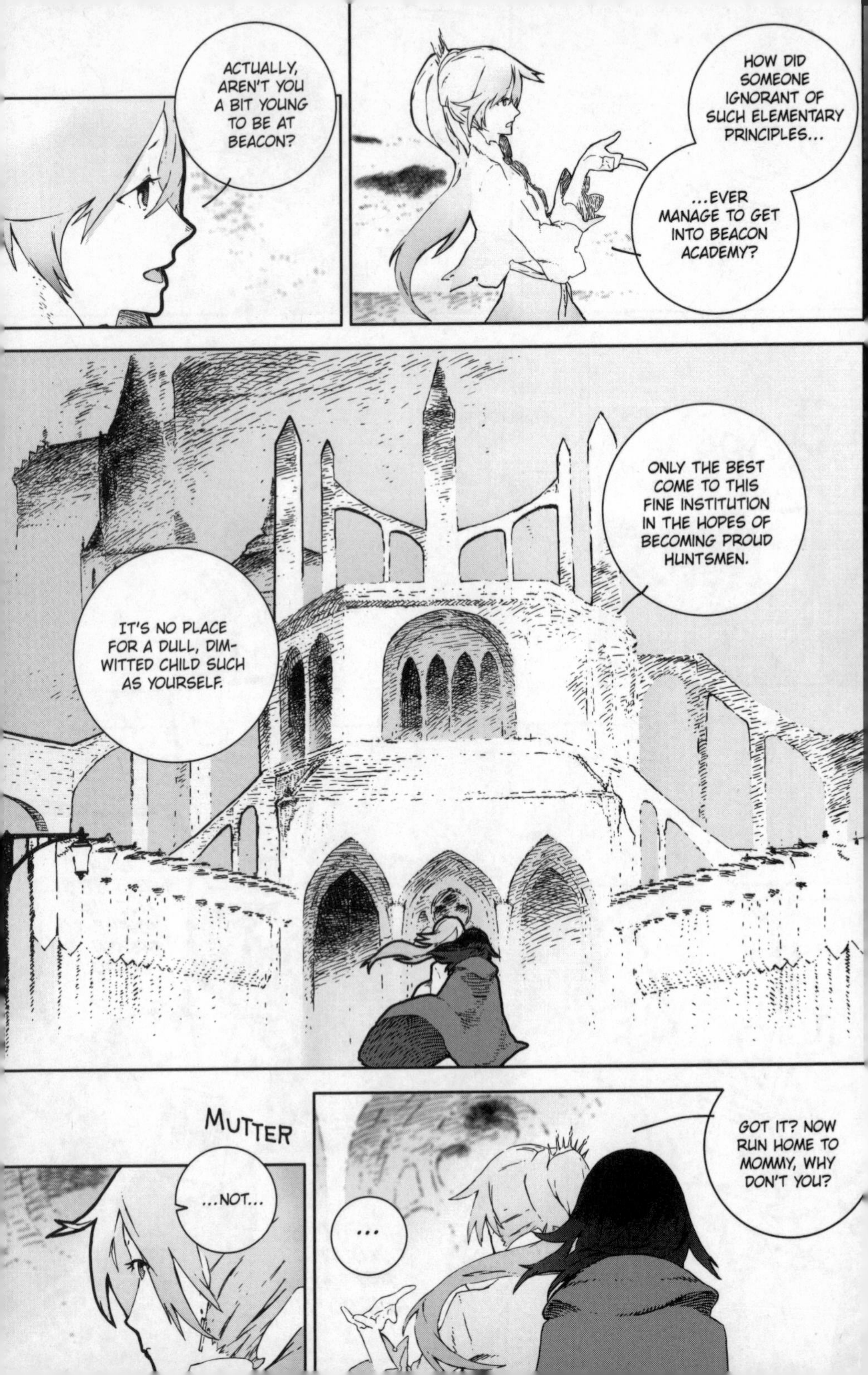

HOW DID SOMEONE IGNORANT OF SUCH ELEMENTARY PRINCIPLES...
...EVER MANAGE TO GET INTO BEACON ACADEMY?
ACTUALLY, AREN'T YOU A BIT YOUNG TO BE AT BEACON?
ONLY THE BEST COME TO THIS FINE INSTITUTION IN THE HOPES OF BECOMING PROUD HUNTSMEN.
IT'S NO PLACE FOR A DULL, DIM-WITTED CHILD SUCH AS YOURSELF.
GOT IT? NOW RUN HOME TO MOMMY, WHY DON'T YOU?
...
MUTTER
...NOT...

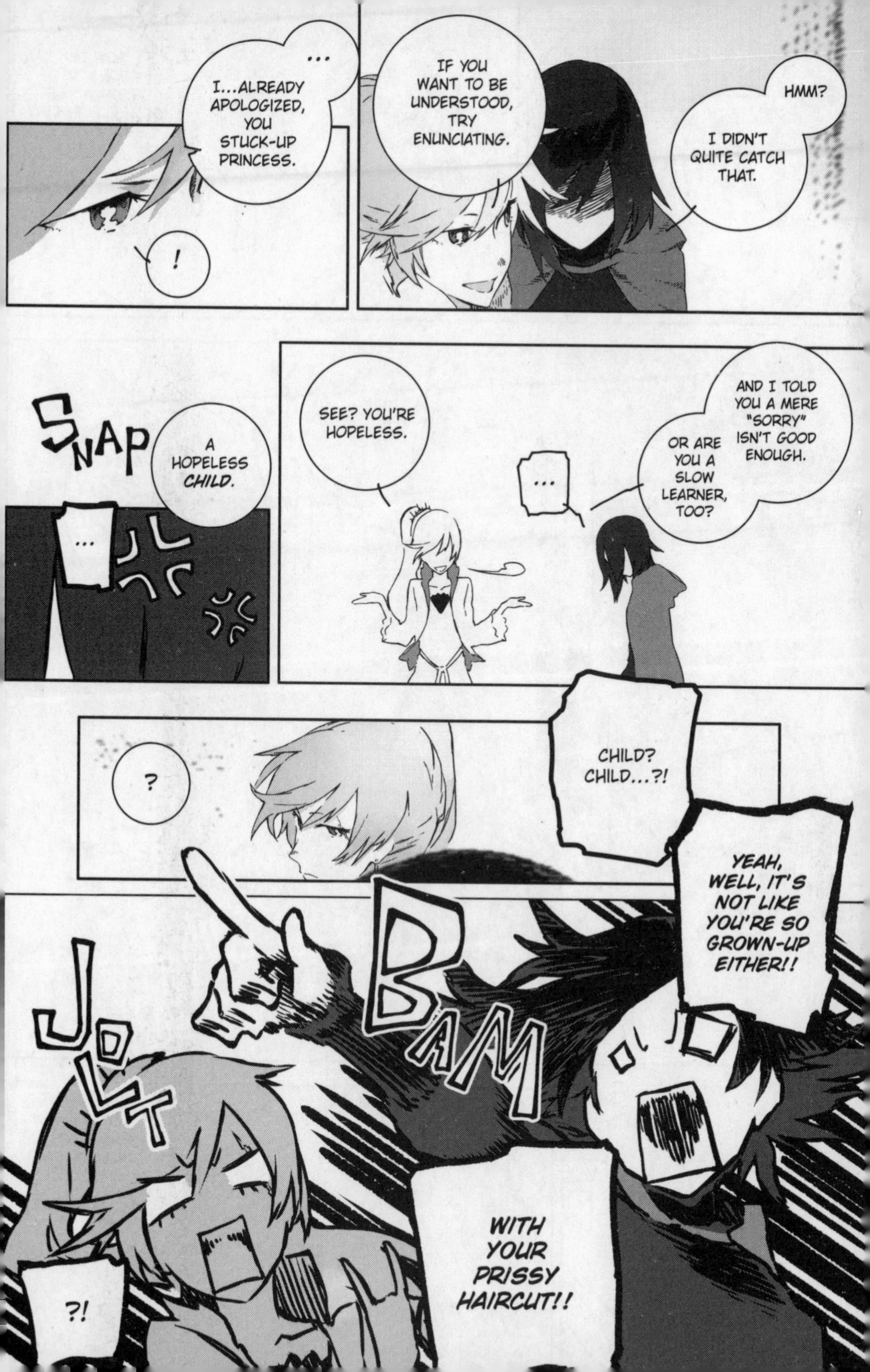
HMM?
I DIDN'T QUITE CATCH THAT.
IF YOU WANT TO BE UNDERSTOOD, TRY ENUNCIATING.
...
I...ALREADY APOLOGIZED, YOU STUCK-UP PRINCESS.
!
AND I TOLD YOU A MERE "SORRY" ISN'T GOOD ENOUGH.
OR ARE YOU A SLOW LEARNER, TOO?
...
SEE? YOU'RE HOPELESS.
A HOPELESS CHILD.
SNAP
...
CHILD? CHILD...?!
?
YEAH, WELL, IT'S NOT LIKE YOU'RE SO GROWN-UP EITHER!!
BAM
WITH YOUR PRISSY HAIRCUT!!
JOLT
?!

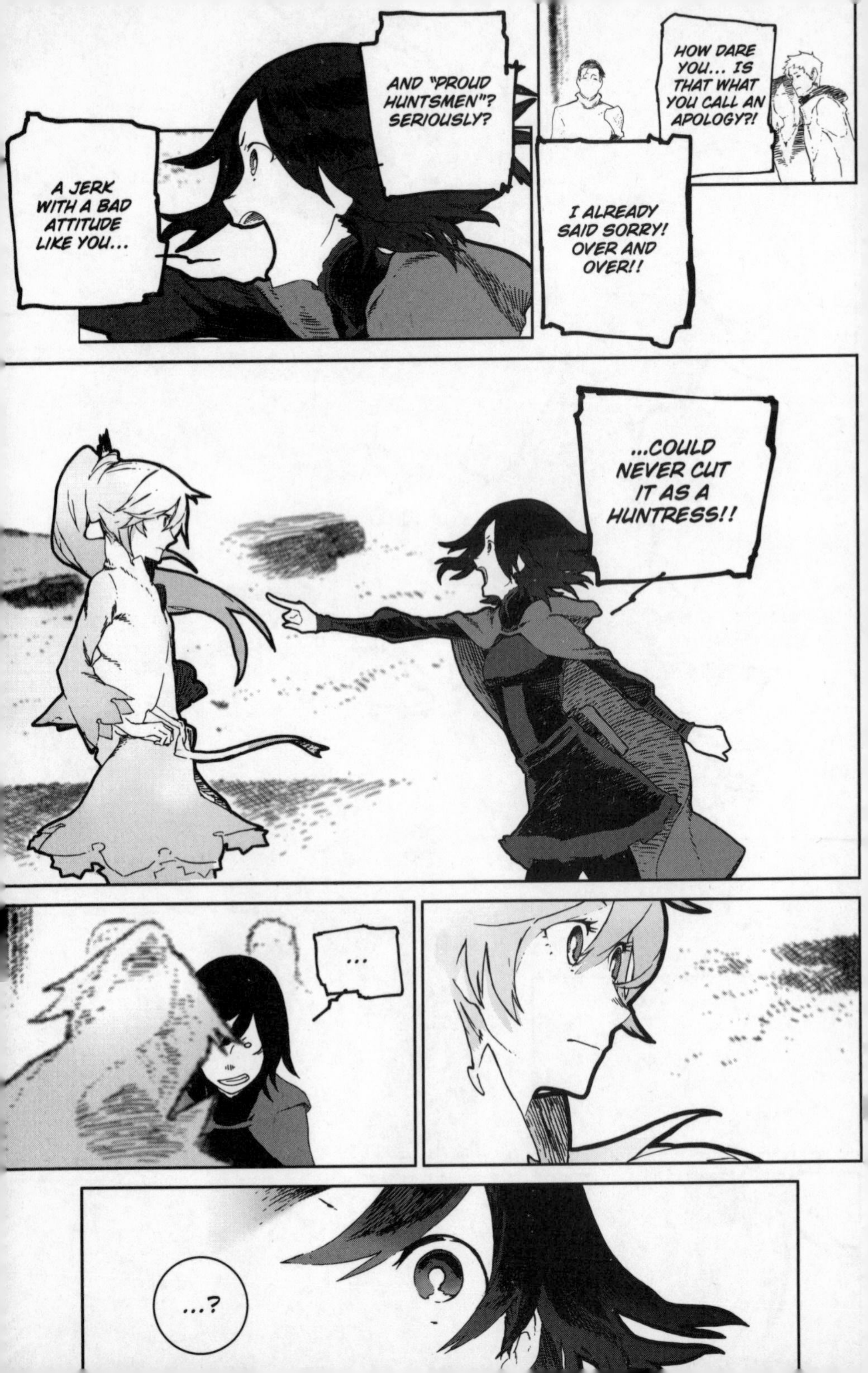
HOW DARE YOU... IS THAT WHAT YOU CALL AN APOLOGY?!
I ALREADY SAID SORRY! OVER AND OVER!!
AND "PROUD HUNTSMEN"? SERIOUSLY?
A JERK WITH A BAD ATTITUDE LIKE YOU...
...COULD NEVER CUT IT AS A HUNTRESS!!
...
...?

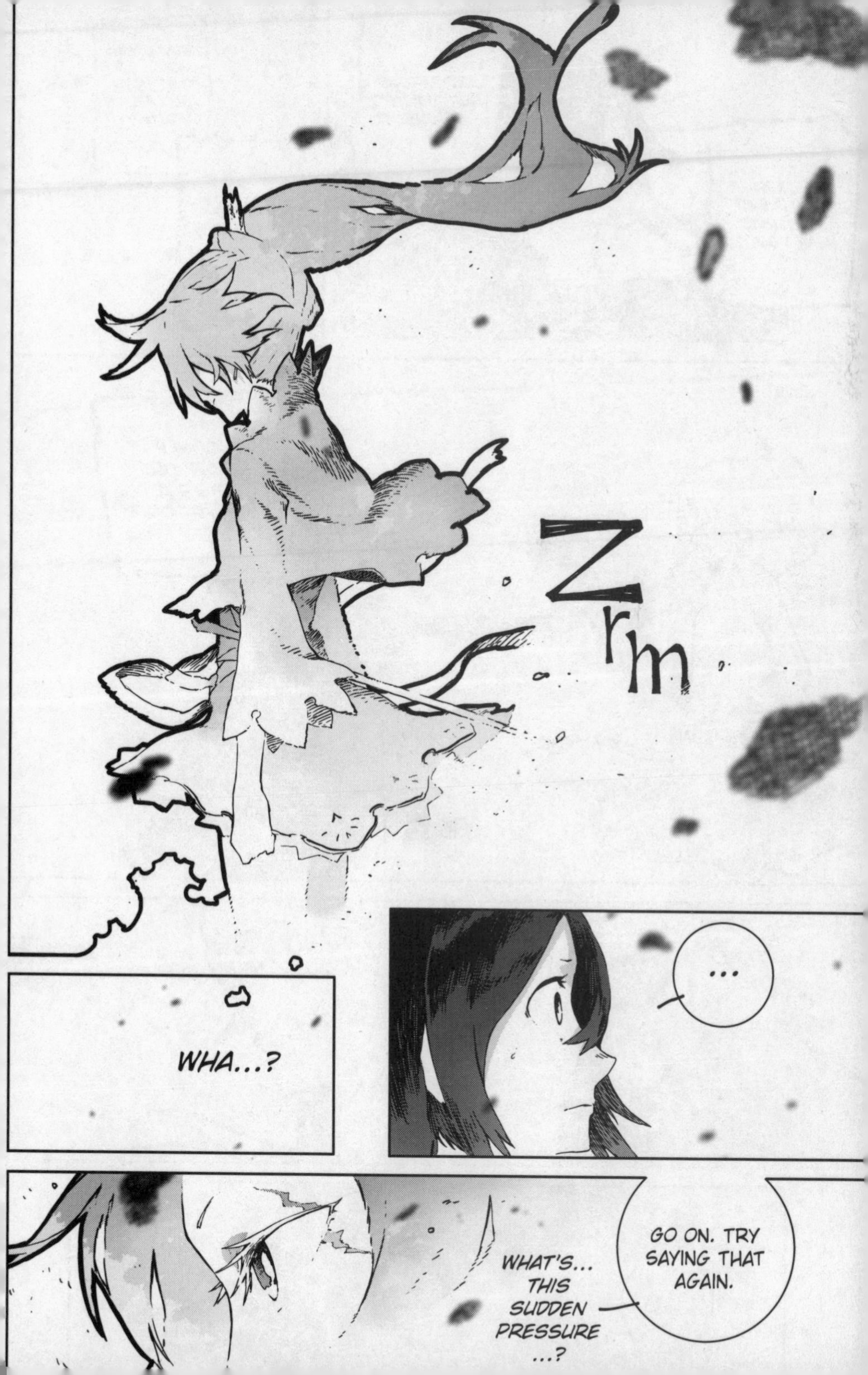
Zrm
...
WHA...?
GO ON. TRY SAYING THAT AGAIN.
WHAT'S... THIS SUDDEN PRESSURE ...?

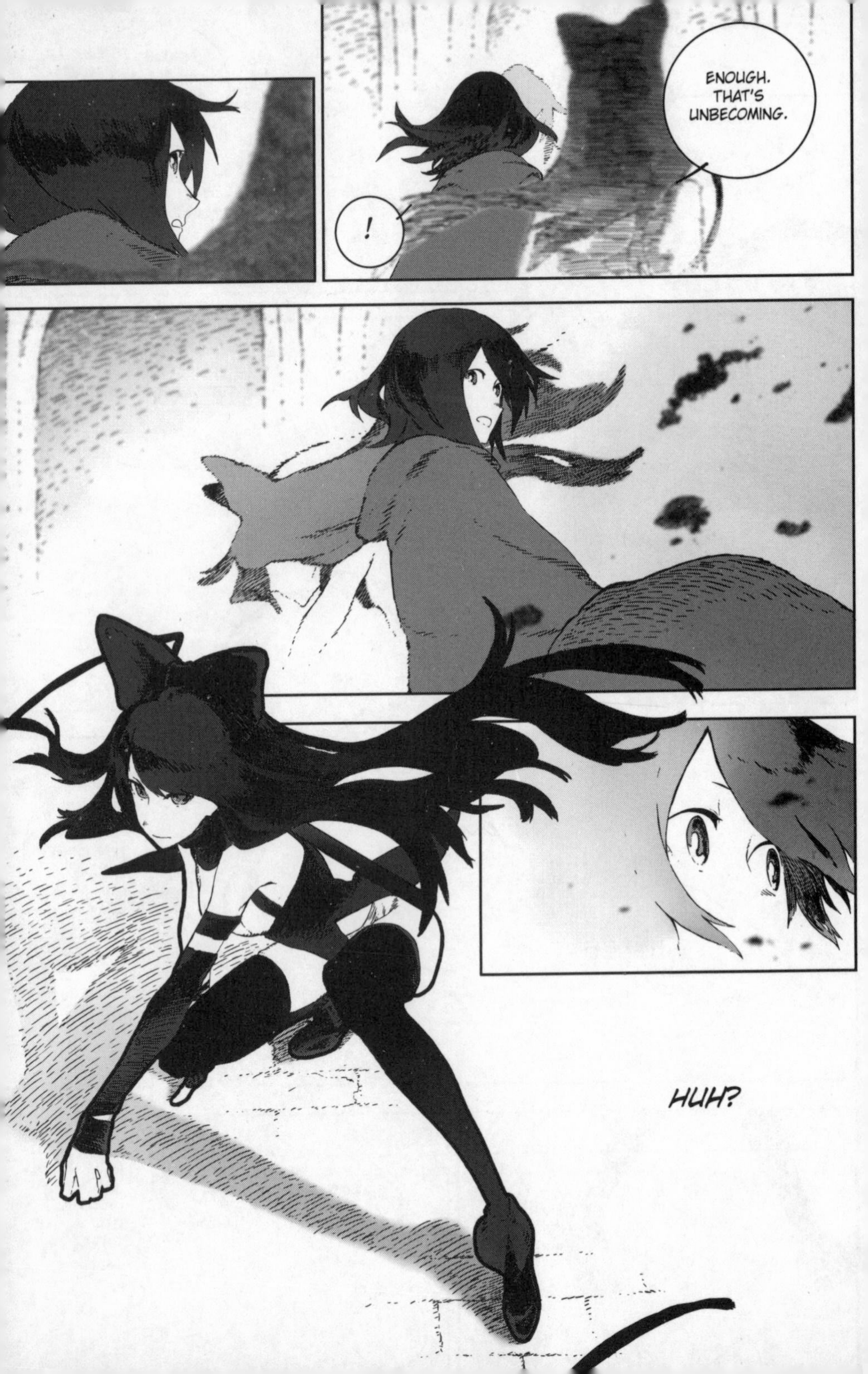
ENOUGH. THAT'S UNBECOMING.
!
HUH?

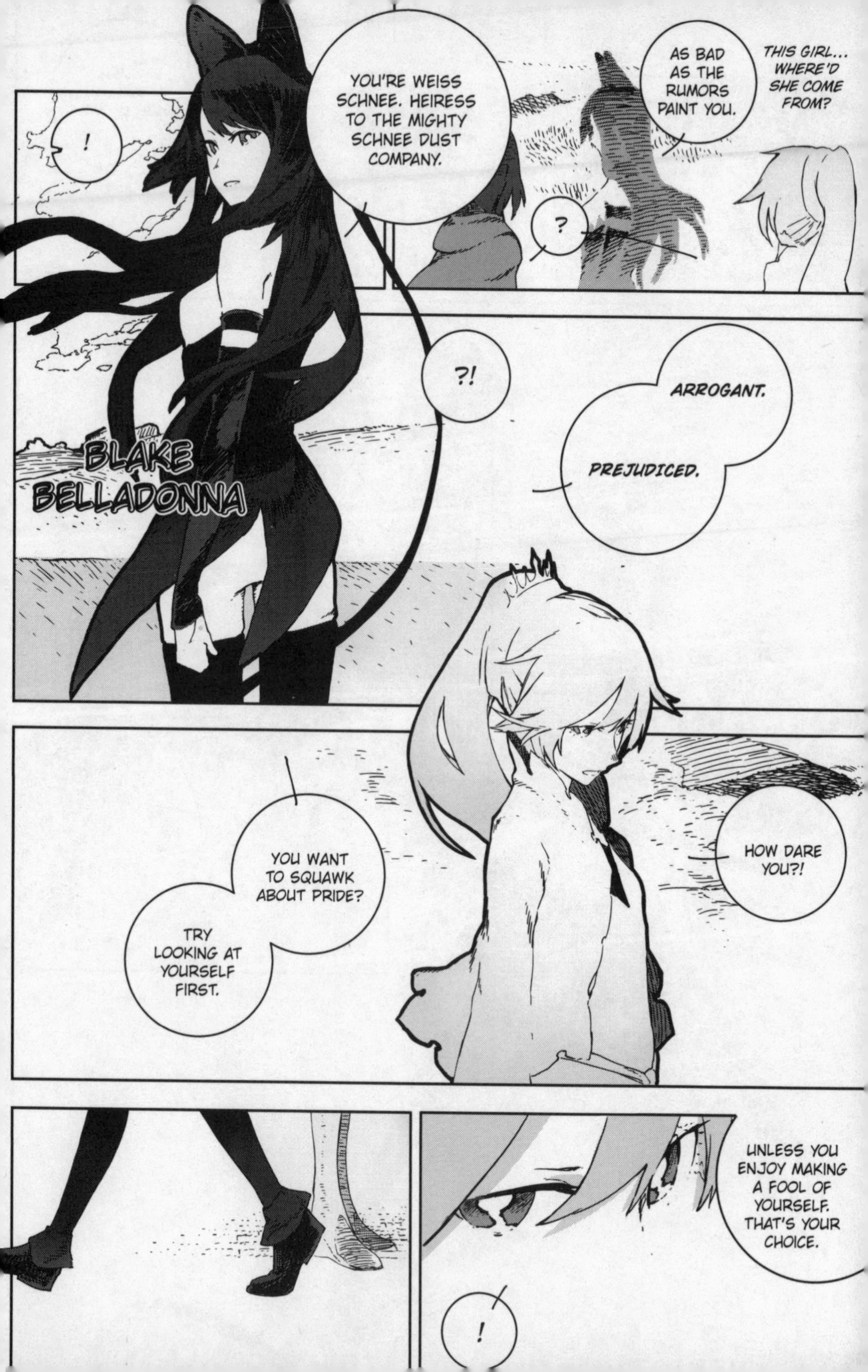
THIS GIRL... WHERE'D SHE COME FROM?
AS BAD AS THE RUMORS PAINT YOU.
?
YOU'RE WEISS SCHNEE. HEIRESS TO THE MIGHTY SCHNEE DUST COMPANY.
!
BLAKE BELLADONNA
ARROGANT.
PREJUDICED.
?!
HOW DARE YOU?!
YOU WANT TO SQUAWK ABOUT PRIDE?
TRY LOOKING AT YOURSELF FIRST.
UNLESS YOU ENJOY MAKING A FOOL OF YOURSELF. THAT'S YOUR CHOICE.
!

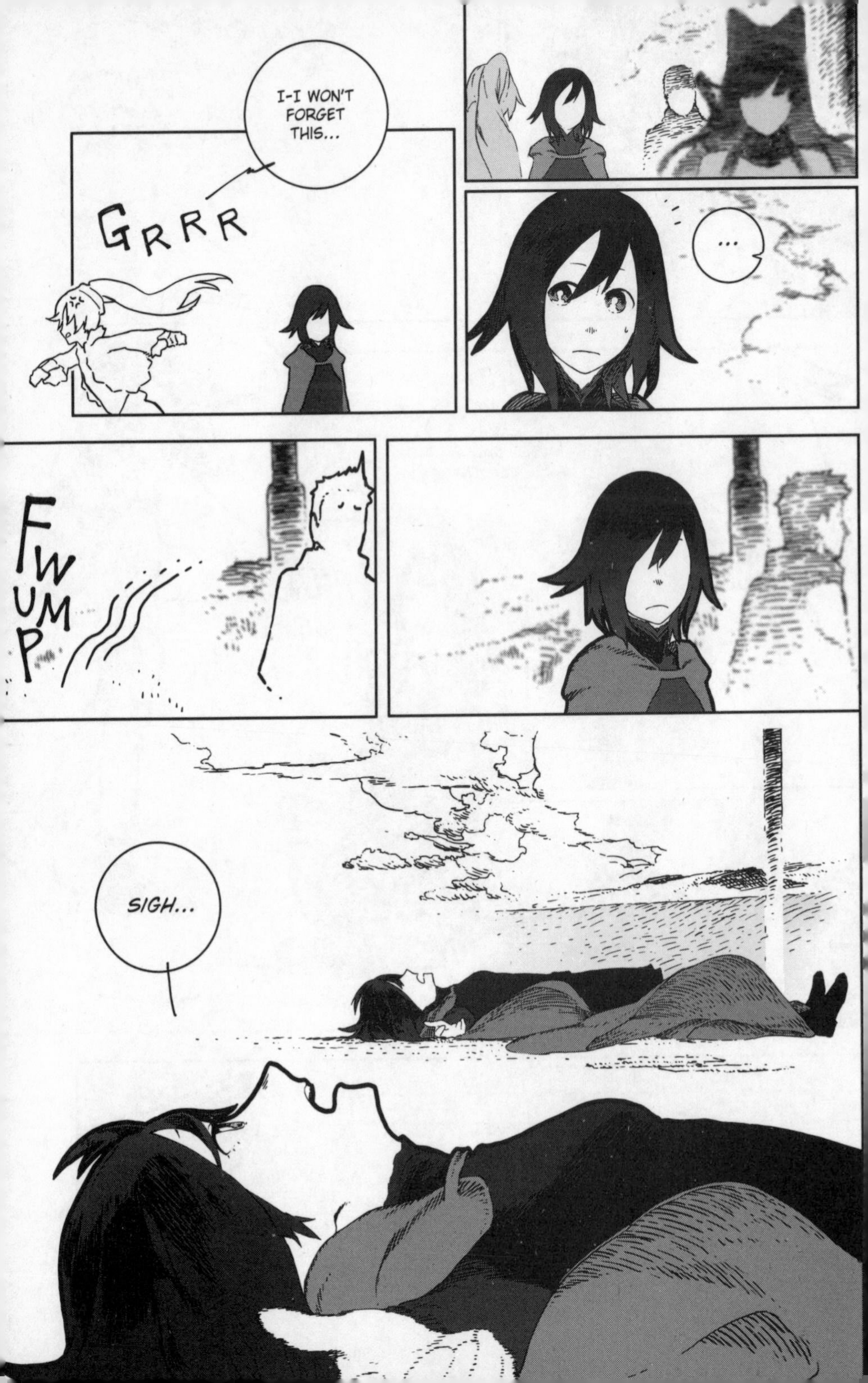
...
I-I WON'T FORGET THIS...
GRRR
FWUMP
SIGH...

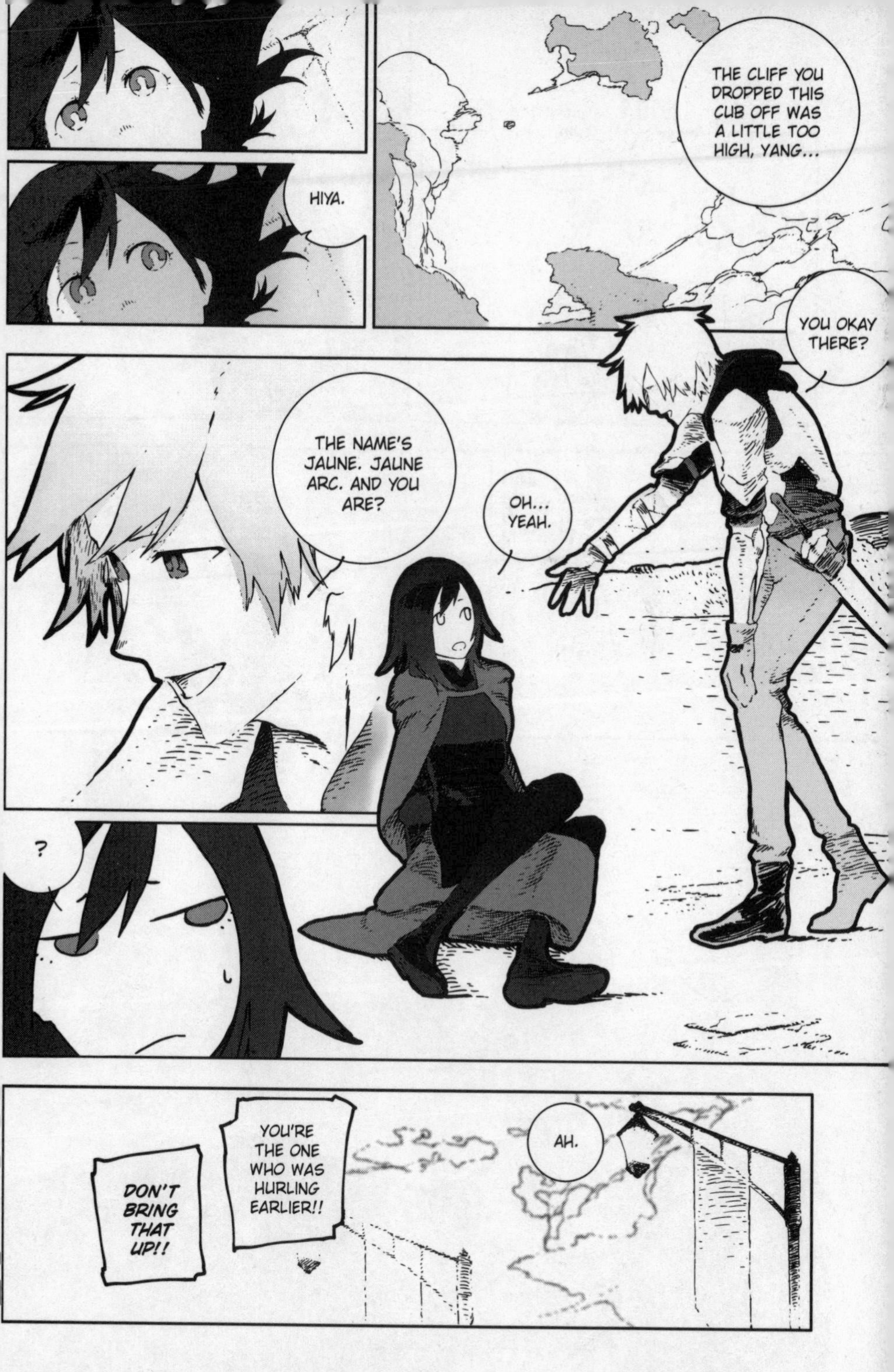
THE CLIFF YOU DROPPED THIS CUB OFF WAS A LITTLE TOO HIGH, YANG...
HIYA.
YOU OKAY THERE?
OH... YEAH.
THE NAME'S JAUNE. JAUNE ARC. AND YOU ARE?
?
AH.
YOU'RE THE ONE WHO WAS HURLING EARLIER!!
DON'T BRING THAT UP!!

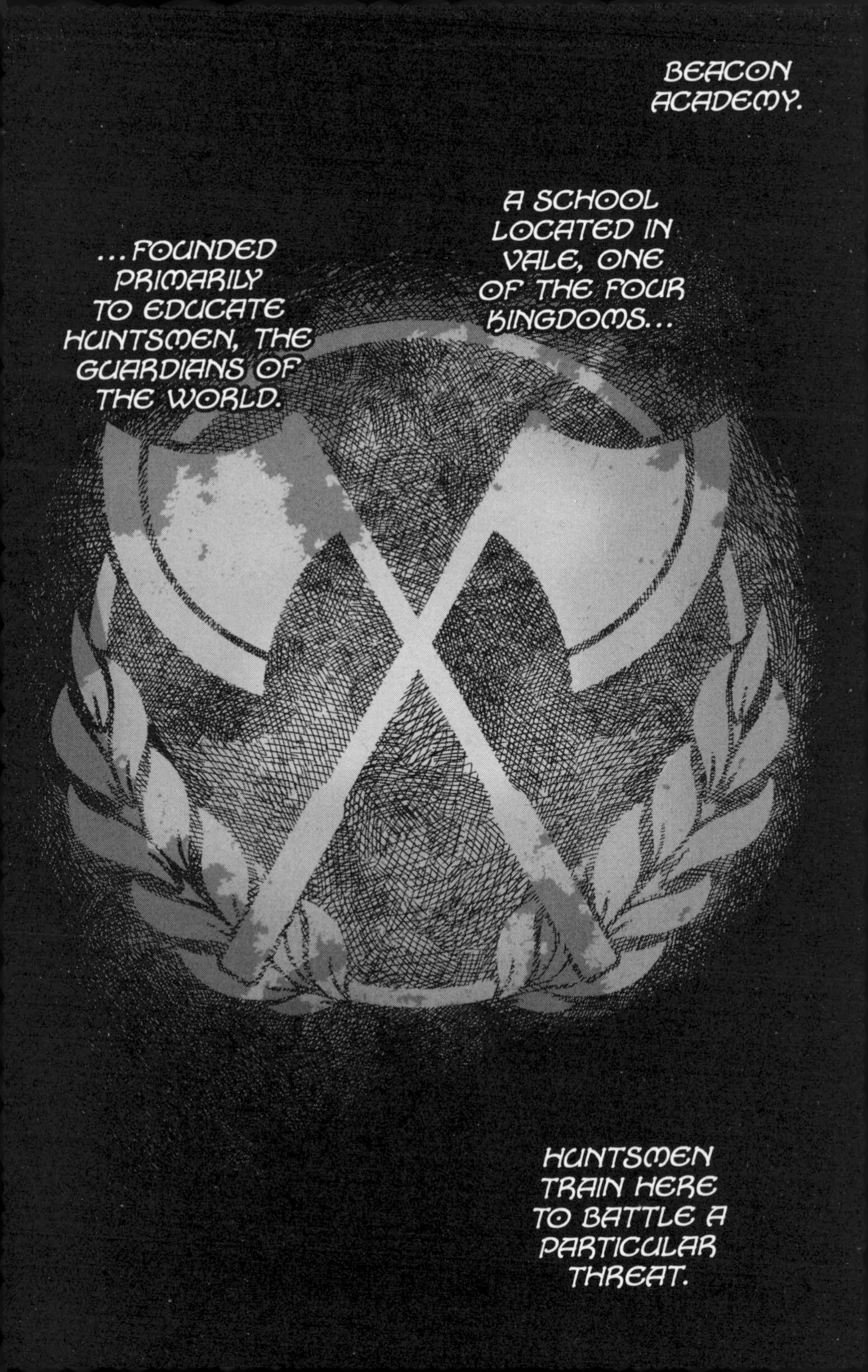
BEACON ACADEMY.
A SCHOOL LOCATED IN VALE, ONE OF THE FOUR KINGDOMS...
...FOUNDED PRIMARILY TO EDUCATE HUNTSMEN, THE GUARDIANS OF THE WORLD.
HUNTSMEN TRAIN HERE TO BATTLE A PARTICULAR THREAT.

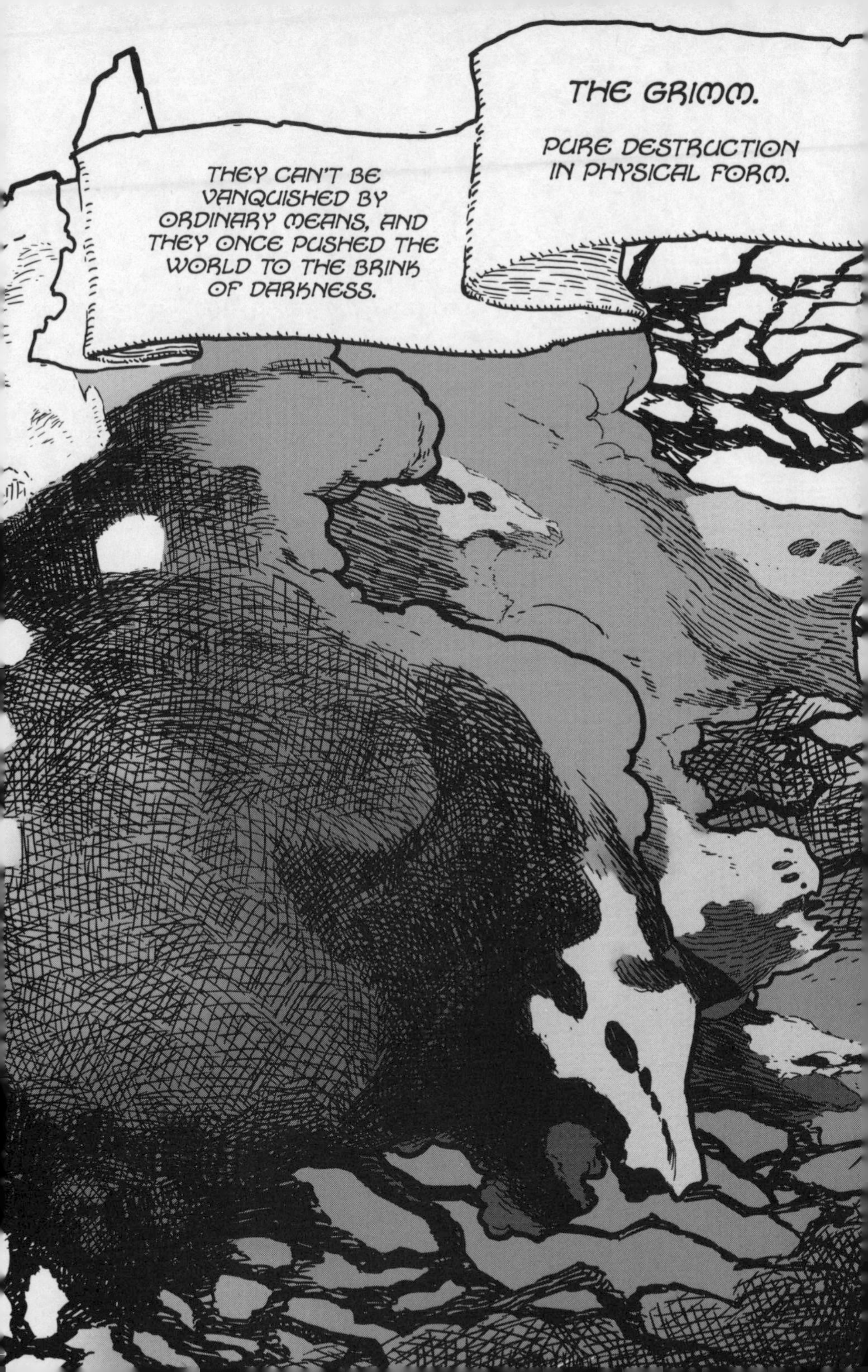
THE GRIMM.
PURE DESTRUCTION IN PHYSICAL FORM.
THEY CAN'T BE VANQUISHED BY ORDINARY MEANS, AND THEY ONCE PUSHED THE WORLD TO THE BRINK OF DARKNESS.

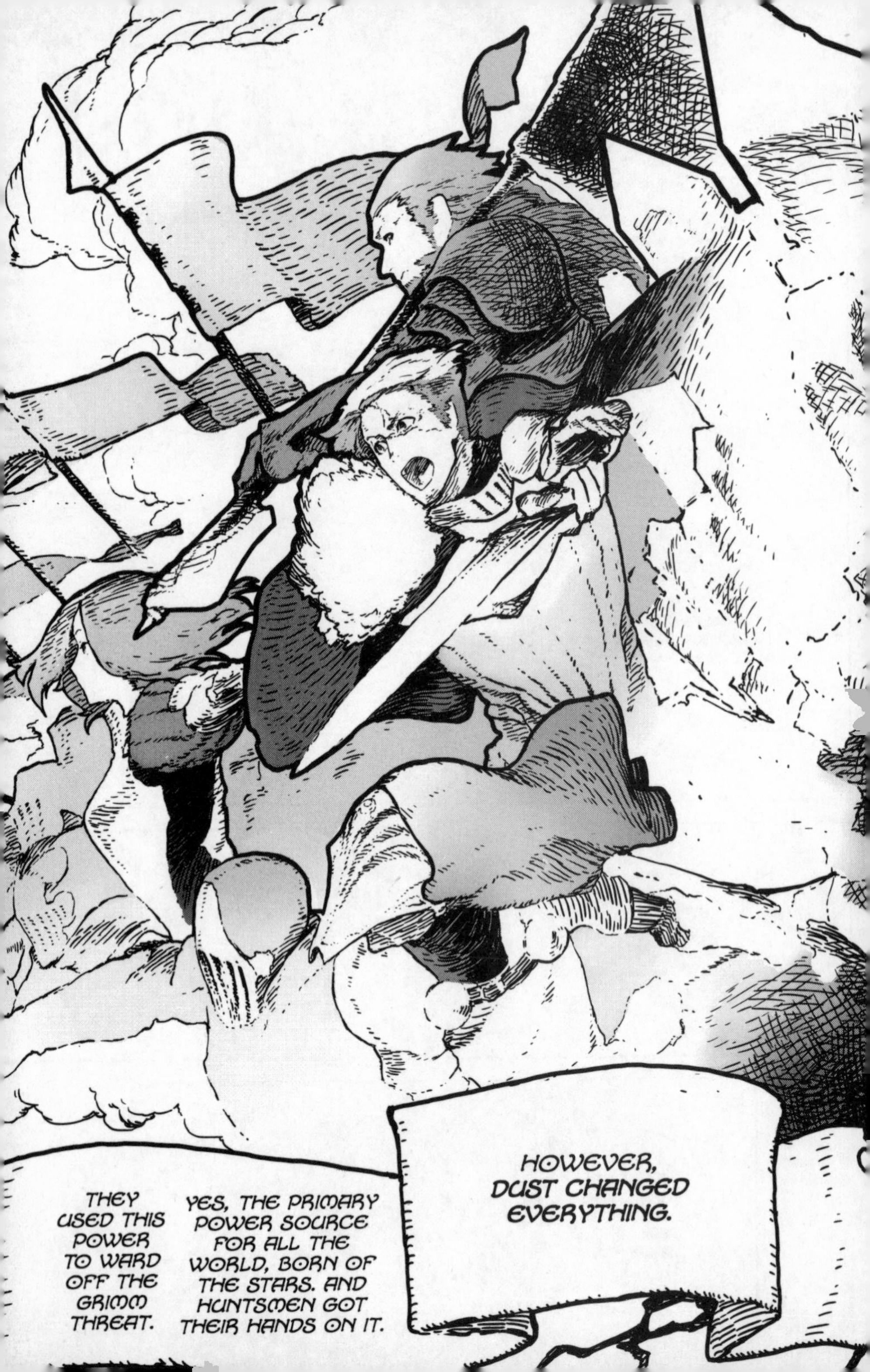
HOWEVER, DUST CHANGED EVERYTHING.
YES, THE PRIMARY POWER SOURCE FOR ALL THE WORLD, BORN OF THE STARS. AND HUNTSMEN GOT THEIR HANDS ON IT.
THEY USED THIS POWER TO WARD OFF THE GRIMM THREAT.

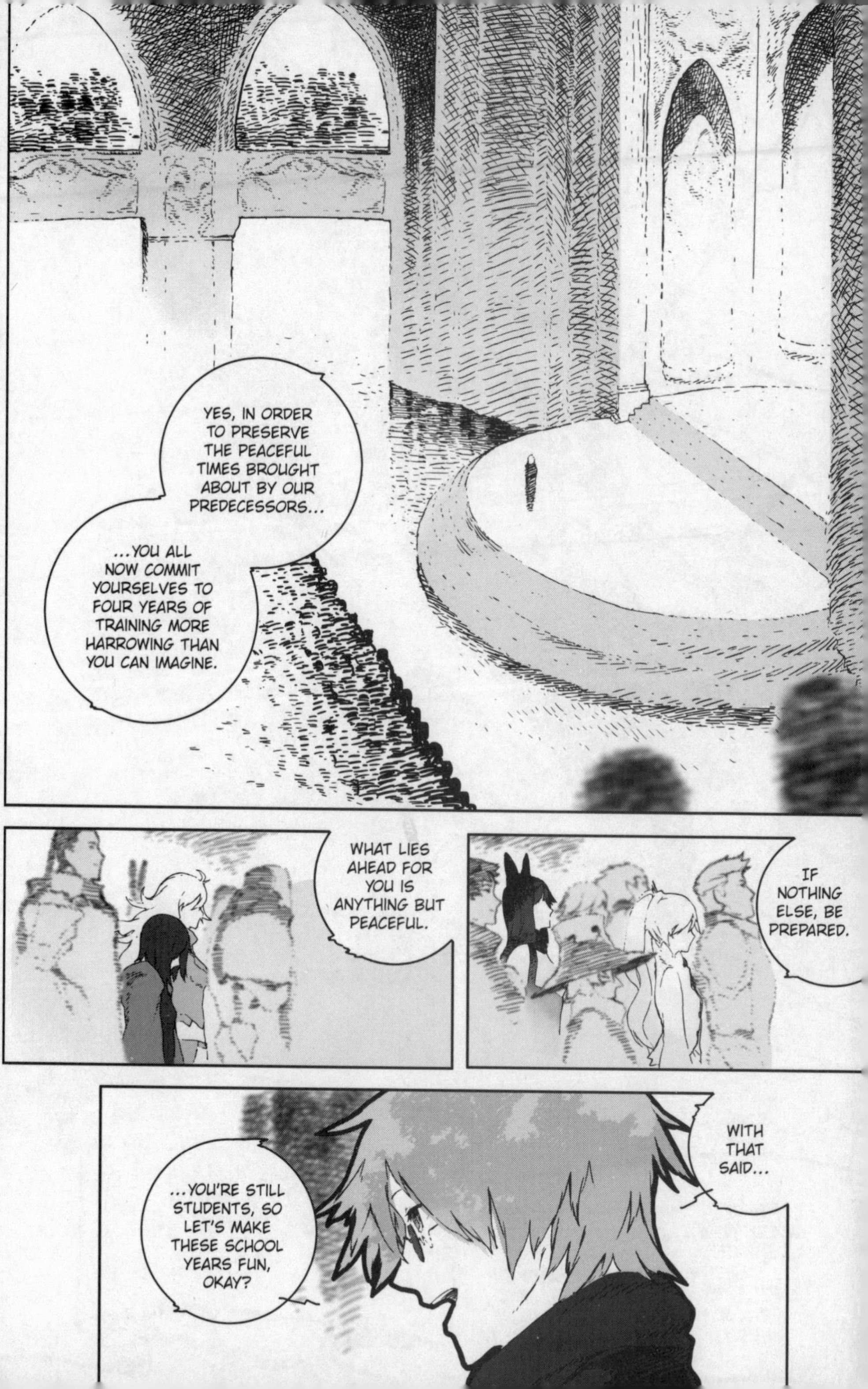
YES, IN ORDER TO PRESERVE THE PEACEFUL TIMES BROUGHT ABOUT BY OUR PREDECESSORS...
...YOU ALL NOW COMMIT YOURSELVES TO FOUR YEARS OF TRAINING MORE HARROWING THAN YOU CAN IMAGINE.
IF NOTHING ELSE, BE PREPARED.
WHAT LIES AHEAD FOR YOU IS ANYTHING BUT PEACEFUL.
WITH THAT SAID...
...YOU'RE STILL STUDENTS, SO LET'S MAKE THESE SCHOOL YEARS FUN, OKAY?

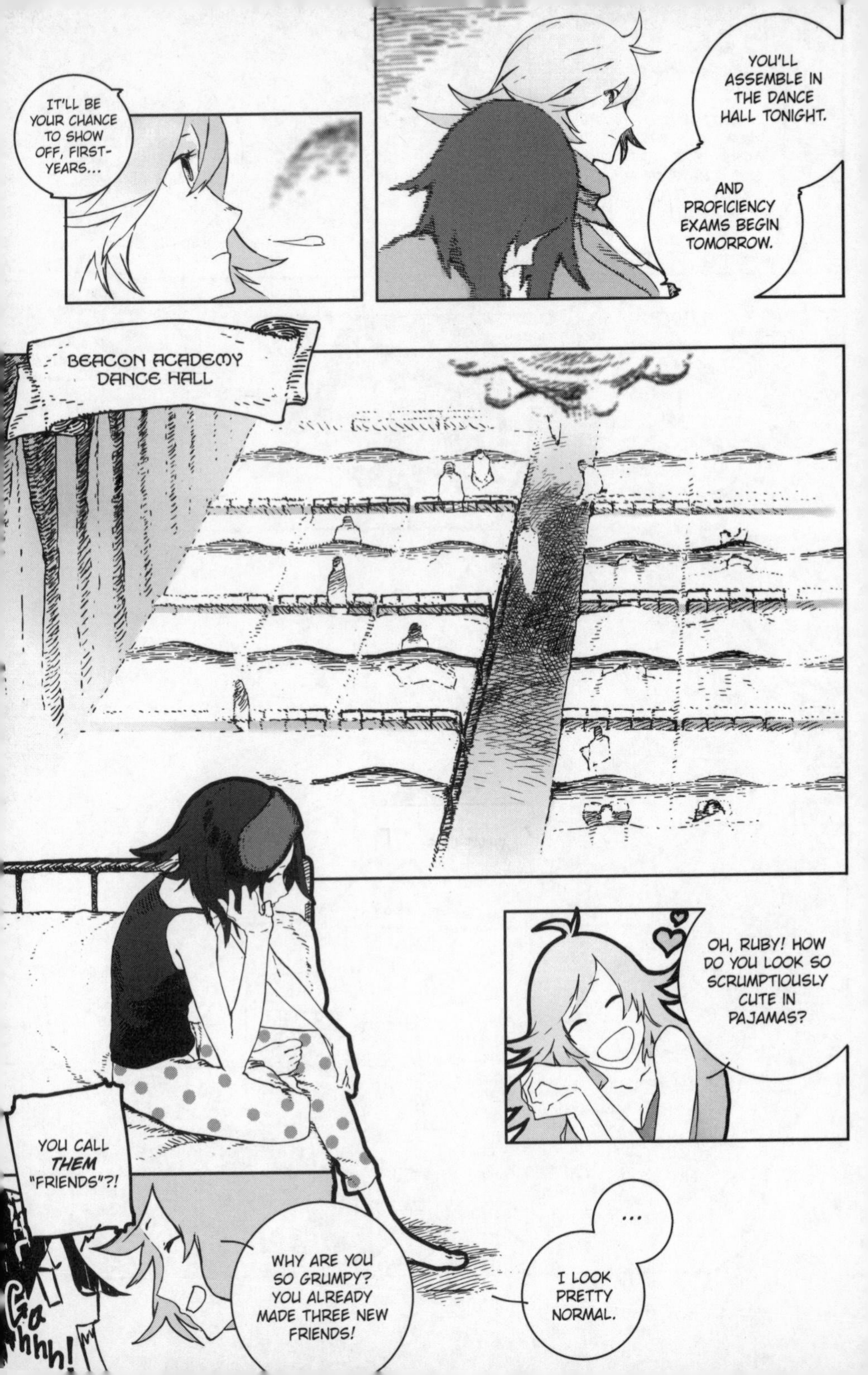
YOU'LL ASSEMBLE IN THE DANCE HALL TONIGHT.
AND PROFICIENCY EXAMS BEGIN TOMORROW.
IT'LL BE YOUR CHANCE TO SHOW OFF, FIRST-YEARS...
BEACON ACADEMY DANCE HALL
OH, RUBY! HOW DO YOU LOOK SO SCRUMPTIOUSLY CUTE IN PAJAMAS?
...
I LOOK PRETTY NORMAL.
WHY ARE YOU SO GRUMPY? YOU ALREADY MADE THREE NEW FRIENDS!
YOU CALL *THEM* "FRIENDS"?!

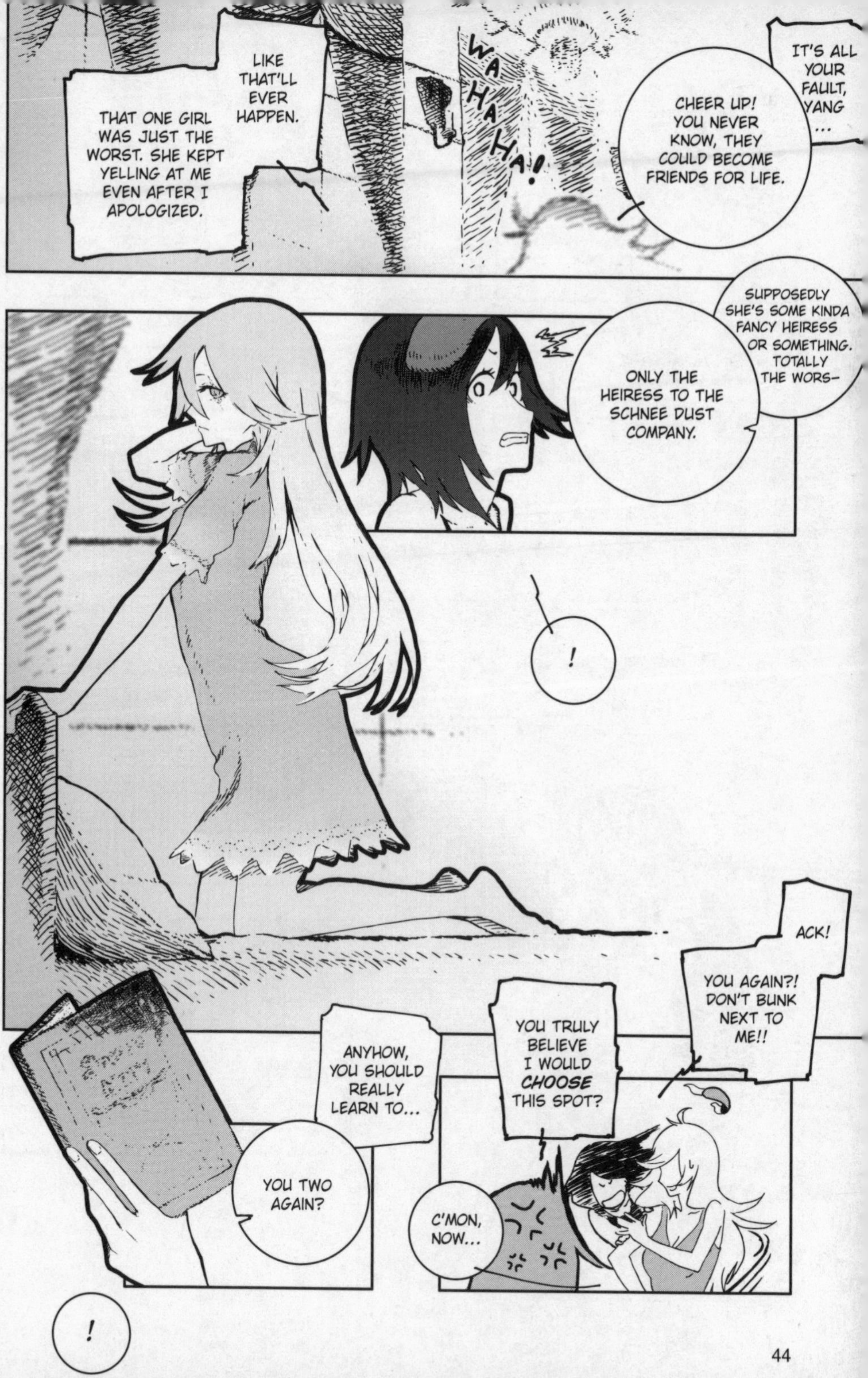
IT'S ALL YOUR FAULT, YANG...
CHEER UP! YOU NEVER KNOW, THEY COULD BECOME FRIENDS FOR LIFE.
WAHAHA!
LIKE THAT'LL EVER HAPPEN.
THAT ONE GIRL WAS JUST THE WORST. SHE KEPT YELLING AT ME EVEN AFTER I APOLOGIZED.
SUPPOSEDLY SHE'S SOME KINDA FANCY HEIRESS OR SOMETHING. TOTALLY THE WORS–
ONLY THE HEIRESS TO THE SCHNEE DUST COMPANY.
!
ACK!
YOU AGAIN?! DON'T BUNK NEXT TO ME!!
YOU TRULY BELIEVE I WOULD *CHOOSE* THIS SPOT?
C'MON, NOW...
ANYHOW, YOU SHOULD REALLY LEARN TO...
YOU TWO AGAIN?
!

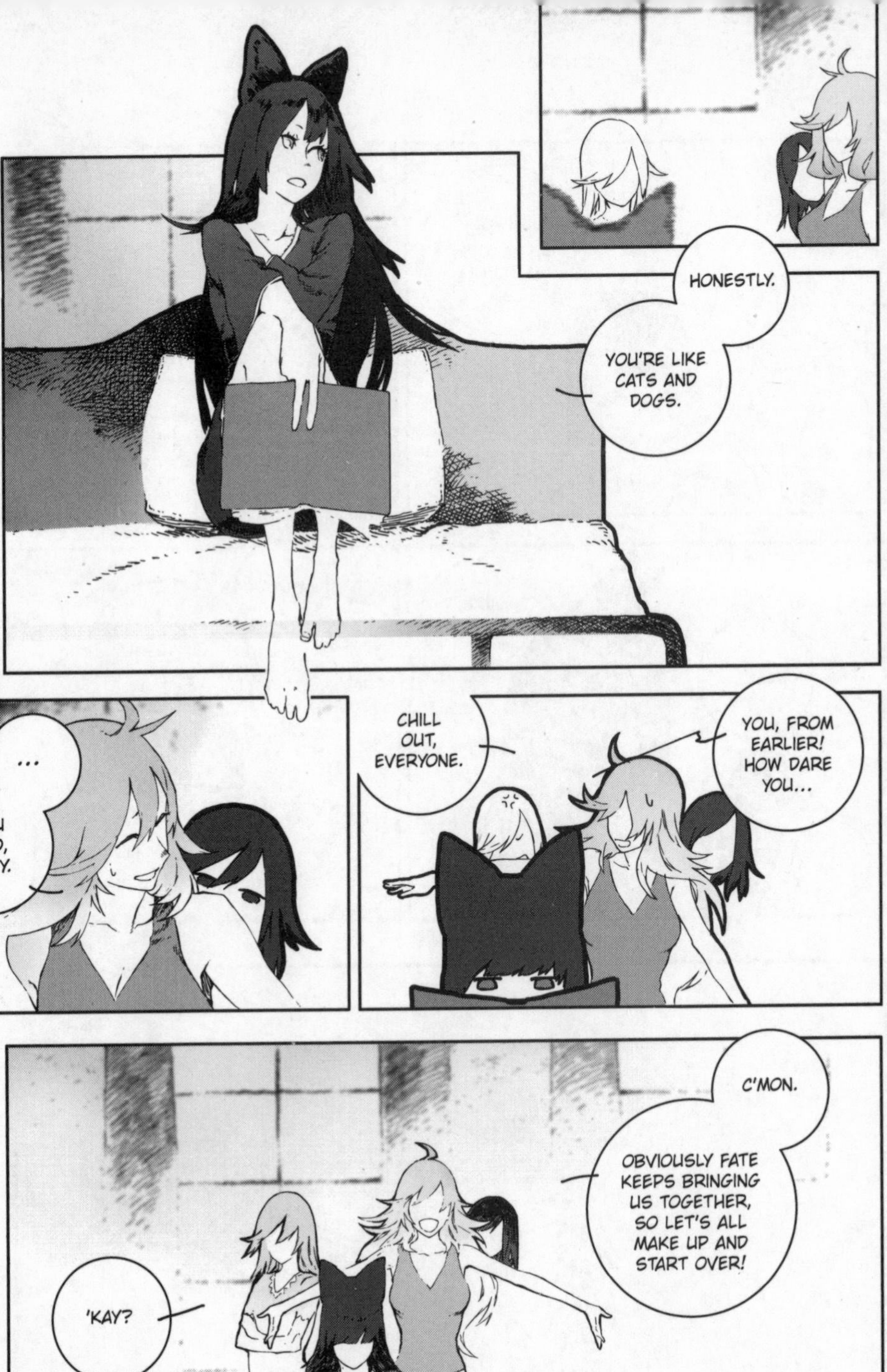
HONESTLY.
YOU'RE LIKE CATS AND DOGS.
YOU, FROM EARLIER! HOW DARE YOU...
CHILL OUT, EVERYONE.
...
YOU TOO, RUBY.
C'MON.
OBVIOUSLY FATE KEEPS BRINGING US TOGETHER, SO LET'S ALL MAKE UP AND START OVER!
'KAY?

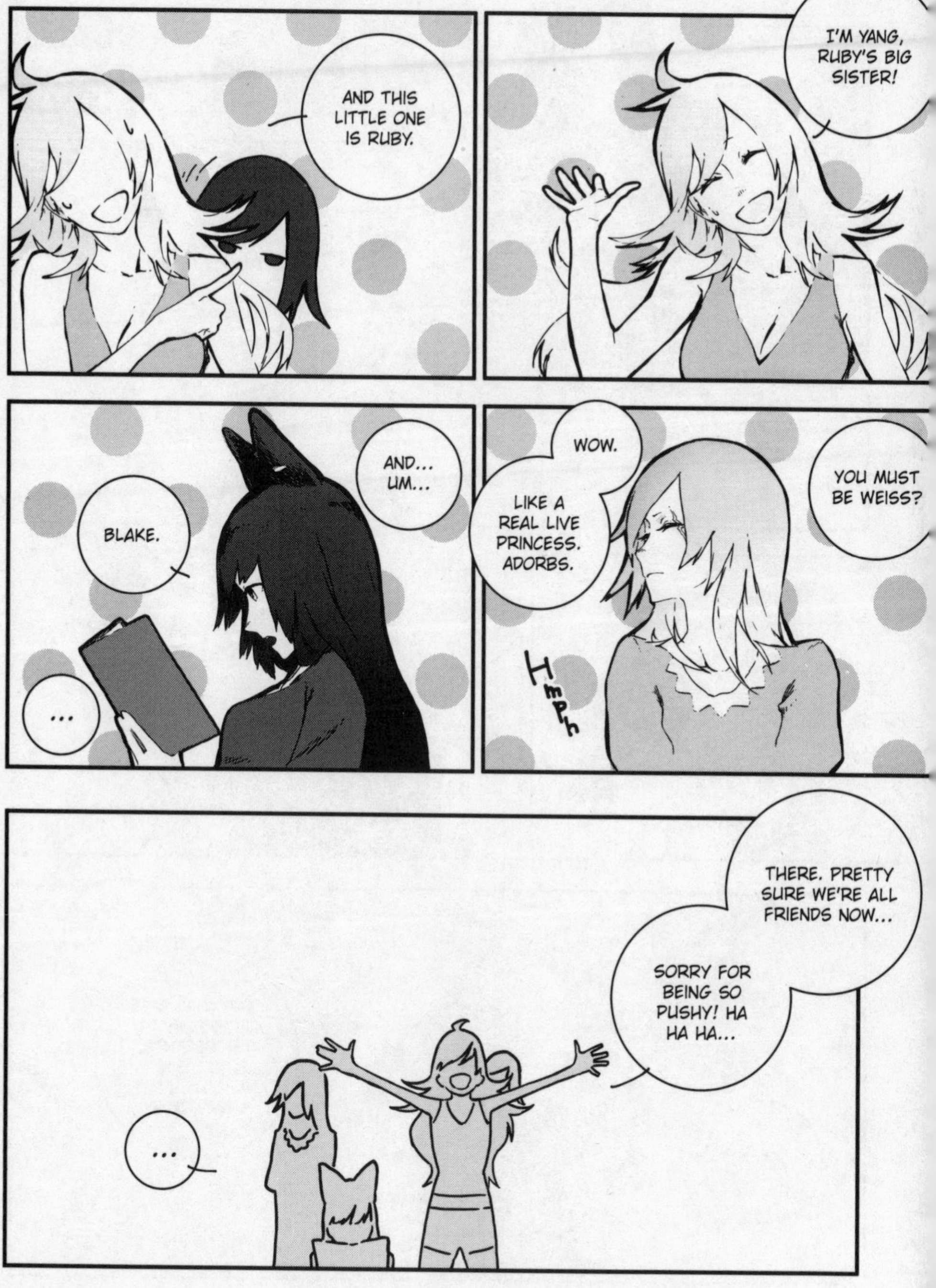
I'M YANG, RUBY'S BIG SISTER!
AND THIS LITTLE ONE IS RUBY.
YOU MUST BE WEISS?
WOW.
LIKE A REAL LIVE PRINCESS. ADORBS.
Hmph
AND... UM...
BLAKE.
...
THERE. PRETTY SURE WE'RE ALL FRIENDS NOW...
SORRY FOR BEING SO PUSHY! HA HA HA...
...

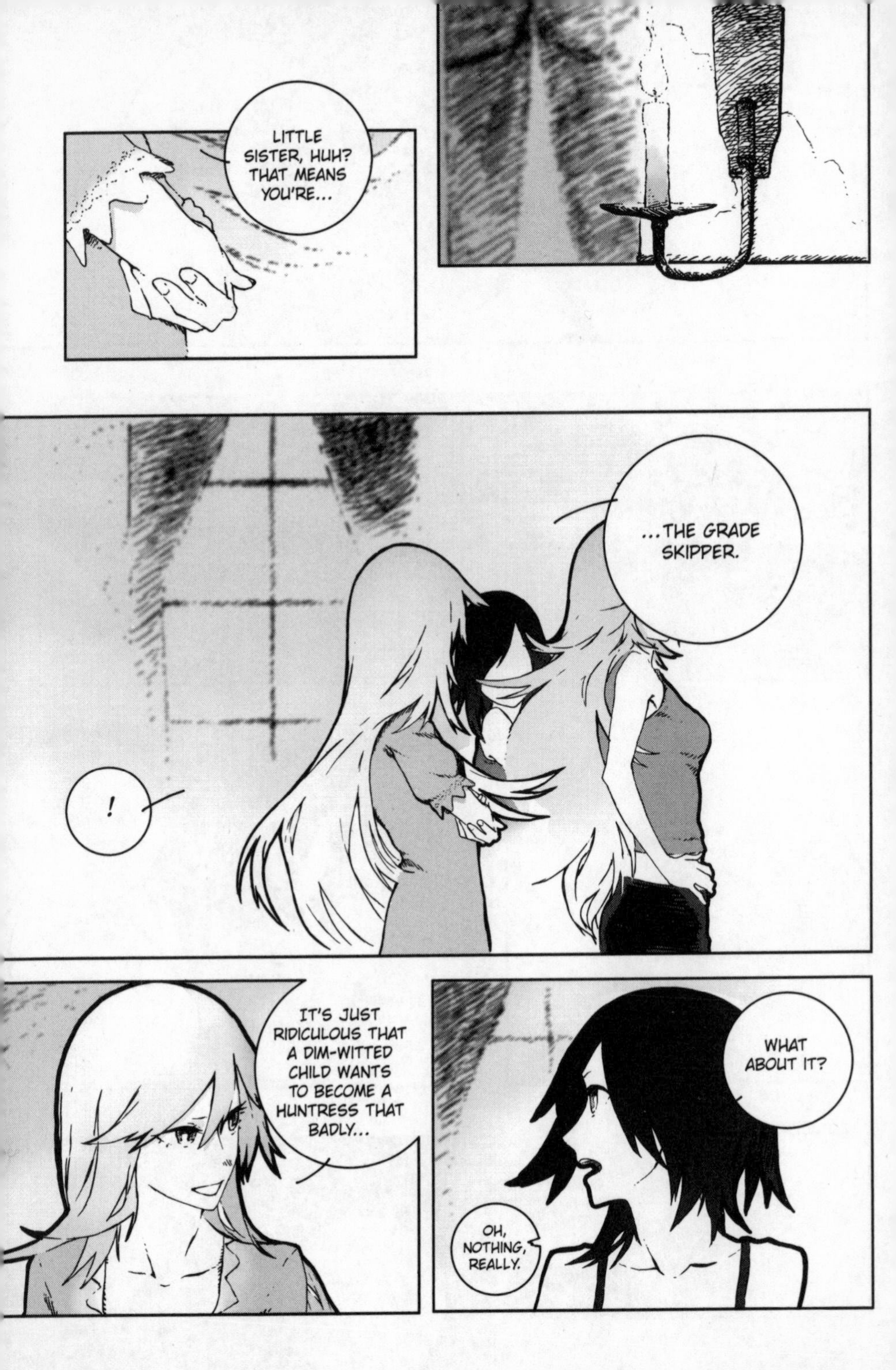
LITTLE SISTER, HUH? THAT MEANS YOU'RE...
...THE GRADE SKIPPER.
!
WHAT ABOUT IT?
OH, NOTHING, REALLY.
IT'S JUST RIDICULOUS THAT A DIM-WITTED CHILD WANTS TO BECOME A HUNTRESS THAT BADLY...

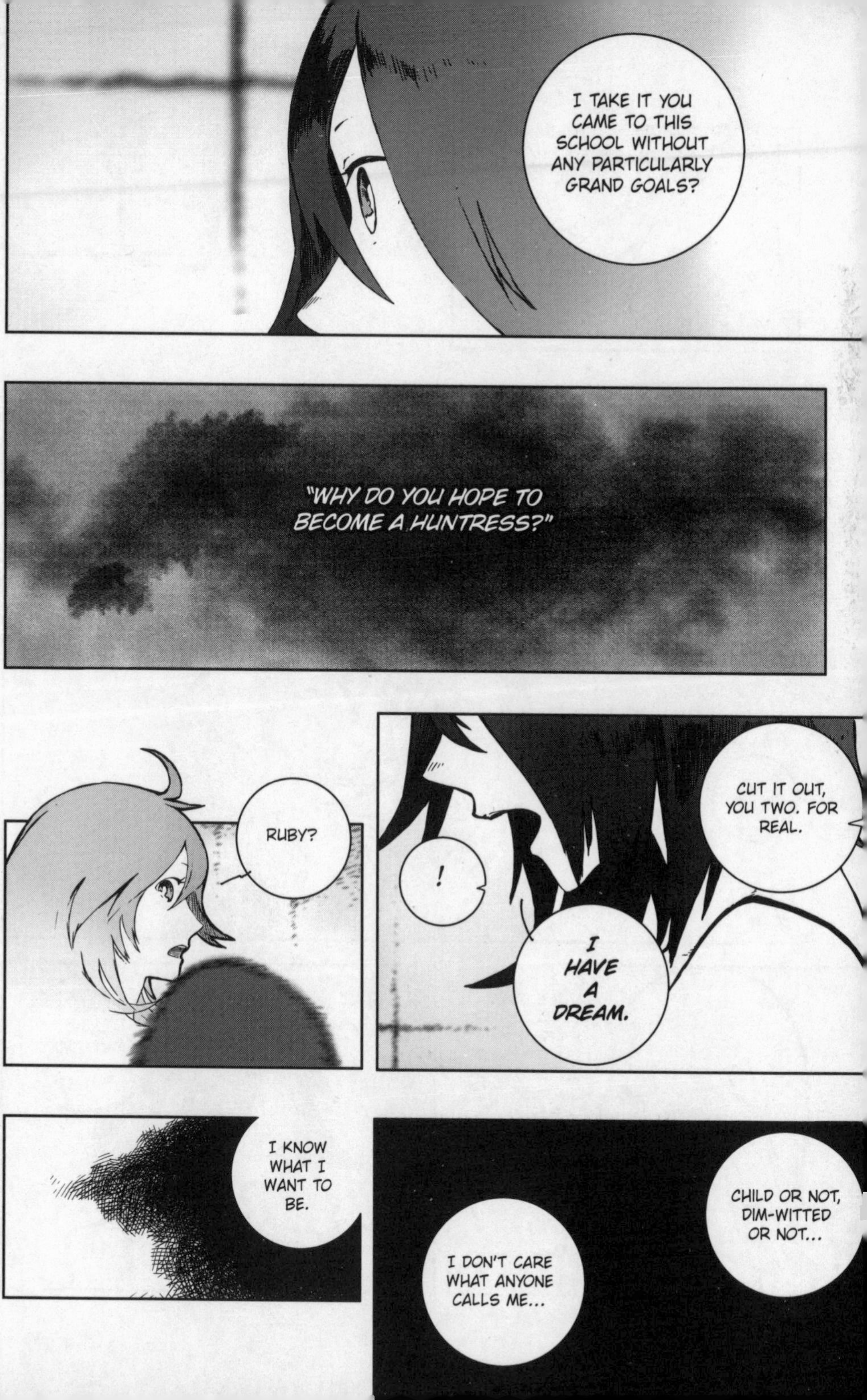
I TAKE IT YOU CAME TO THIS SCHOOL WITHOUT ANY PARTICULARLY GRAND GOALS?
"WHY DO YOU HOPE TO BECOME A HUNTRESS?"
CUT IT OUT, YOU TWO. FOR REAL.
!
I HAVE A DREAM.
RUBY?
CHILD OR NOT, DIM-WITTED OR NOT...
I DON'T CARE WHAT ANYONE CALLS ME...
I KNOW WHAT I WANT TO BE.

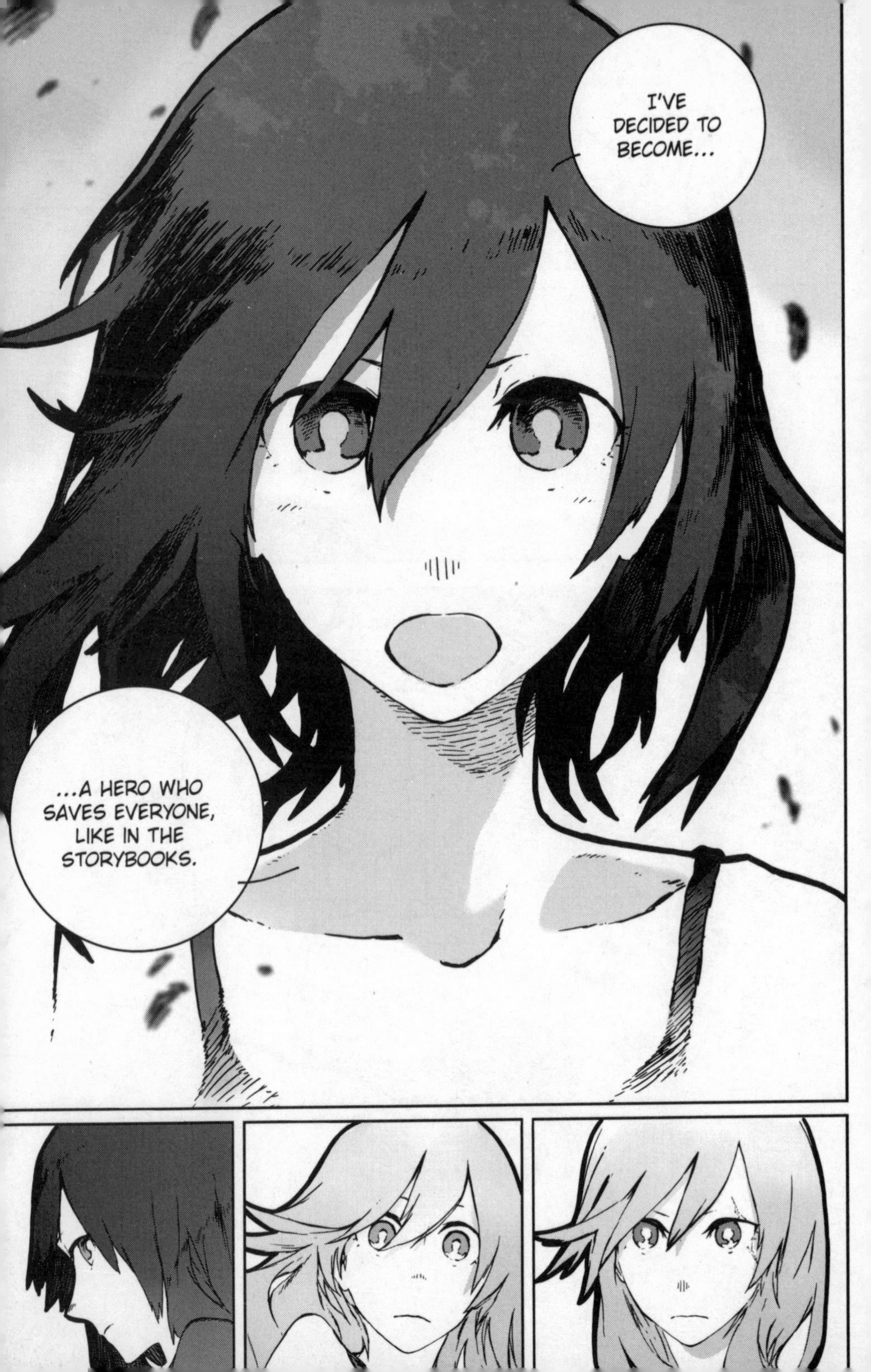
I'VE DECIDED TO BECOME...
...A HERO WHO SAVES EVERYONE, LIKE IN THE STORYBOOKS.

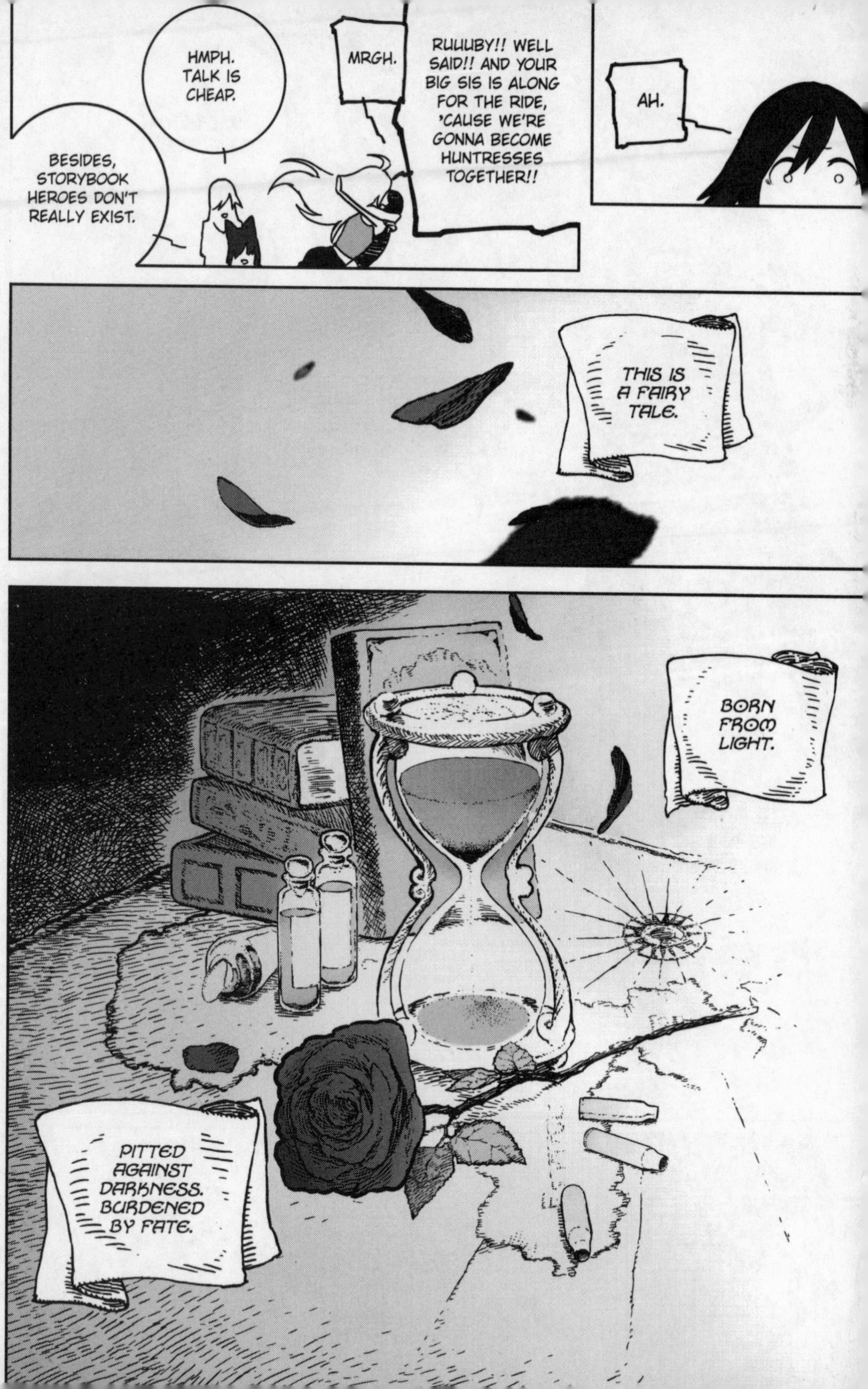
AH.
RUUUBY!! WELL SAID!! AND YOUR BIG SIS IS ALONG FOR THE RIDE, 'CAUSE WE'RE GONNA BECOME HUNTRESSES TOGETHER!!
MRGH.
HMPH. TALK IS CHEAP.
BESIDES, STORYBOOK HEROES DON'T REALLY EXIST.
THIS IS A FAIRY TALE.
BORN FROM LIGHT.
PITTED AGAINST DARKNESS. BURDENED BY FATE.

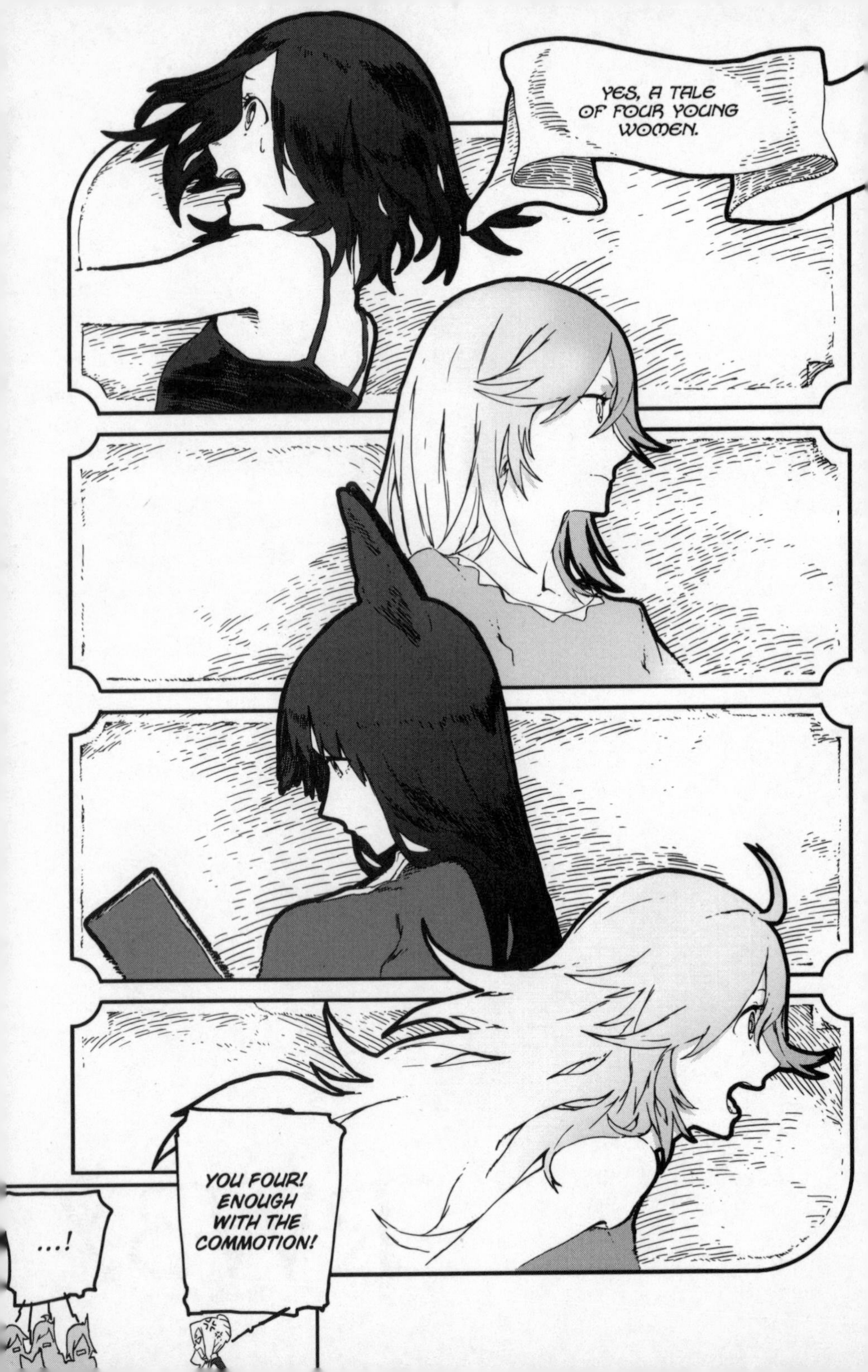
YES, A TALE OF FOUR YOUNG WOMEN.
YOU FOUR! ENOUGH WITH THE COMMOTION!
...!

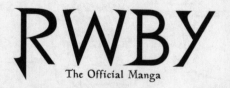
RWBY
The Official Manga

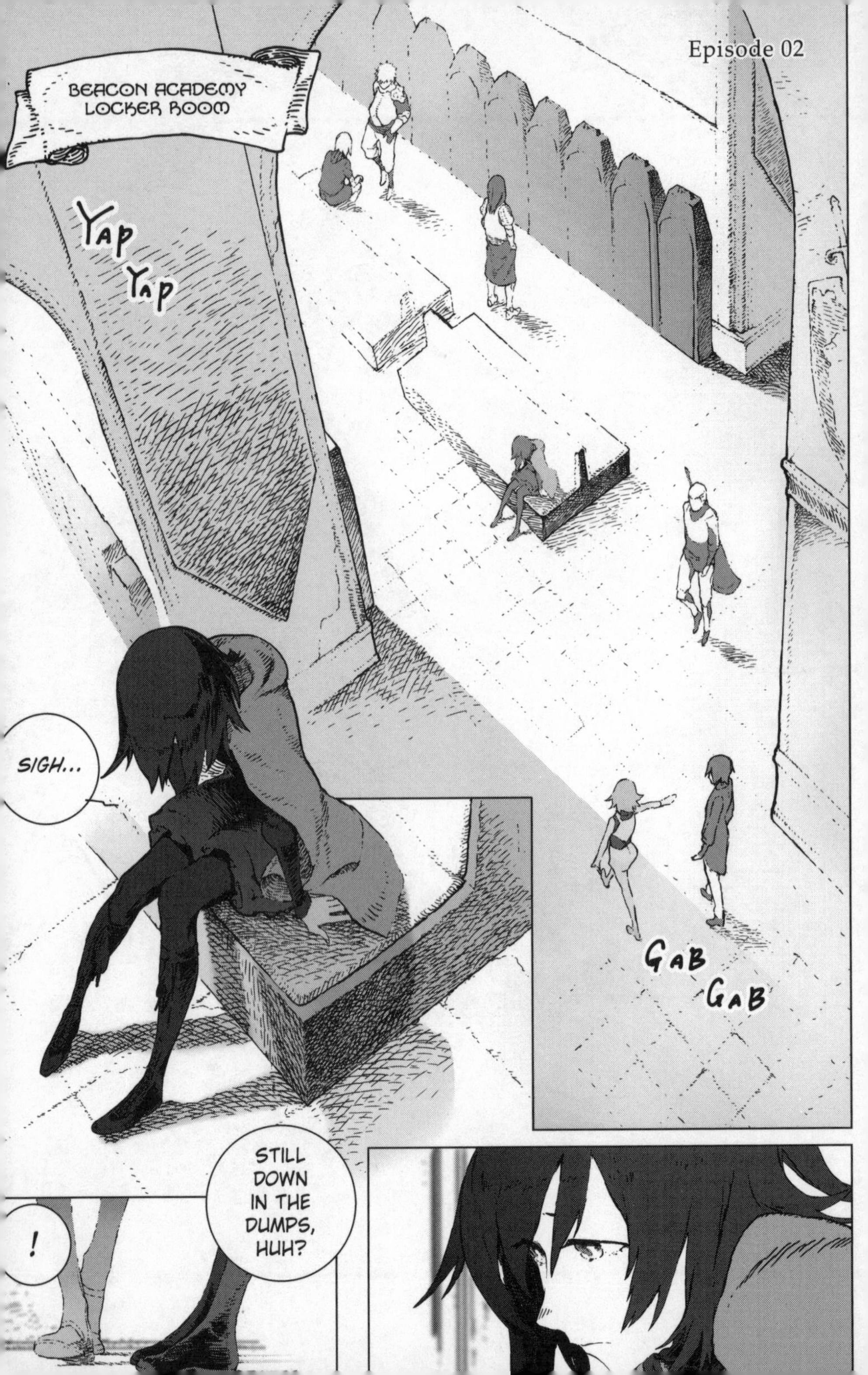
BEACON ACADEMY
LOCKER ROOM
YAP YAP
GAB GAB
SIGH...
STILL DOWN IN THE DUMPS, HUH?
!

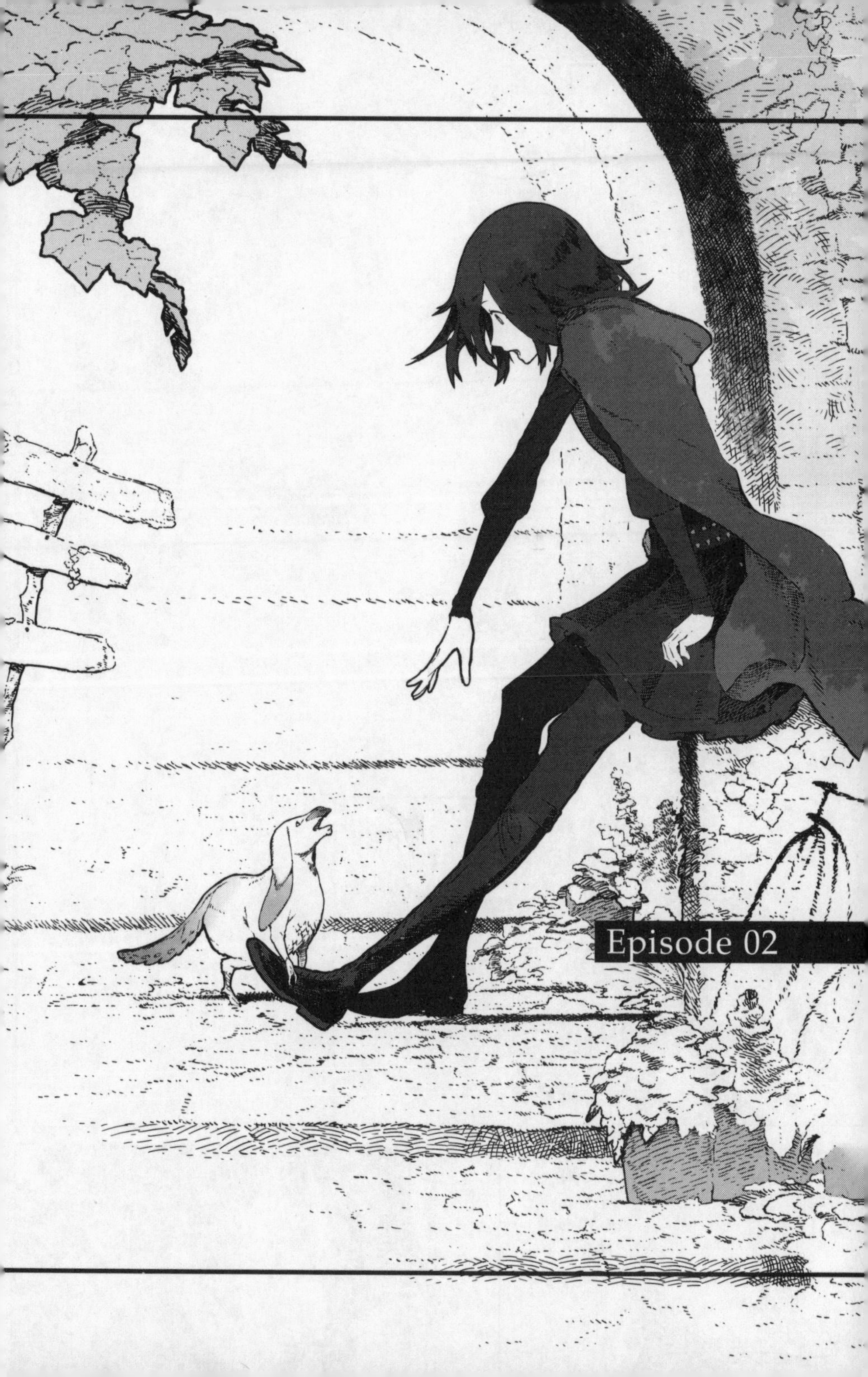
Episode 02

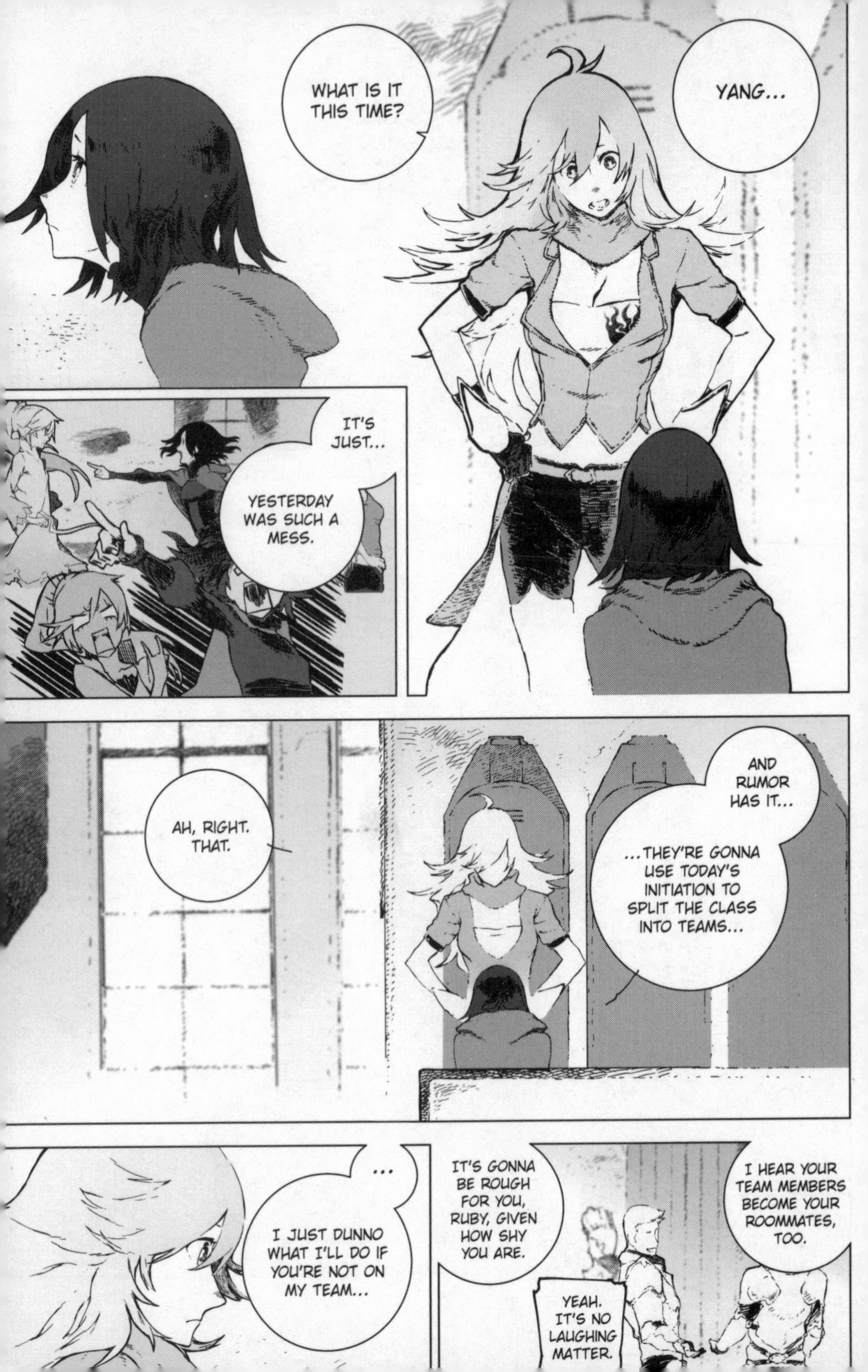
YANG...
WHAT IS IT THIS TIME?
IT'S JUST...
YESTERDAY WAS SUCH A MESS.
AND RUMOR HAS IT...
...THEY'RE GONNA USE TODAY'S INITIATION TO SPLIT THE CLASS INTO TEAMS...
AH, RIGHT. THAT.
I HEAR YOUR TEAM MEMBERS BECOME YOUR ROOMMATES, TOO.
IT'S GONNA BE ROUGH FOR YOU, RUBY, GIVEN HOW SHY YOU ARE.
YEAH. IT'S NO LAUGHING MATTER.
...
I JUST DUNNO WHAT I'LL DO IF YOU'RE NOT ON MY TEAM...

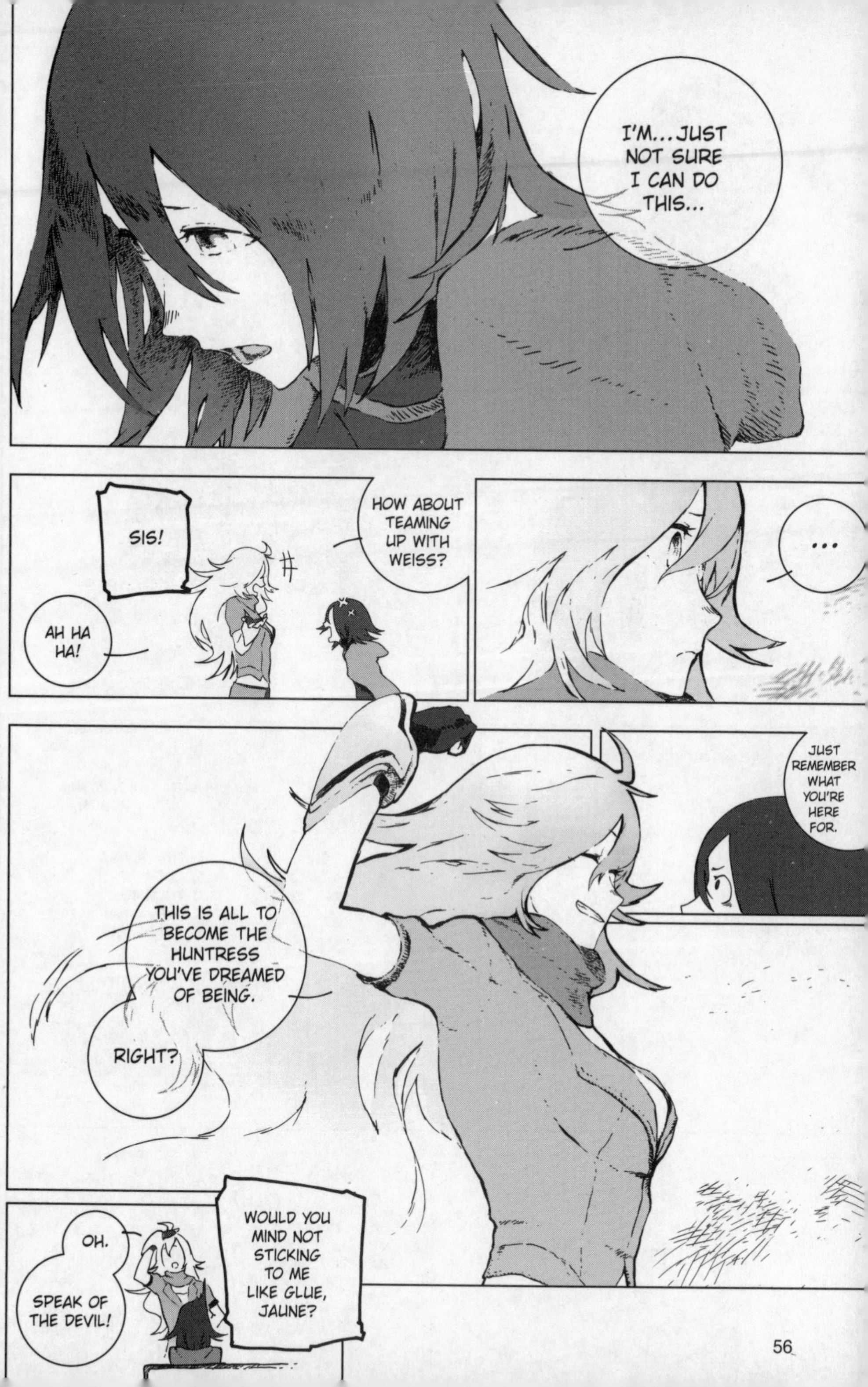
I'M...JUST NOT SURE I CAN DO THIS...
...
HOW ABOUT TEAMING UP WITH WEISS?
SIS!
AH HA HA!
JUST REMEMBER WHAT YOU'RE HERE FOR.
THIS IS ALL TO BECOME THE HUNTRESS YOU'VE DREAMED OF BEING.
RIGHT?
WOULD YOU MIND NOT STICKING TO ME LIKE GLUE, JAUNE?
OH.
SPEAK OF THE DEVIL!

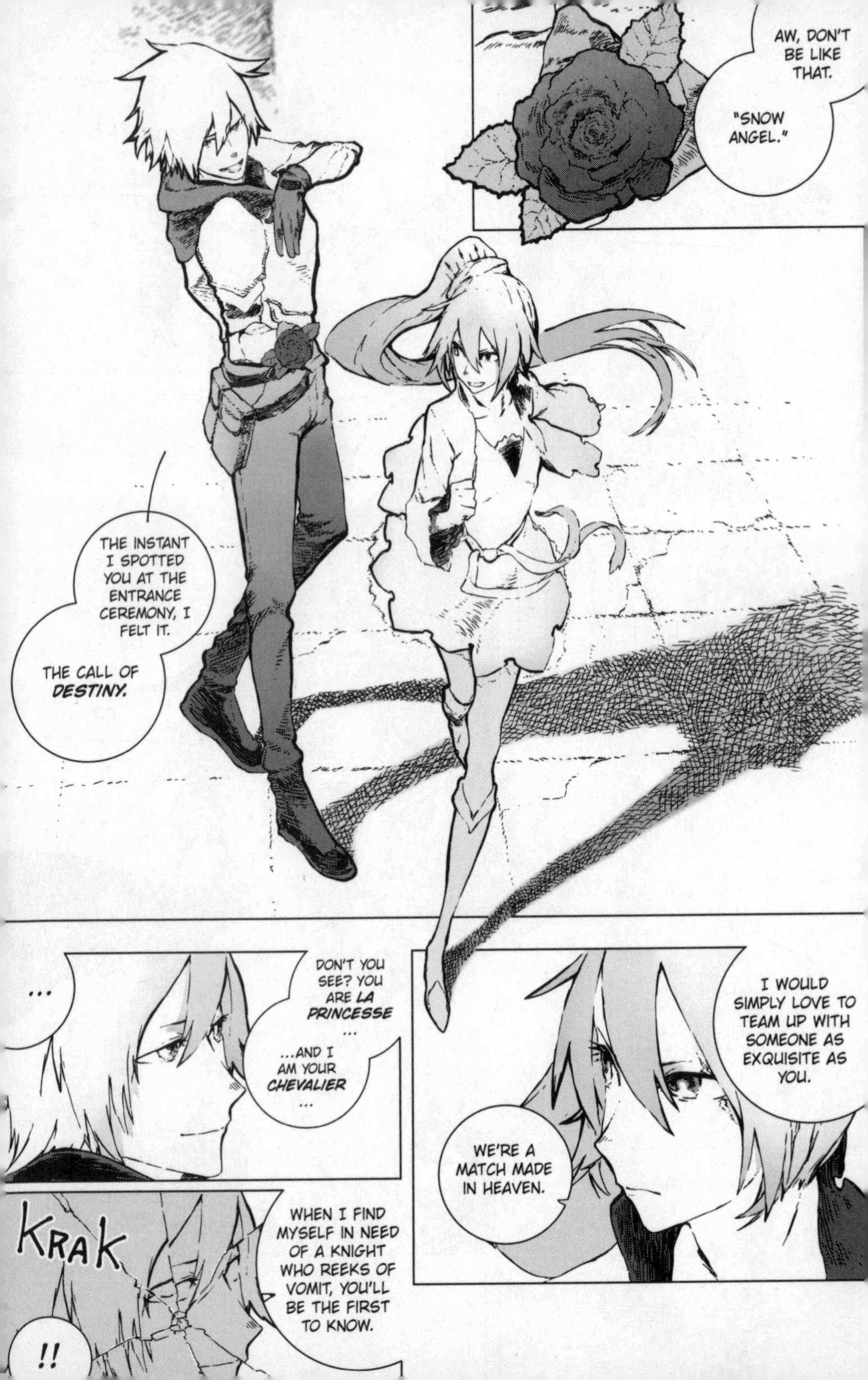
AW, DON'T BE LIKE THAT.
"SNOW ANGEL."
THE INSTANT I SPOTTED YOU AT THE ENTRANCE CEREMONY, I FELT IT.
THE CALL OF *DESTINY.*
I WOULD SIMPLY LOVE TO TEAM UP WITH SOMEONE AS EXQUISITE AS YOU.
WE'RE A MATCH MADE IN HEAVEN.
DON'T YOU SEE? YOU ARE *LA PRINCESSE* ...
...AND I AM YOUR *CHEVALIER* ...
...
WHEN I FIND MYSELF IN NEED OF A KNIGHT WHO REEKS OF VOMIT, YOU'LL BE THE FIRST TO KNOW.
KRAK
!!

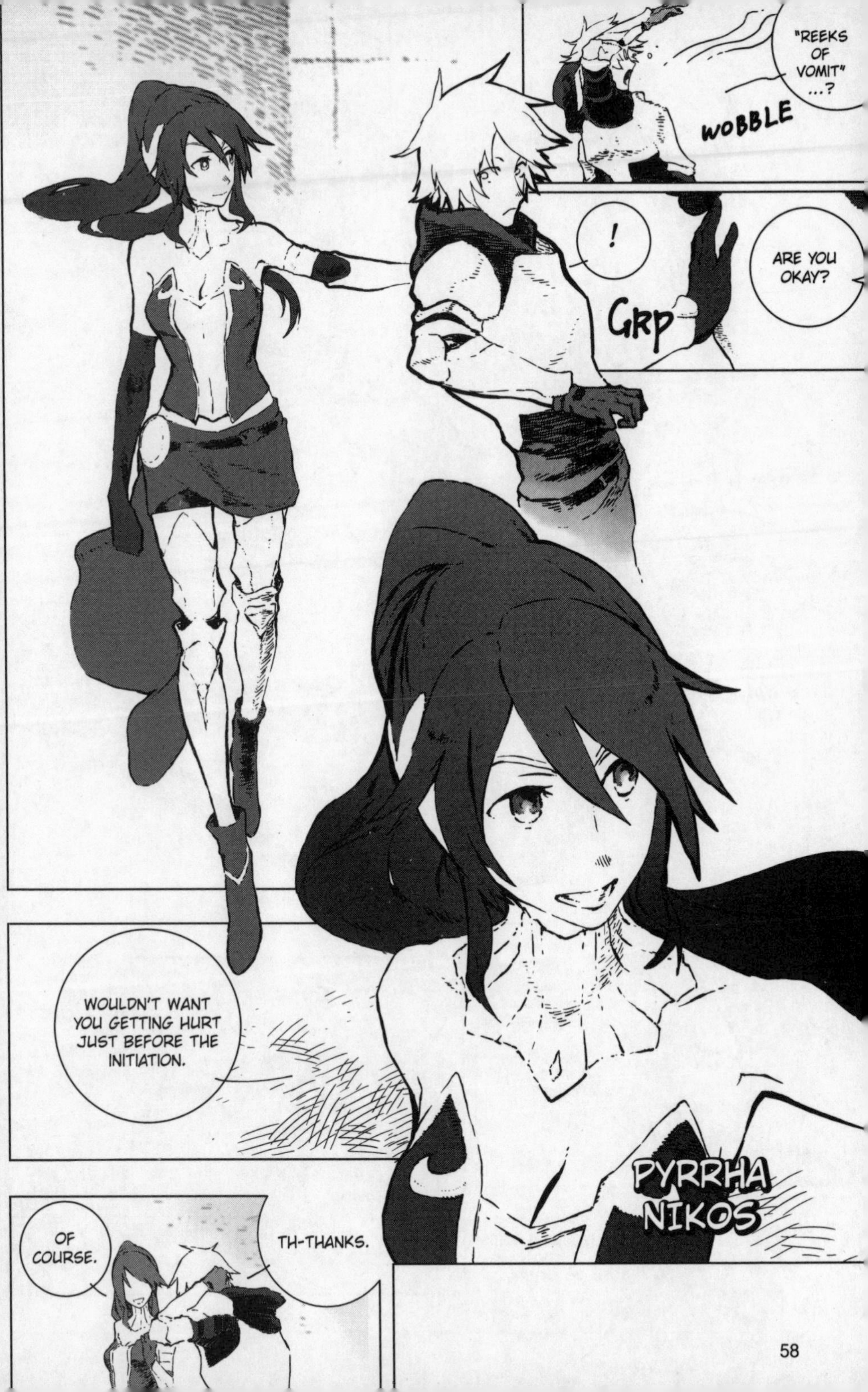
"REEKS OF VOMIT" ...?
WOBBLE
ARE YOU OKAY?
!
GRP
PYRRHA NIKOS
WOULDN'T WANT YOU GETTING HURT JUST BEFORE THE INITIATION.
TH-THANKS.
OF COURSE.

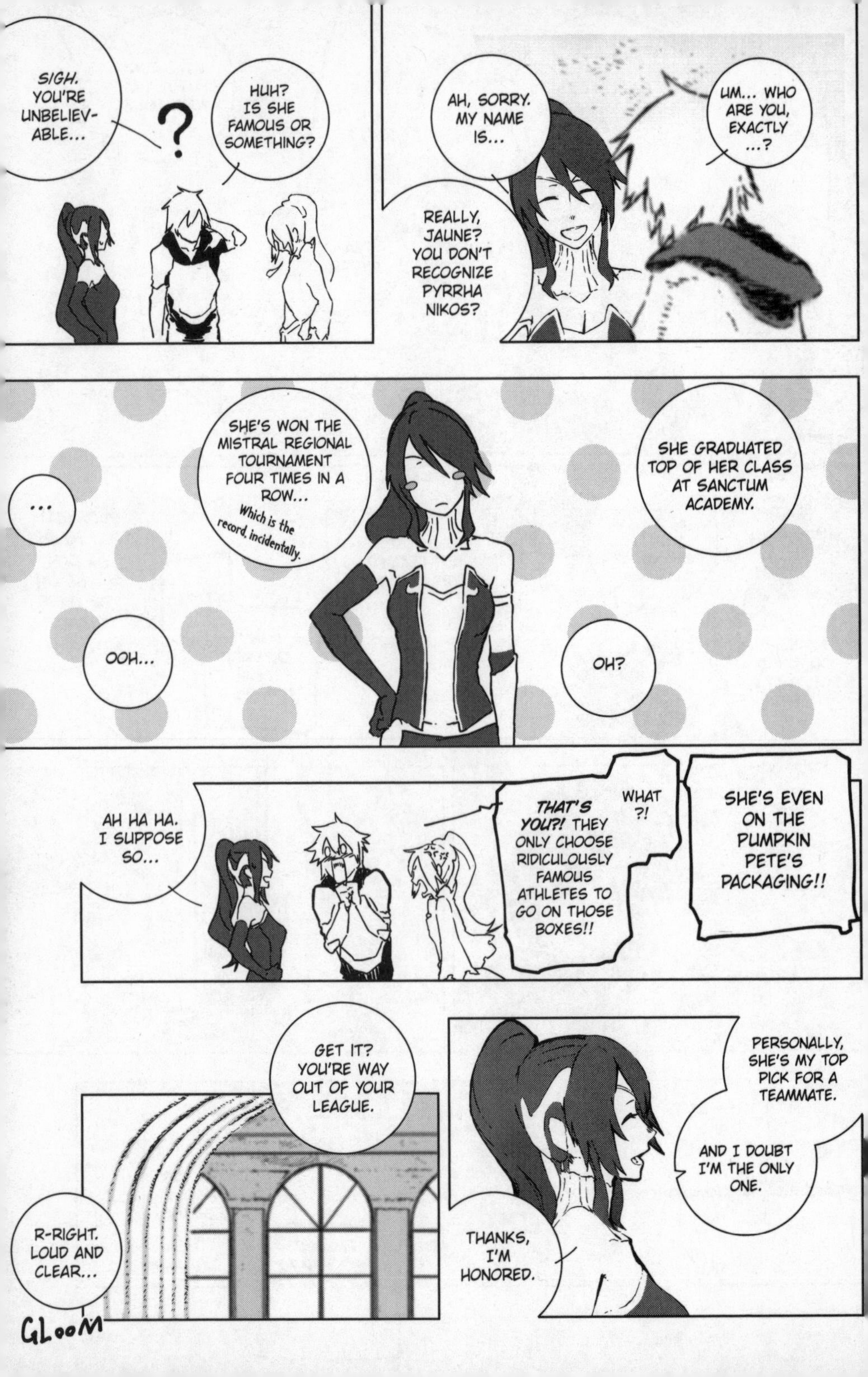
UM... WHO ARE YOU, EXACTLY ...?
AH, SORRY. MY NAME IS...
REALLY, JAUNE? YOU DON'T RECOGNIZE PYRRHA NIKOS?
HUH? IS SHE FAMOUS OR SOMETHING?
?
SIGH. YOU'RE UNBELIEV-ABLE...
SHE GRADUATED TOP OF HER CLASS AT SANCTUM ACADEMY.
SHE'S WON THE MISTRAL REGIONAL TOURNAMENT FOUR TIMES IN A ROW...
Which is the record, incidentally.
...
OH?
OOH...
SHE'S EVEN ON THE PUMPKIN PETE'S PACKAGING!!
WHAT ?!
THAT'S YOU?! THEY ONLY CHOOSE RIDICULOUSLY FAMOUS ATHLETES TO GO ON THOSE BOXES!!
AH HA HA. I SUPPOSE SO...
PERSONALLY, SHE'S MY TOP PICK FOR A TEAMMATE.
AND I DOUBT I'M THE ONLY ONE.
THANKS, I'M HONORED.
GET IT? YOU'RE WAY OUT OF YOUR LEAGUE.
R-RIGHT. LOUD AND CLEAR...
GLOOM

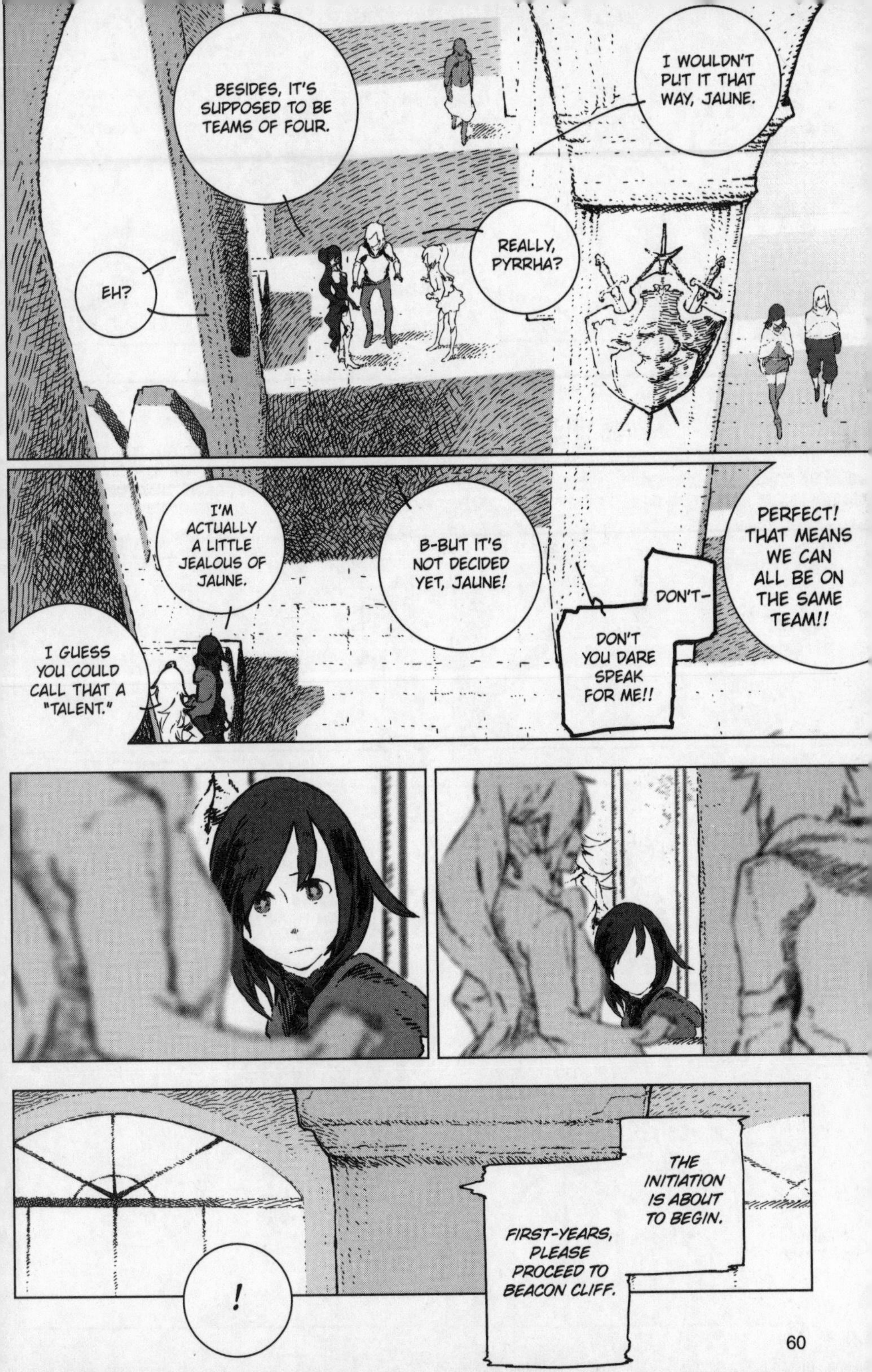
I WOULDN'T PUT IT THAT WAY, JAUNE.
BESIDES, IT'S SUPPOSED TO BE TEAMS OF FOUR.
REALLY, PYRRHA?
EH?
PERFECT! THAT MEANS WE CAN ALL BE ON THE SAME TEAM!!
DON'T-
DON'T YOU DARE SPEAK FOR ME!!
B-BUT IT'S NOT DECIDED YET, JAUNE!
I'M ACTUALLY A LITTLE JEALOUS OF JAUNE.
I GUESS YOU COULD CALL THAT A "TALENT."
THE INITIATION IS ABOUT TO BEGIN.
FIRST-YEARS, PLEASE PROCEED TO BEACON CLIFF.
!

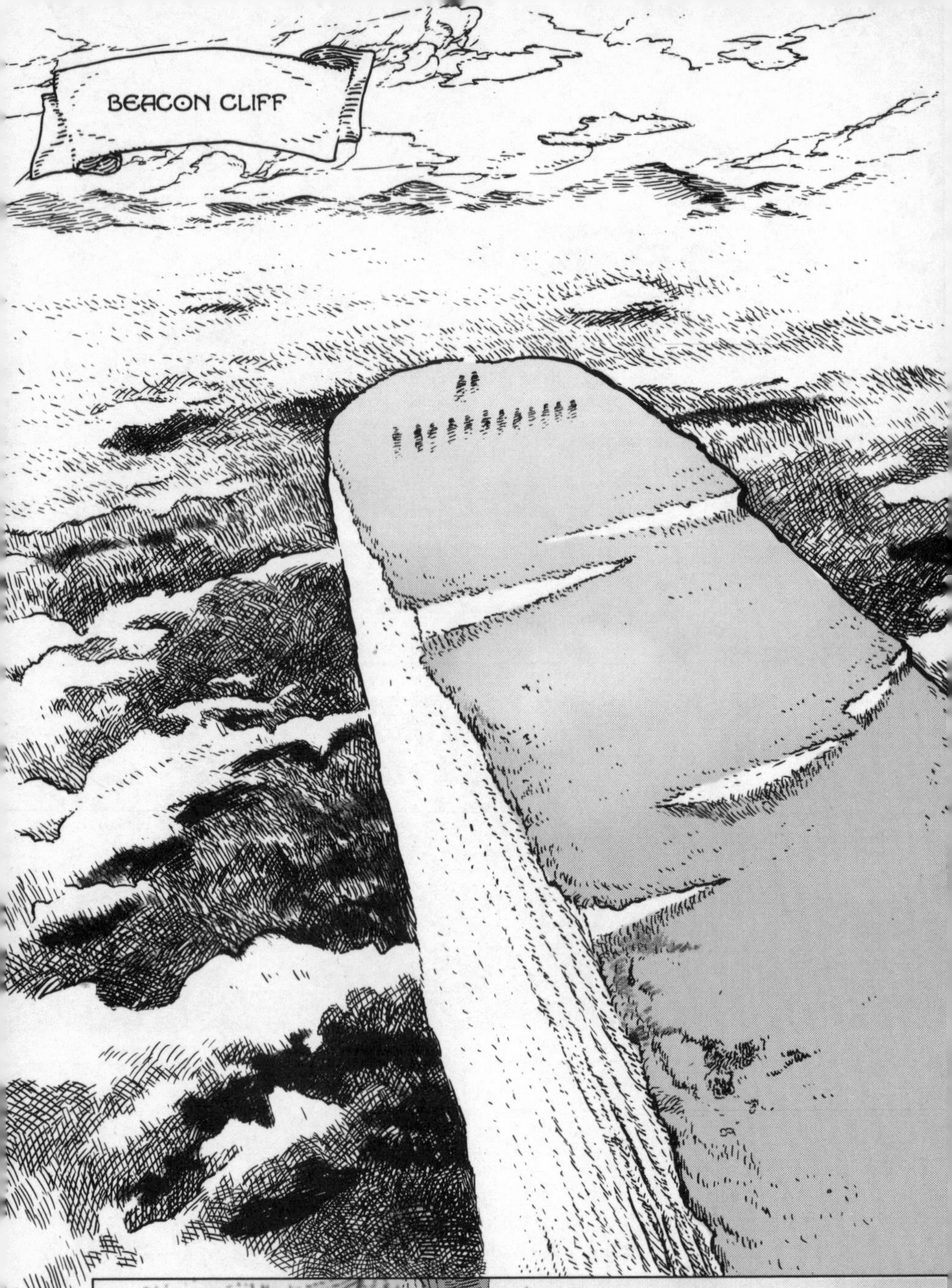
BEACON CLIFF
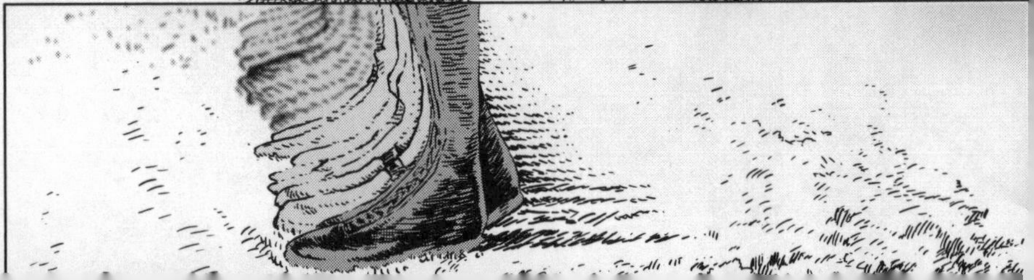

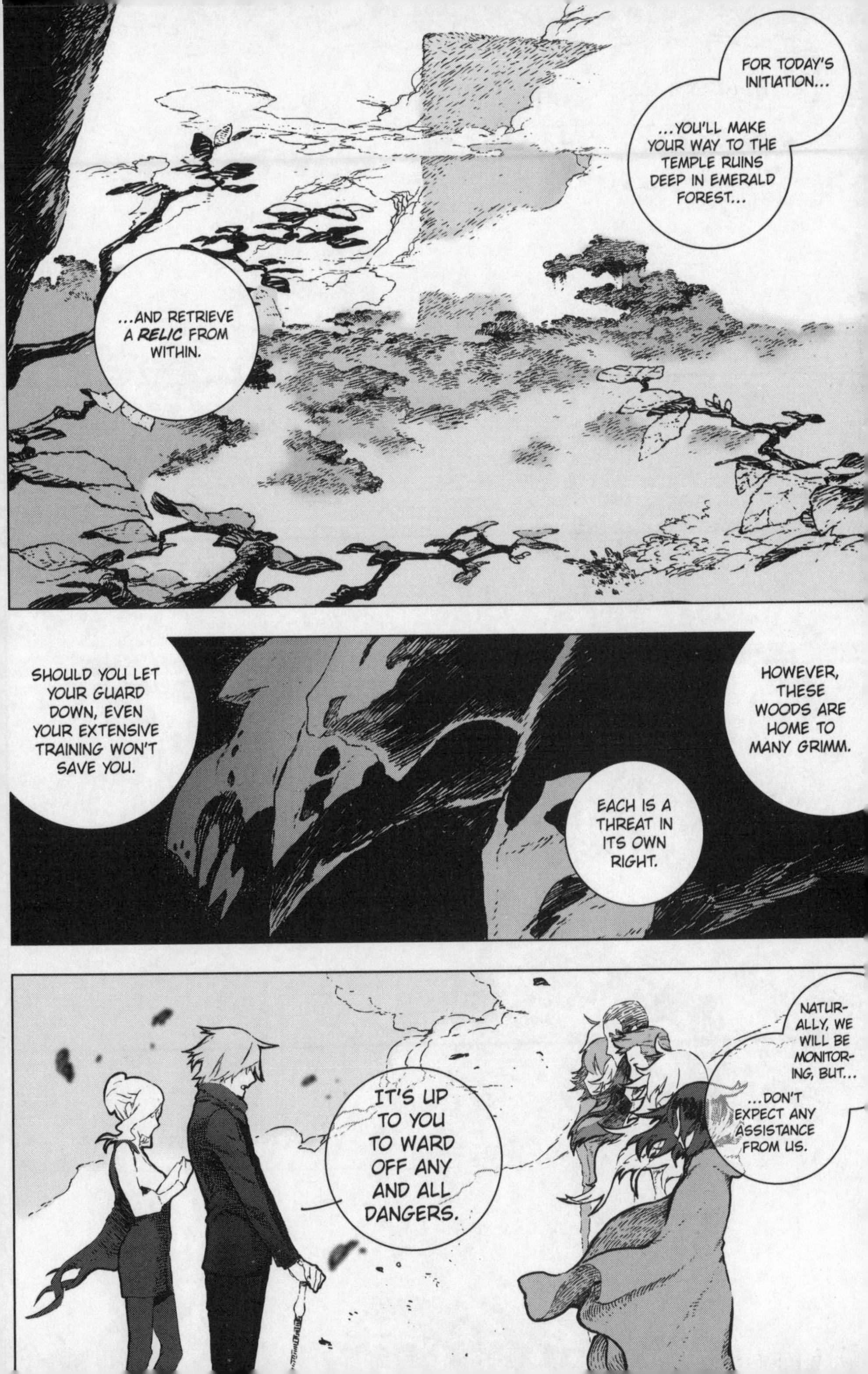
FOR TODAY'S INITIATION...
...YOU'LL MAKE YOUR WAY TO THE TEMPLE RUINS DEEP IN EMERALD FOREST...
...AND RETRIEVE A *RELIC* FROM WITHIN.
HOWEVER, THESE WOODS ARE HOME TO MANY GRIMM.
EACH IS A THREAT IN ITS OWN RIGHT.
SHOULD YOU LET YOUR GUARD DOWN, EVEN YOUR EXTENSIVE TRAINING WON'T SAVE YOU.
NATURALLY, WE WILL BE MONITORING, BUT...
...DON'T EXPECT ANY ASSISTANCE FROM US.
IT'S UP TO YOU TO WARD OFF ANY AND ALL DANGERS.

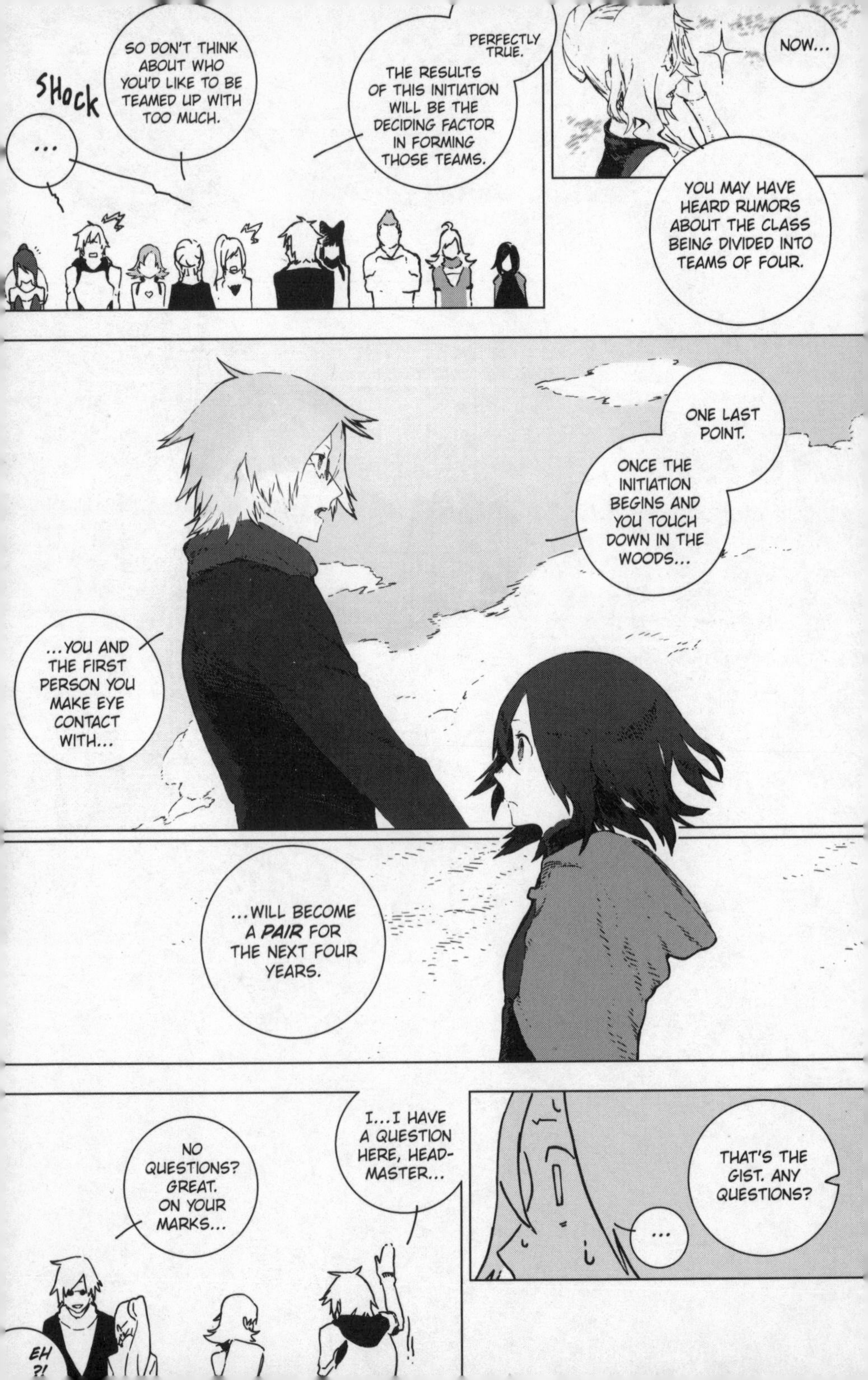
NOW...
YOU MAY HAVE HEARD RUMORS ABOUT THE CLASS BEING DIVIDED INTO TEAMS OF FOUR.
PERFECTLY TRUE.
THE RESULTS OF THIS INITIATION WILL BE THE DECIDING FACTOR IN FORMING THOSE TEAMS.
SO DON'T THINK ABOUT WHO YOU'D LIKE TO BE TEAMED UP WITH TOO MUCH.
SHOCK
...
ONE LAST POINT.
ONCE THE INITIATION BEGINS AND YOU TOUCH DOWN IN THE WOODS...
...YOU AND THE FIRST PERSON YOU MAKE EYE CONTACT WITH...
...WILL BECOME A PAIR FOR THE NEXT FOUR YEARS.
THAT'S THE GIST. ANY QUESTIONS?
...
I...I HAVE A QUESTION HERE, HEAD-MASTER...
NO QUESTIONS? GREAT. ON YOUR MARKS...
EH?!

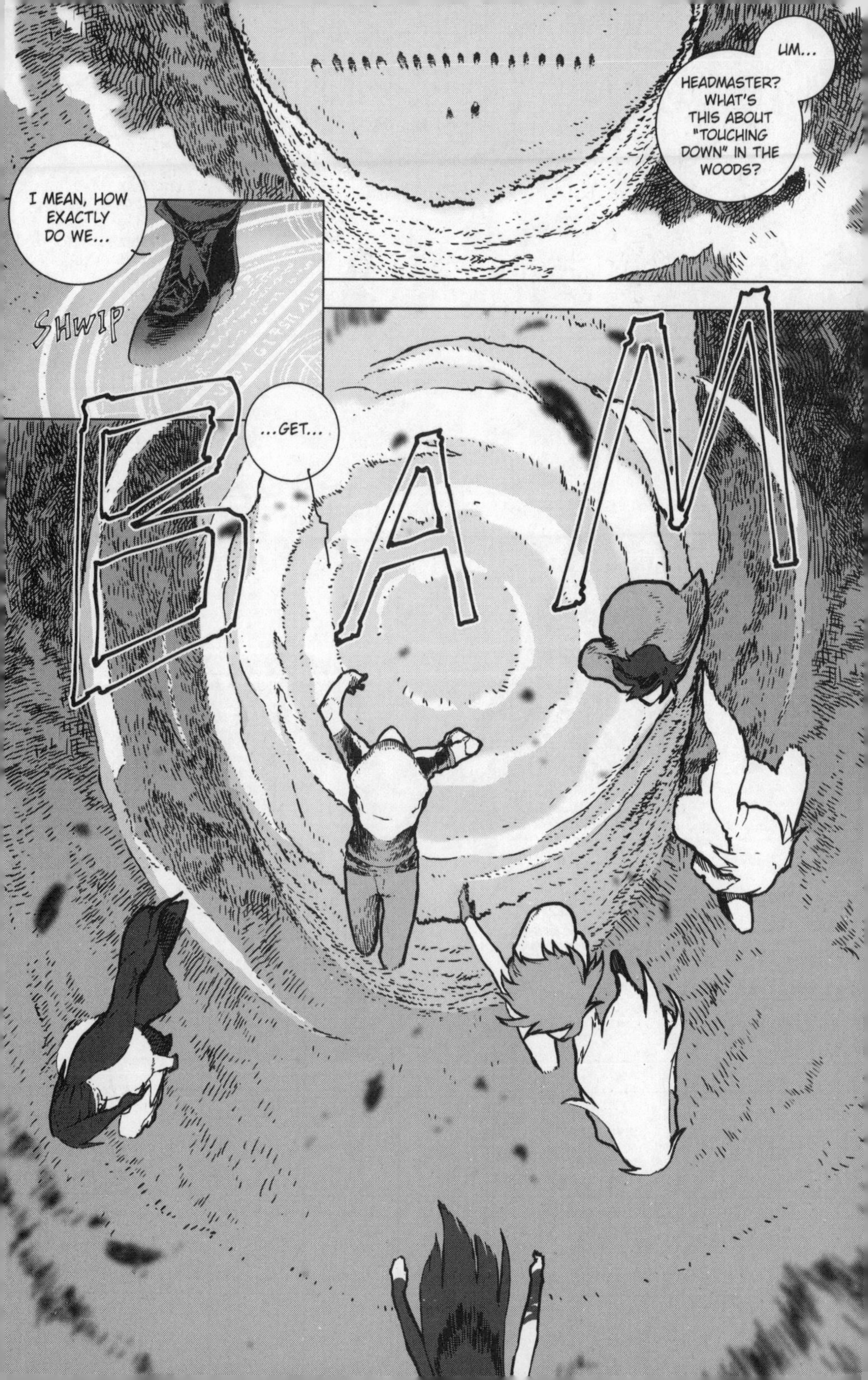
UM...
HEADMASTER? WHAT'S THIS ABOUT "TOUCHING DOWN" IN THE WOODS?
I MEAN, HOW EXACTLY DO WE...
SHWIP
...GET...
BAM

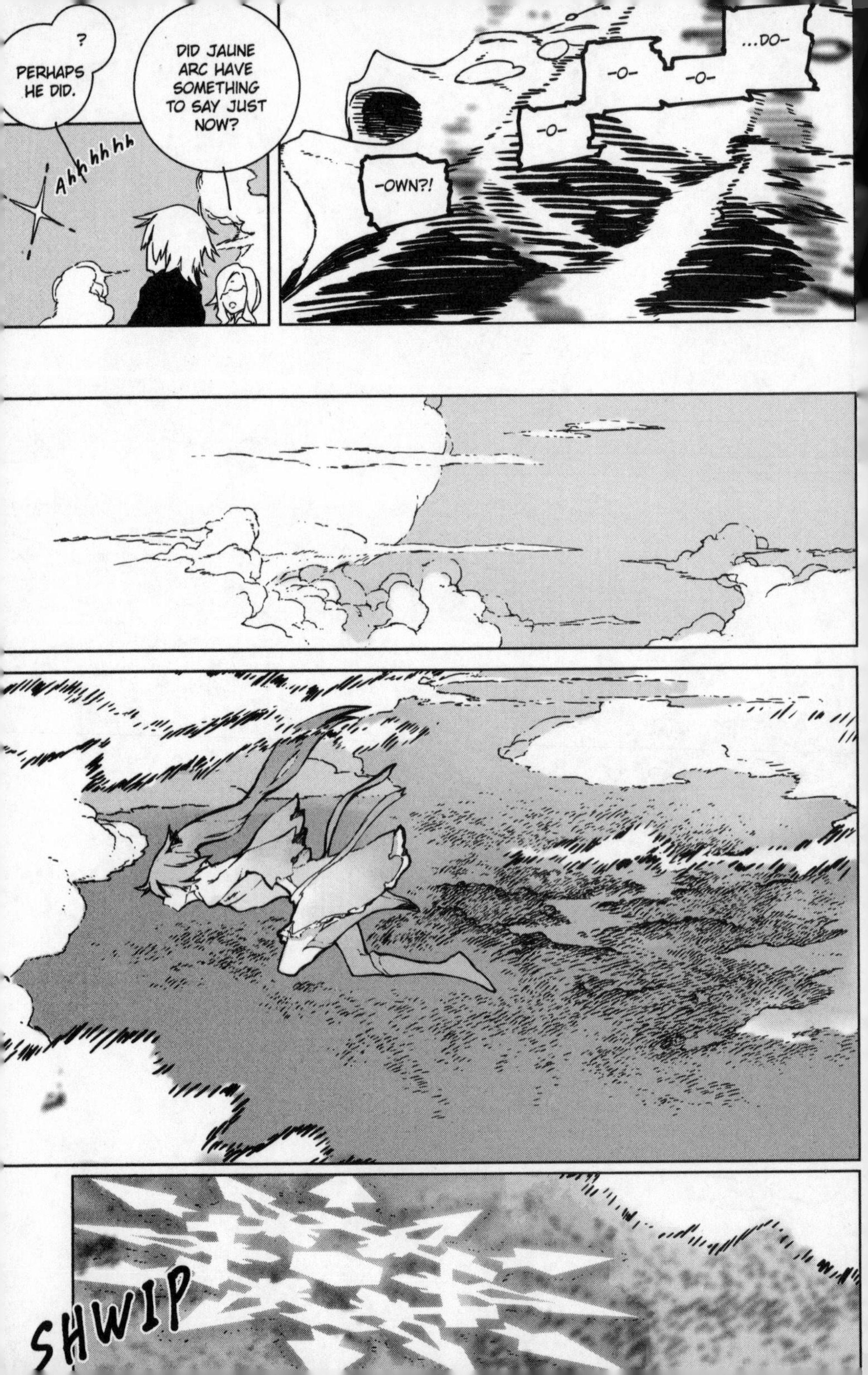
...DO-
-O-
-O-
-O-
-OWN?!
DID JAUNE ARC HAVE SOMETHING TO SAY JUST NOW?
? PERHAPS HE DID.
Ahhhhhh
SHWIP

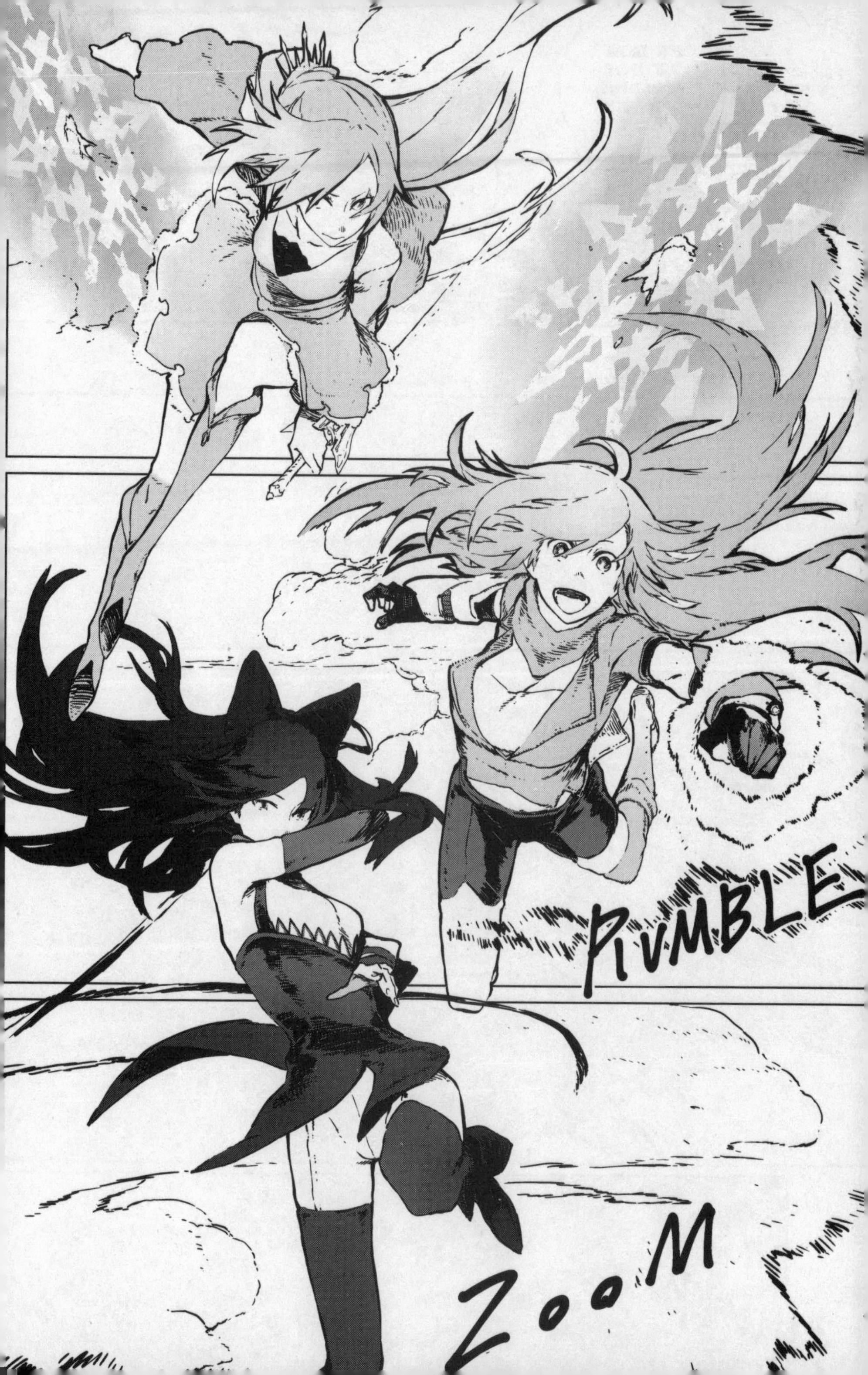
RUMBLE
ZOOM

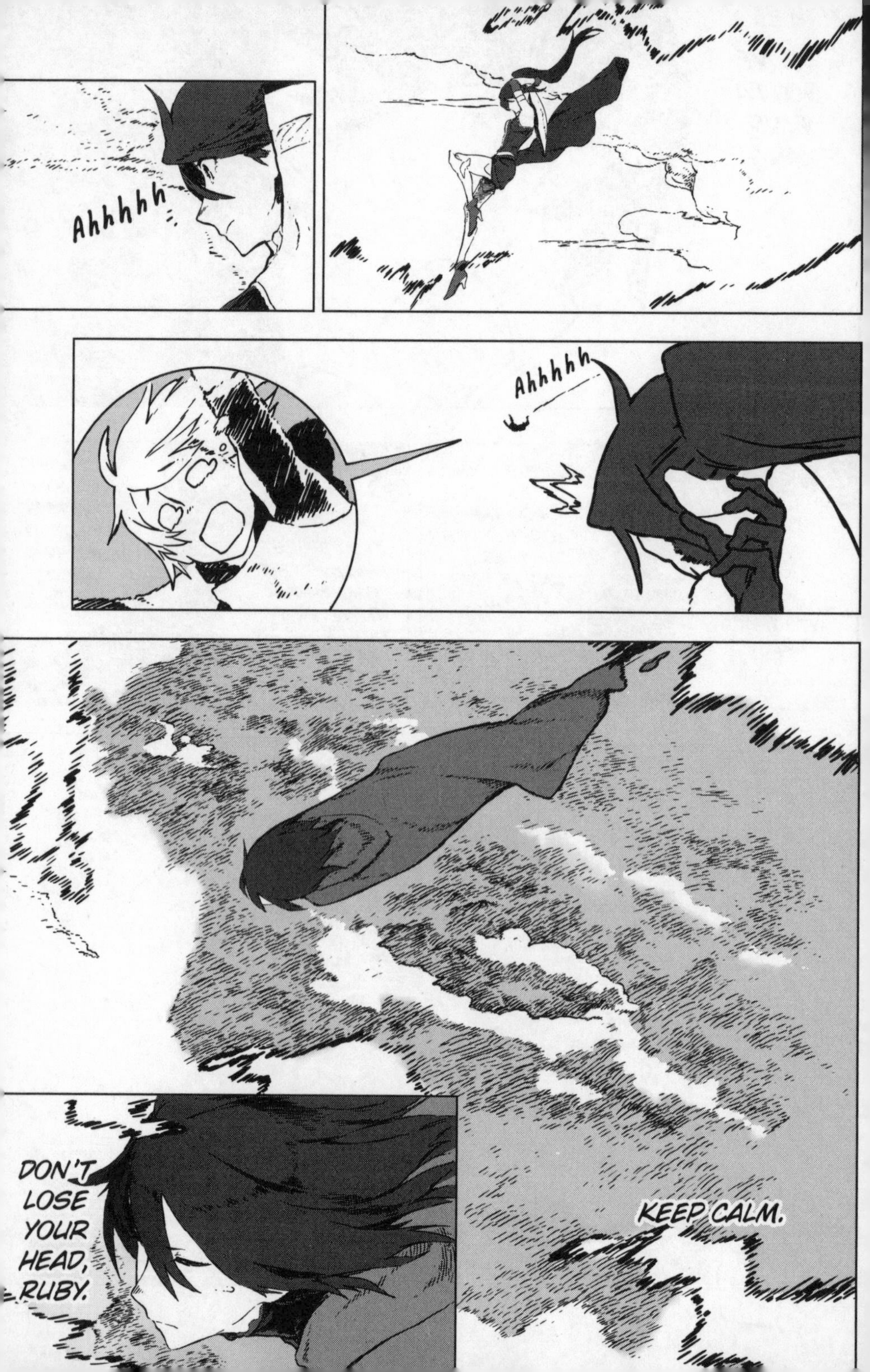
Ahhhhh
Ahhhhh
KEEP CALM.
DON'T LOSE YOUR HEAD, RUBY.

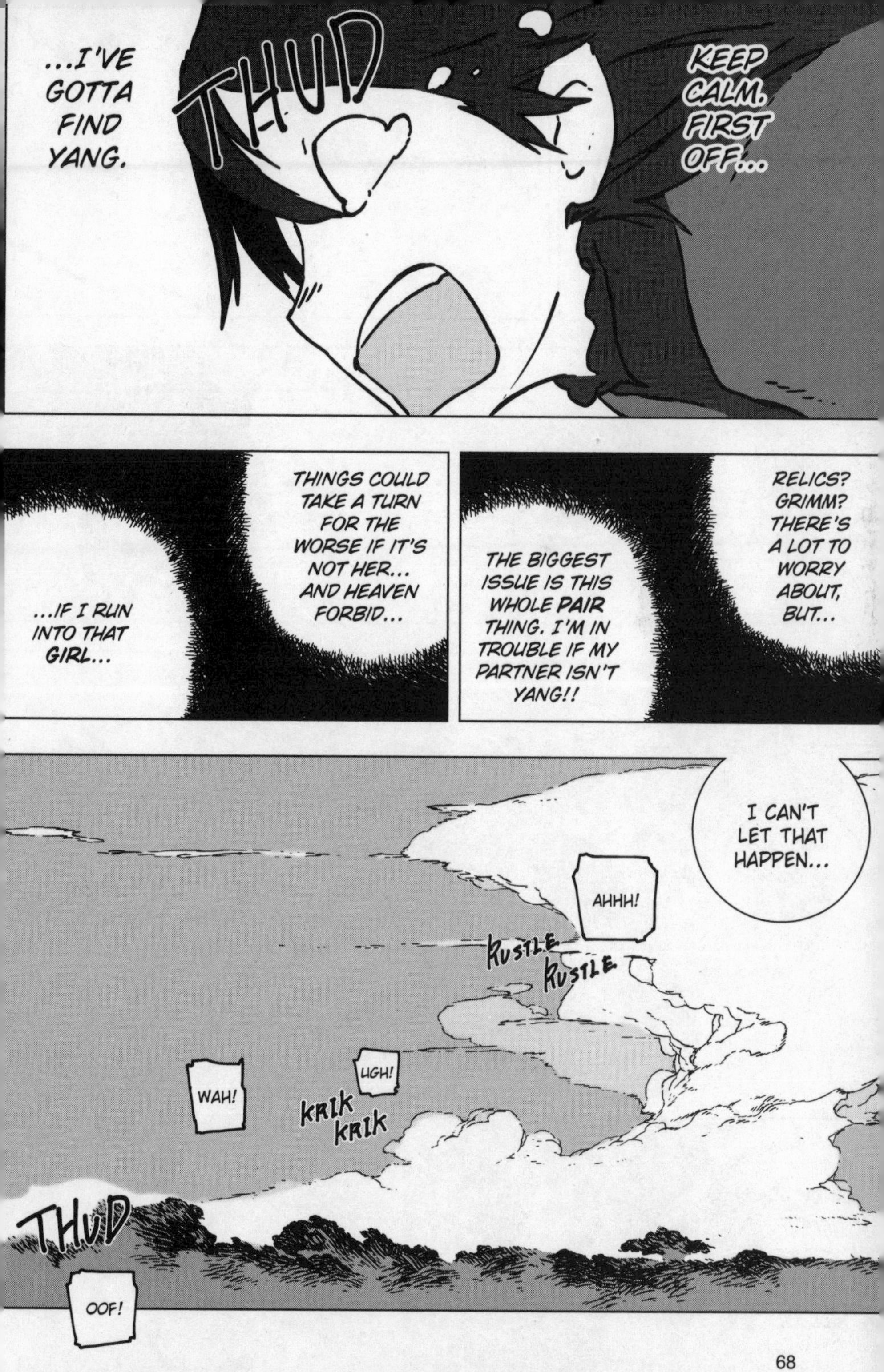
KEEP CALM. FIRST OFF...
THUD
...I'VE GOTTA FIND YANG.
RELICS? GRIMM? THERE'S A LOT TO WORRY ABOUT, BUT...
THE BIGGEST ISSUE IS THIS WHOLE PAIR THING. I'M IN TROUBLE IF MY PARTNER ISN'T YANG!!
THINGS COULD TAKE A TURN FOR THE WORSE IF IT'S NOT HER... AND HEAVEN FORBID...
...IF I RUN INTO THAT GIRL...
I CAN'T LET THAT HAPPEN...
AHHH!
RUSTLE
RUSTLE
UGH!
KRIK
KRIK
WAH!
THUD
OOF!

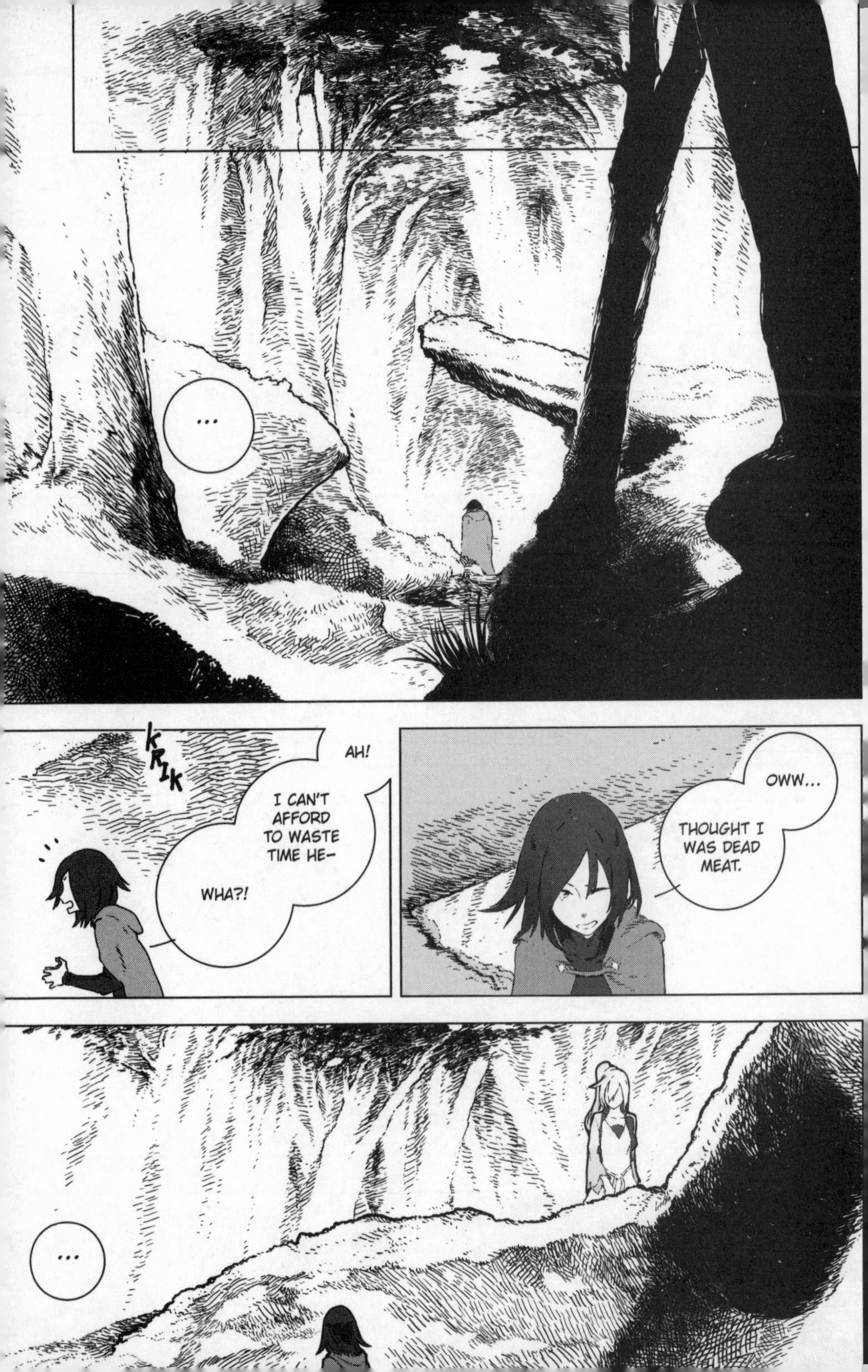
...
OWW...
THOUGHT I WAS DEAD MEAT.
AH!
KRIK
I CAN'T AFFORD TO WASTE TIME HE-
WHA?!
...

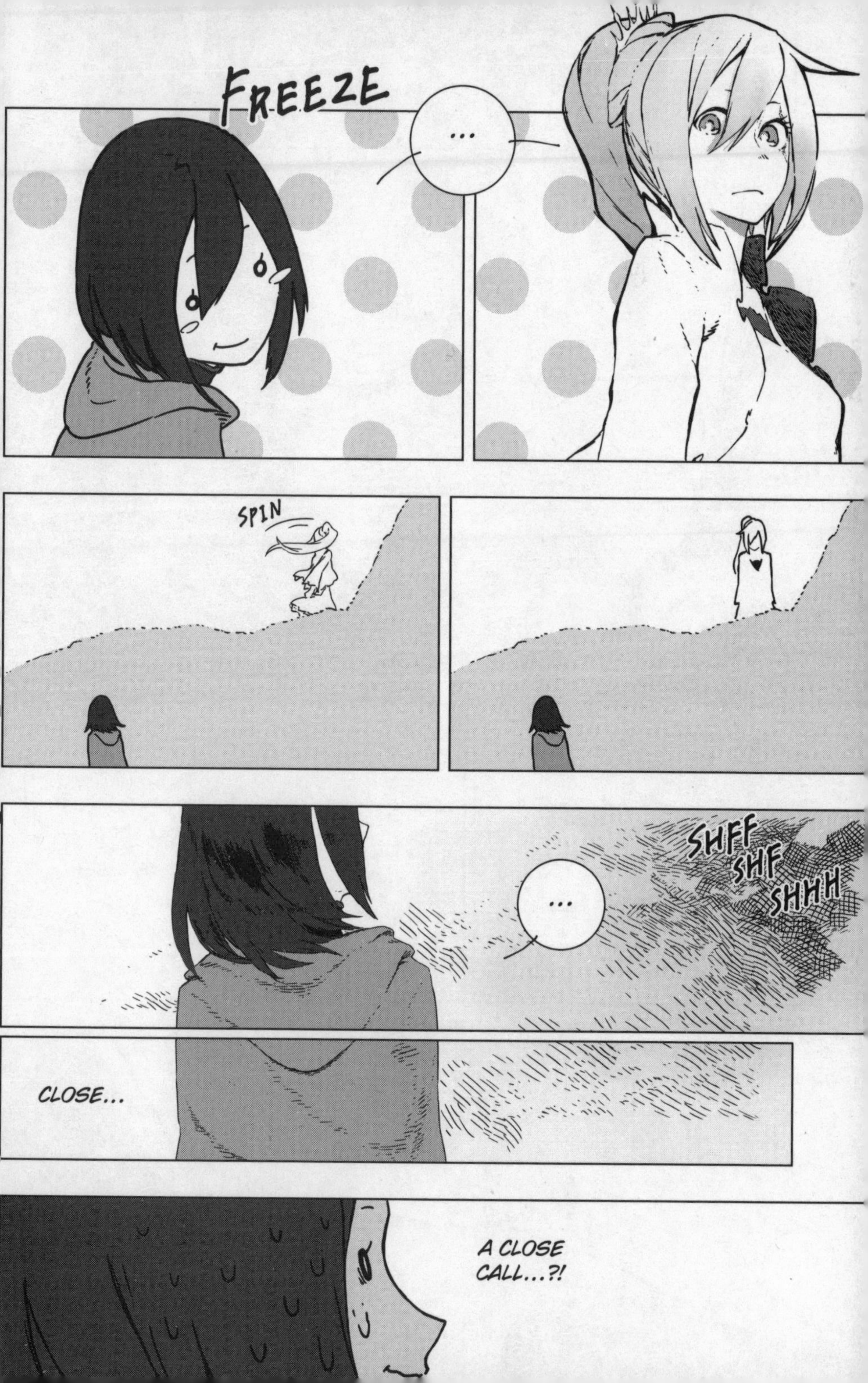
...
FREEZE
SPIN
SHFF
SHF
SHHH
...
CLOSE...
A CLOSE CALL...?!

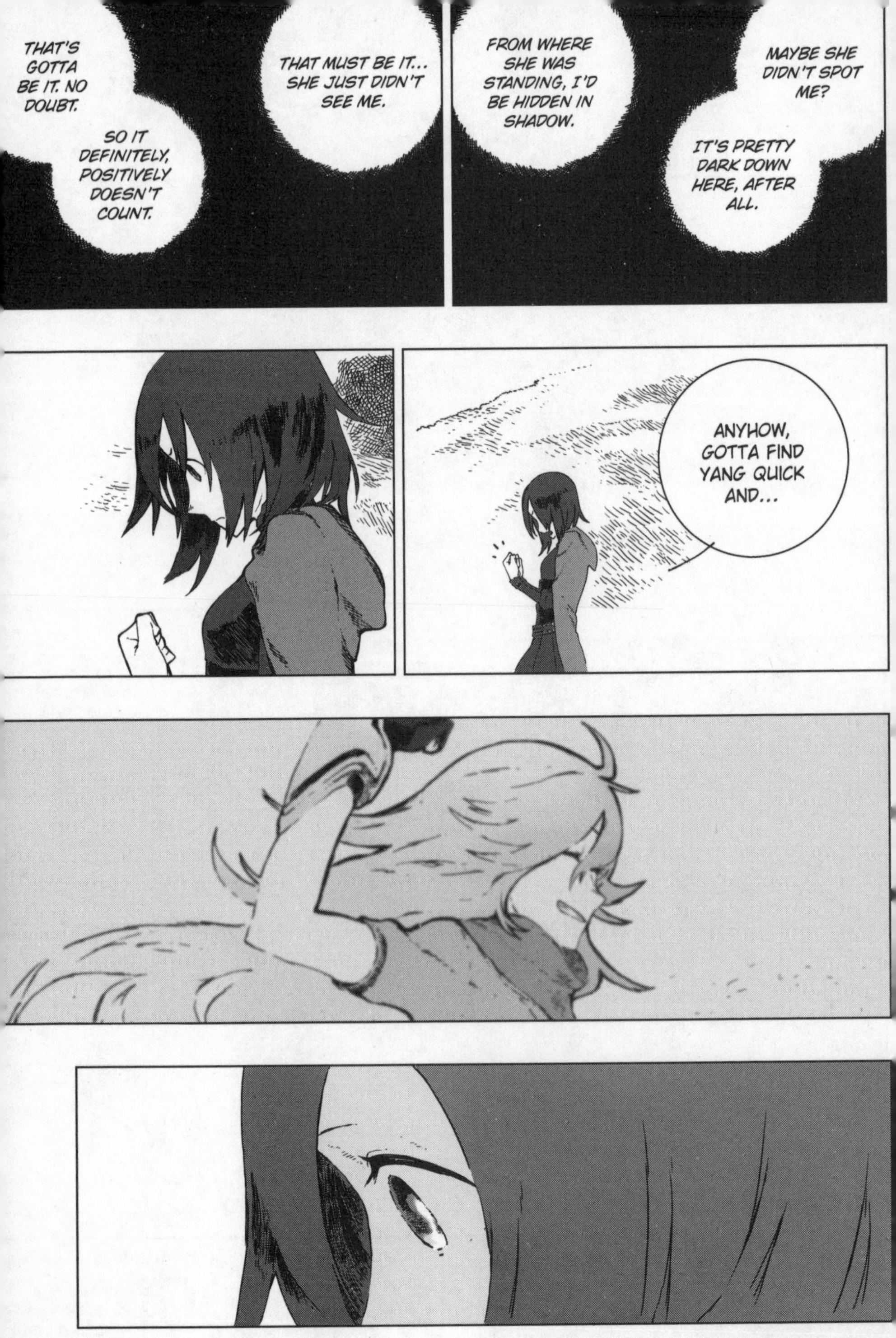
MAYBE SHE DIDN'T SPOT ME?
IT'S PRETTY DARK DOWN HERE, AFTER ALL.
FROM WHERE SHE WAS STANDING, I'D BE HIDDEN IN SHADOW.
THAT MUST BE IT... SHE JUST DIDN'T SEE ME.
THAT'S GOTTA BE IT. NO DOUBT.
SO IT DEFINITELY, POSITIVELY DOESN'T COUNT.
ANYHOW, GOTTA FIND YANG QUICK AND...

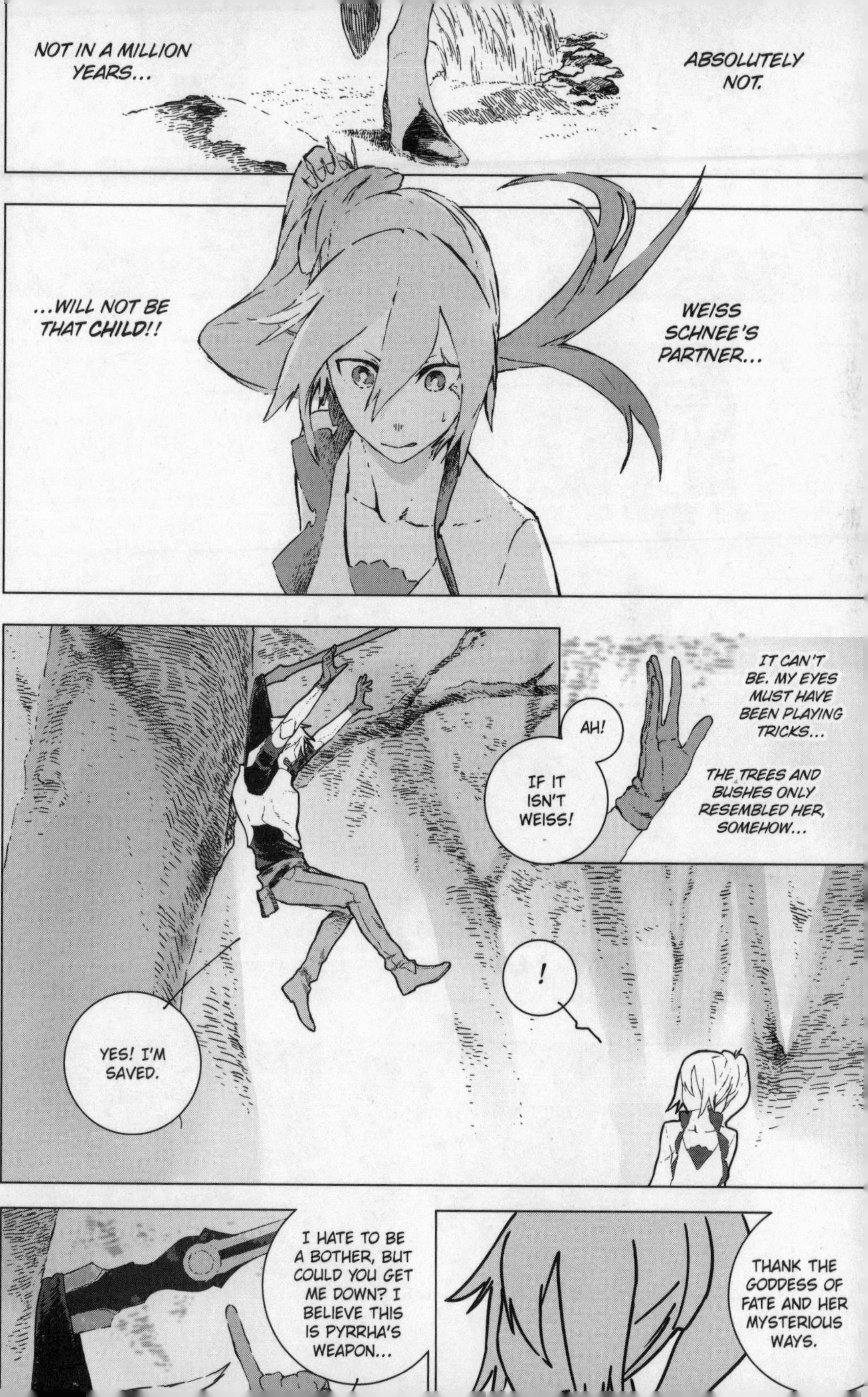
ABSOLUTELY NOT.
NOT IN A MILLION YEARS...
WEISS SCHNEE'S PARTNER...
...WILL NOT BE THAT CHILD!!
IT CAN'T BE. MY EYES MUST HAVE BEEN PLAYING TRICKS...
THE TREES AND BUSHES ONLY RESEMBLED HER, SOMEHOW...
AH!
IF IT ISN'T WEISS!
!
YES! I'M SAVED.
THANK THE GODDESS OF FATE AND HER MYSTERIOUS WAYS.
I HATE TO BE A BOTHER, BUT COULD YOU GET ME DOWN? I BELIEVE THIS IS PYRRHA'S WEAPON...

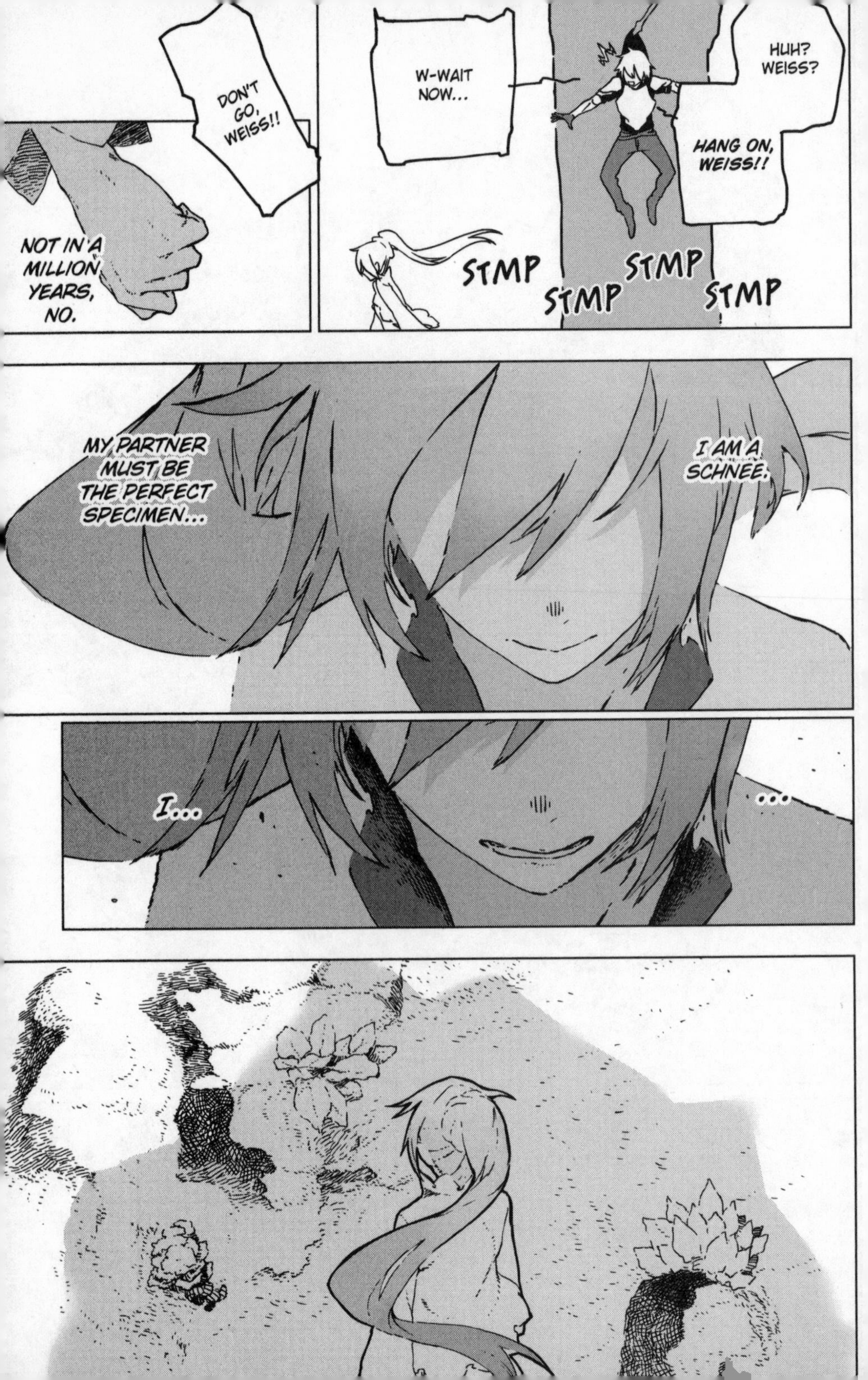
HUH? WEISS?
HANG ON, WEISS!!
W-WAIT NOW...
STMP
STMP
STMP
STMP
DON'T GO, WEISS!!
NOT IN A MILLION YEARS, NO.
I AM A SCHNEE.
MY PARTNER MUST BE THE PERFECT SPECIMEN...
...
I...

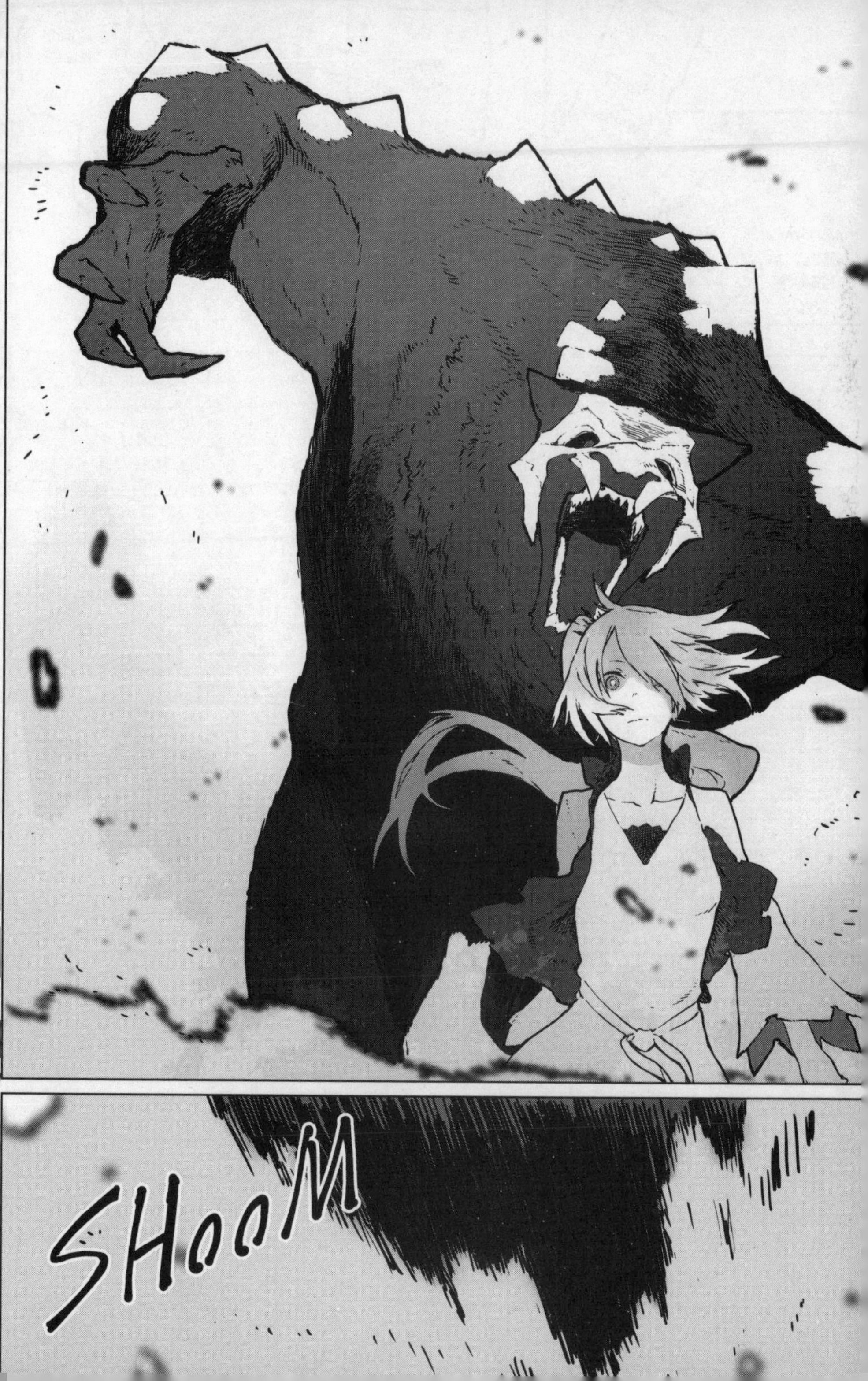
SHOOM

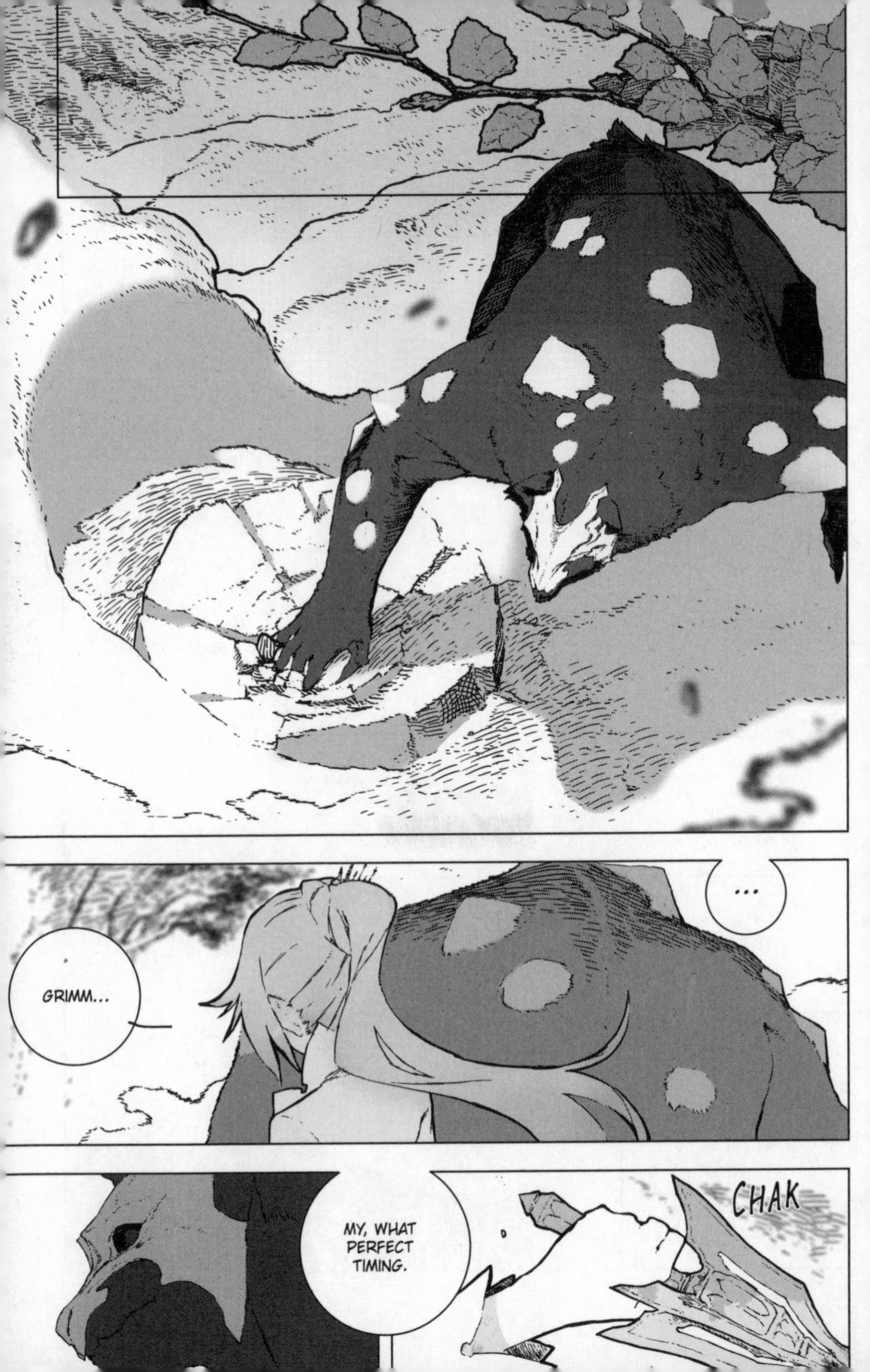
...
GRIMM...
CHAK
MY, WHAT PERFECT TIMING.

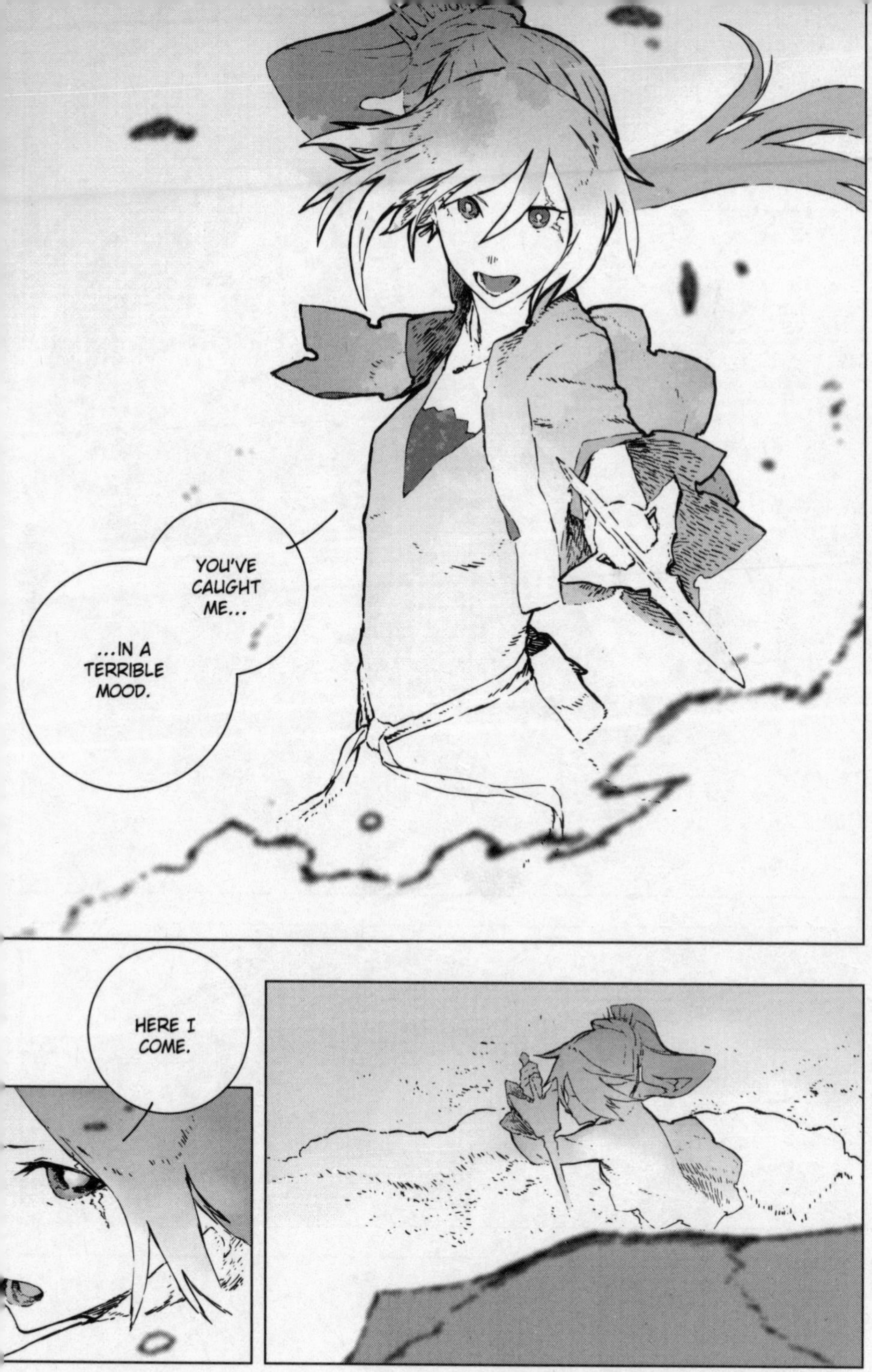
YOU'VE CAUGHT ME...
...IN A TERRIBLE MOOD.
HERE I COME.

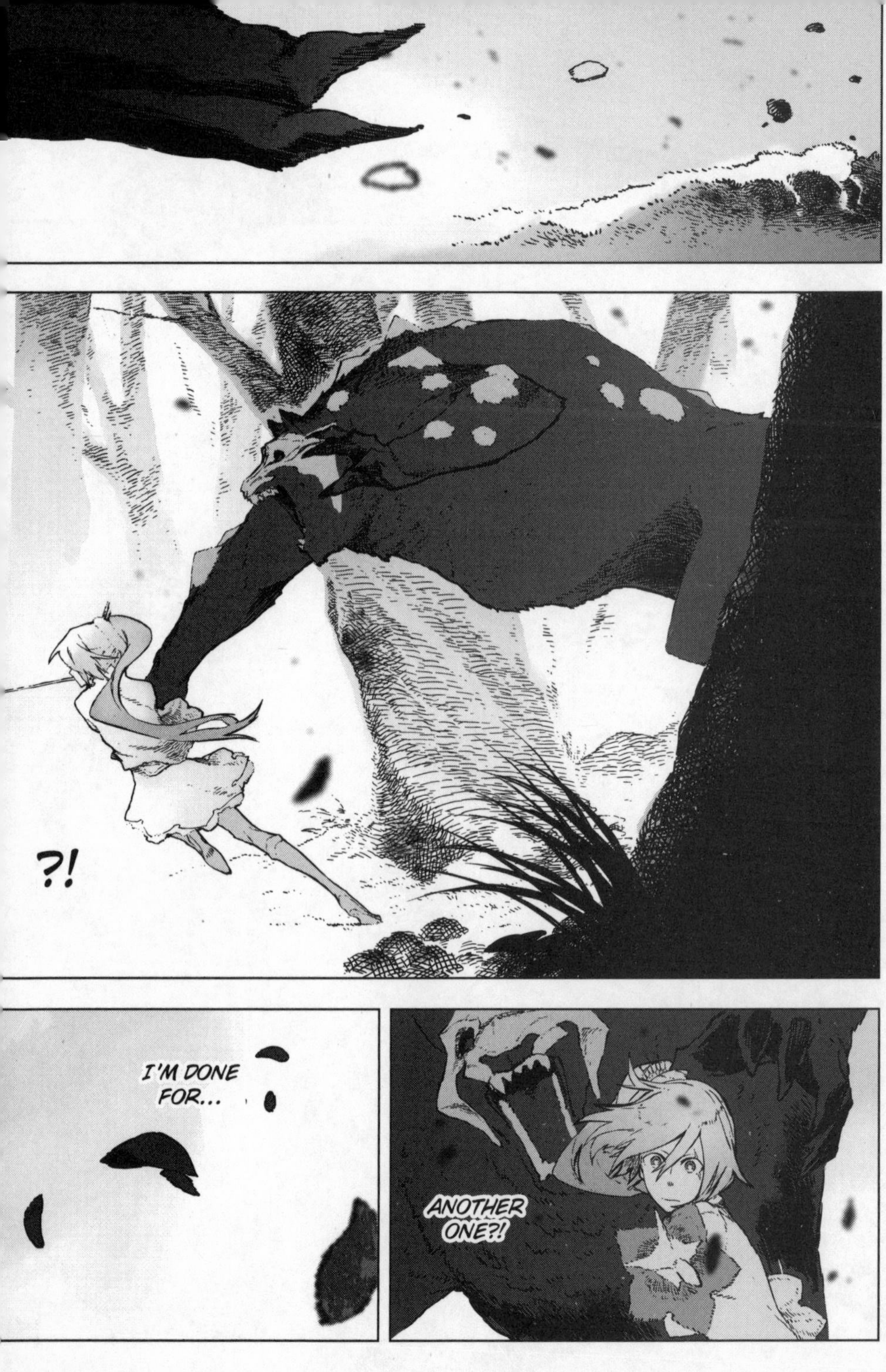
?!
ANOTHER ONE?!
I'M DONE FOR...

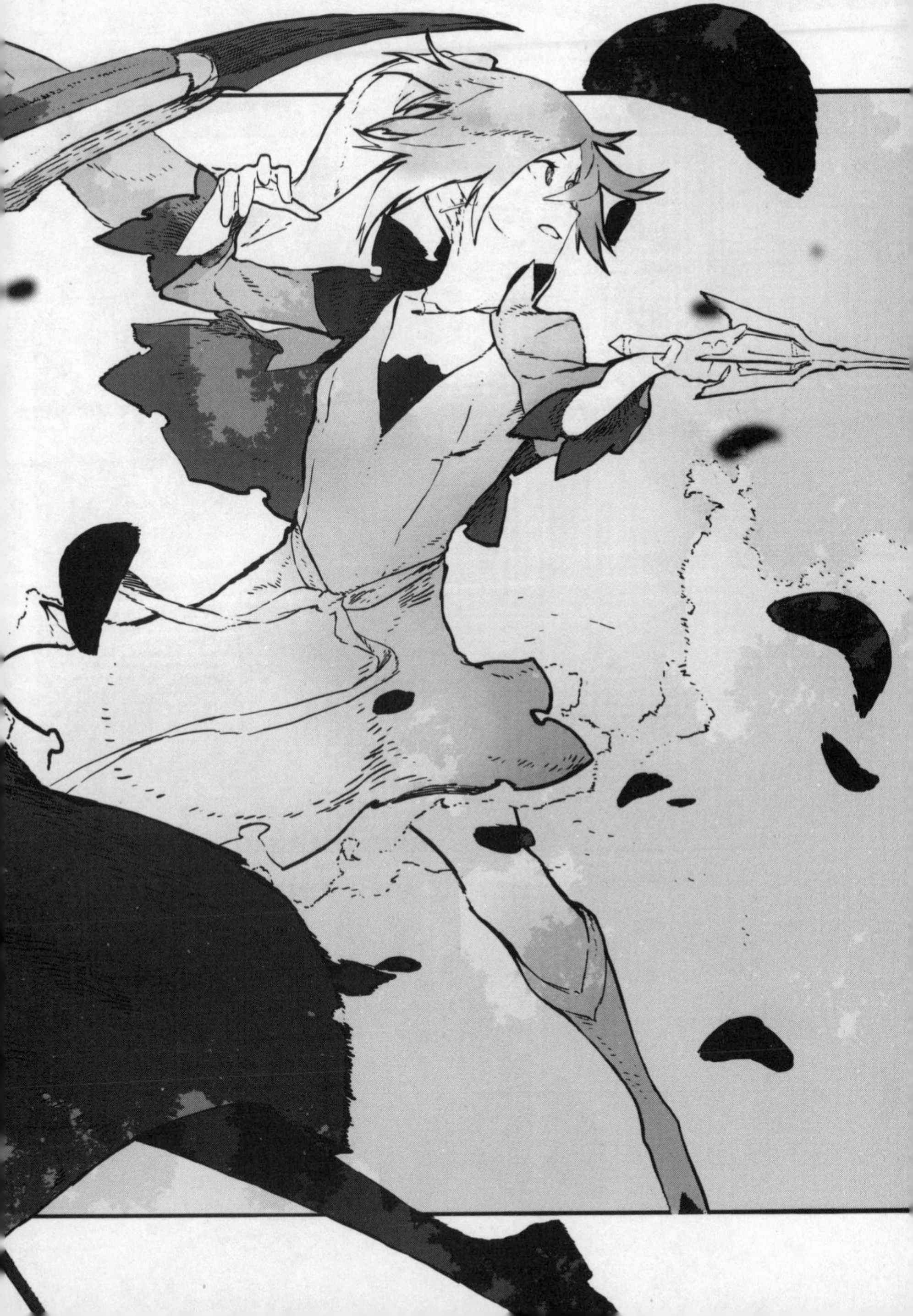

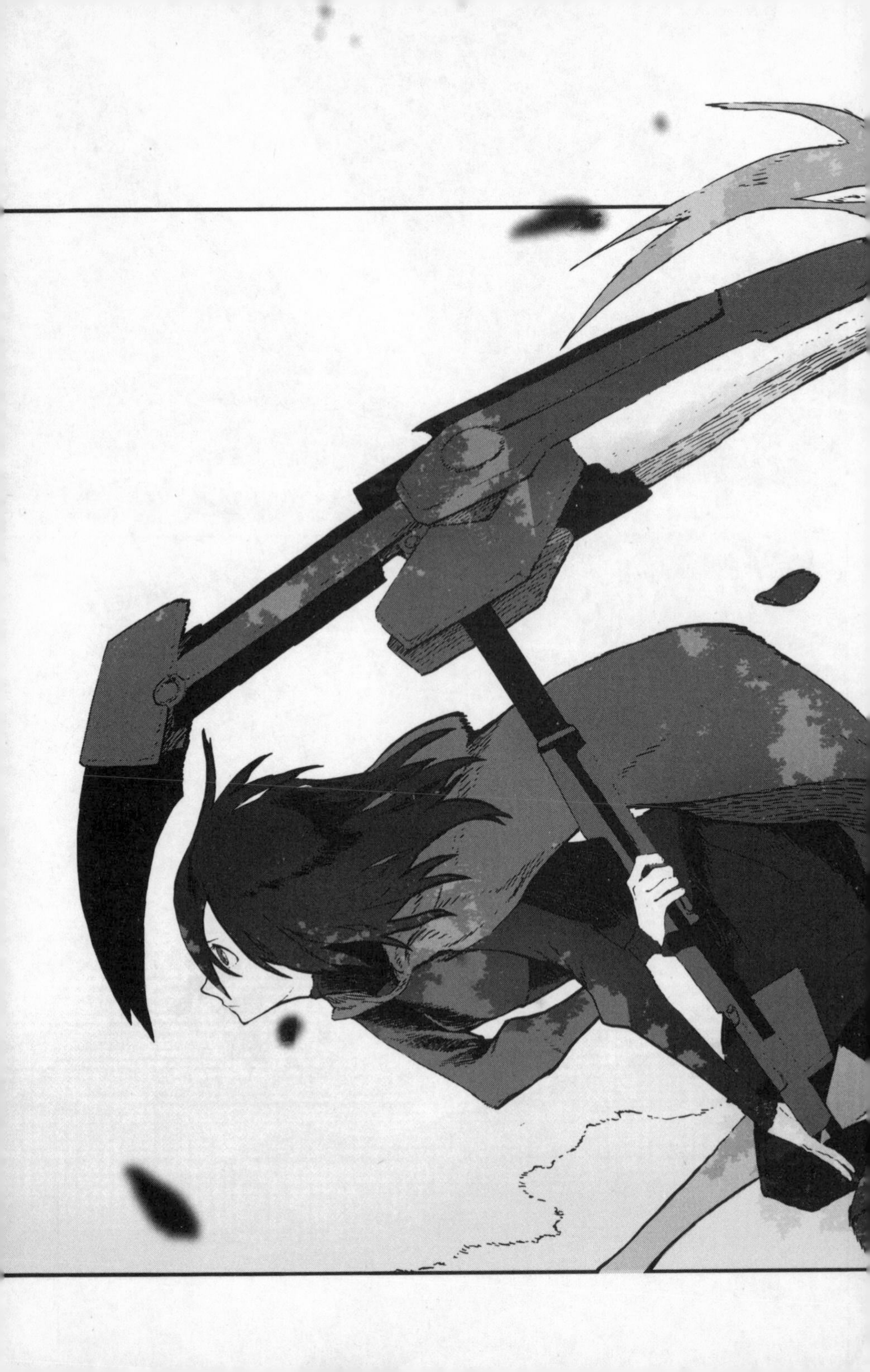

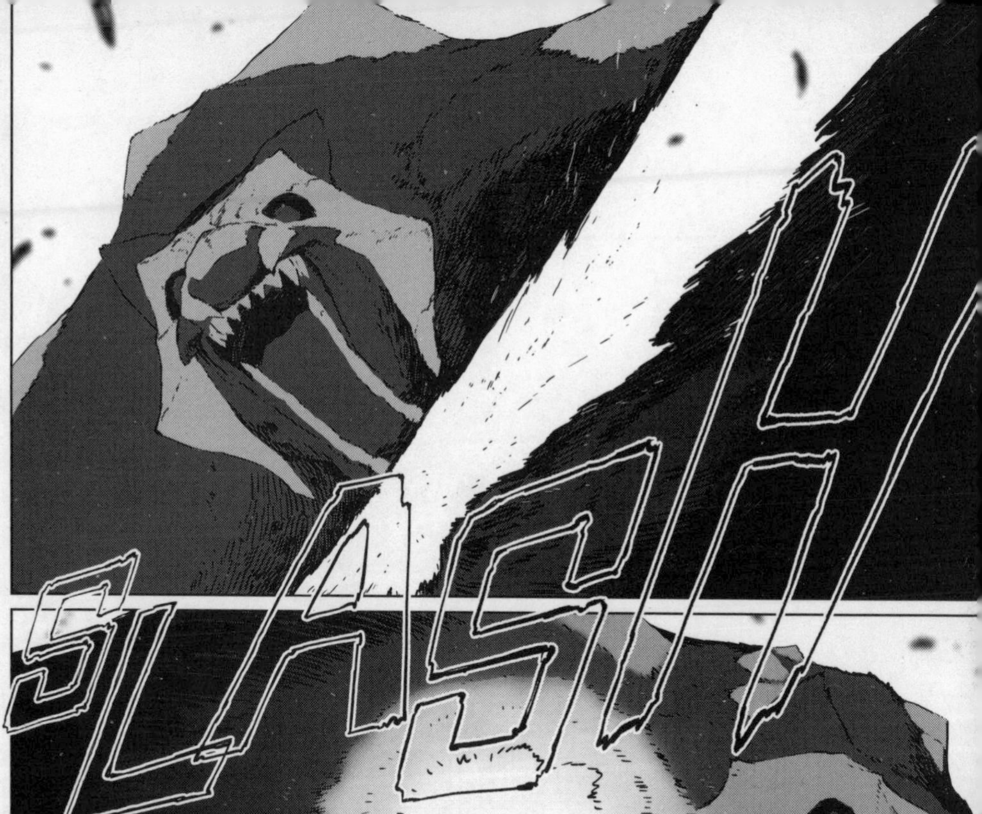
SLASH
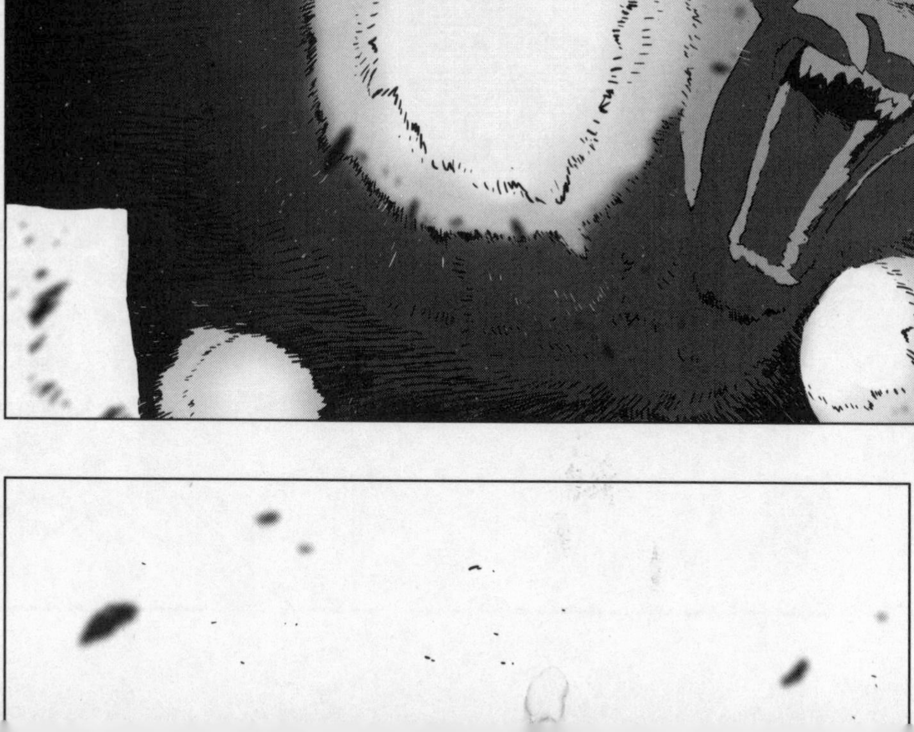

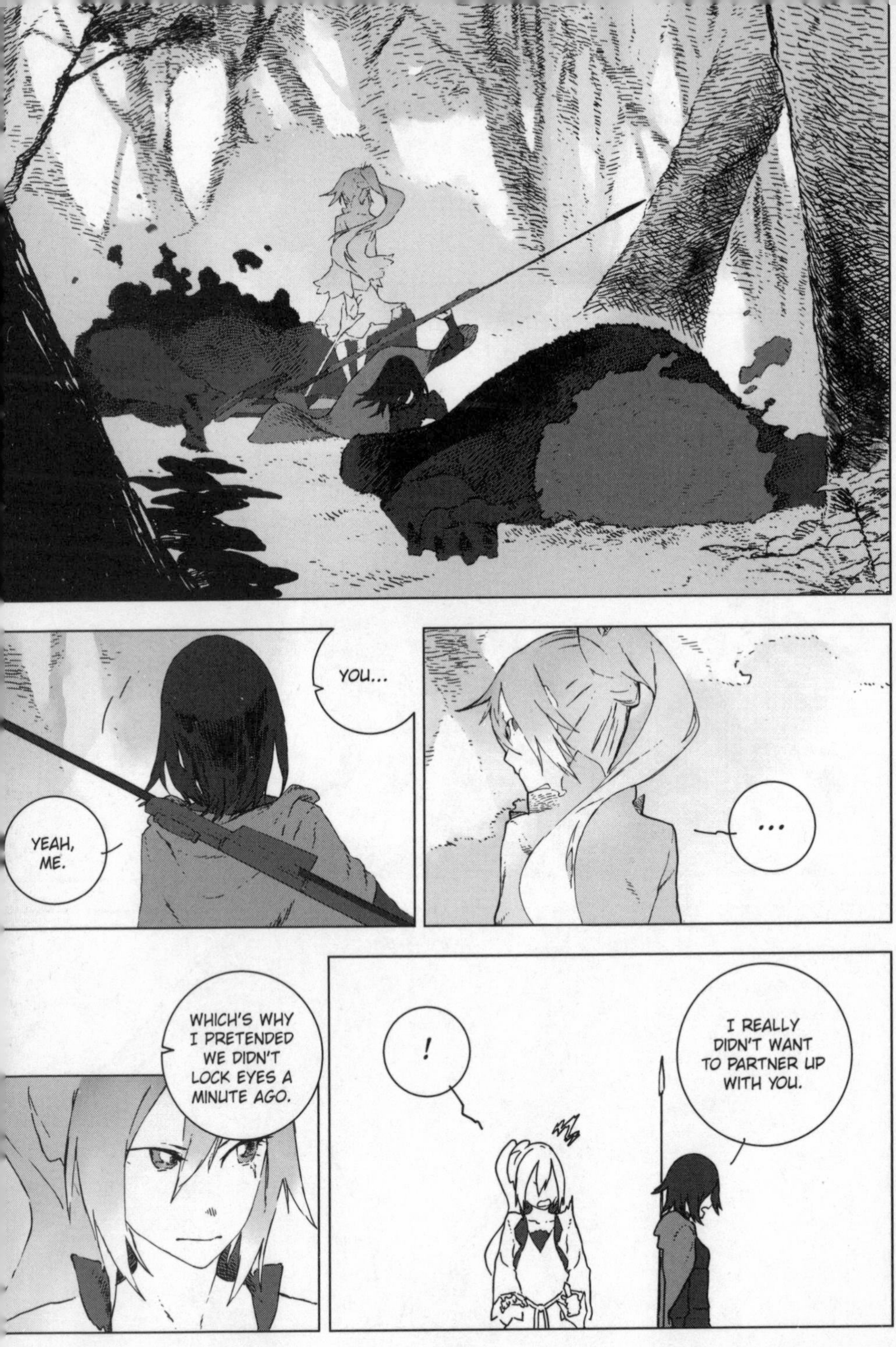
...
YOU...
YEAH, ME.
I REALLY DIDN'T WANT TO PARTNER UP WITH YOU.
!
WHICH'S WHY I PRETENDED WE DIDN'T LOCK EYES A MINUTE AGO.

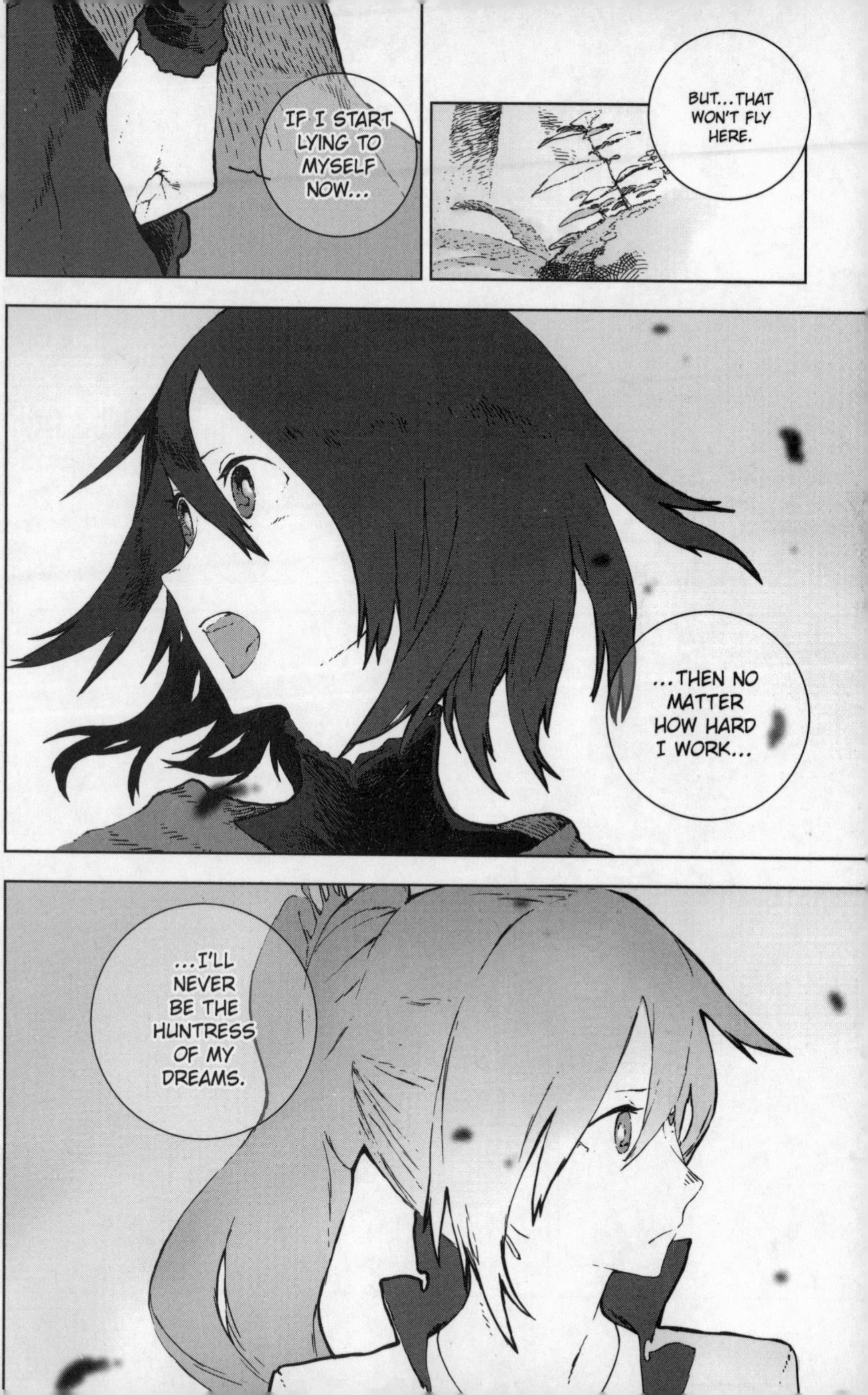
BUT...THAT WON'T FLY HERE.
IF I START LYING TO MYSELF NOW...
...THEN NO MATTER HOW HARD I WORK...
...I'LL NEVER BE THE HUNTRESS OF MY DREAMS.

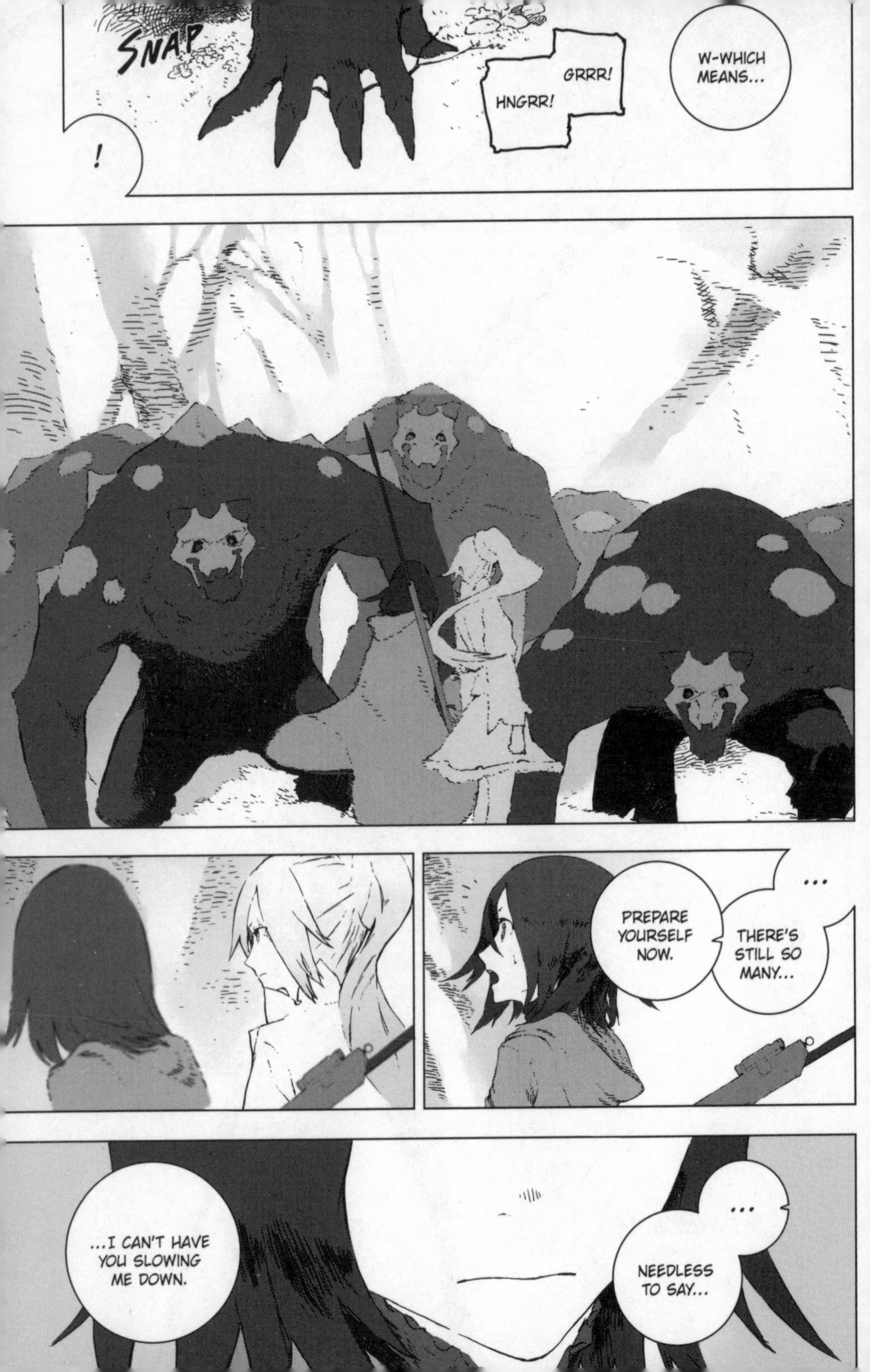
W-WHICH MEANS...
GRRR!
HNGRR!
SNAP
!
...
THERE'S STILL SO MANY...
PREPARE YOURSELF NOW.
...
NEEDLESS TO SAY...
...I CAN'T HAVE YOU SLOWING ME DOWN.

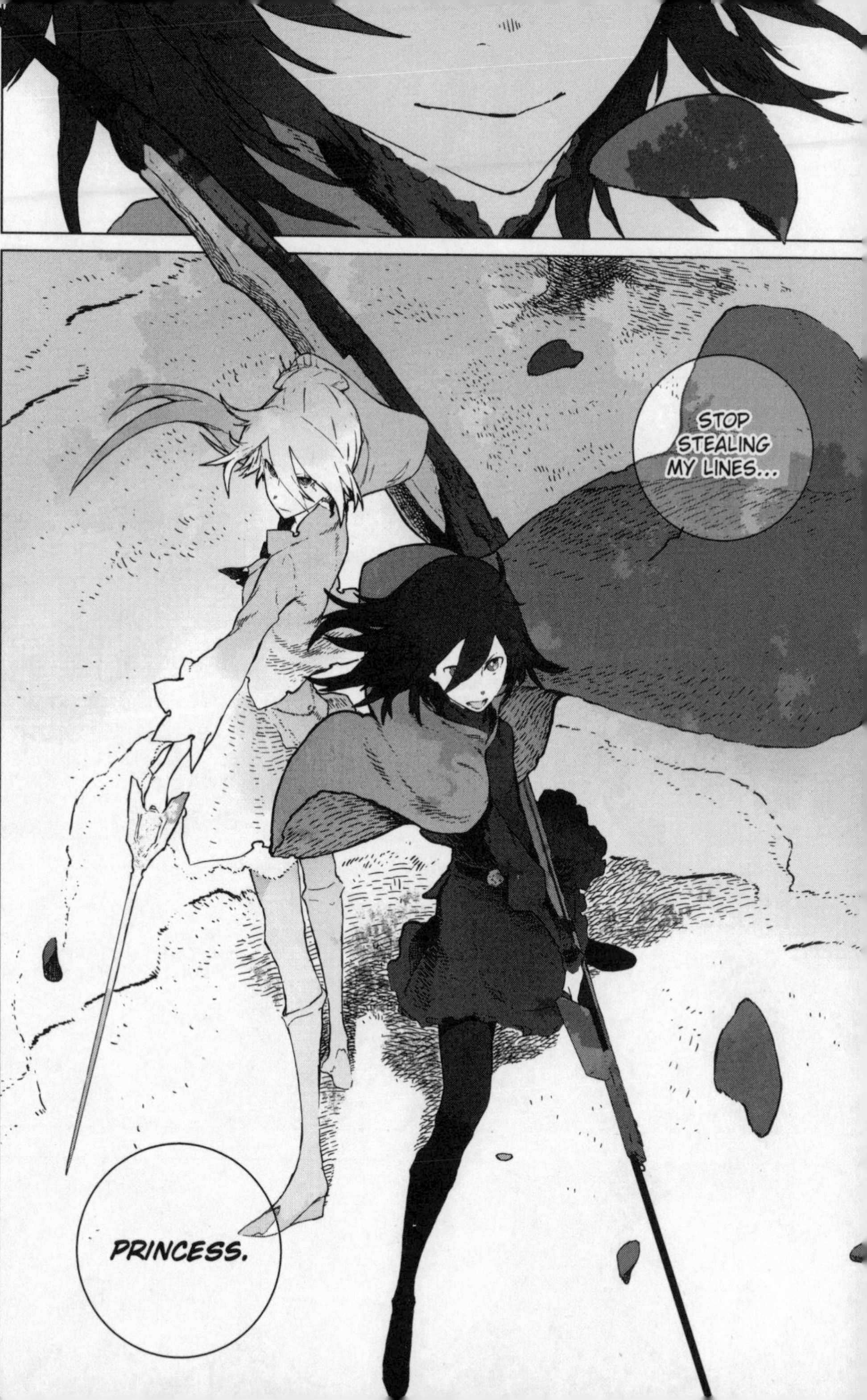
STOP STEALING MY LINES...
PRINCESS.

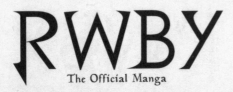

RWBY
The Official Manga

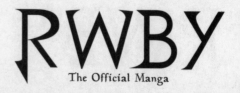

RWBY
The Official Manga

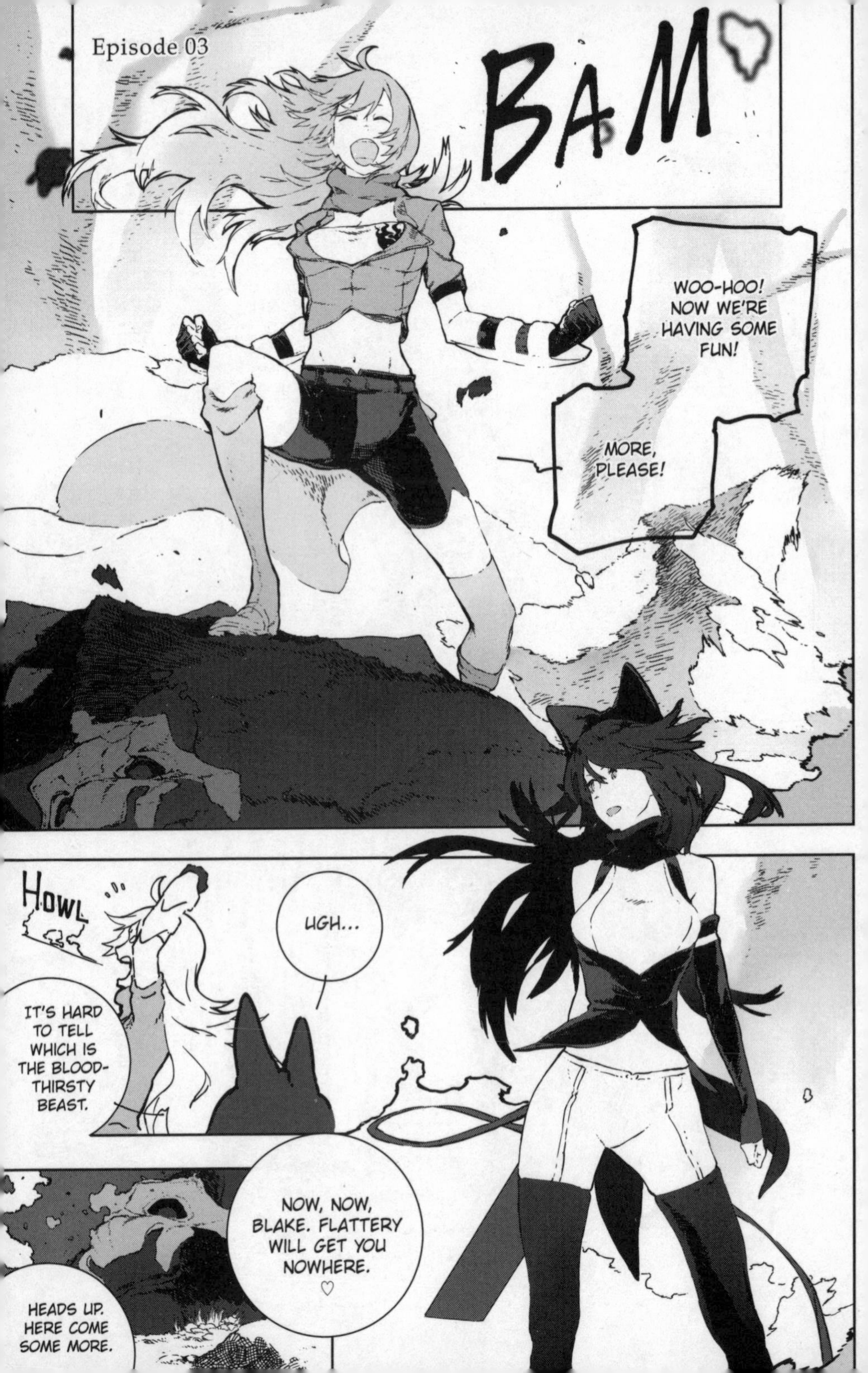
Episode 03
BAM
WOO-HOO! NOW WE'RE HAVING SOME FUN!
MORE, PLEASE!
UGH...
HOWL
IT'S HARD TO TELL WHICH IS THE BLOOD-THIRSTY BEAST.
NOW, NOW, BLAKE. FLATTERY WILL GET YOU NOWHERE. ♡
HEADS UP. HERE COME SOME MORE.

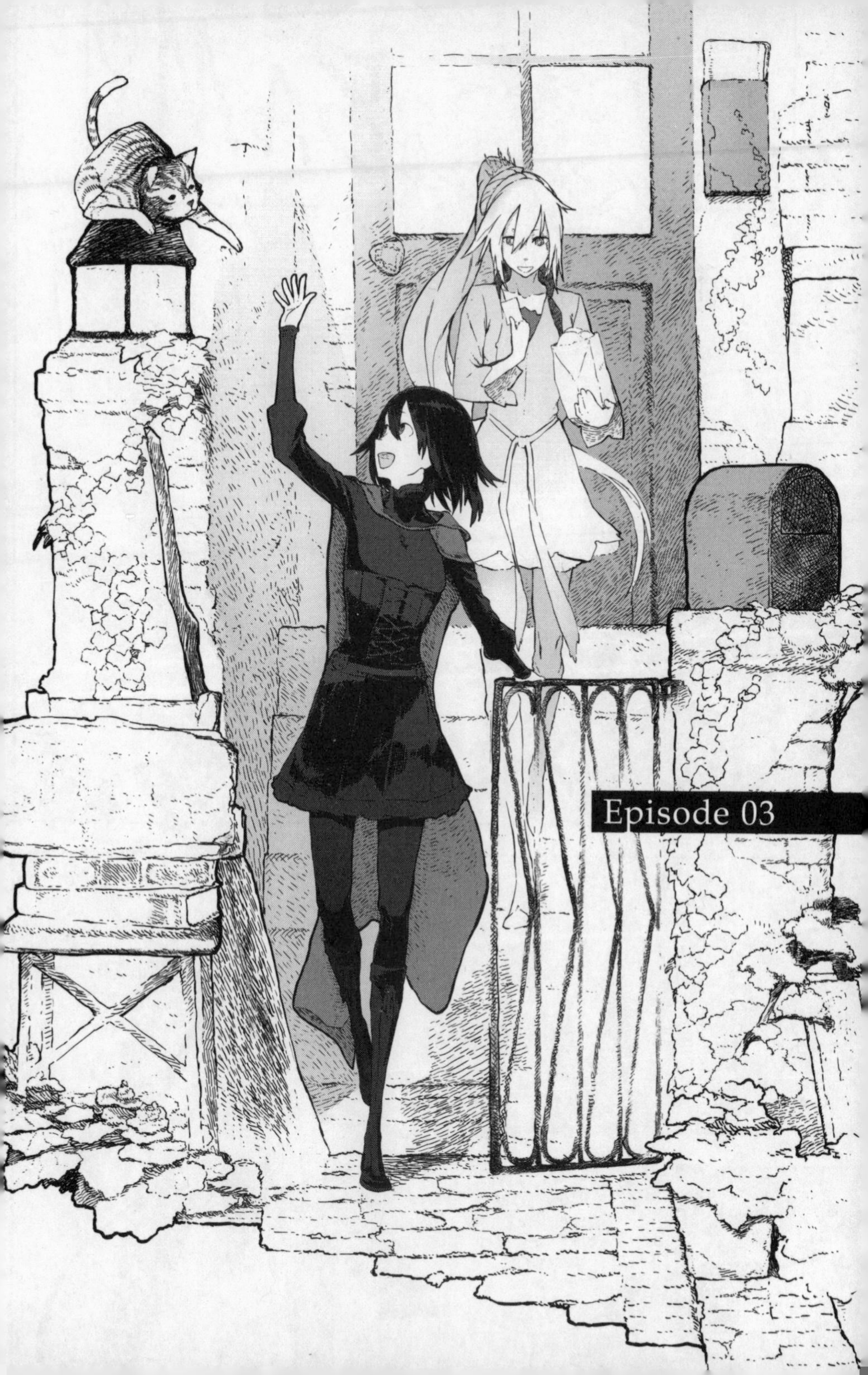
Episode 03

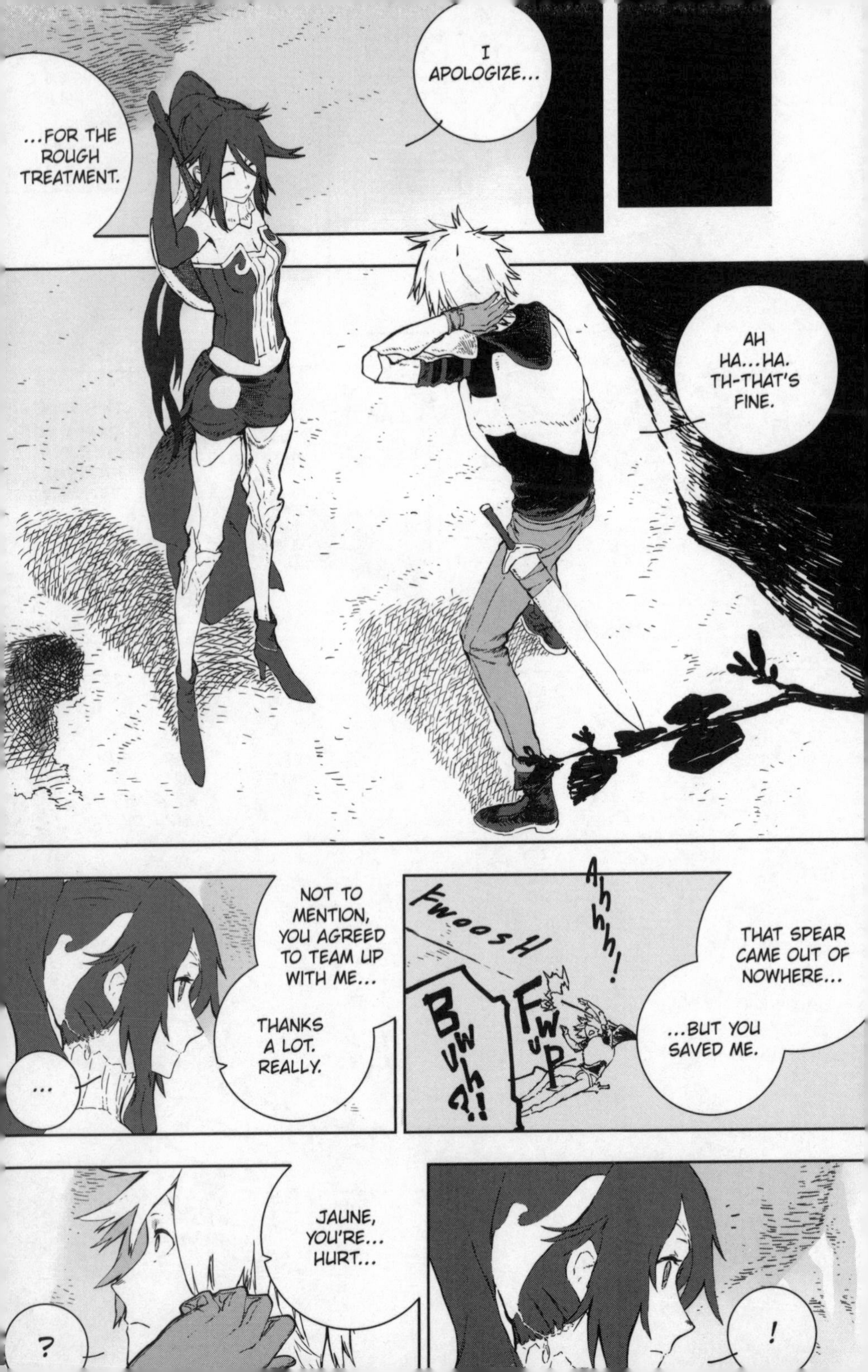
I APOLOGIZE...
...FOR THE ROUGH TREATMENT.
AH HA...HA. TH-THAT'S FINE.
Ahhh!
FWOOSH
THAT SPEAR CAME OUT OF NOWHERE...
...BUT YOU SAVED ME.
FWUP
BWUH?!
NOT TO MENTION, YOU AGREED TO TEAM UP WITH ME...
THANKS A LOT. REALLY.
...
!
JAUNE, YOU'RE... HURT...
?

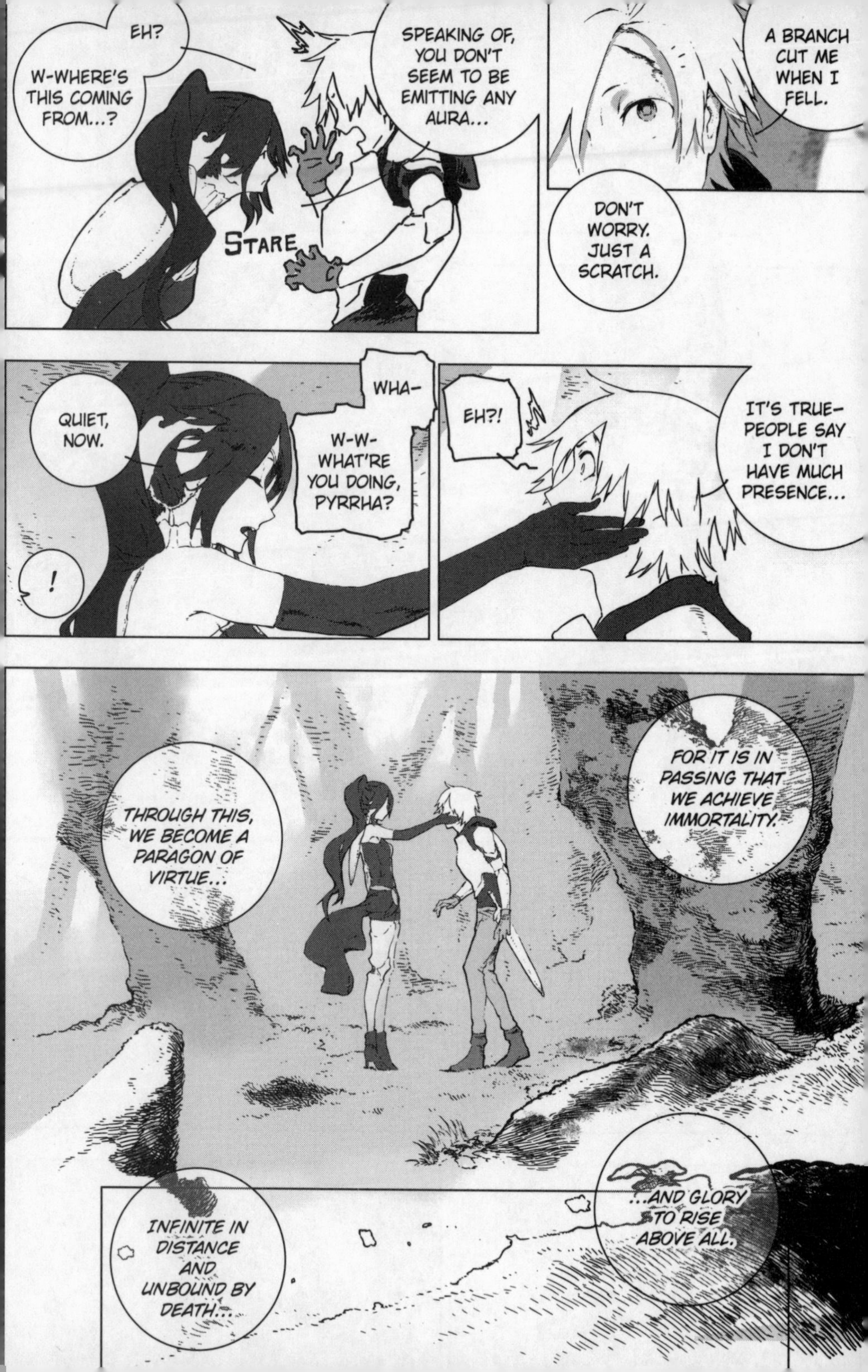
A BRANCH CUT ME WHEN I FELL.
DON'T WORRY. JUST A SCRATCH.
SPEAKING OF, YOU DON'T SEEM TO BE EMITTING ANY AURA...
EH?
W-WHERE'S THIS COMING FROM...?
STARE
IT'S TRUE—PEOPLE SAY I DON'T HAVE MUCH PRESENCE...
EH?!
WHA-
W-W-WHAT'RE YOU DOING, PYRRHA?
QUIET, NOW.
!
FOR IT IS IN PASSING THAT WE ACHIEVE IMMORTALITY.
THROUGH THIS, WE BECOME A PARAGON OF VIRTUE...
INFINITE IN DISTANCE AND UNBOUND BY DEATH...
...AND GLORY TO RISE ABOVE ALL.

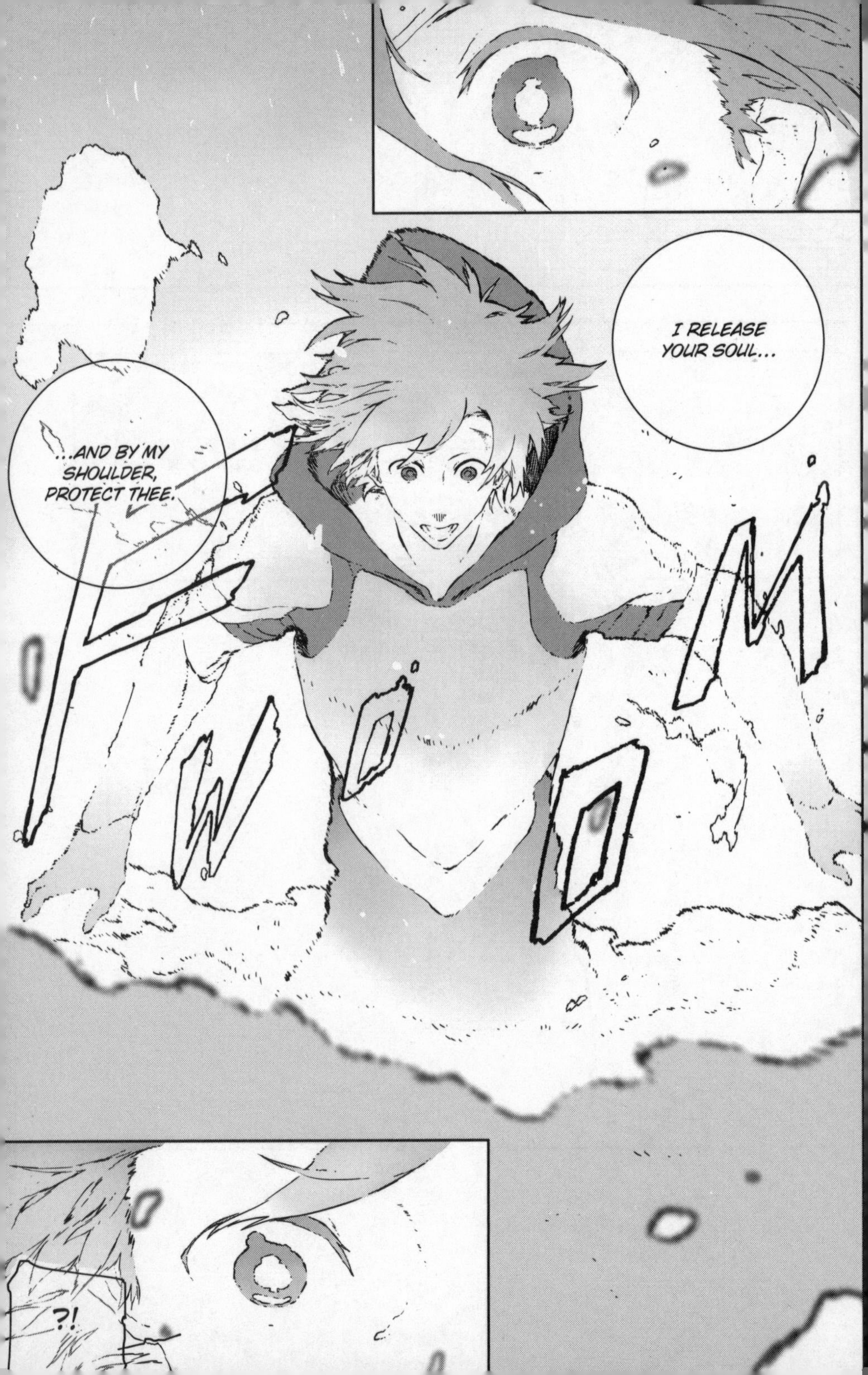
I RELEASE YOUR SOUL...
...AND BY MY SHOULDER, PROTECT THEE.
FWOOM
?!

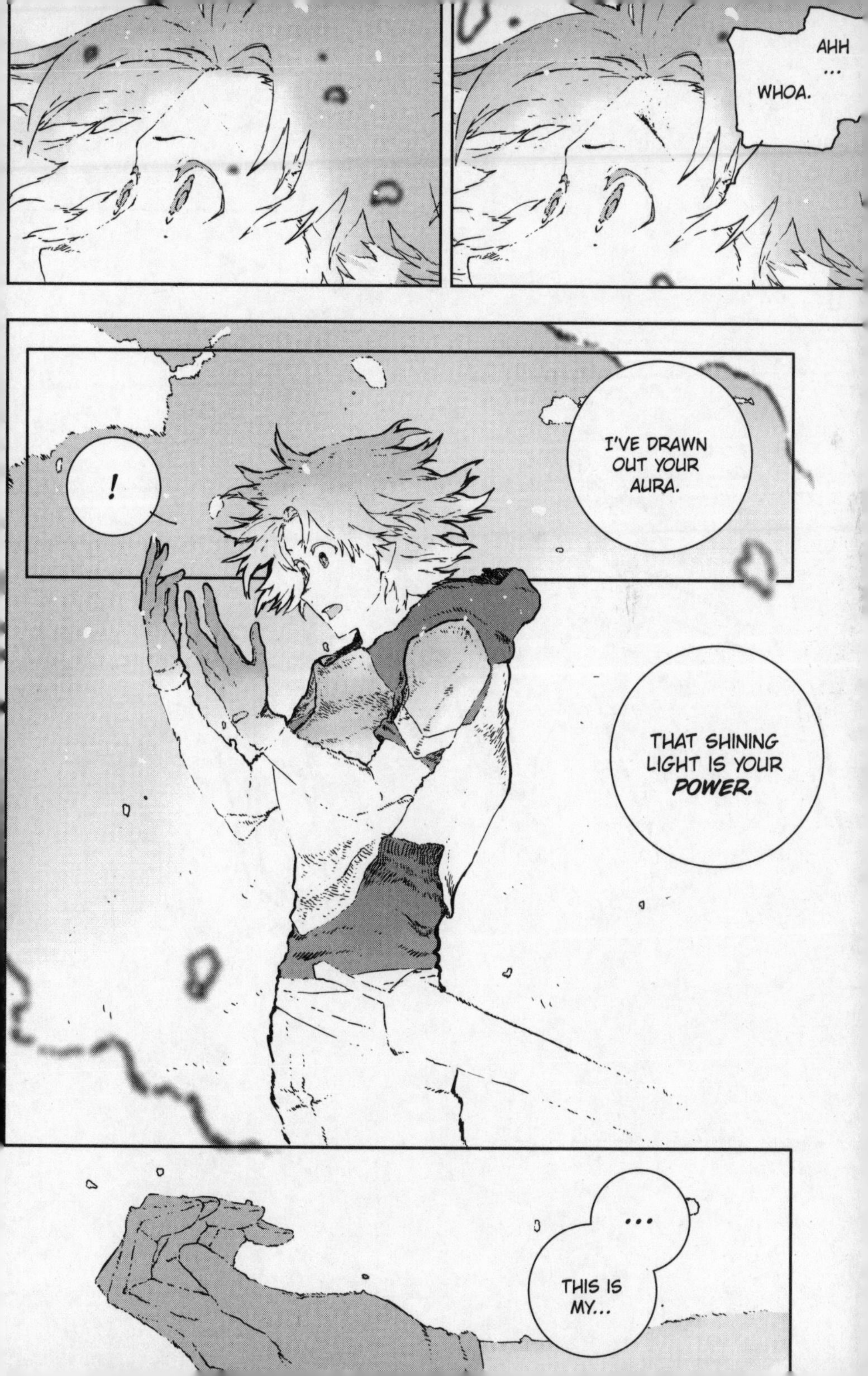
AHH ... WHOA.
I'VE DRAWN OUT YOUR AURA.
!
THAT SHINING LIGHT IS YOUR *POWER.*
...
THIS IS MY...

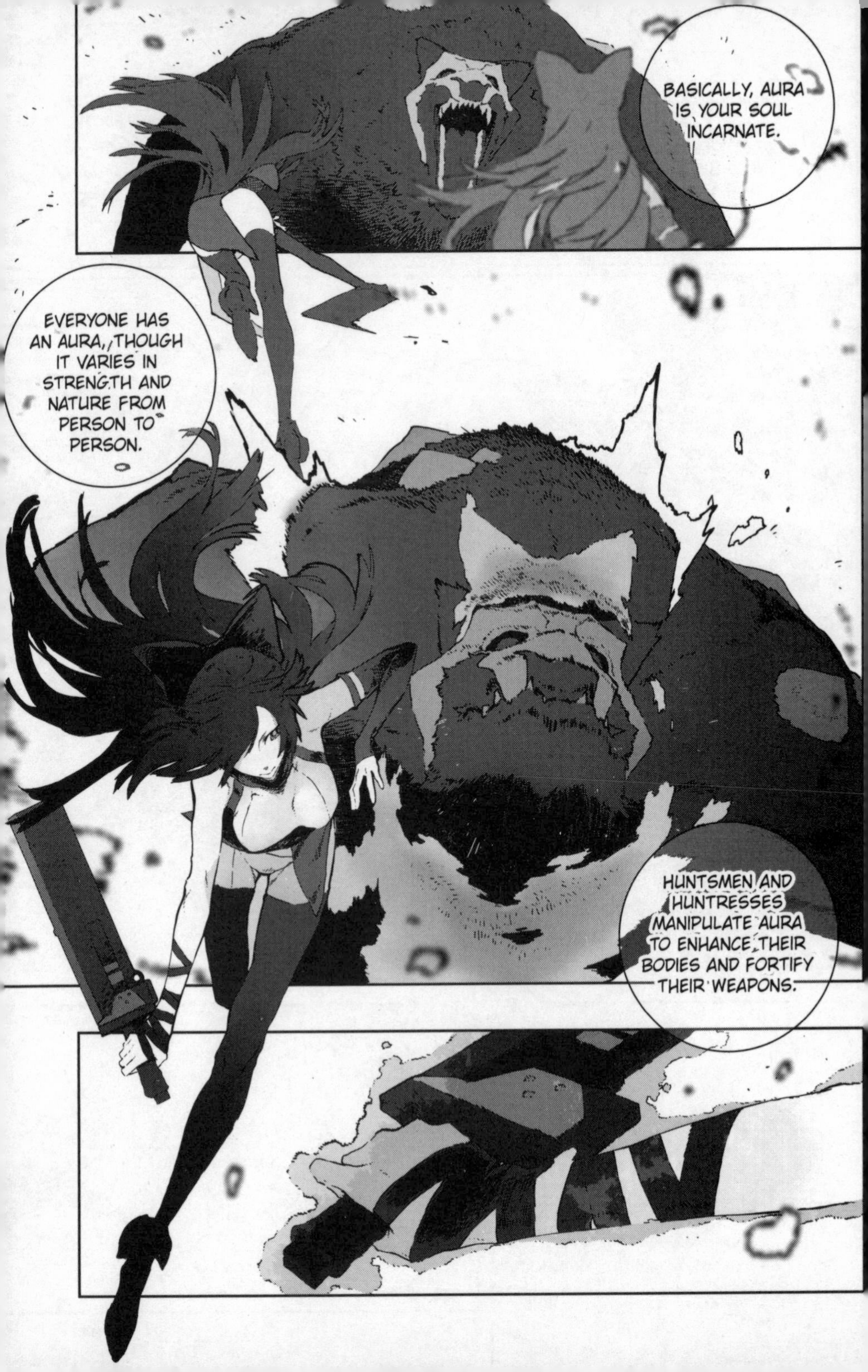
BASICALLY, AURA IS YOUR SOUL INCARNATE.
EVERYONE HAS AN AURA, THOUGH IT VARIES IN STRENGTH AND NATURE FROM PERSON TO PERSON.
HUNTSMEN AND HUNTRESSES MANIPULATE AURA TO ENHANCE THEIR BODIES AND FORTIFY THEIR WEAPONS.

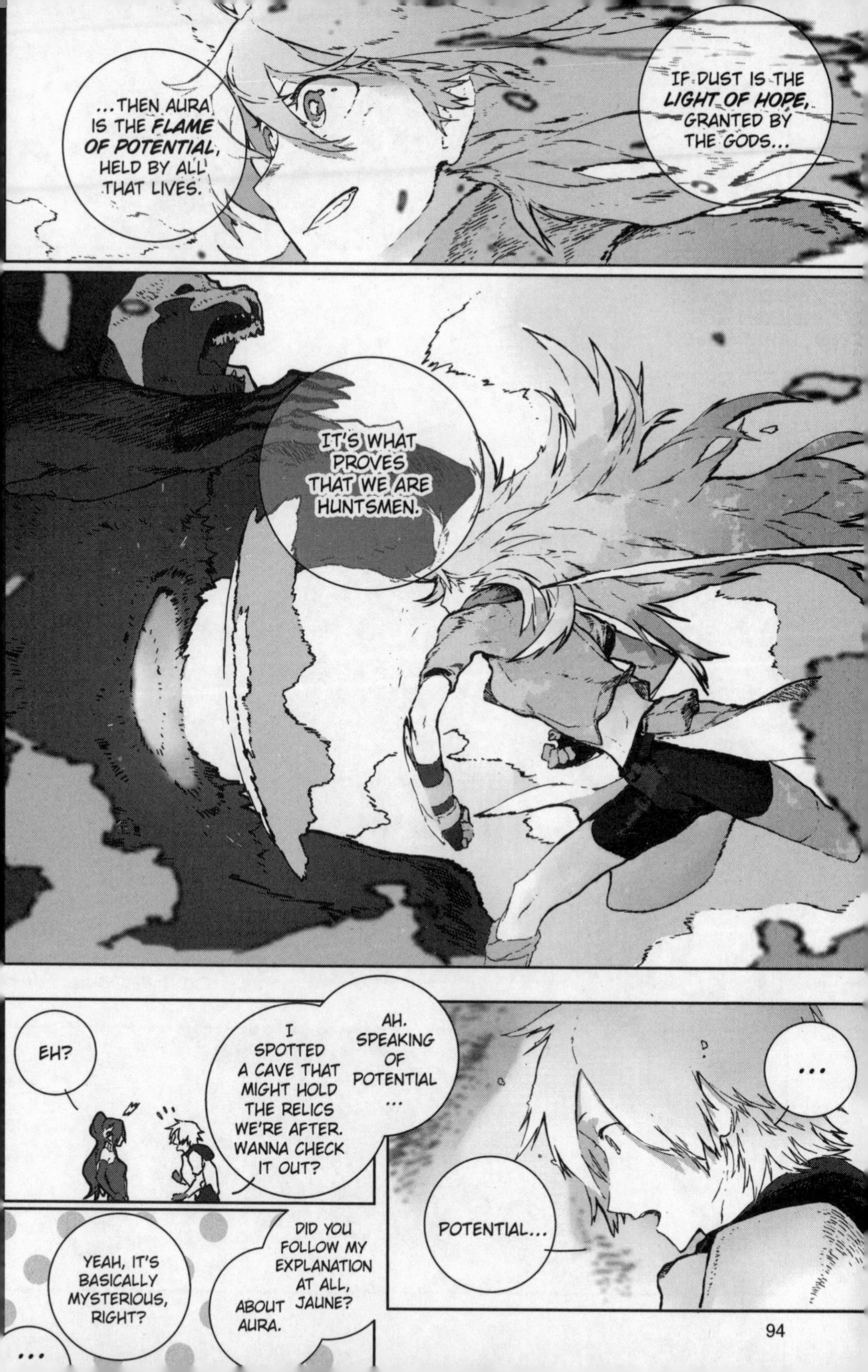
IF DUST IS THE *LIGHT OF HOPE*, GRANTED BY THE GODS...
...THEN AURA IS THE *FLAME OF POTENTIAL*, HELD BY ALL THAT LIVES.
IT'S WHAT PROVES THAT WE ARE HUNTSMEN.
...
POTENTIAL...
AH. SPEAKING OF POTENTIAL...
I SPOTTED A CAVE THAT MIGHT HOLD THE RELICS WE'RE AFTER. WANNA CHECK IT OUT?
EH?
DID YOU FOLLOW MY EXPLANATION AT ALL, JAUNE?
ABOUT AURA.
YEAH, IT'S BASICALLY MYSTERIOUS, RIGHT?
...

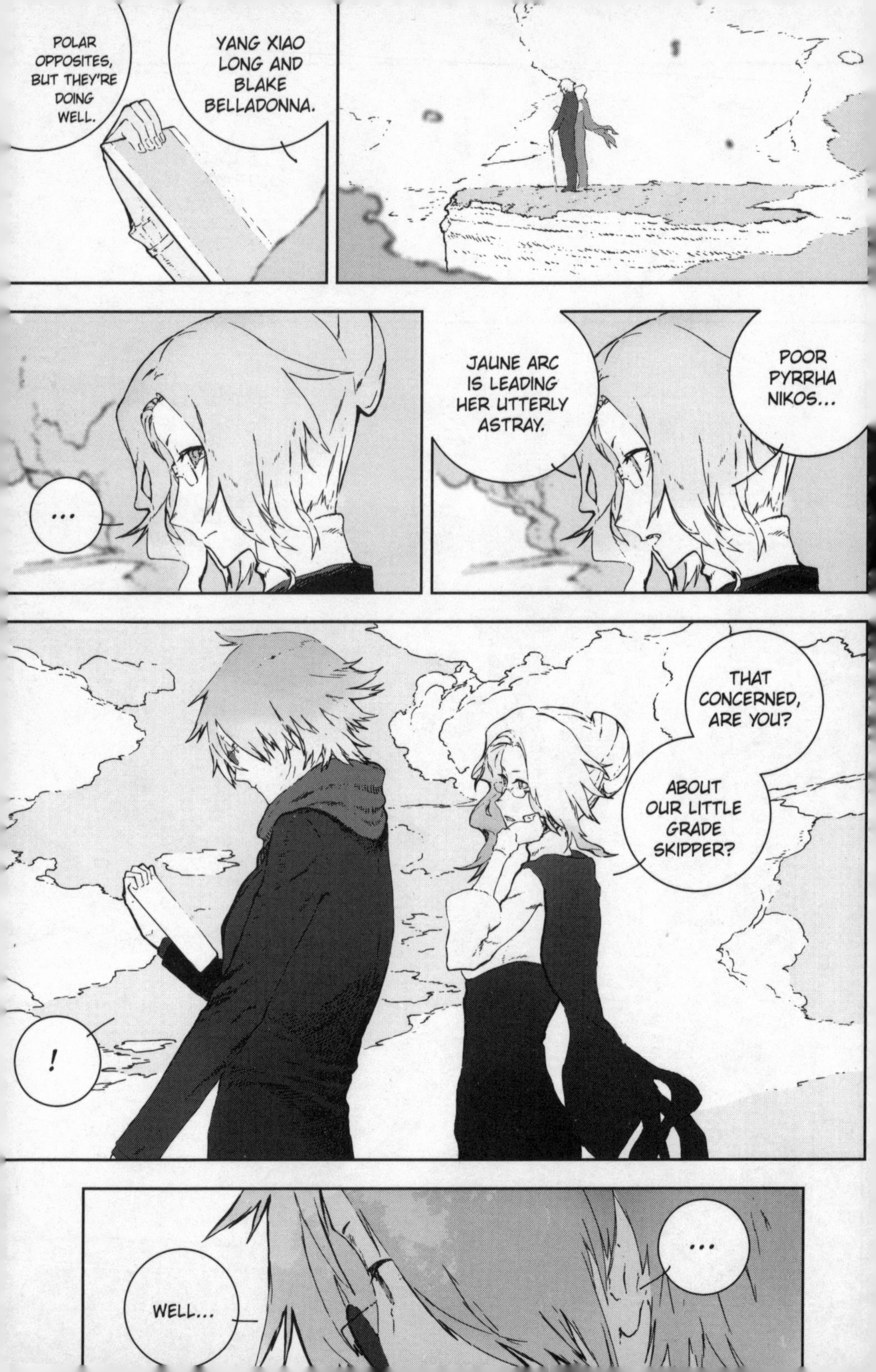
YANG XIAO LONG AND BLAKE BELLADONNA.
POLAR OPPOSITES, BUT THEY'RE DOING WELL.
POOR PYRRHA NIKOS...
JAUNE ARC IS LEADING HER UTTERLY ASTRAY.
...
THAT CONCERNED, ARE YOU?
ABOUT OUR LITTLE GRADE SKIPPER?
!
...
WELL...

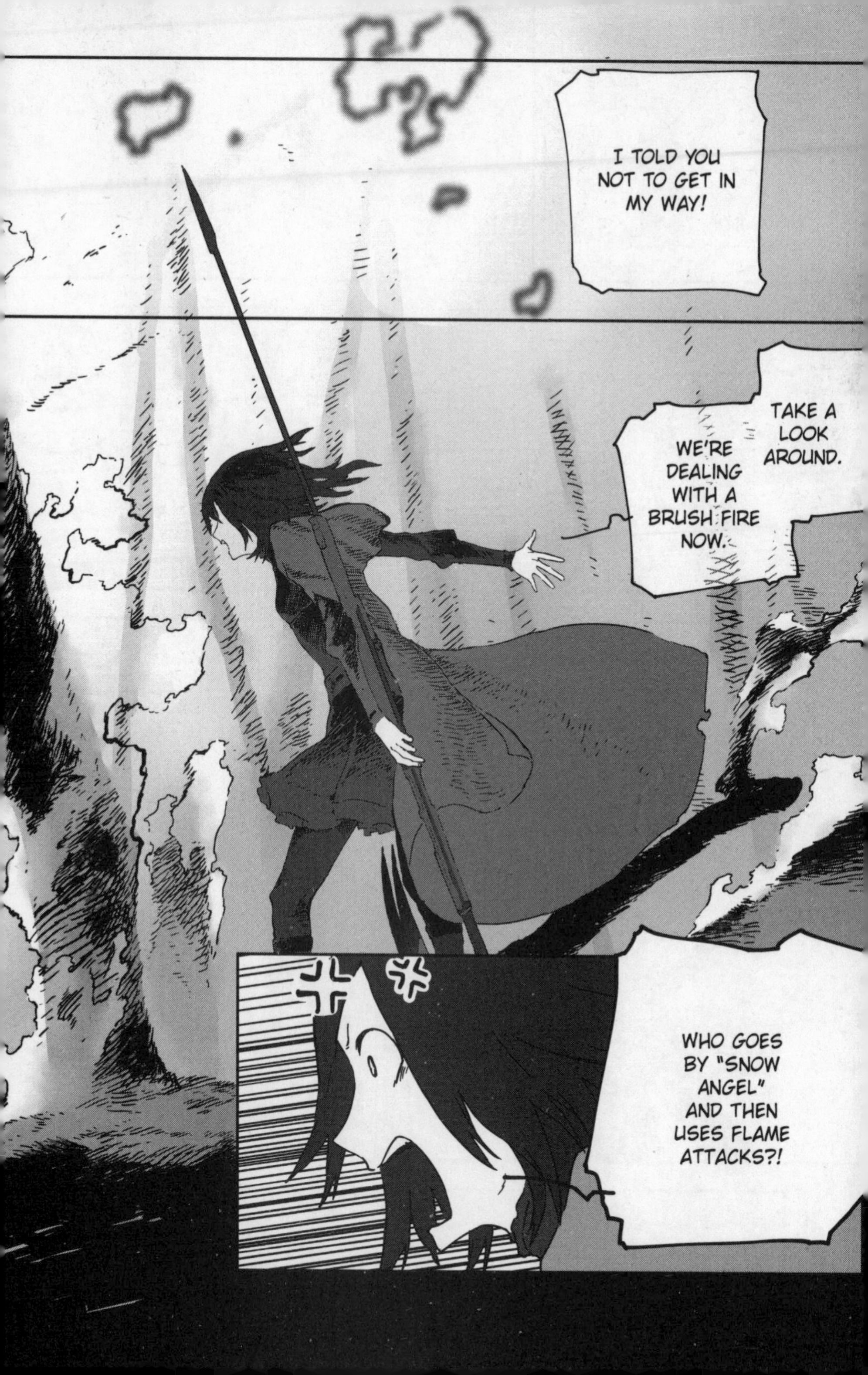
I TOLD YOU NOT TO GET IN MY WAY!
TAKE A LOOK AROUND.
WE'RE DEALING WITH A BRUSH FIRE NOW.
WHO GOES BY "SNOW ANGEL" AND THEN USES FLAME ATTACKS?!

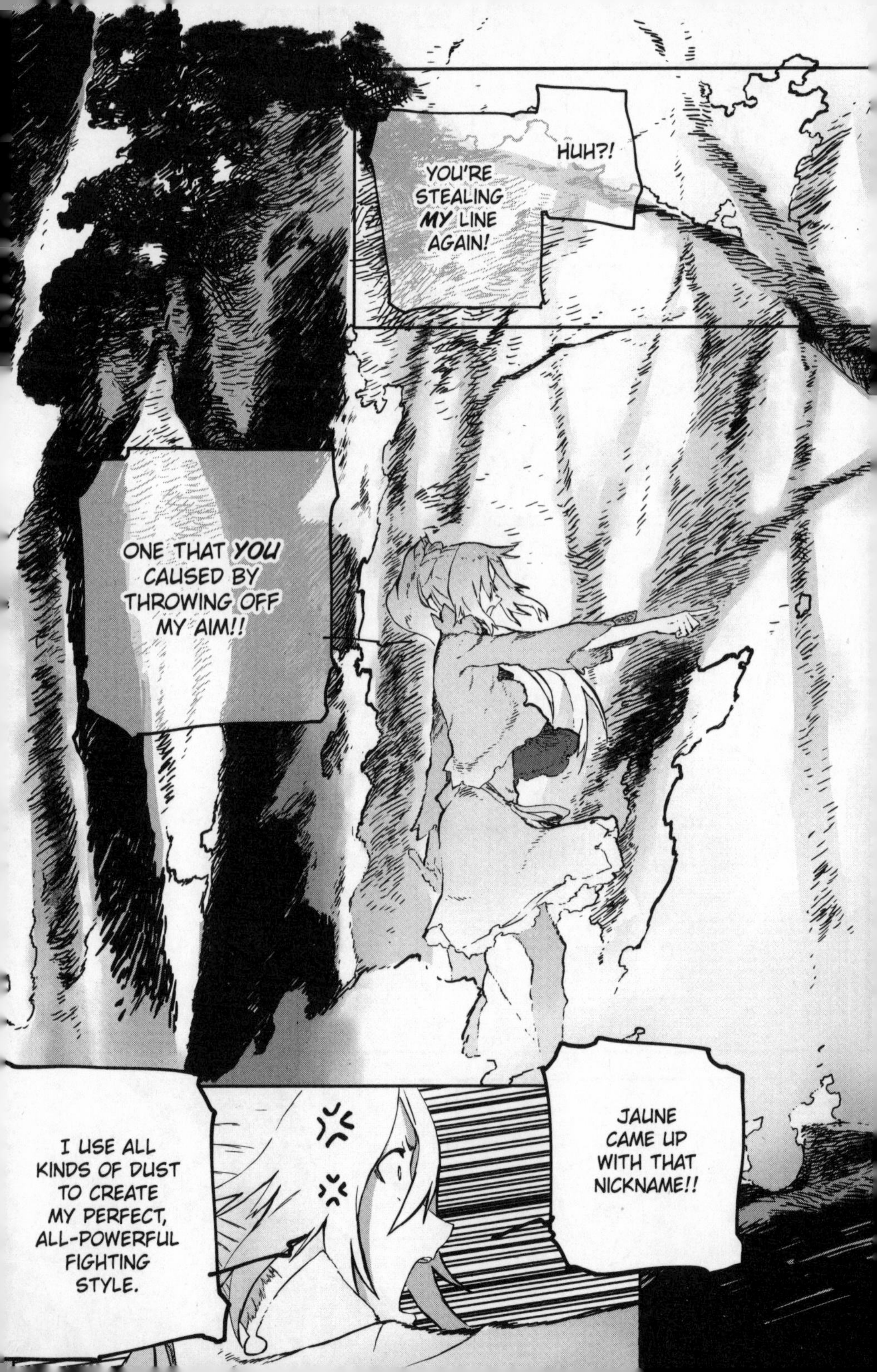
HUH?!
YOU'RE STEALING MY LINE AGAIN!
ONE THAT YOU CAUSED BY THROWING OFF MY AIM!!
JAUNE CAME UP WITH THAT NICKNAME!!
I USE ALL KINDS OF DUST TO CREATE MY PERFECT, ALL-POWERFUL FIGHTING STYLE.

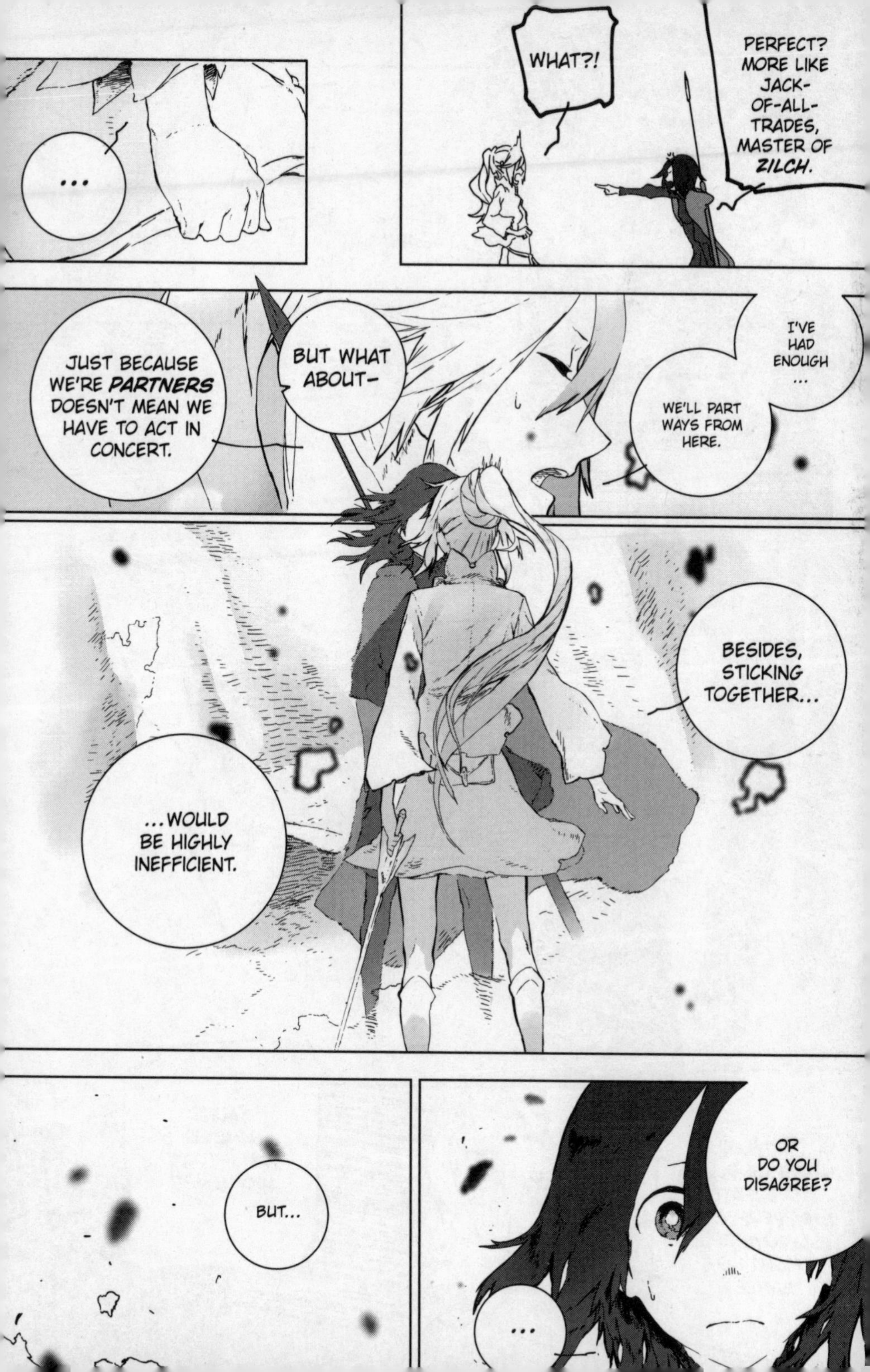
PERFECT? MORE LIKE JACK-OF-ALL-TRADES, MASTER OF ZILCH.
WHAT?!
...
I'VE HAD ENOUGH...
WE'LL PART WAYS FROM HERE.
BUT WHAT ABOUT-
JUST BECAUSE WE'RE PARTNERS DOESN'T MEAN WE HAVE TO ACT IN CONCERT.
BESIDES, STICKING TOGETHER...
...WOULD BE HIGHLY INEFFICIENT.
OR DO YOU DISAGREE?
...
BUT...

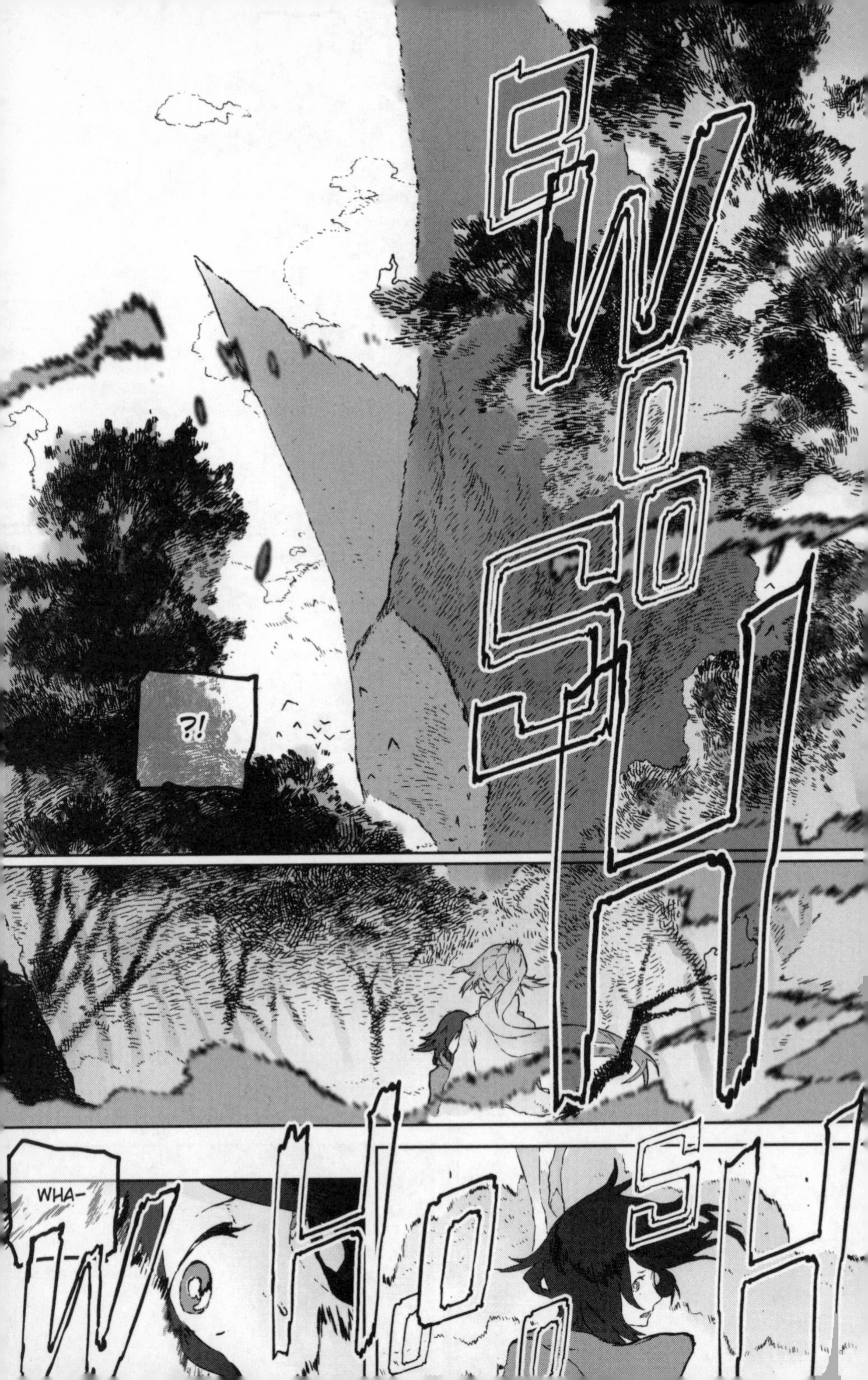
WOOSH!!
?!
WHA-
WHOOSH!

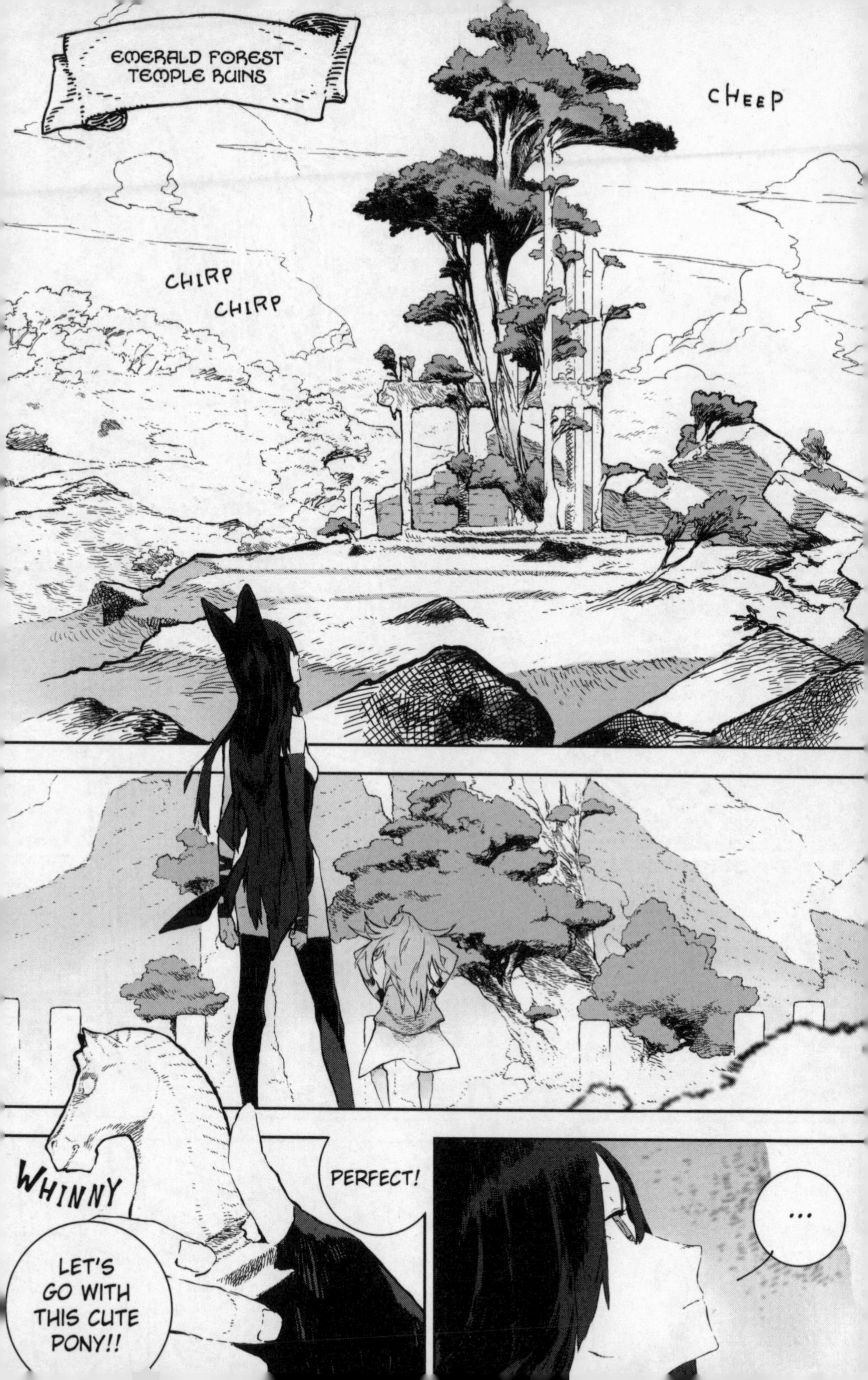
EMERALD FOREST
TEMPLE RUINS
CHEEP
CHIRP
CHIRP
...
PERFECT!
WHINNY
LET'S GO WITH THIS CUTE PONY!!

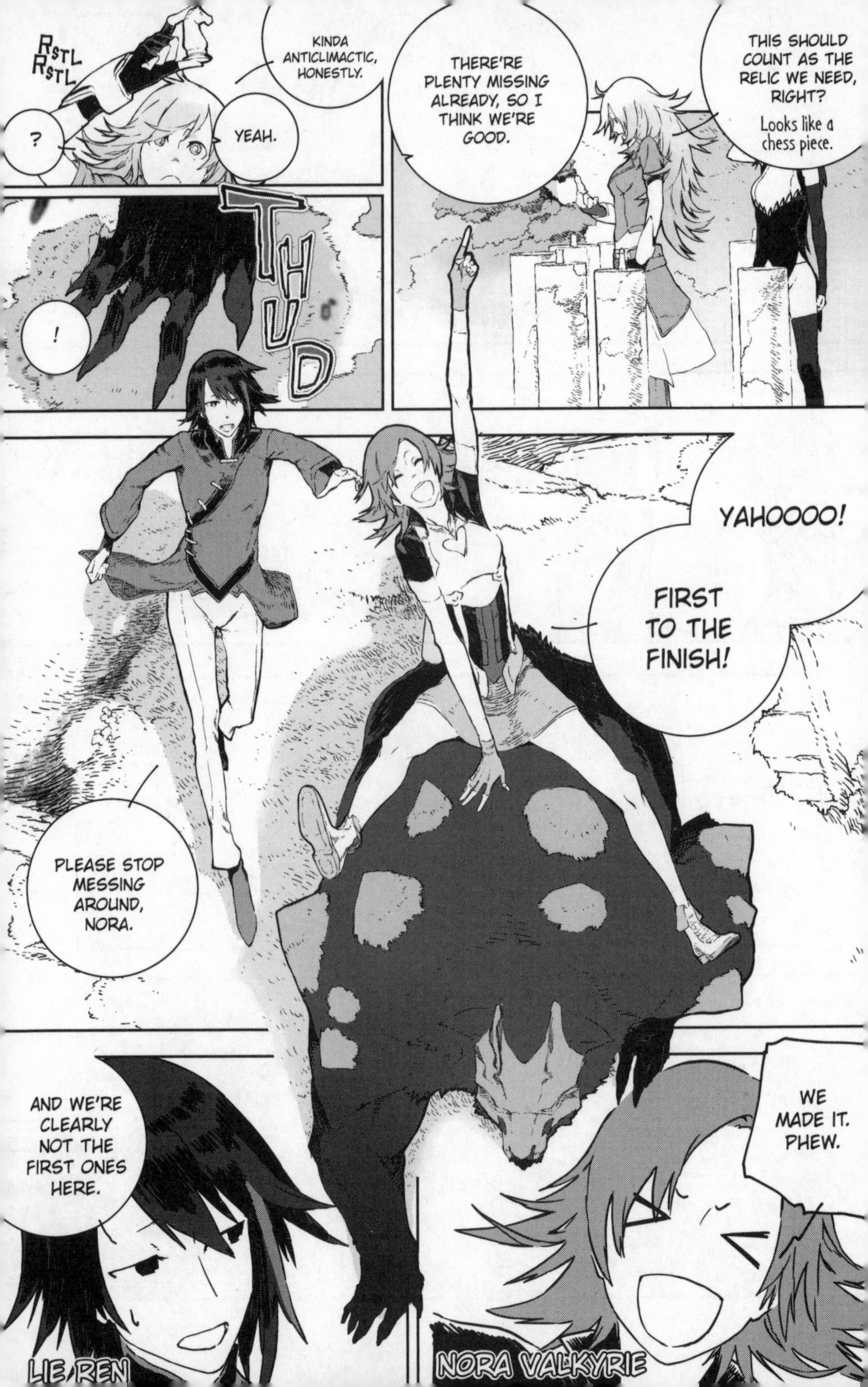
THIS SHOULD COUNT AS THE RELIC WE NEED, RIGHT?
Looks like a chess piece.
THERE'RE PLENTY MISSING ALREADY, SO I THINK WE'RE GOOD.
RSTL RSTL
KINDA ANTICLIMACTIC, HONESTLY.
YEAH.
?
THUD
!
YAHOOOO!
FIRST TO THE FINISH!
PLEASE STOP MESSING AROUND, NORA.
WE MADE IT. PHEW.
NORA VALKYRIE
AND WE'RE CLEARLY NOT THE FIRST ONES HERE.
LIE REN

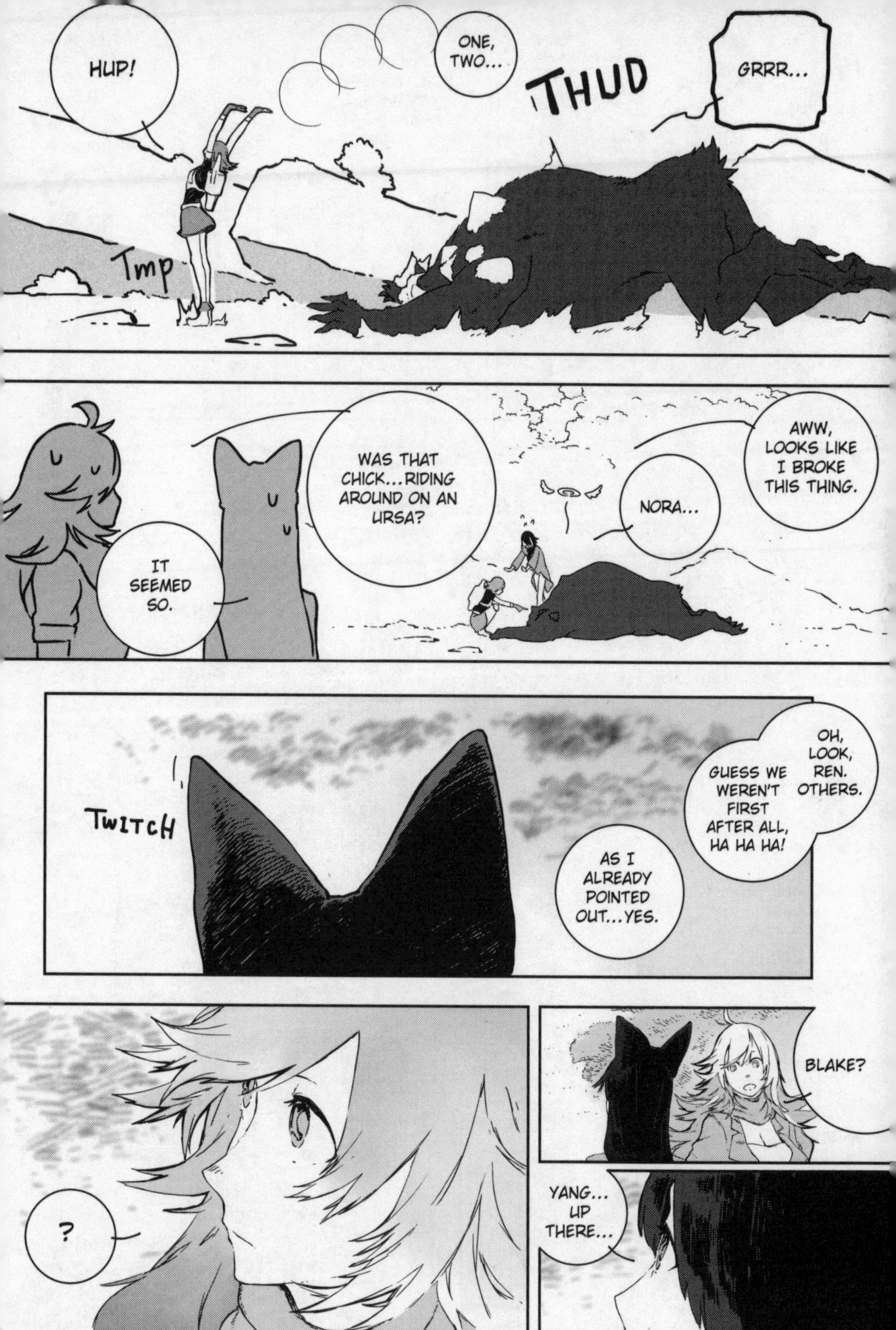
GRRR...
THUD
ONE, TWO...
HUP!
Tmp
AWW, LOOKS LIKE I BROKE THIS THING.
NORA...
WAS THAT CHICK...RIDING AROUND ON AN URSA?
IT SEEMED SO.
OH, LOOK, REN. OTHERS.
GUESS WE WEREN'T FIRST AFTER ALL, HA HA HA!
AS I ALREADY POINTED OUT...YES.
TWITCH
BLAKE?
YANG... UP THERE...
?

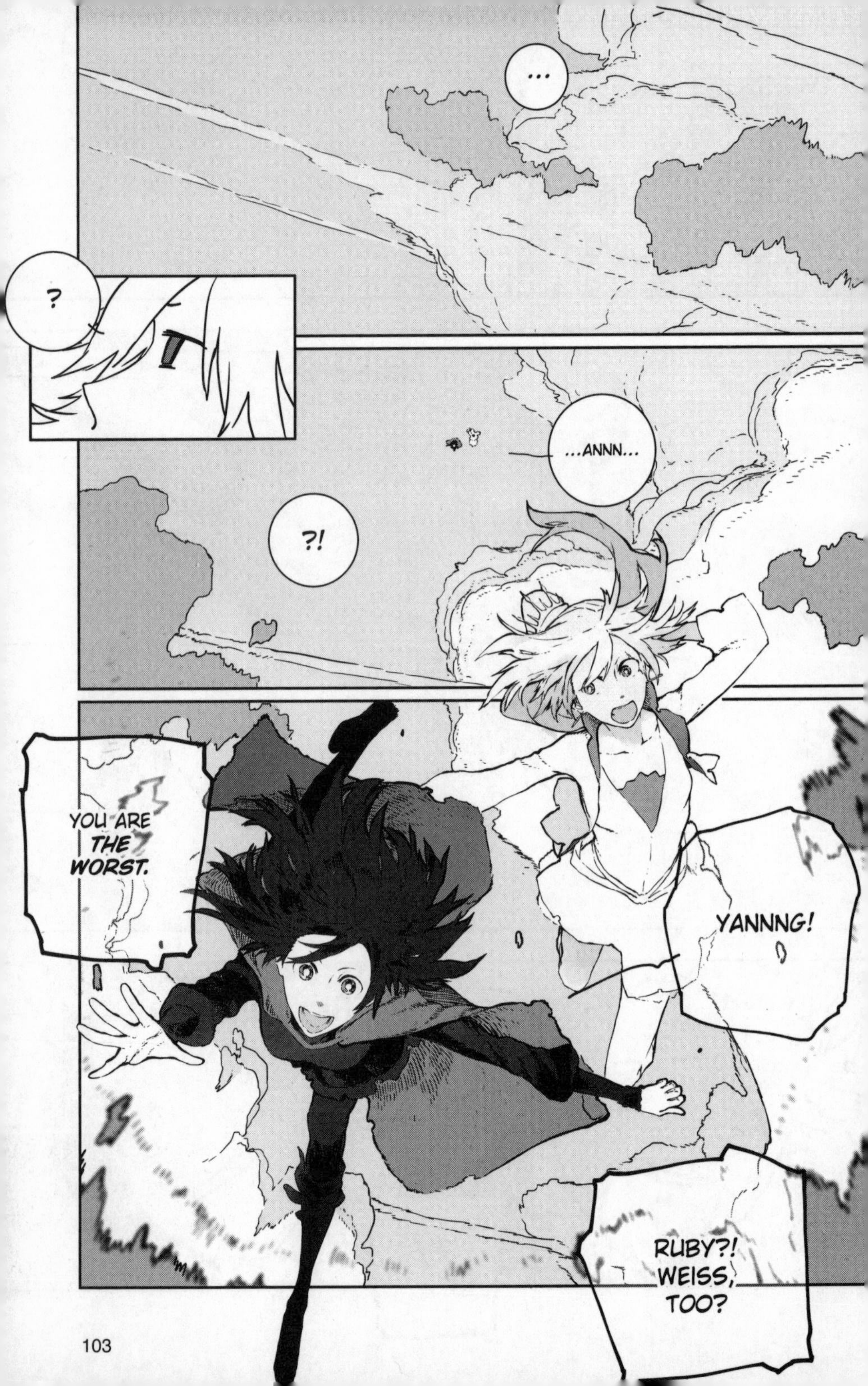
...
?
...ANNN...
?!
YANNNG!
RUBY?! WEISS, TOO?
YOU ARE *THE WORST.*

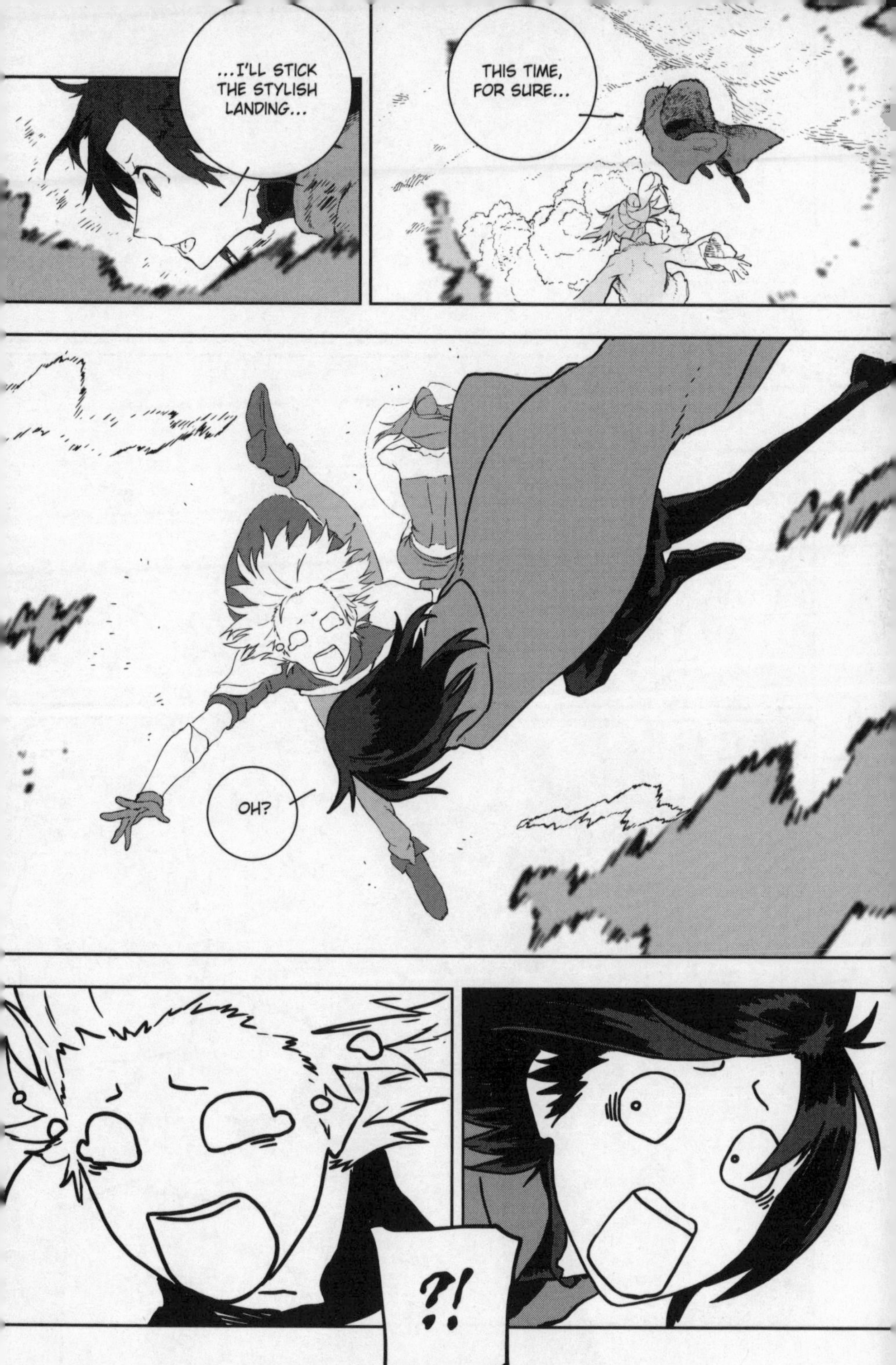
THIS TIME, FOR SURE...
...I'LL STICK THE STYLISH LANDING...
OH?
?!

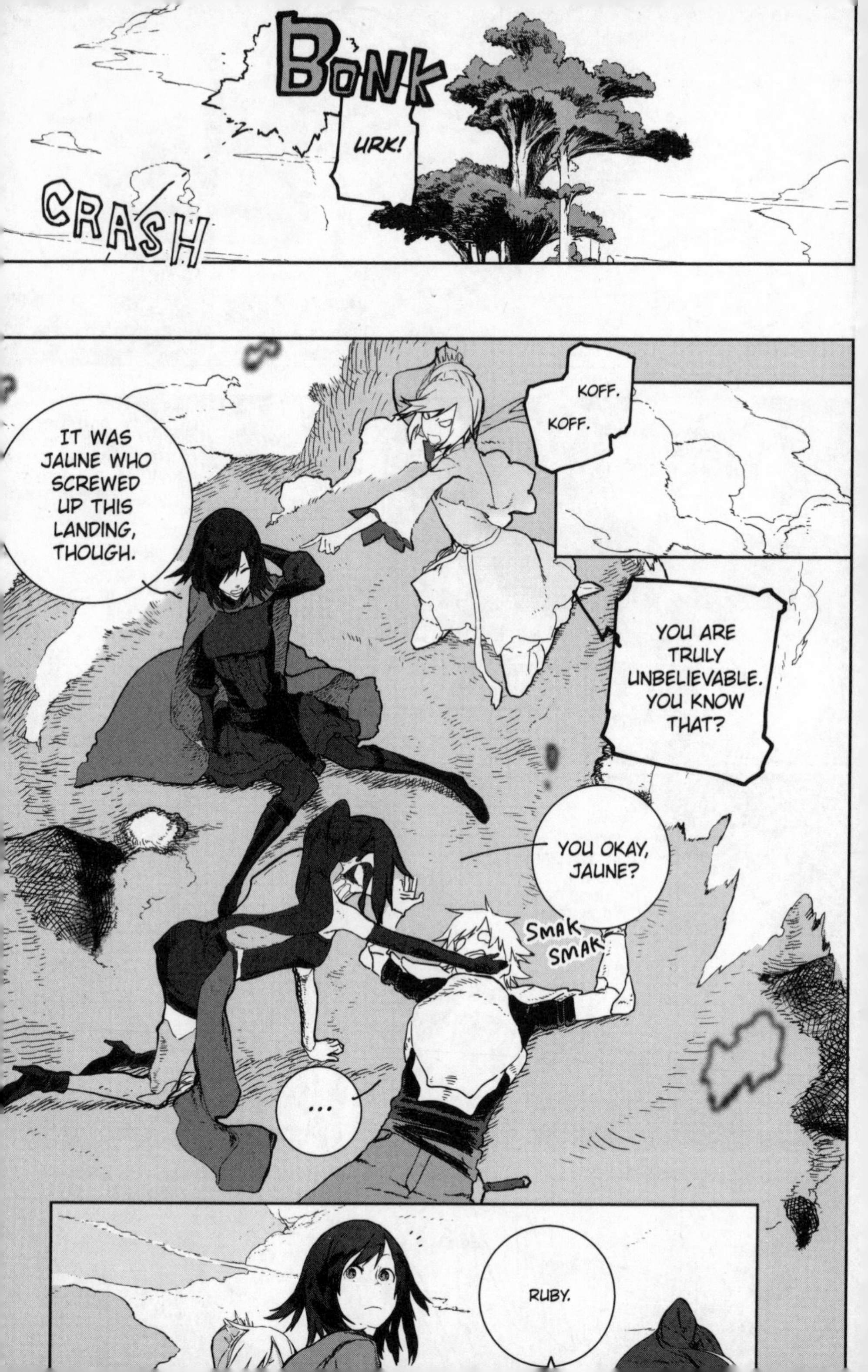
BONK
URK!
CRASH
KOFF. KOFF.
IT WAS JAUNE WHO SCREWED UP THIS LANDING, THOUGH.
YOU ARE TRULY UNBELIEVABLE. YOU KNOW THAT?
YOU OKAY, JAUNE?
SMAK SMAK
...
RUBY.

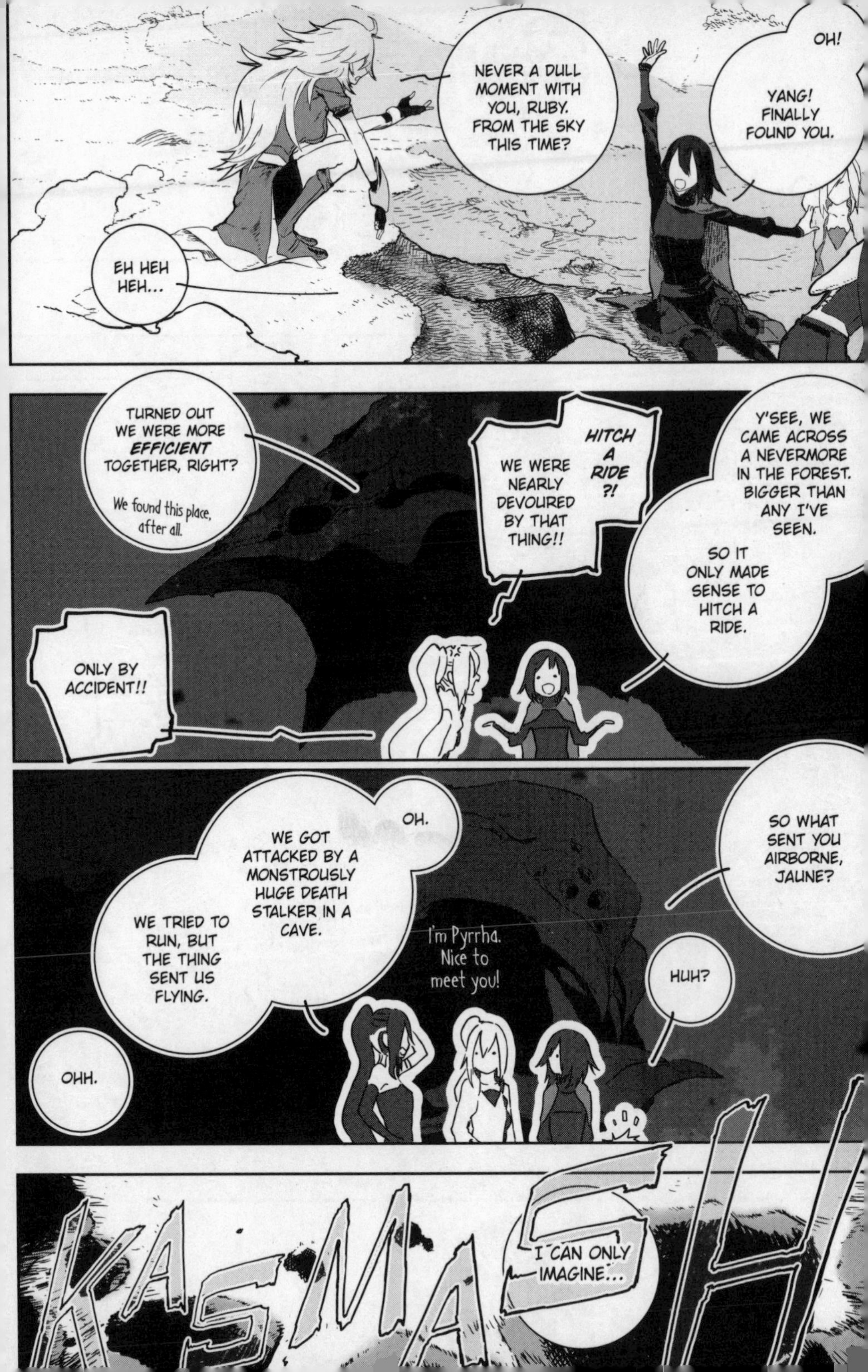
OH!
YANG! FINALLY FOUND YOU.
NEVER A DULL MOMENT WITH YOU, RUBY. FROM THE SKY THIS TIME?
EH HEH HEH...
Y'SEE, WE CAME ACROSS A NEVERMORE IN THE FOREST. BIGGER THAN ANY I'VE SEEN.
SO IT ONLY MADE SENSE TO HITCH A RIDE.
HITCH A RIDE?!
WE WERE NEARLY DEVOURED BY THAT THING!!
TURNED OUT WE WERE MORE EFFICIENT TOGETHER, RIGHT?
We found this place, after all.
ONLY BY ACCIDENT!!
SO WHAT SENT YOU AIRBORNE, JAUNE?
HUH?
I'm Pyrrha. Nice to meet you!
OH.
WE GOT ATTACKED BY A MONSTROUSLY HUGE DEATH STALKER IN A CAVE.
WE TRIED TO RUN, BUT THE THING SENT US FLYING.
OHH.
I CAN ONLY IMAGINE...
KASMASH

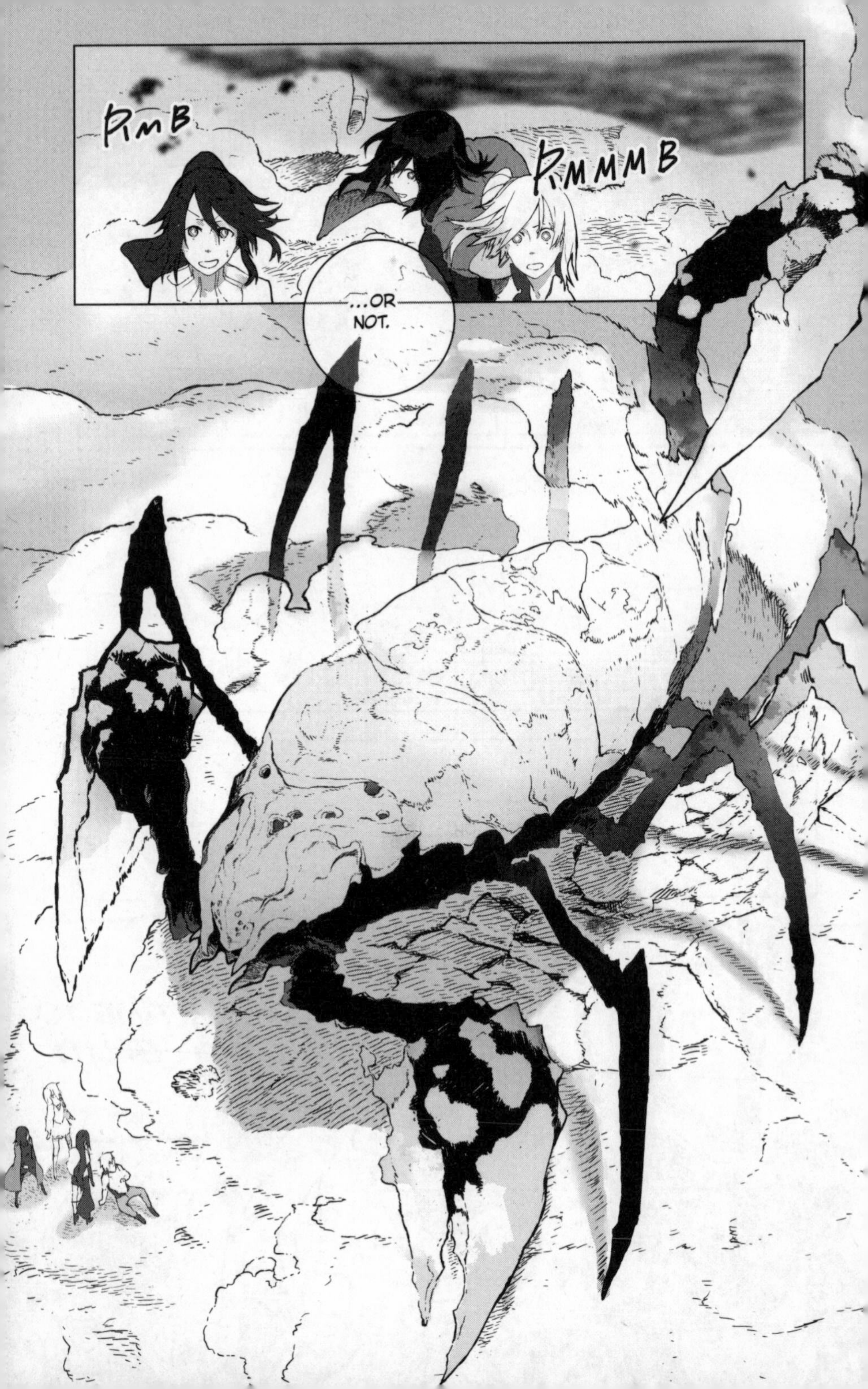
PMMMB
PMB
...OR NOT.

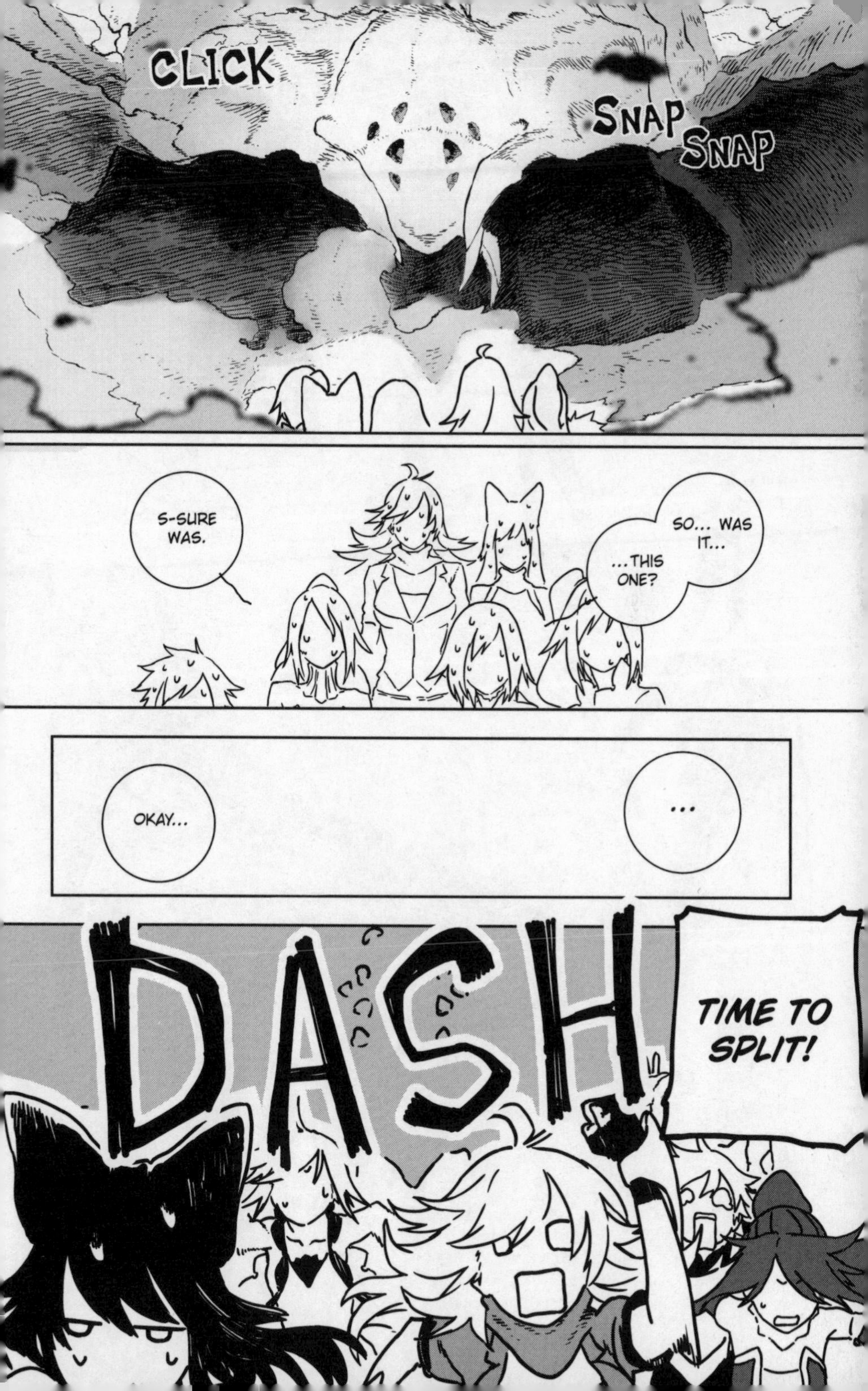
SNAP SNAP
CLICK
SO... WAS IT...
...THIS ONE?
S-SURE WAS.
...
OKAY...
TIME TO SPLIT!
DASH

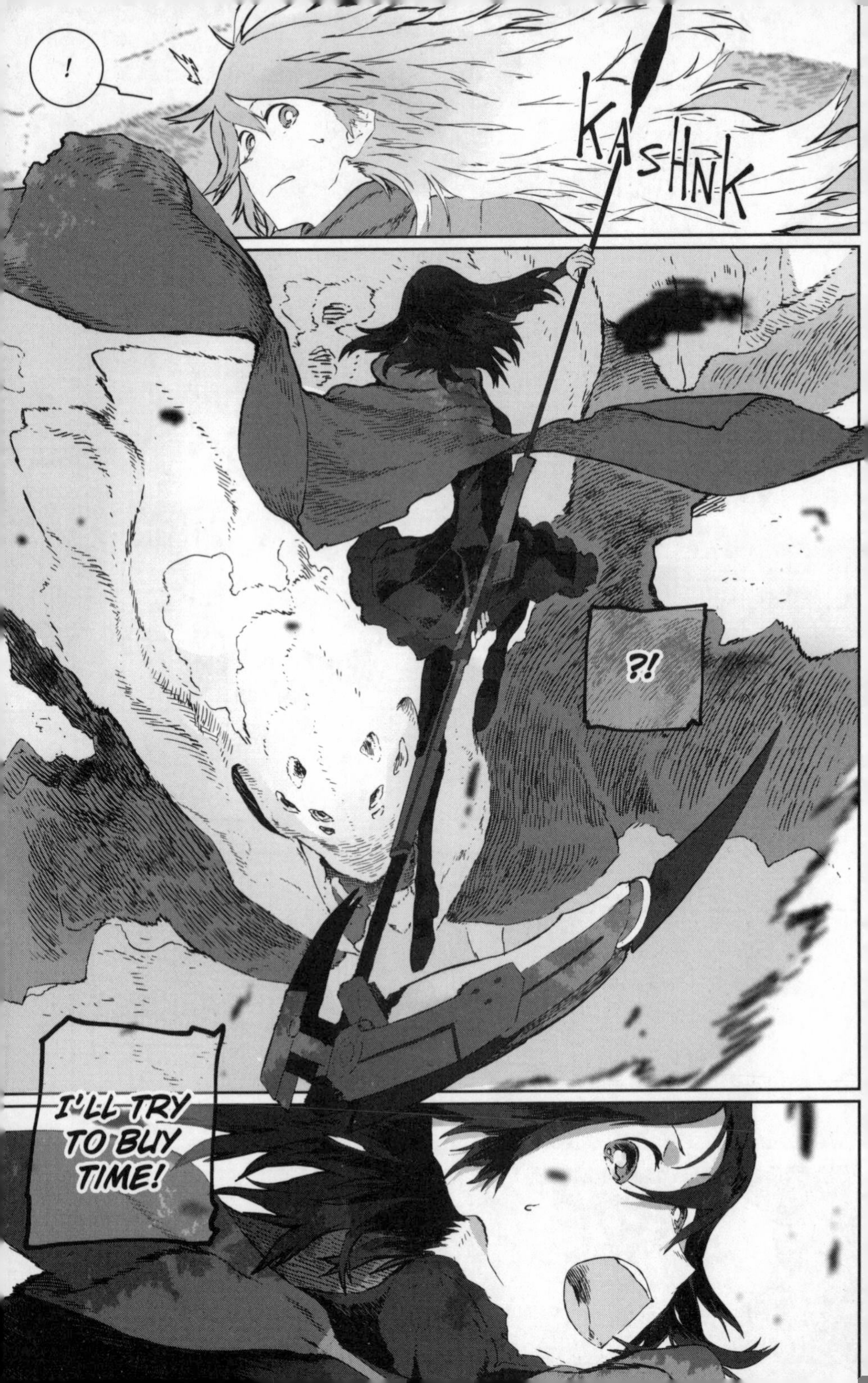
KASHNK
!
?!
I'LL TRY TO BUY TIME!

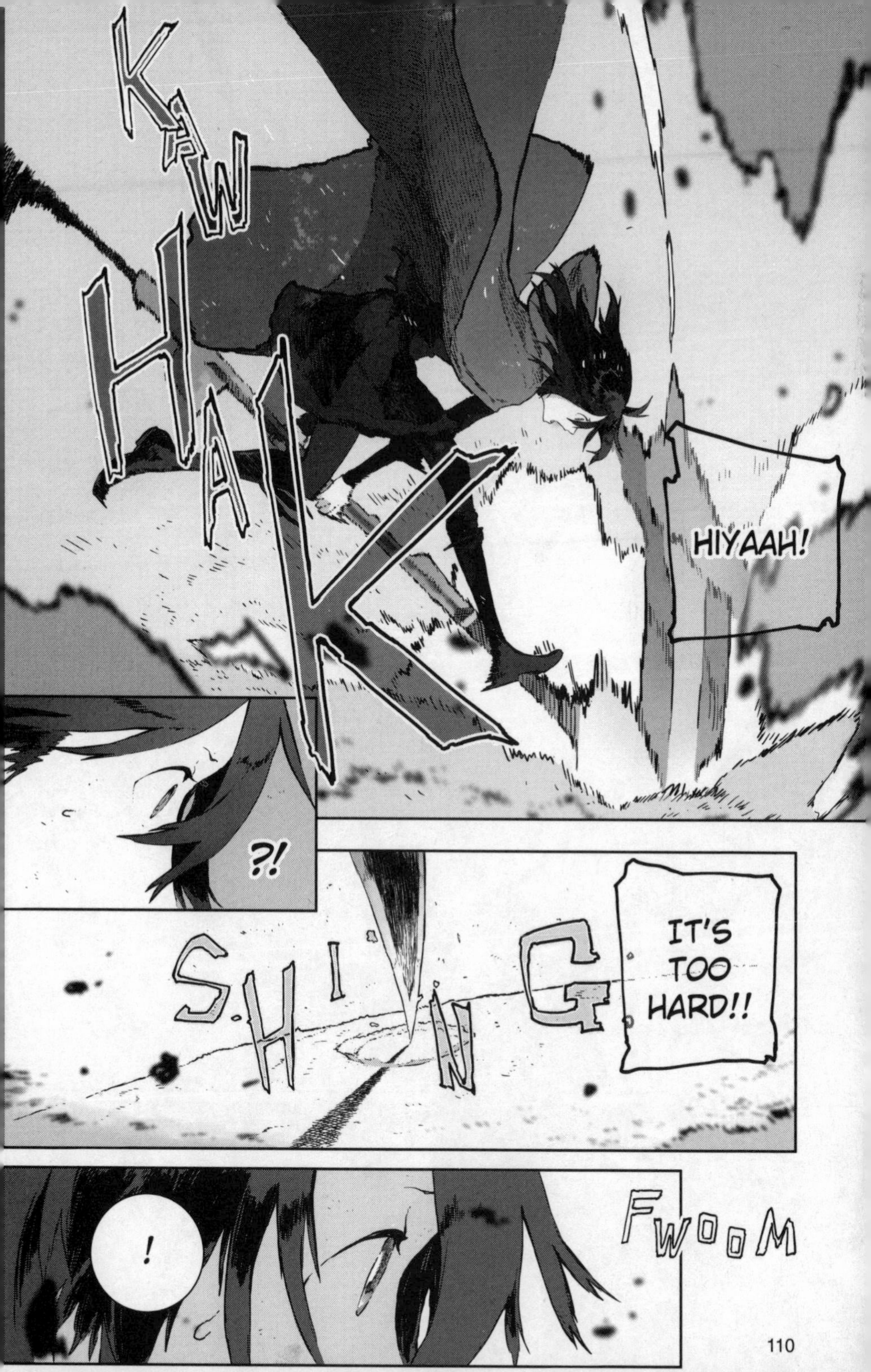
HIYAAH!
KAWHACK
?!
IT'S TOO HARD!!
SHING
FWOOM
!

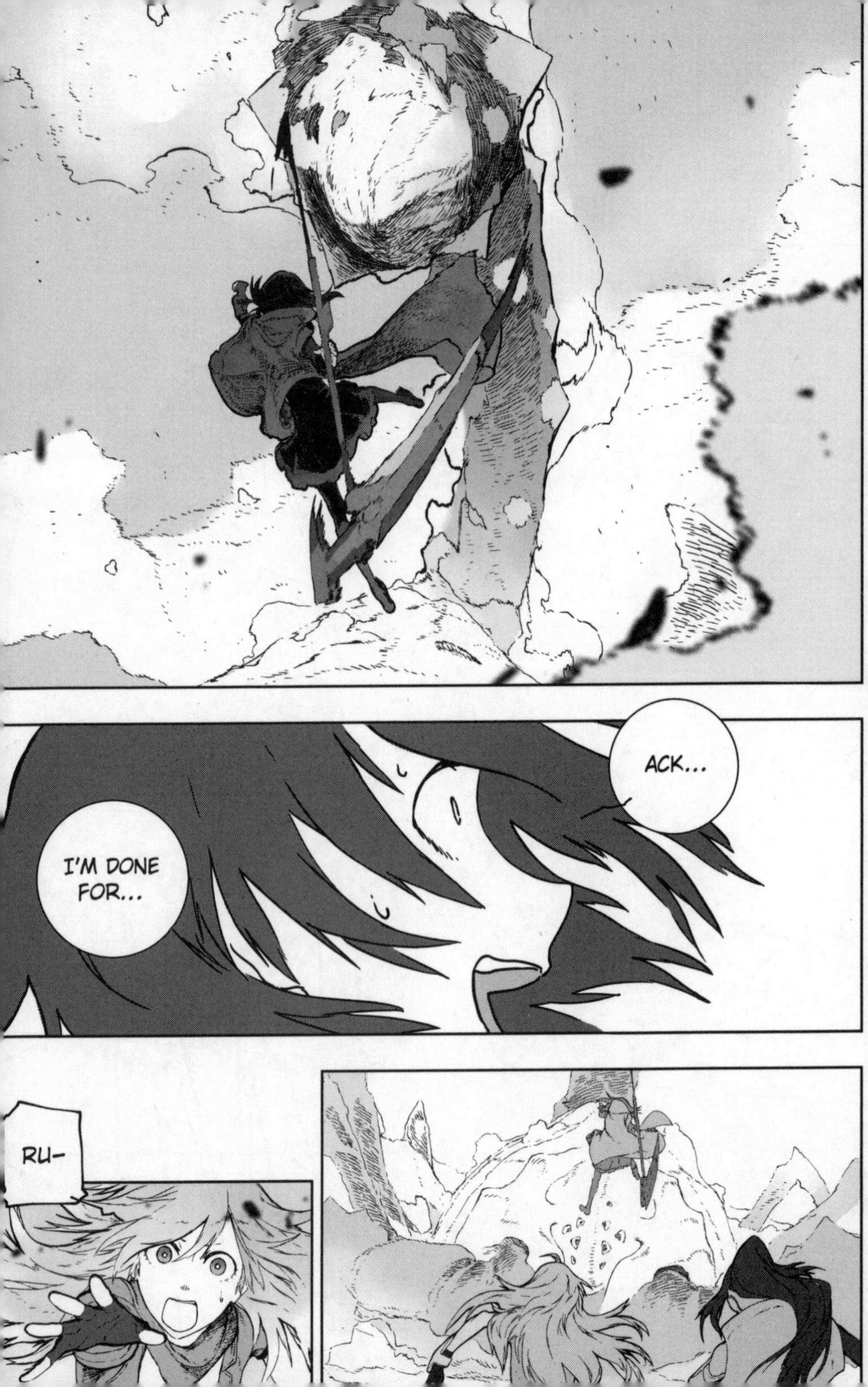
ACK...
I'M DONE FOR...
RU-

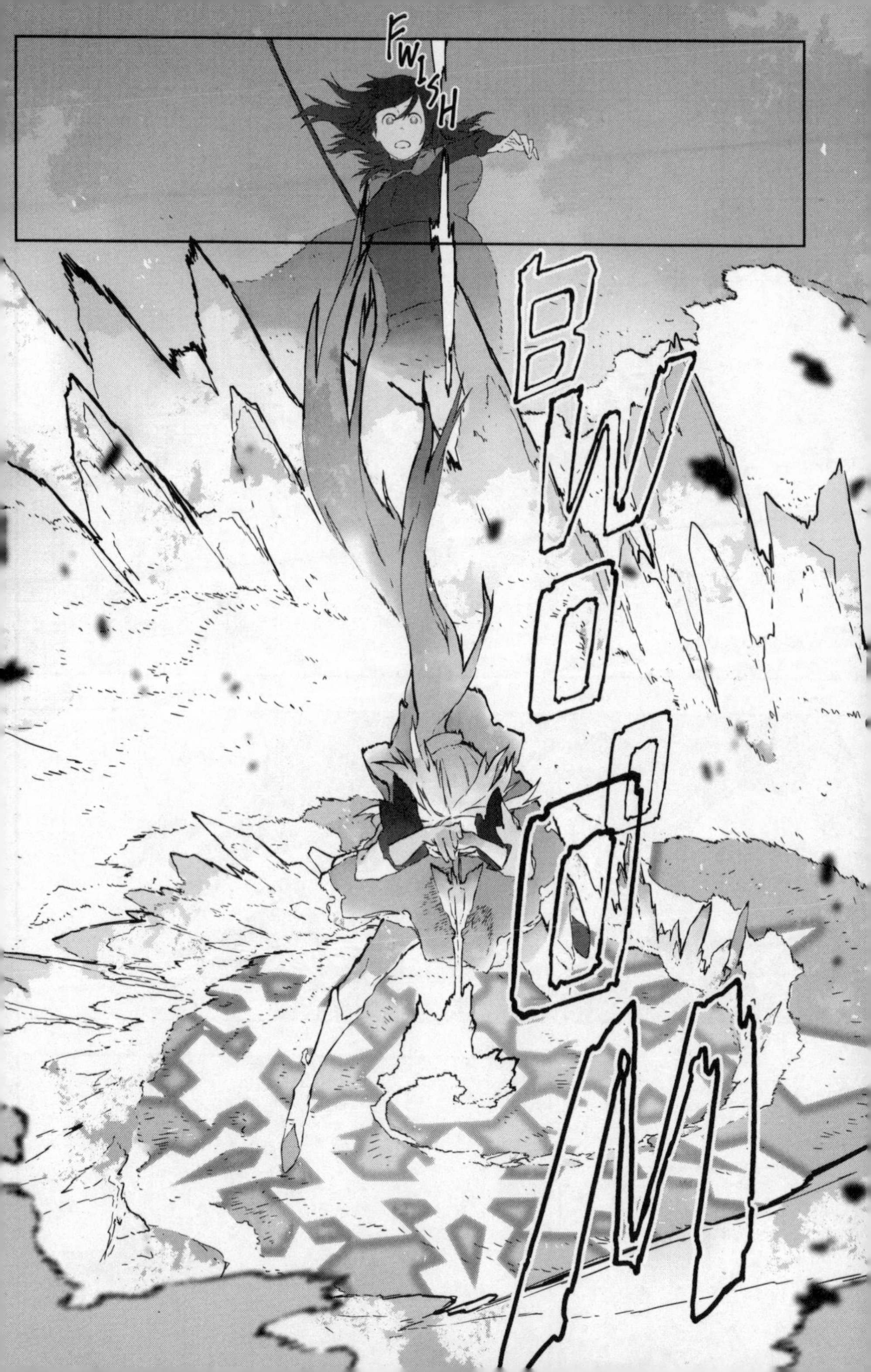
FWISH
BWOOOM

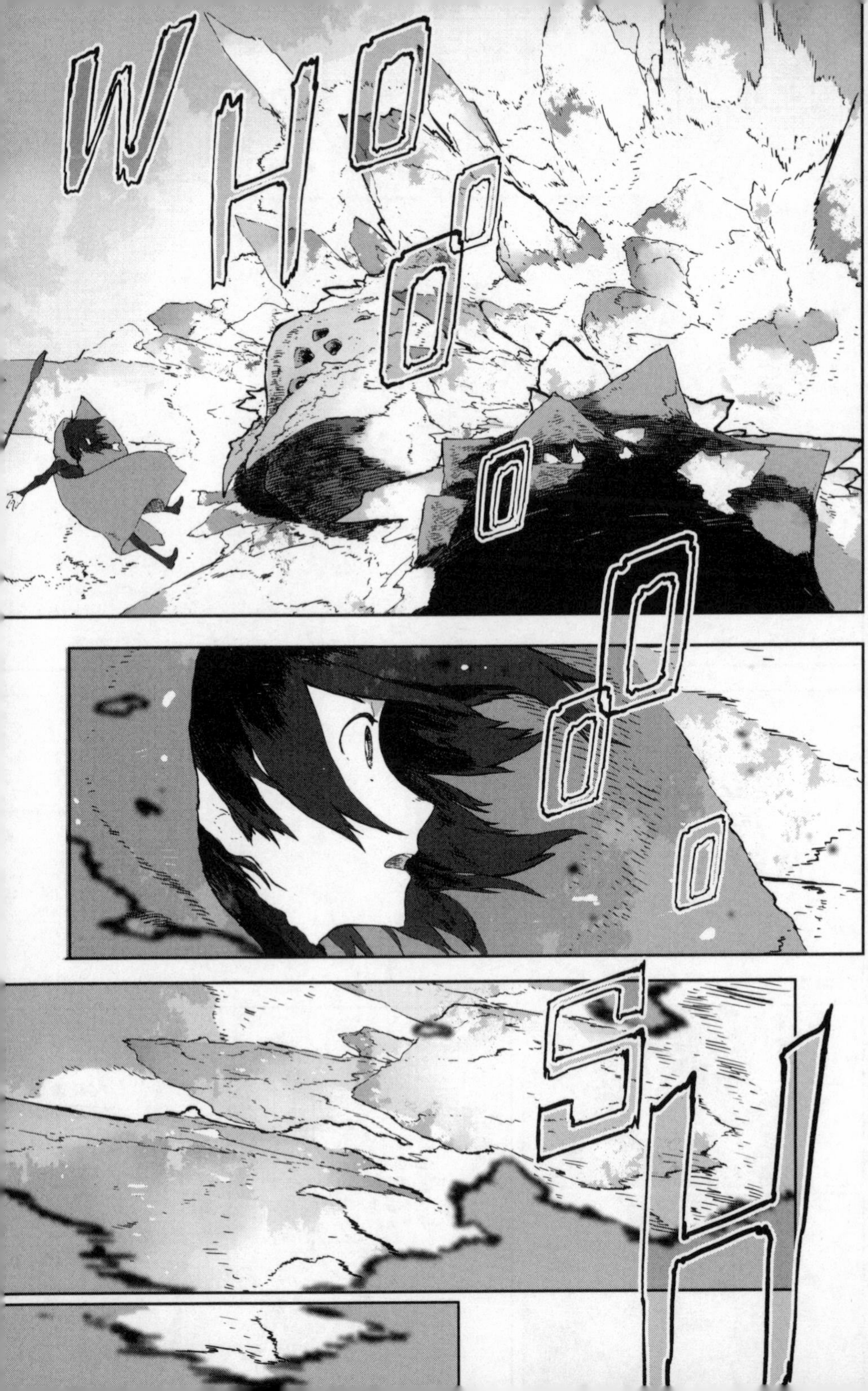
WHOOOOOOOSH

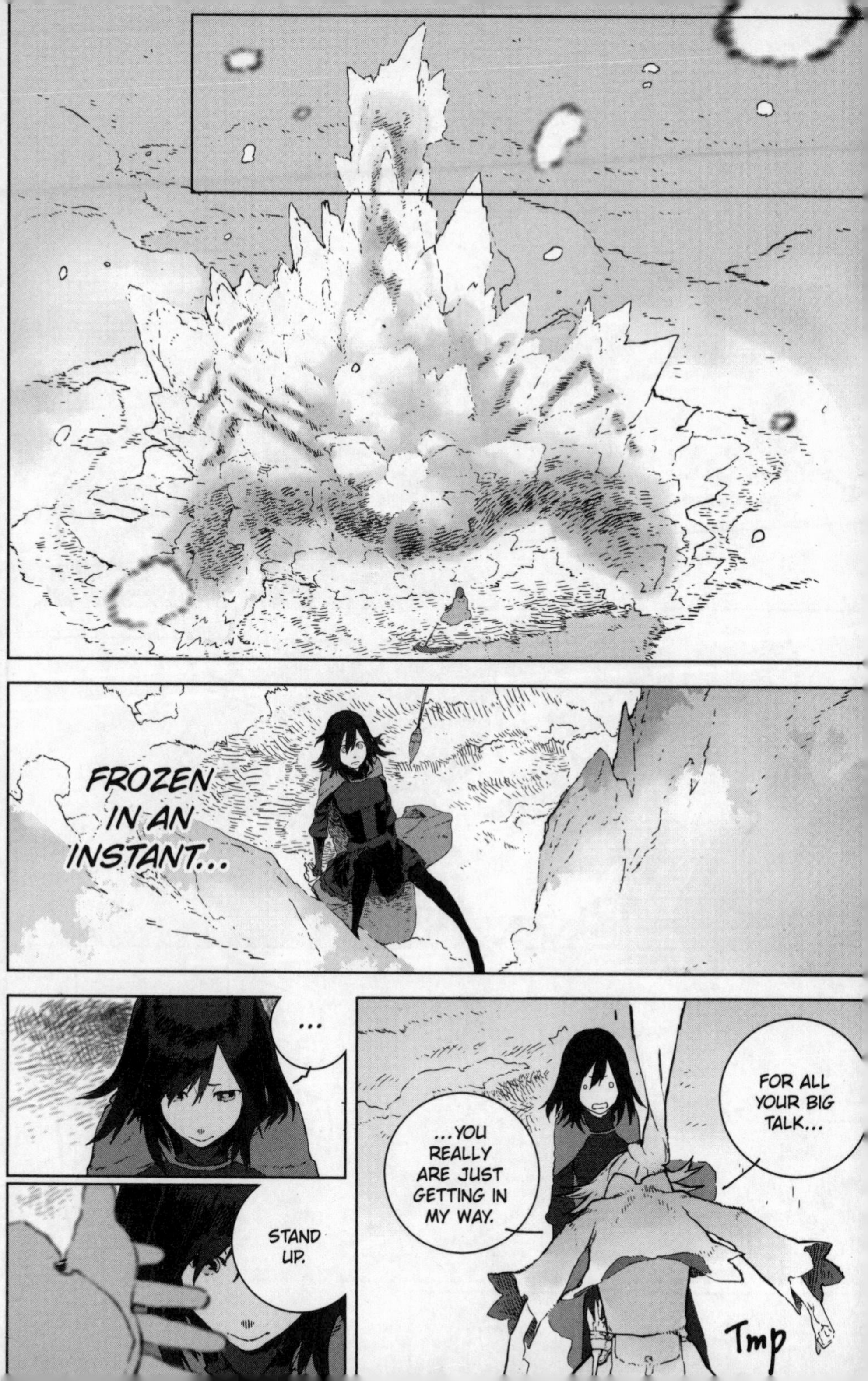
FROZEN IN AN INSTANT...
FOR ALL YOUR BIG TALK...
...YOU REALLY ARE JUST GETTING IN MY WAY.
Tmp
...
STAND UP.

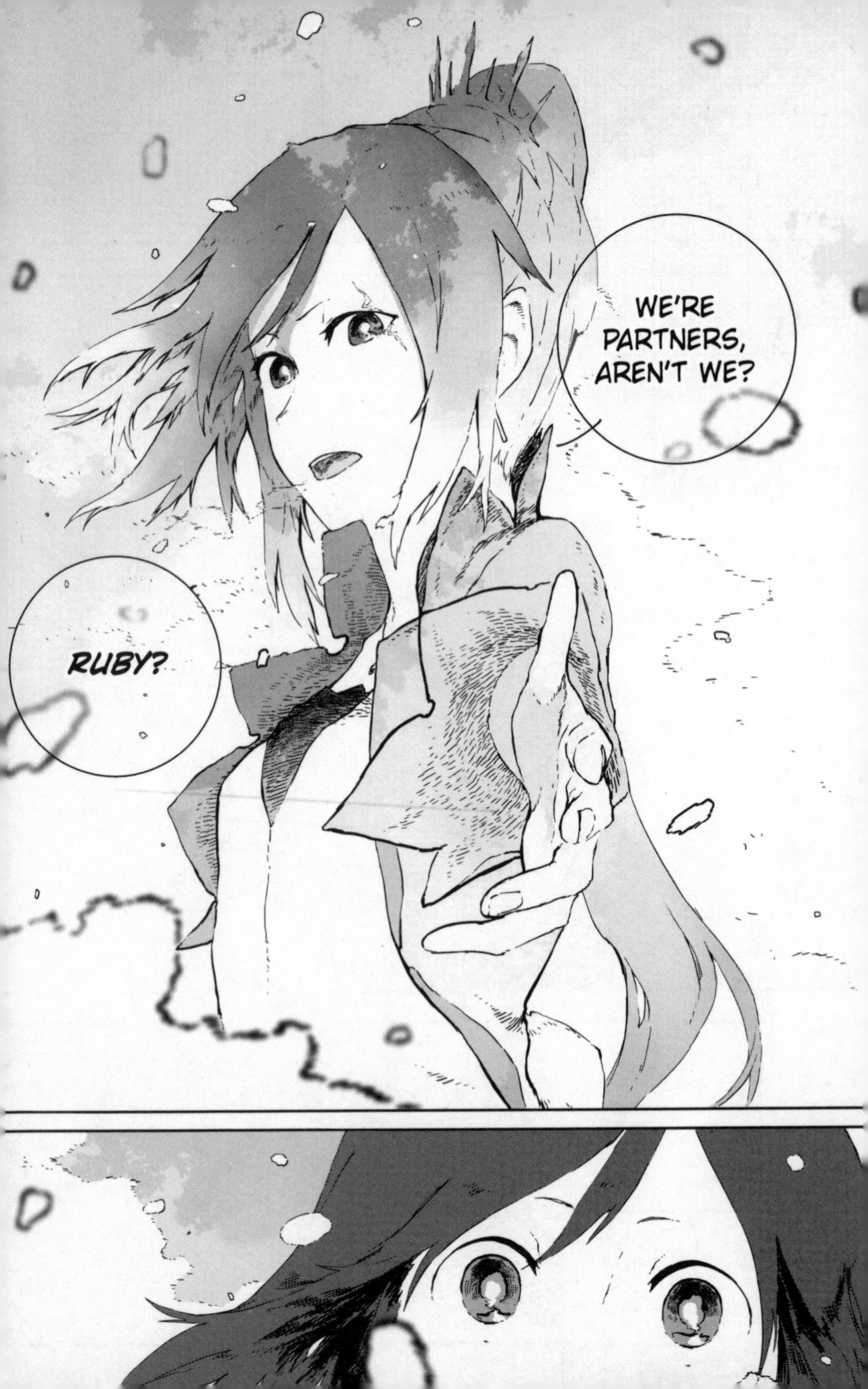
WE'RE PARTNERS, AREN'T WE?
RUBY?

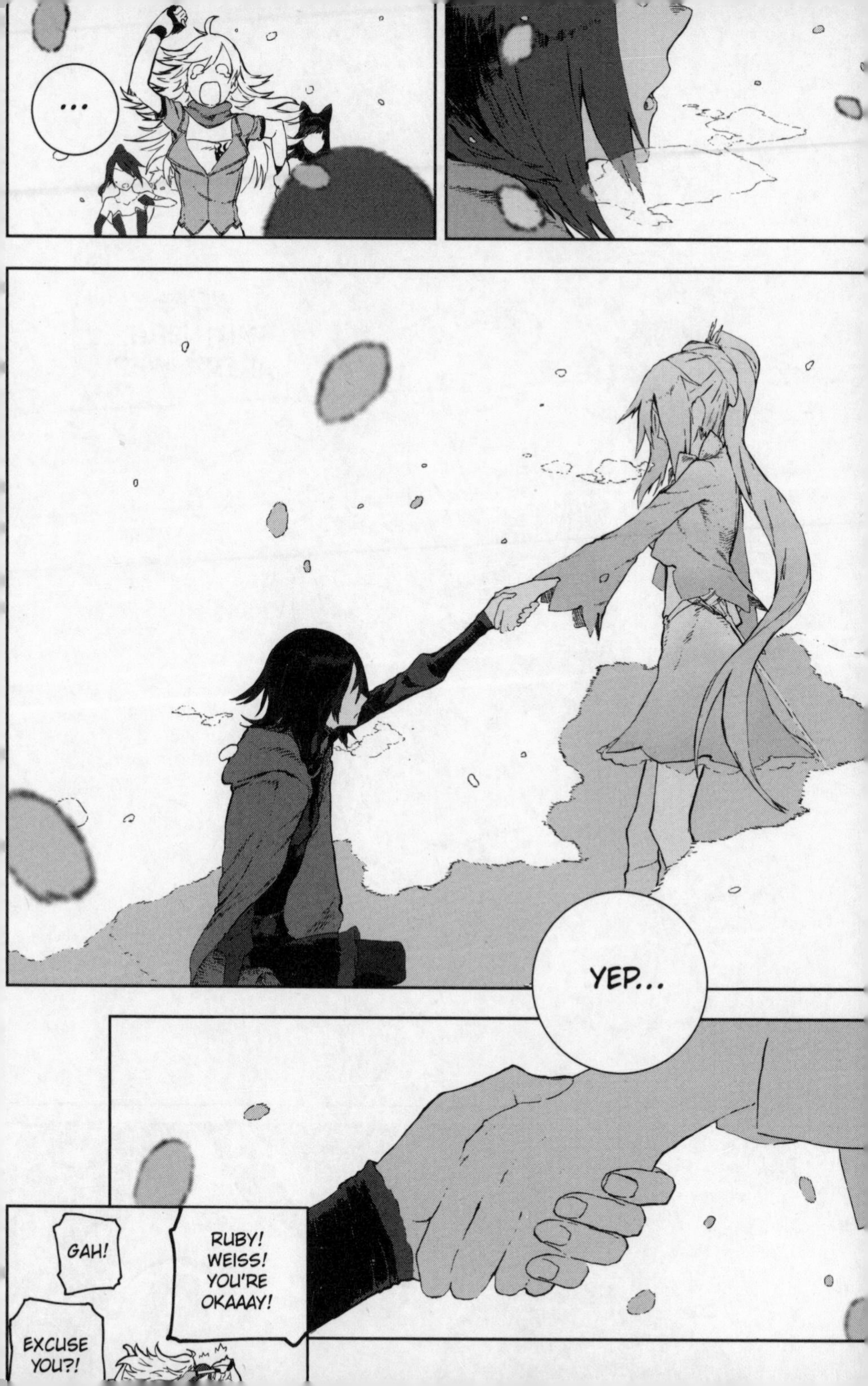
...
YEP...
RUBY! WEISS! YOU'RE OKAAAY!
GAH!
EXCUSE YOU?!

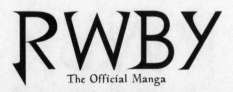

RWBY
The Official Manga

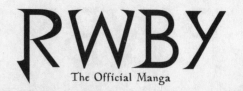

RWBY
The Official Manga

Episode 04

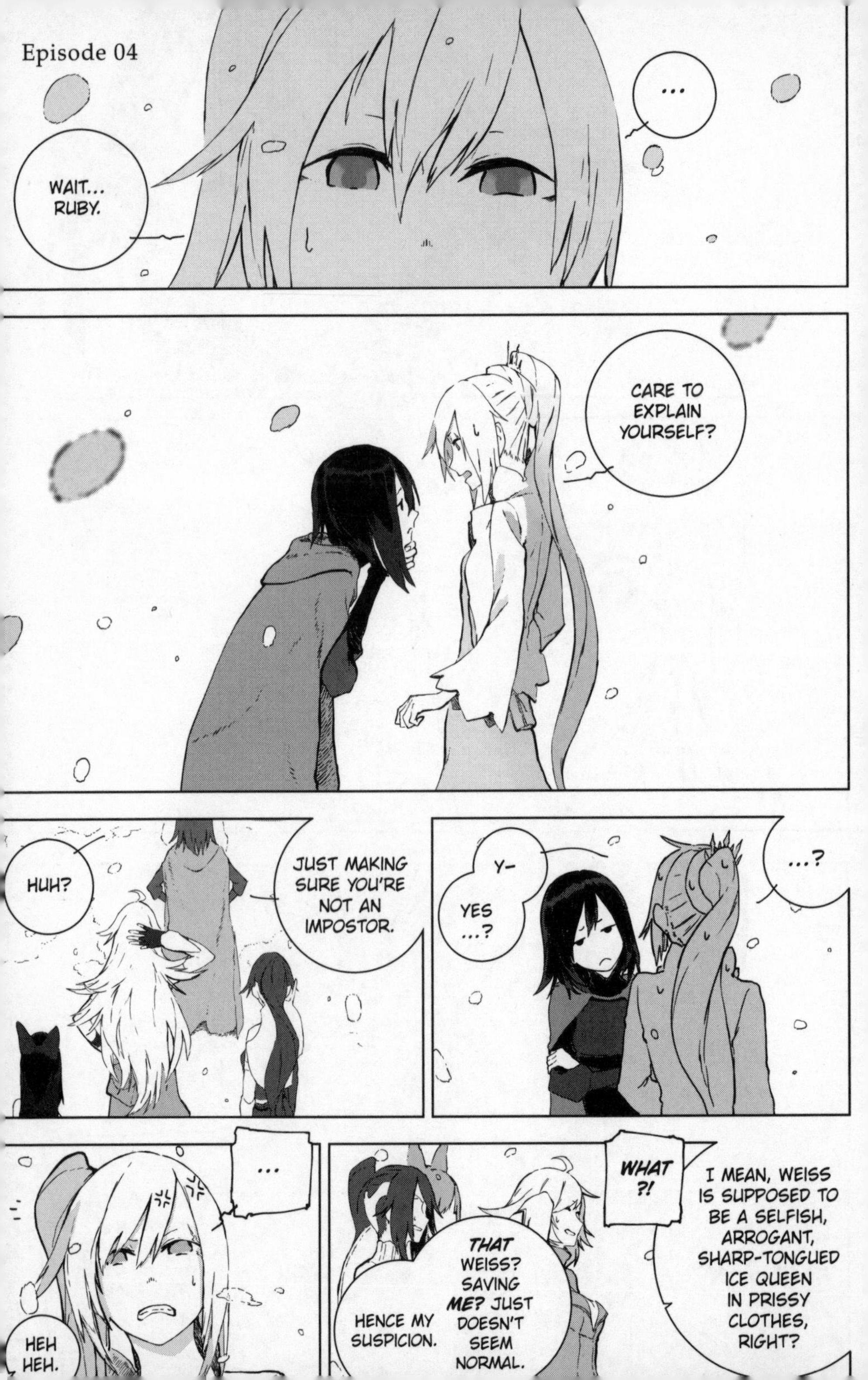
...
WAIT... RUBY.
CARE TO EXPLAIN YOURSELF?
...?
Y-
YES ...?
JUST MAKING SURE YOU'RE NOT AN IMPOSTOR.
HUH?
I MEAN, WEISS IS SUPPOSED TO BE A SELFISH, ARROGANT, SHARP-TONGUED ICE QUEEN IN PRISSY CLOTHES, RIGHT?
WHAT ?!
THAT WEISS? SAVING ME? JUST DOESN'T SEEM NORMAL.
HENCE MY SUSPICION.
...
HEH HEH.

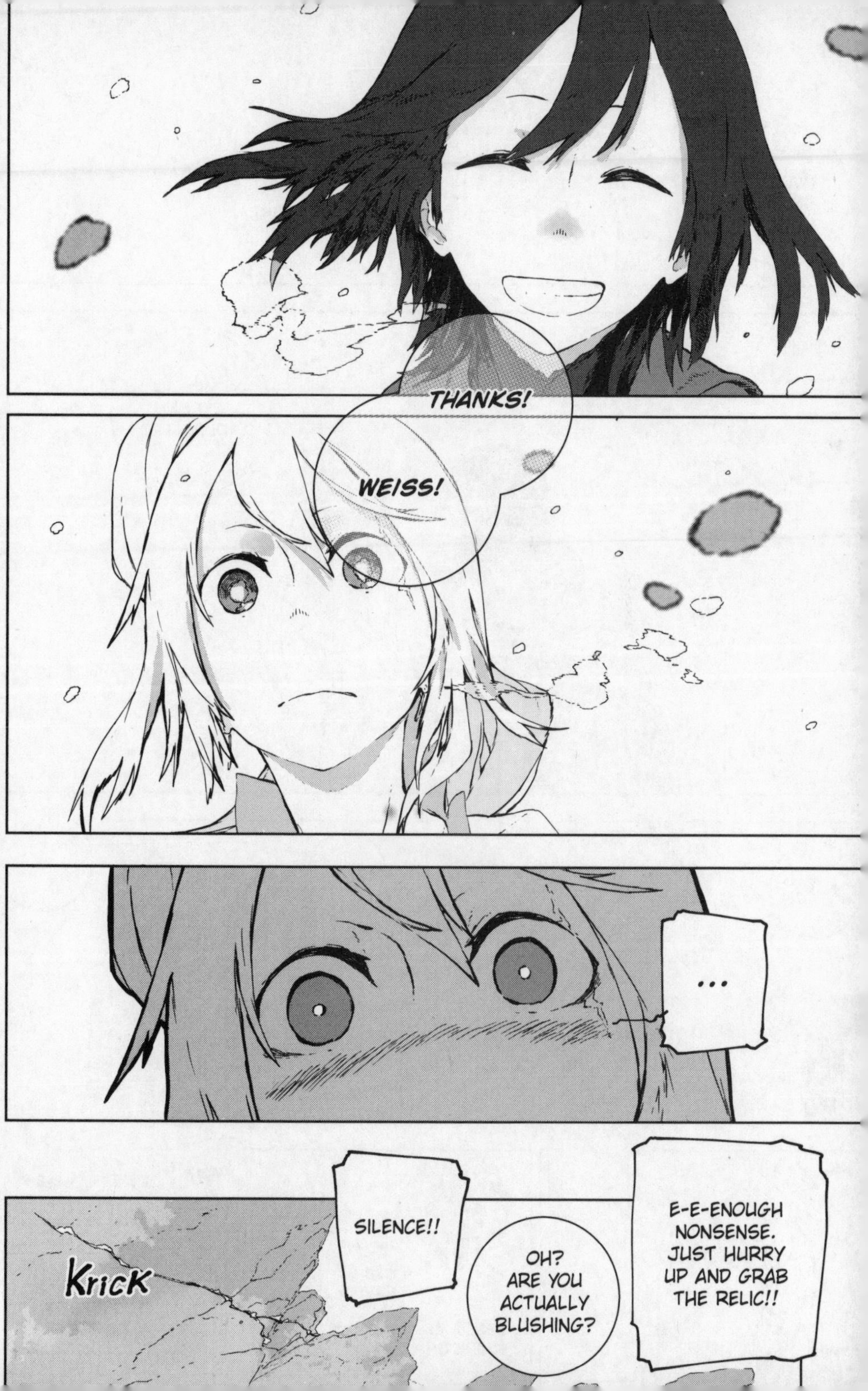
THANKS!
WEISS!
...
E-E-ENOUGH NONSENSE. JUST HURRY UP AND GRAB THE RELIC!!
OH? ARE YOU ACTUALLY BLUSHING?
SILENCE!!
Krick

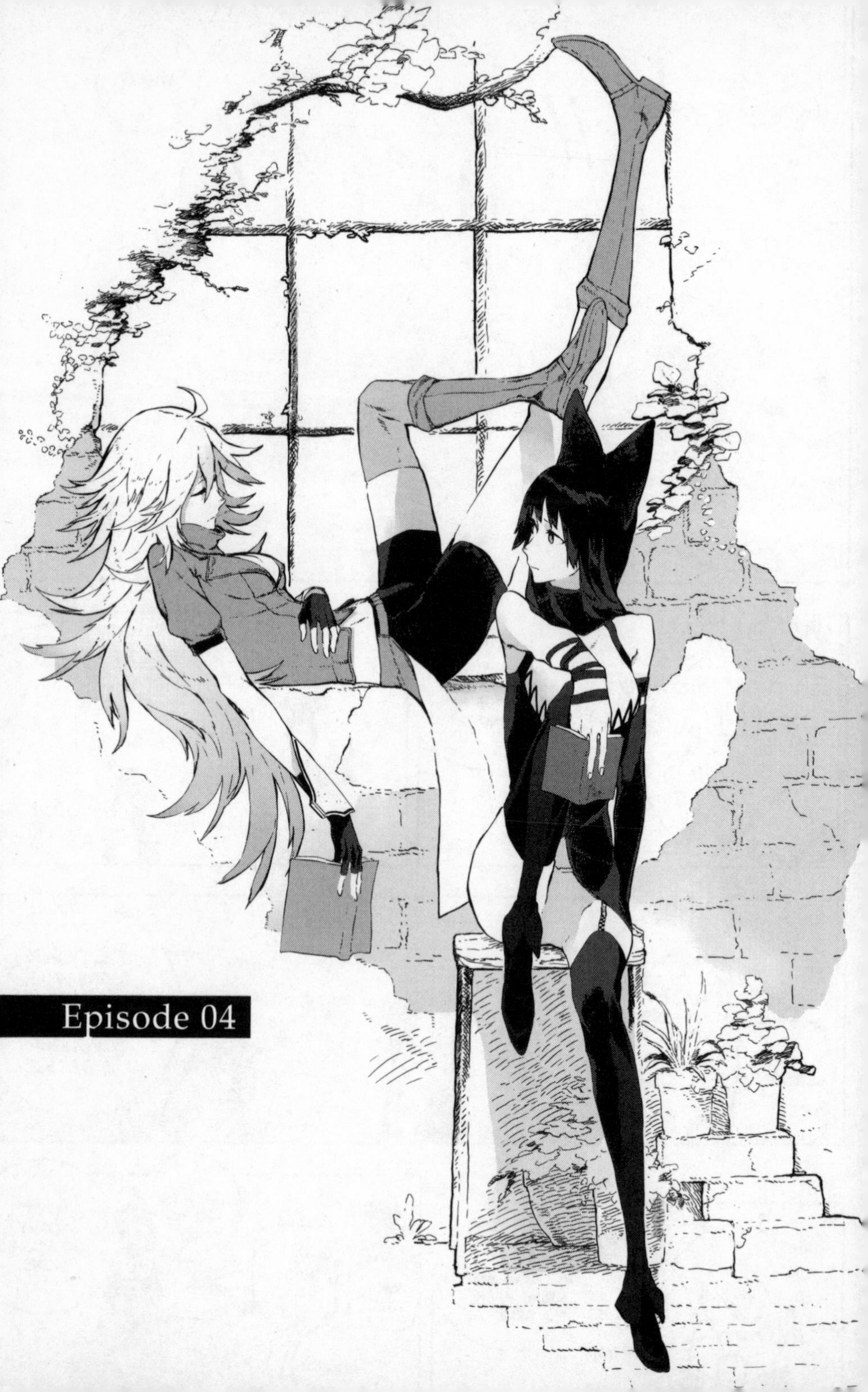

Episode 04

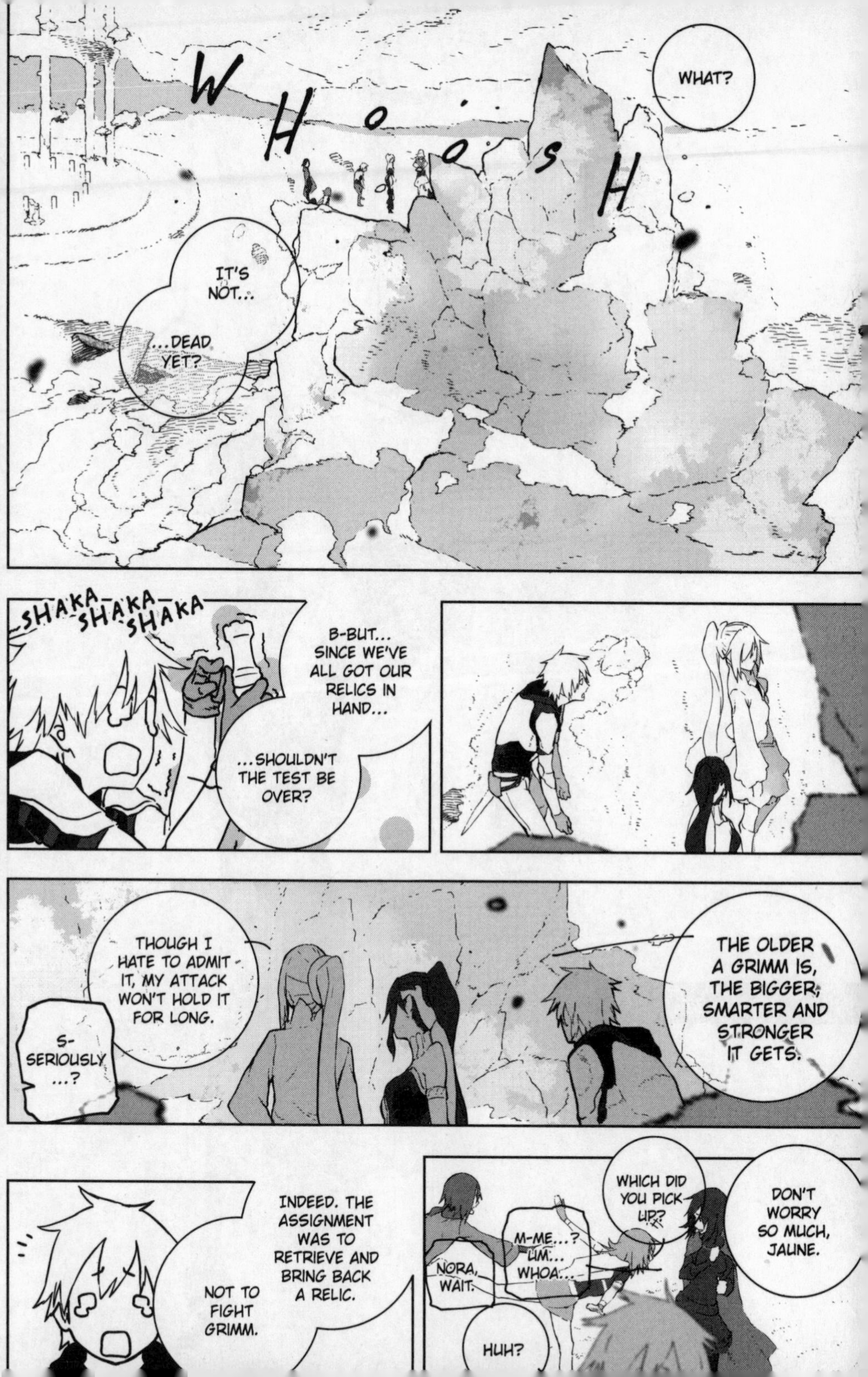
WHAT?
WHOOSH
IT'S NOT...
...DEAD YET?
B-BUT... SINCE WE'VE ALL GOT OUR RELICS IN HAND...
...SHOULDN'T THE TEST BE OVER?
SHAKA SHAKA SHAKA
THE OLDER A GRIMM IS, THE BIGGER, SMARTER AND STRONGER IT GETS.
THOUGH I HATE TO ADMIT IT, MY ATTACK WON'T HOLD IT FOR LONG.
S-SERIOUSLY...?
DON'T WORRY SO MUCH, JAUNE.
WHICH DID YOU PICK UP?
M-ME...? UM... WHOA...
NORA, WAIT.
HUH?
INDEED. THE ASSIGNMENT WAS TO RETRIEVE AND BRING BACK A RELIC.
NOT TO FIGHT GRIMM.

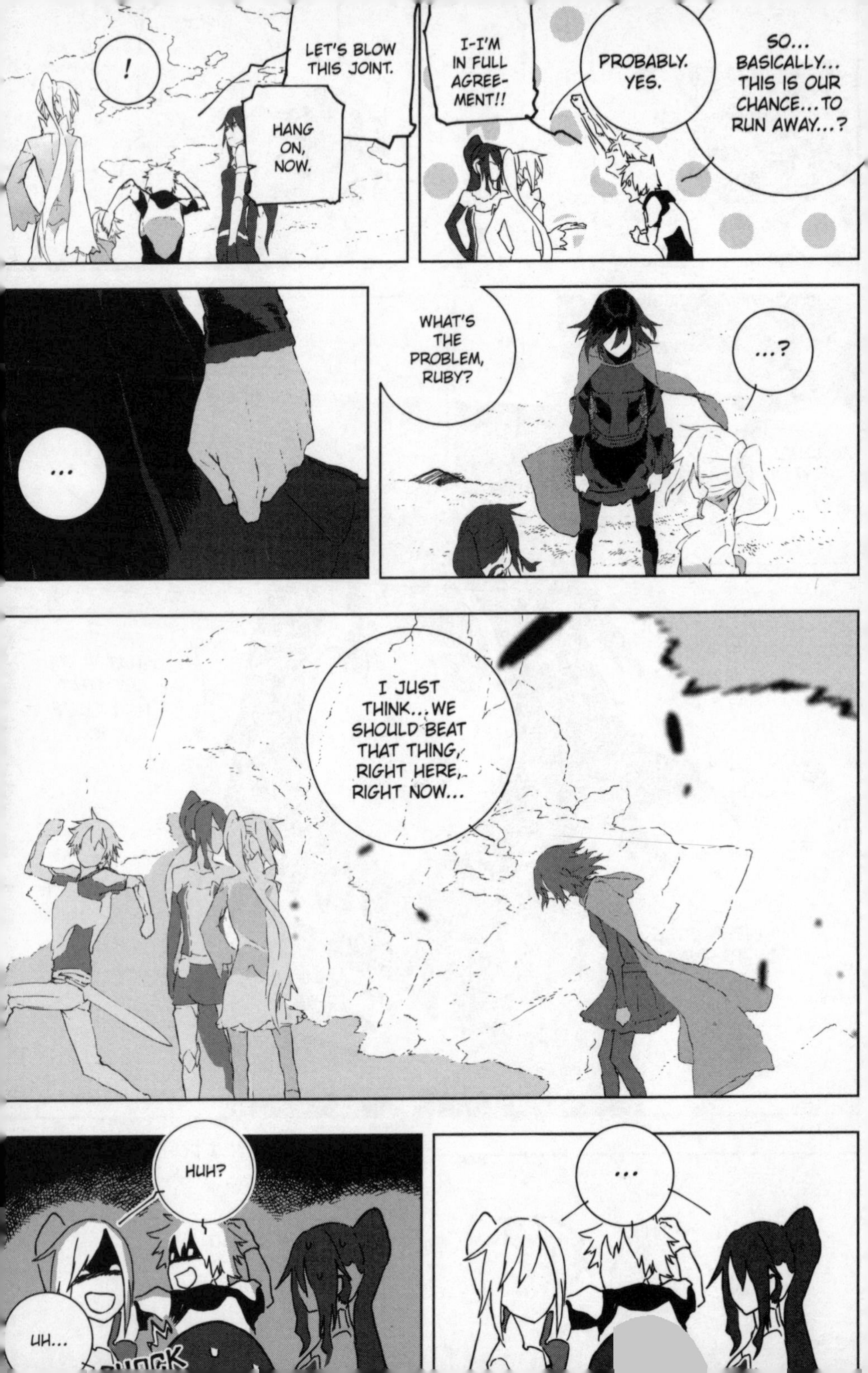
SO... BASICALLY... THIS IS OUR CHANCE...TO RUN AWAY...?
PROBABLY. YES.
I-I'M IN FULL AGREE-MENT!!
LET'S BLOW THIS JOINT.
HANG ON, NOW.
!
...?
WHAT'S THE PROBLEM, RUBY?
...
I JUST THINK...WE SHOULD BEAT THAT THING, RIGHT HERE, RIGHT NOW...
...
HUH?
UH...

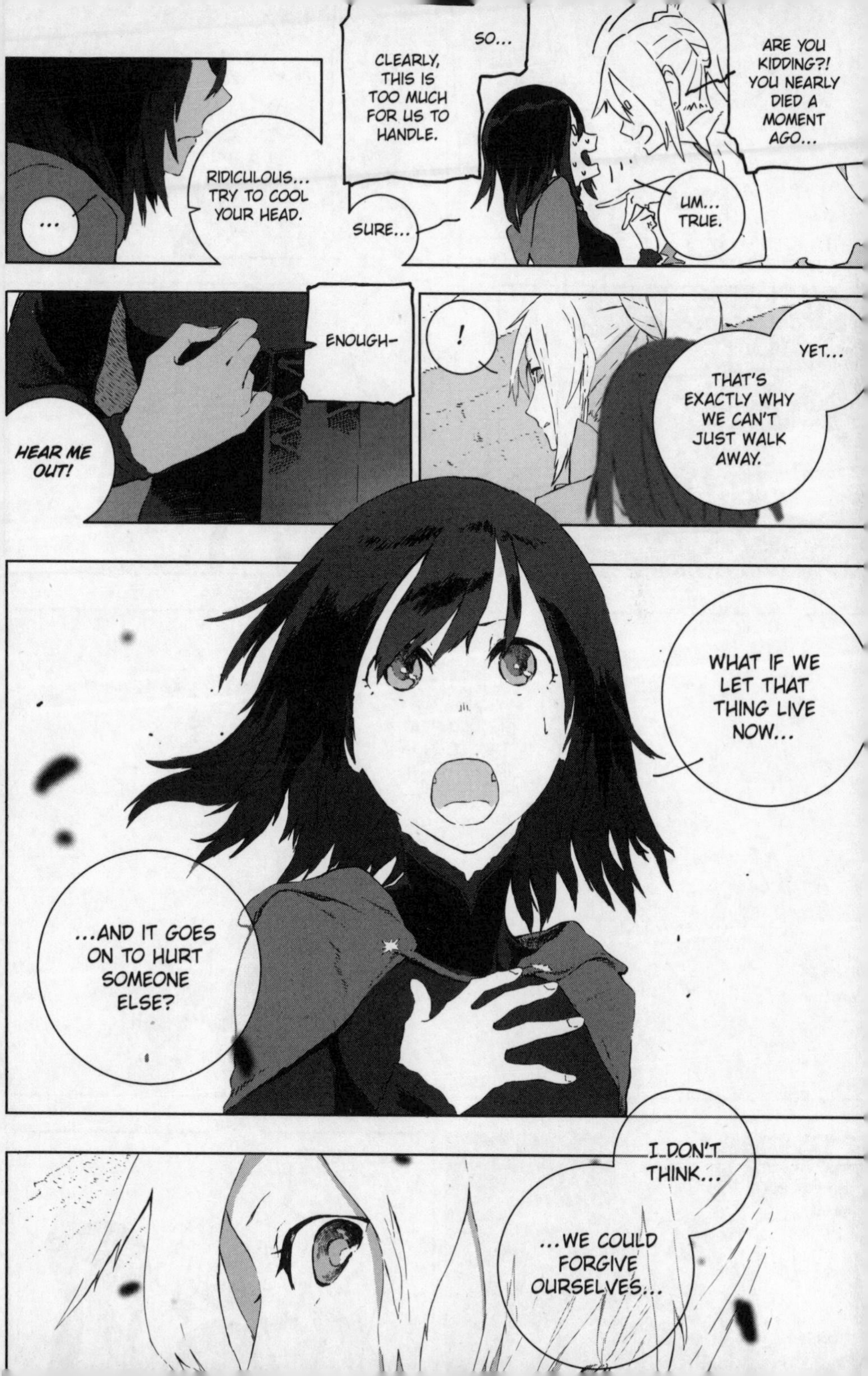
ARE YOU KIDDING?! YOU NEARLY DIED A MOMENT AGO...
SO... CLEARLY, THIS IS TOO MUCH FOR US TO HANDLE.
UM... TRUE.
SURE...
RIDICULOUS... TRY TO COOL YOUR HEAD.
...
YET... THAT'S EXACTLY WHY WE CAN'T JUST WALK AWAY.
!
ENOUGH-
HEAR ME OUT!
WHAT IF WE LET THAT THING LIVE NOW...
...AND IT GOES ON TO HURT SOMEONE ELSE?
I DON'T THINK...
...WE COULD FORGIVE OURSELVES...

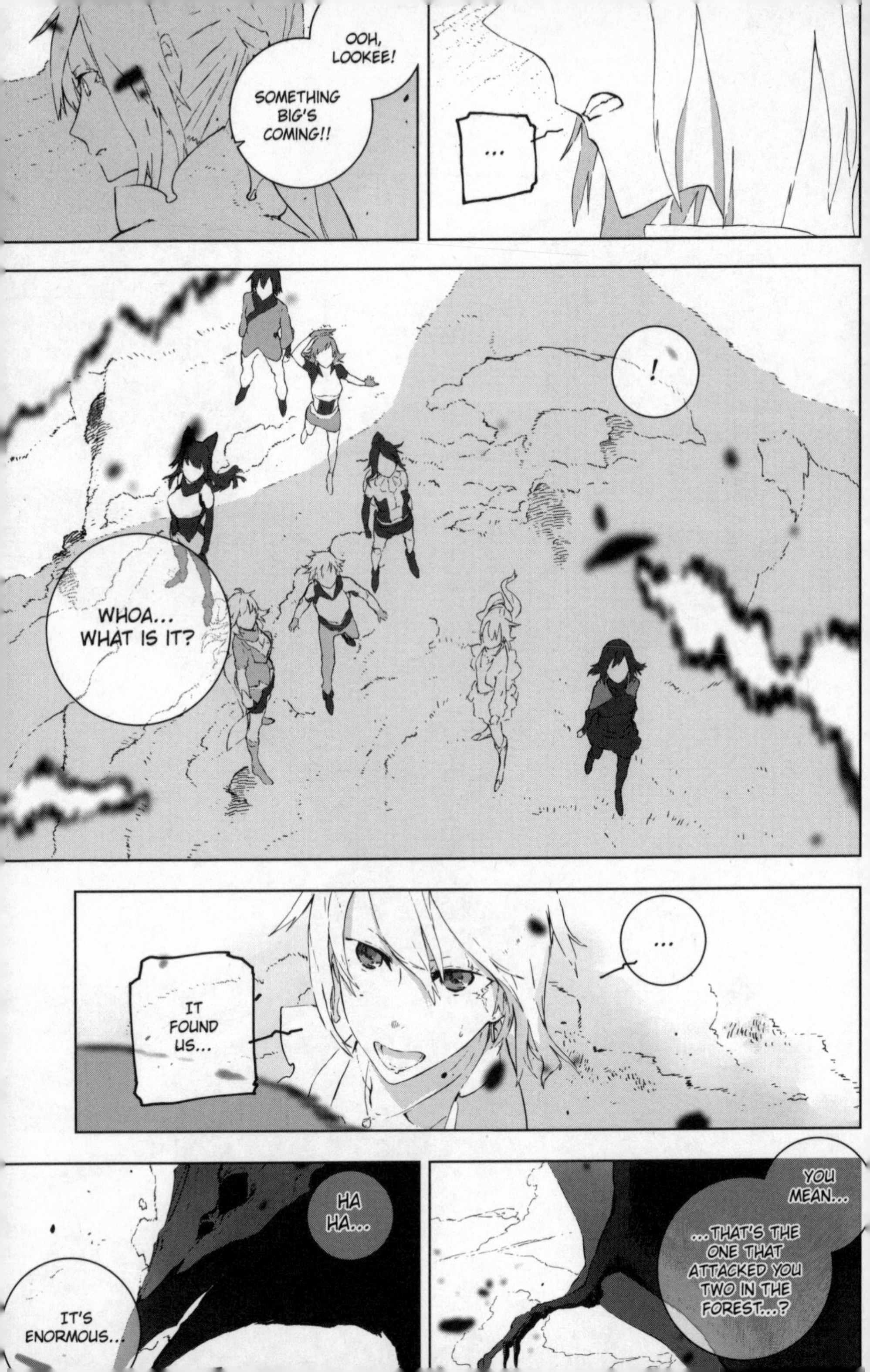
...
OOH, LOOKEE!
SOMETHING BIG'S COMING!!
!
WHOA... WHAT IS IT?
...
IT FOUND US...
YOU MEAN...
...THAT'S THE ONE THAT ATTACKED YOU TWO IN THE FOREST...?
HA HA...
IT'S ENORMOUS...

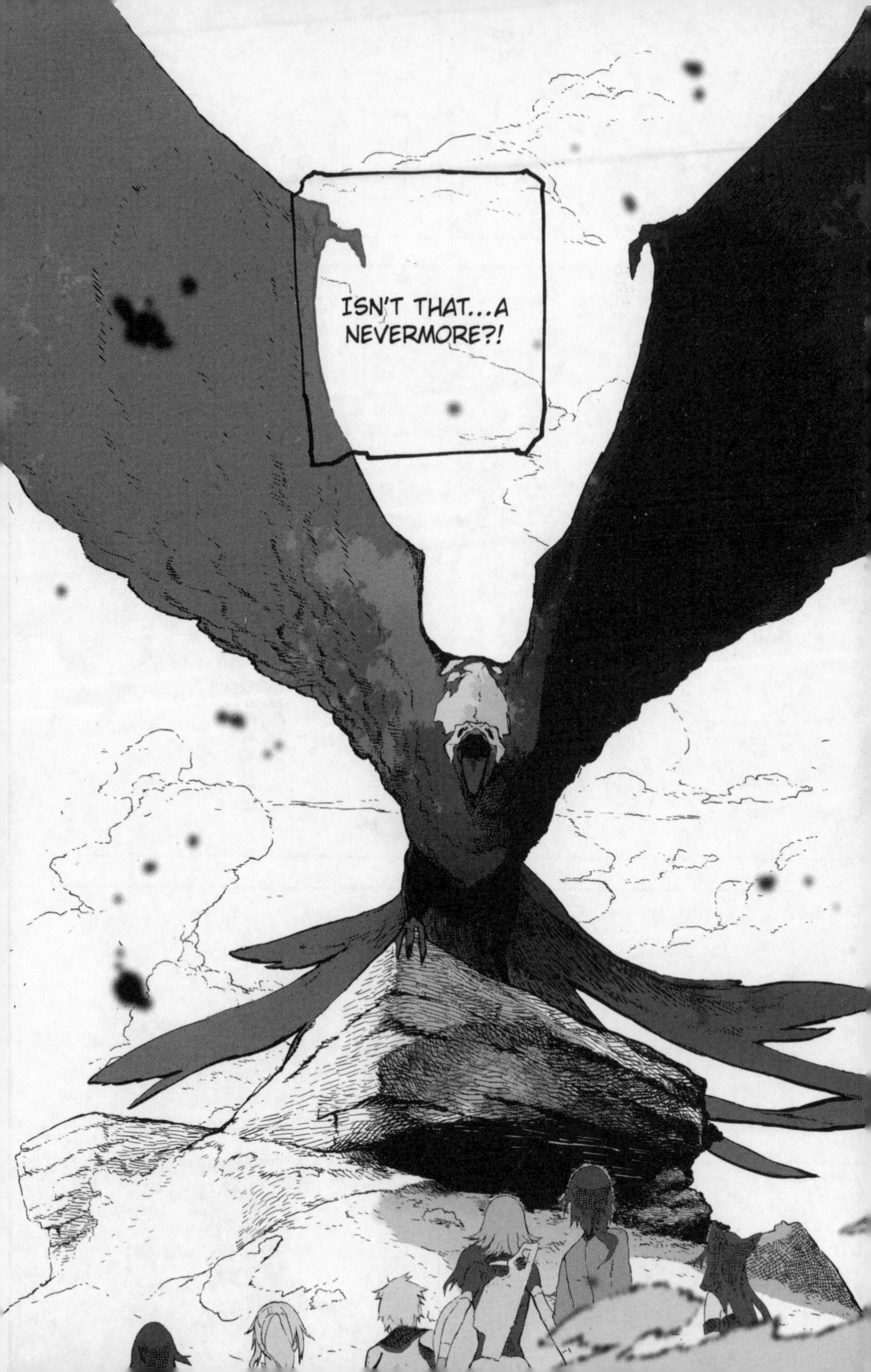
ISN'T THAT...A NEVERMORE?!

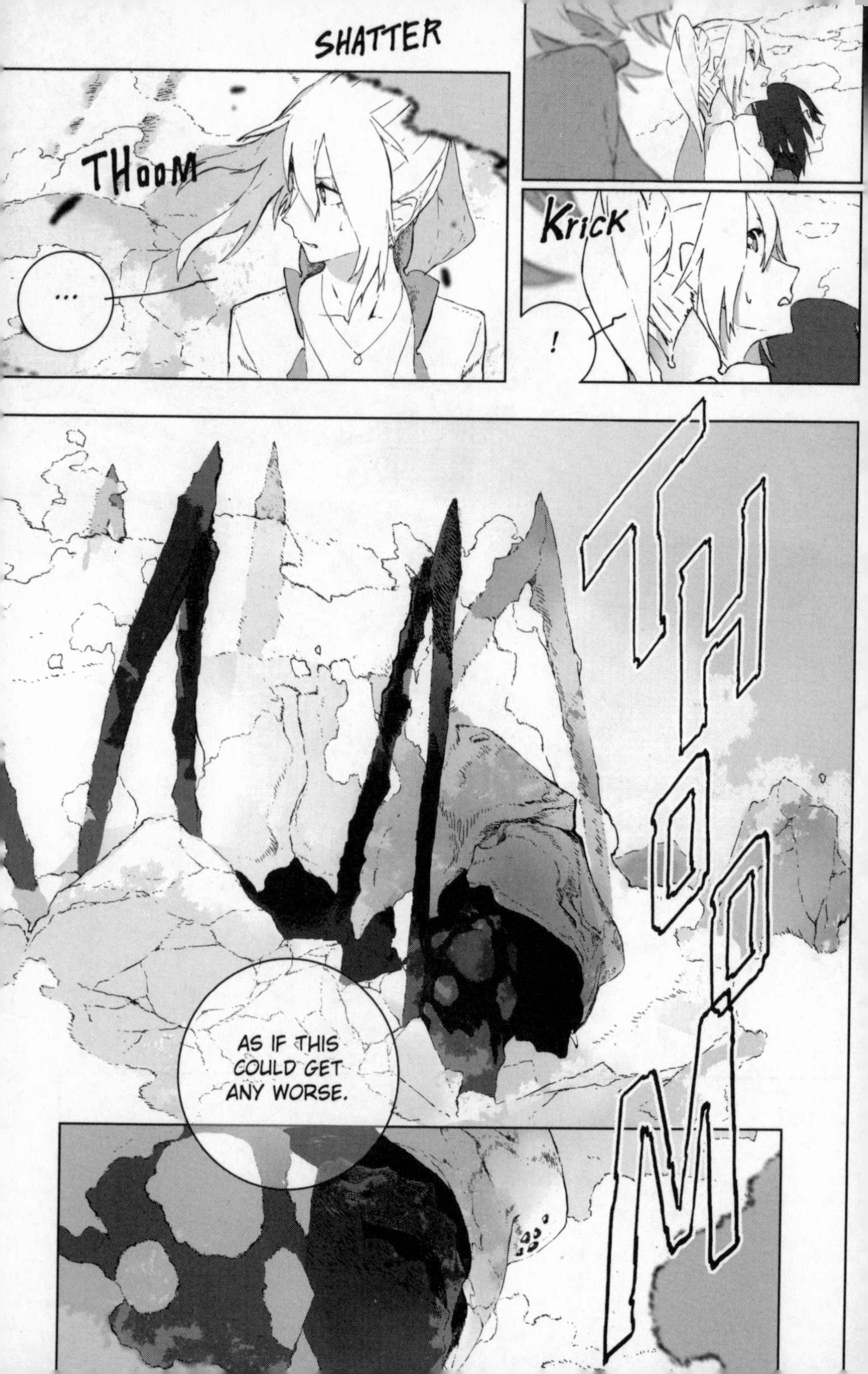
Krick
!
SHATTER
THOOM
...
THOOOM
AS IF THIS COULD GET ANY WORSE.

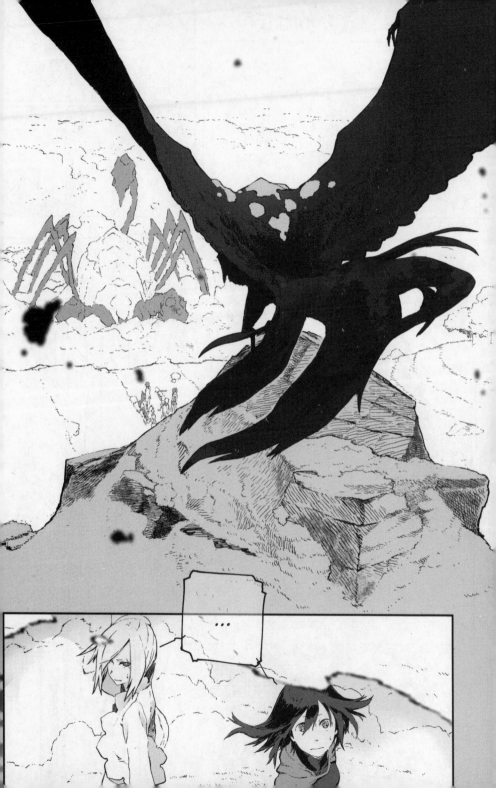

...

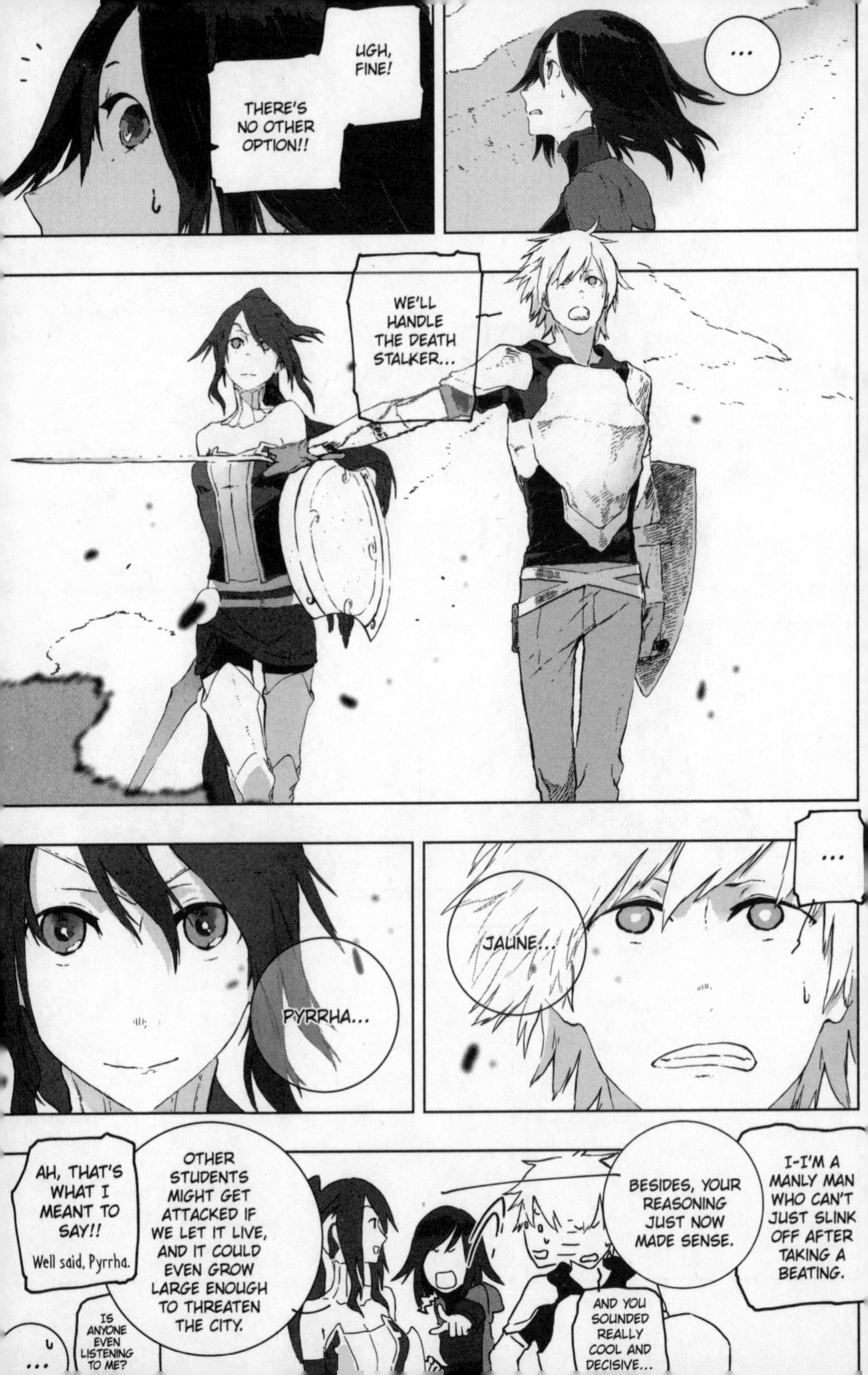
...
UGH, FINE!
THERE'S NO OTHER OPTION!!
WE'LL HANDLE THE DEATH STALKER...
...
JAUNE...
PYRRHA...
I-I'M A MANLY MAN WHO CAN'T JUST SLINK OFF AFTER TAKING A BEATING.
BESIDES, YOUR REASONING JUST NOW MADE SENSE.
AND YOU SOUNDED REALLY COOL AND DECISIVE...
OTHER STUDENTS MIGHT GET ATTACKED IF WE LET IT LIVE, AND IT COULD EVEN GROW LARGE ENOUGH TO THREATEN THE CITY.
AH, THAT'S WHAT I MEANT TO SAY!!
Well said, Pyrrha.
IS ANYONE EVEN LISTENING TO ME?
...

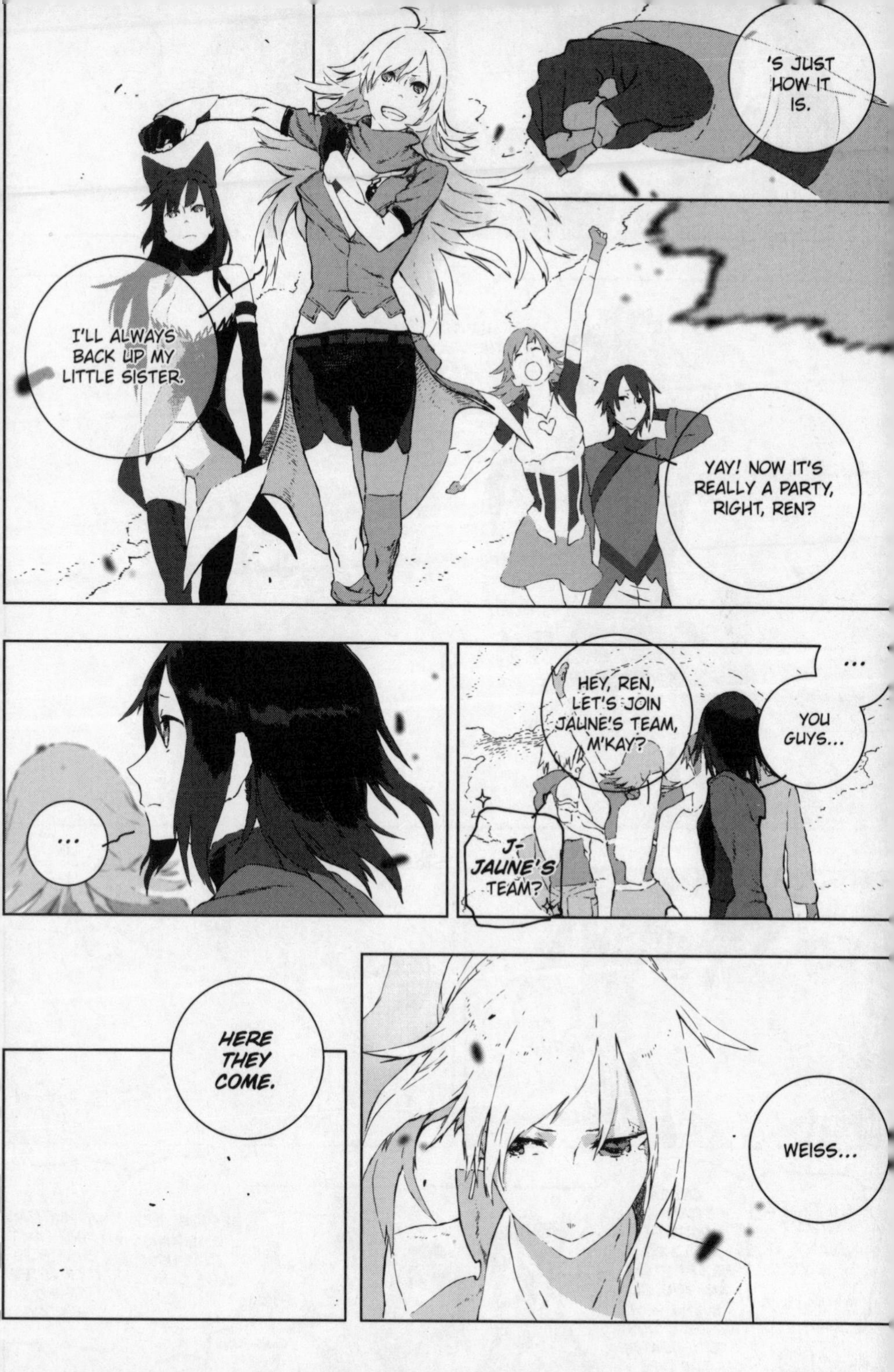

'S JUST HOW IT IS.
I'LL ALWAYS BACK UP MY LITTLE SISTER.
YAY! NOW IT'S REALLY A PARTY, RIGHT, REN?
...
YOU GUYS...
HEY, REN, LET'S JOIN JAUNE'S TEAM, M'KAY?
J-JAUNE'S TEAM?
...
WEISS...
HERE THEY COME.

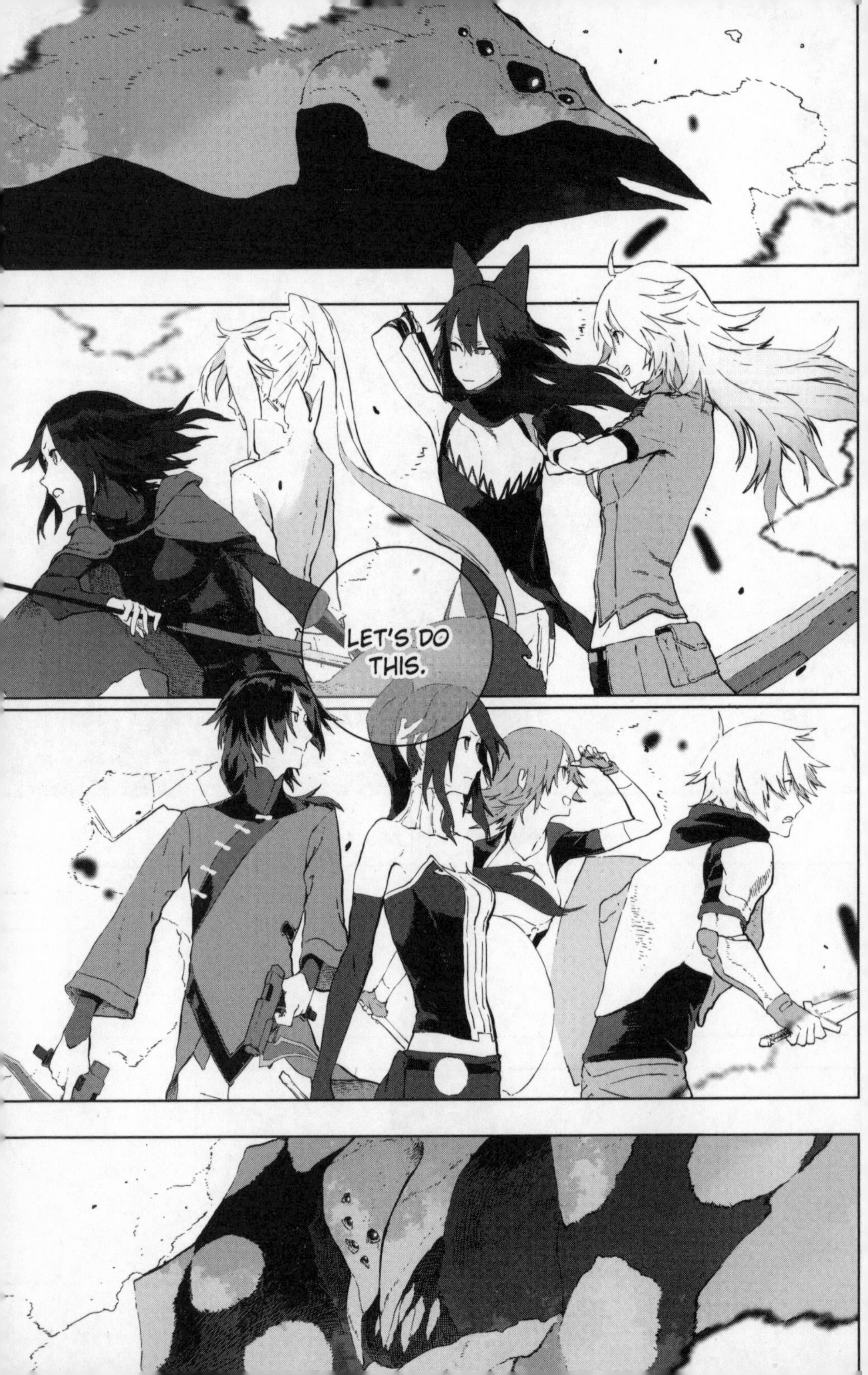
LET'S DO THIS.

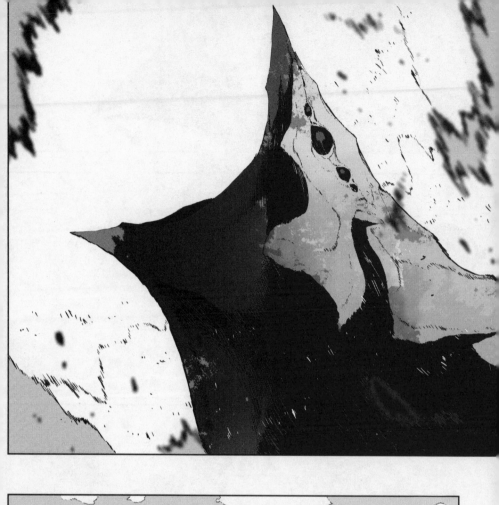

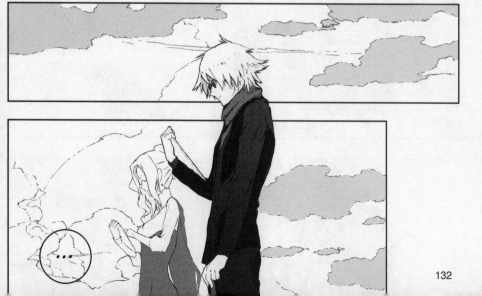

132

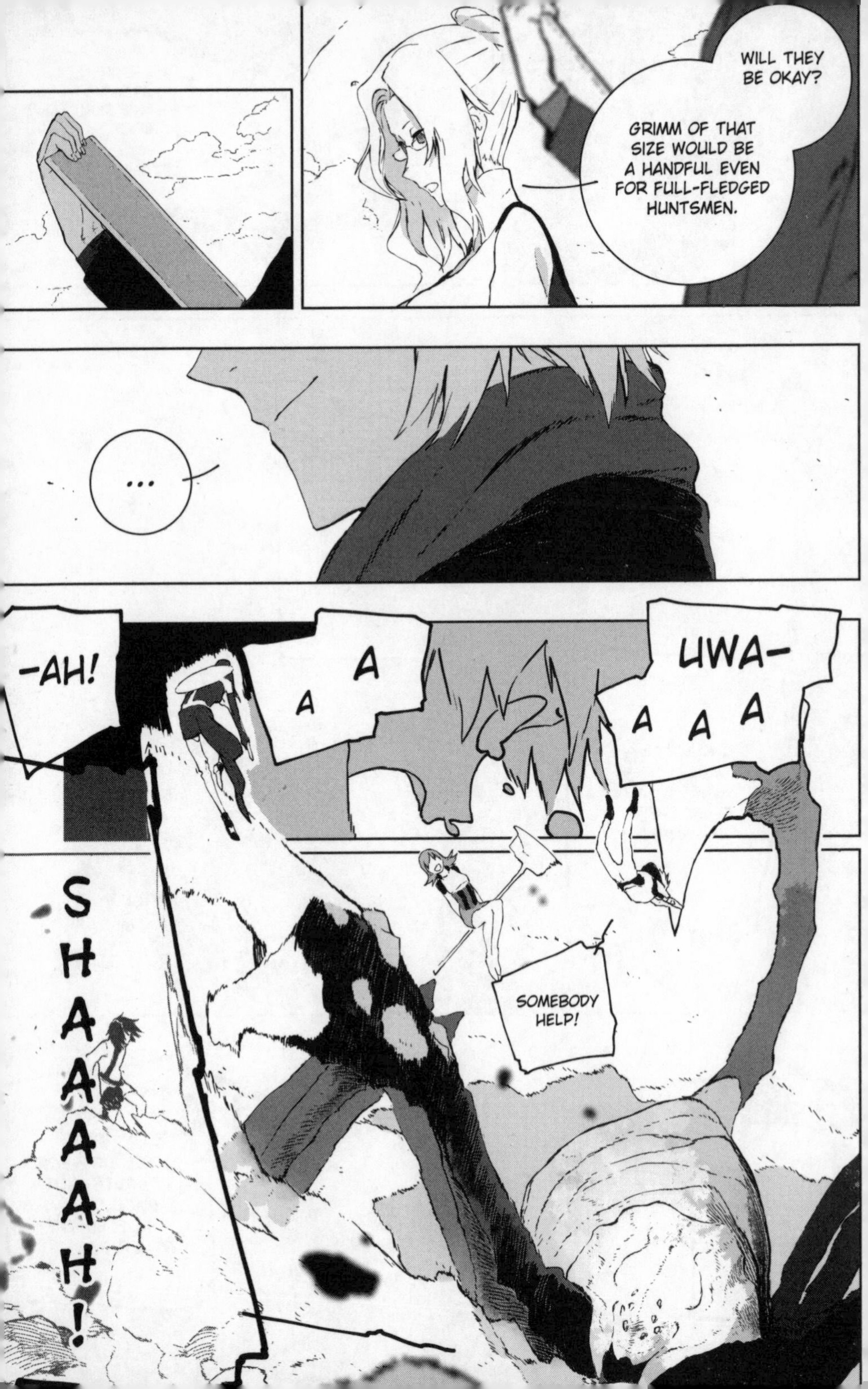
WILL THEY BE OKAY?
GRIMM OF THAT SIZE WOULD BE A HANDFUL EVEN FOR FULL-FLEDGED HUNTSMEN.
...
UWA-
A A A
A A
-AH!
SOMEBODY HELP!
SHAAAAAH!

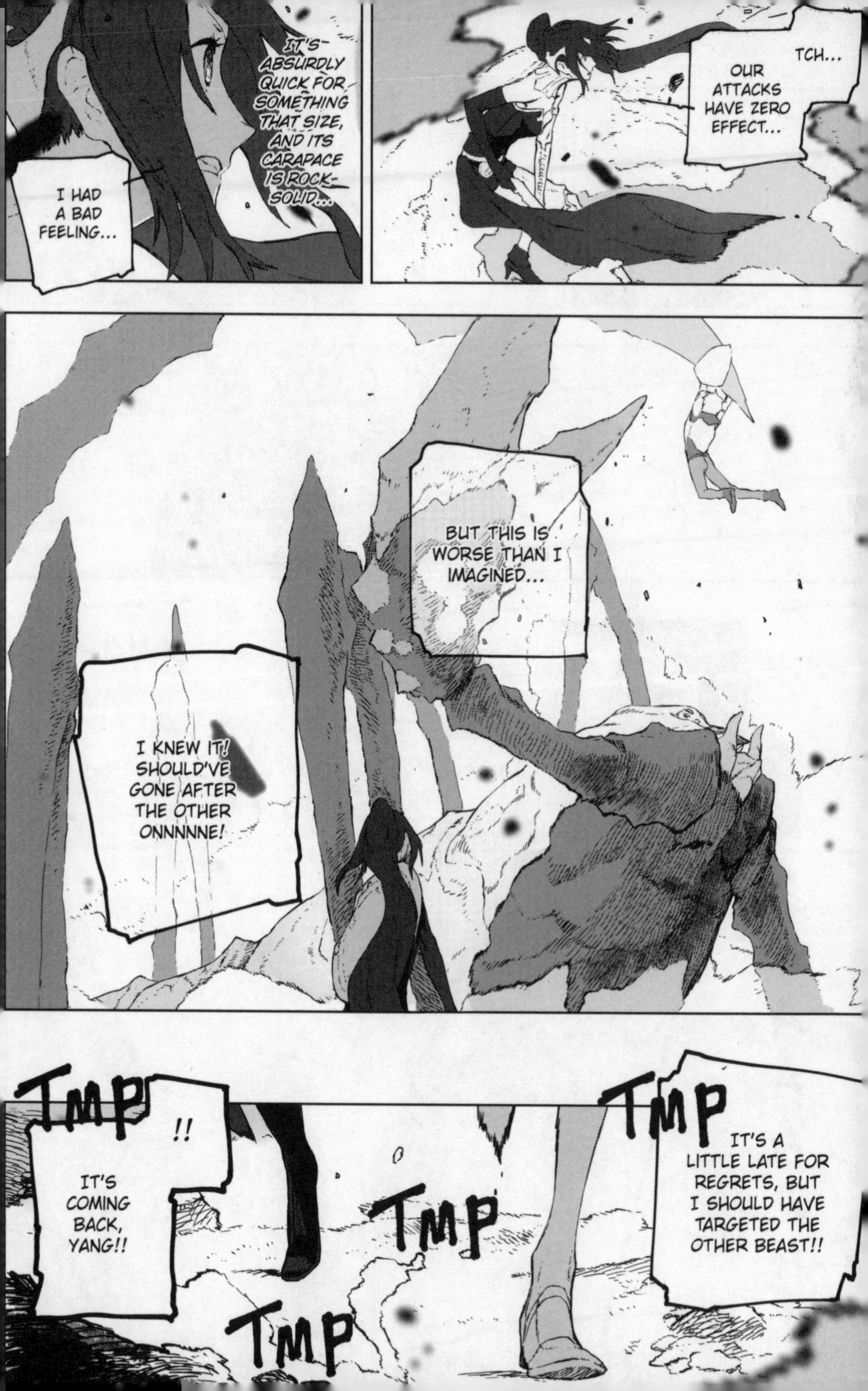
TCH...
OUR ATTACKS HAVE ZERO EFFECT...
IT'S ABSURDLY QUICK FOR SOMETHING THAT SIZE, AND ITS CARAPACE IS ROCK-SOLID...
I HAD A BAD FEELING...
BUT THIS IS WORSE THAN I IMAGINED...
I KNEW IT! SHOULD'VE GONE AFTER THE OTHER ONNNNNE!
TMP
IT'S A LITTLE LATE FOR REGRETS, BUT I SHOULD HAVE TARGETED THE OTHER BEAST!!
TMP
TMP
TMP
!!
IT'S COMING BACK, YANG!!

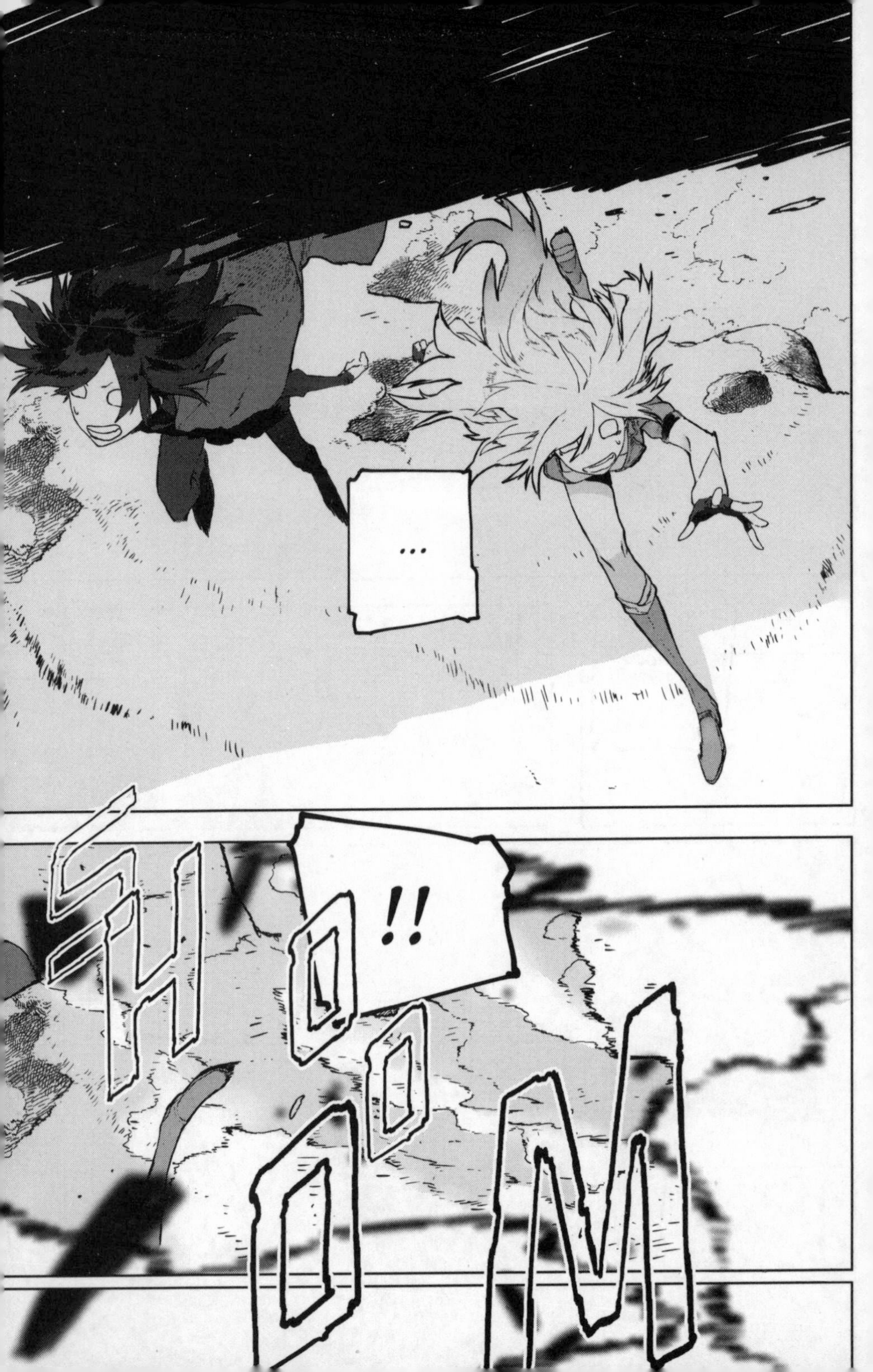
...
!!
SHOOOM

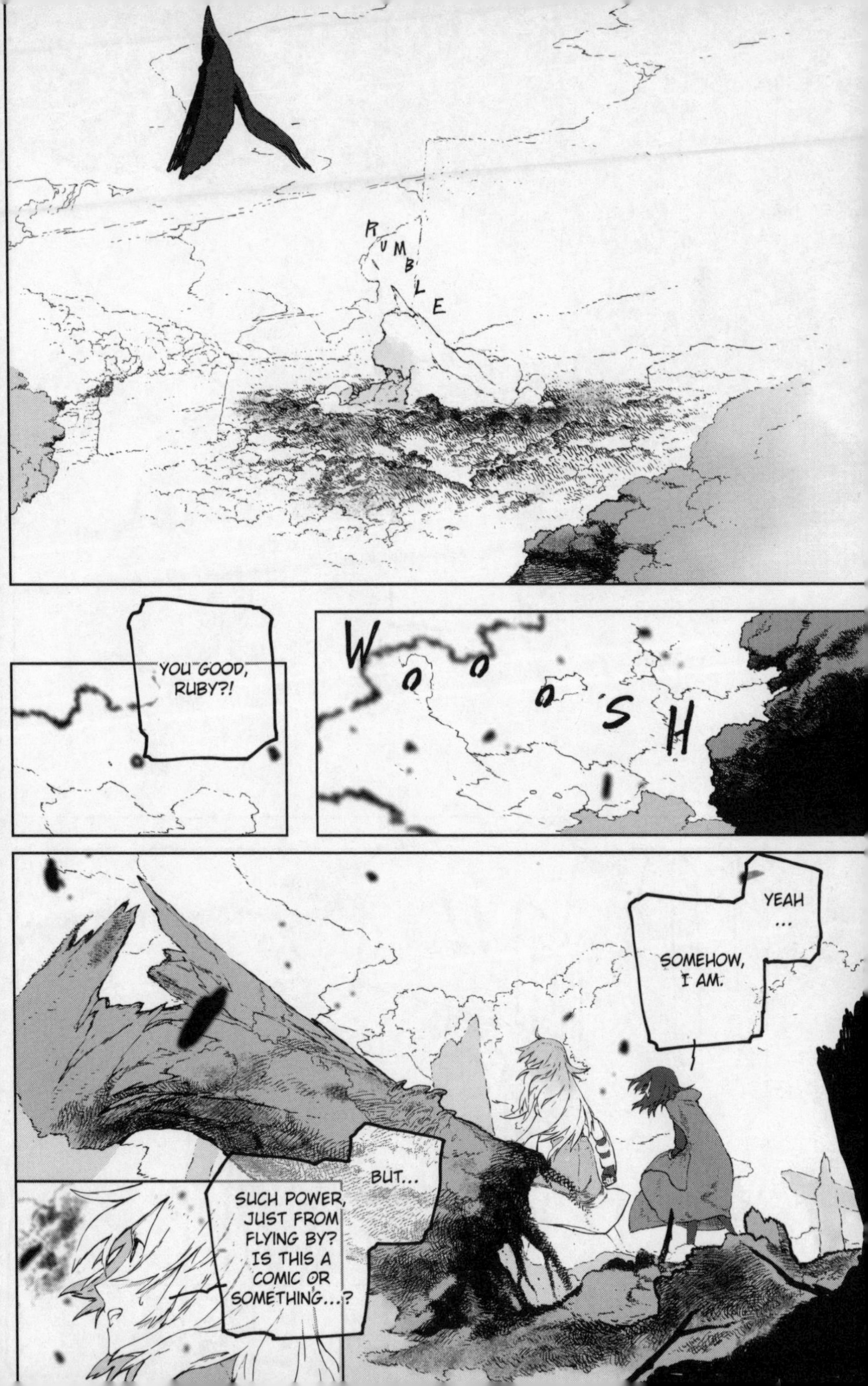
RUMBLE
WOOOSH
YOU GOOD, RUBY?!
YEAH...
SOMEHOW, I AM.
BUT...
SUCH POWER, JUST FROM FLYING BY? IS THIS A COMIC OR SOMETHING...?

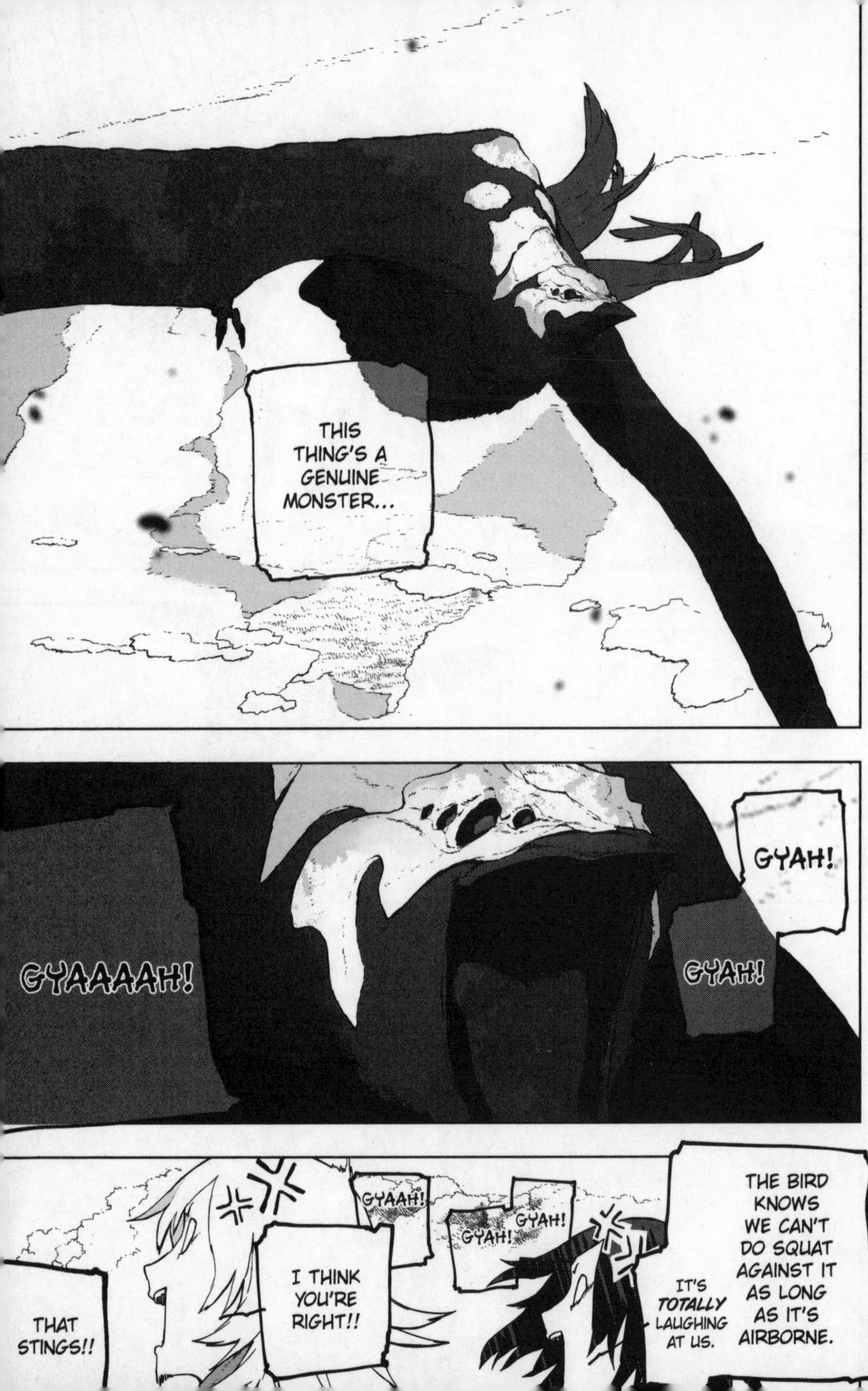
THIS THING'S A GENUINE MONSTER...
GYAH!
GYAH!
GYAAAAH!
THE BIRD KNOWS WE CAN'T DO SQUAT AGAINST IT AS LONG AS IT'S AIRBORNE.
IT'S *TOTALLY* LAUGHING AT US.
GYAH!
GYAH!
GYAAH!
I THINK YOU'RE RIGHT!!
THAT STINGS!!

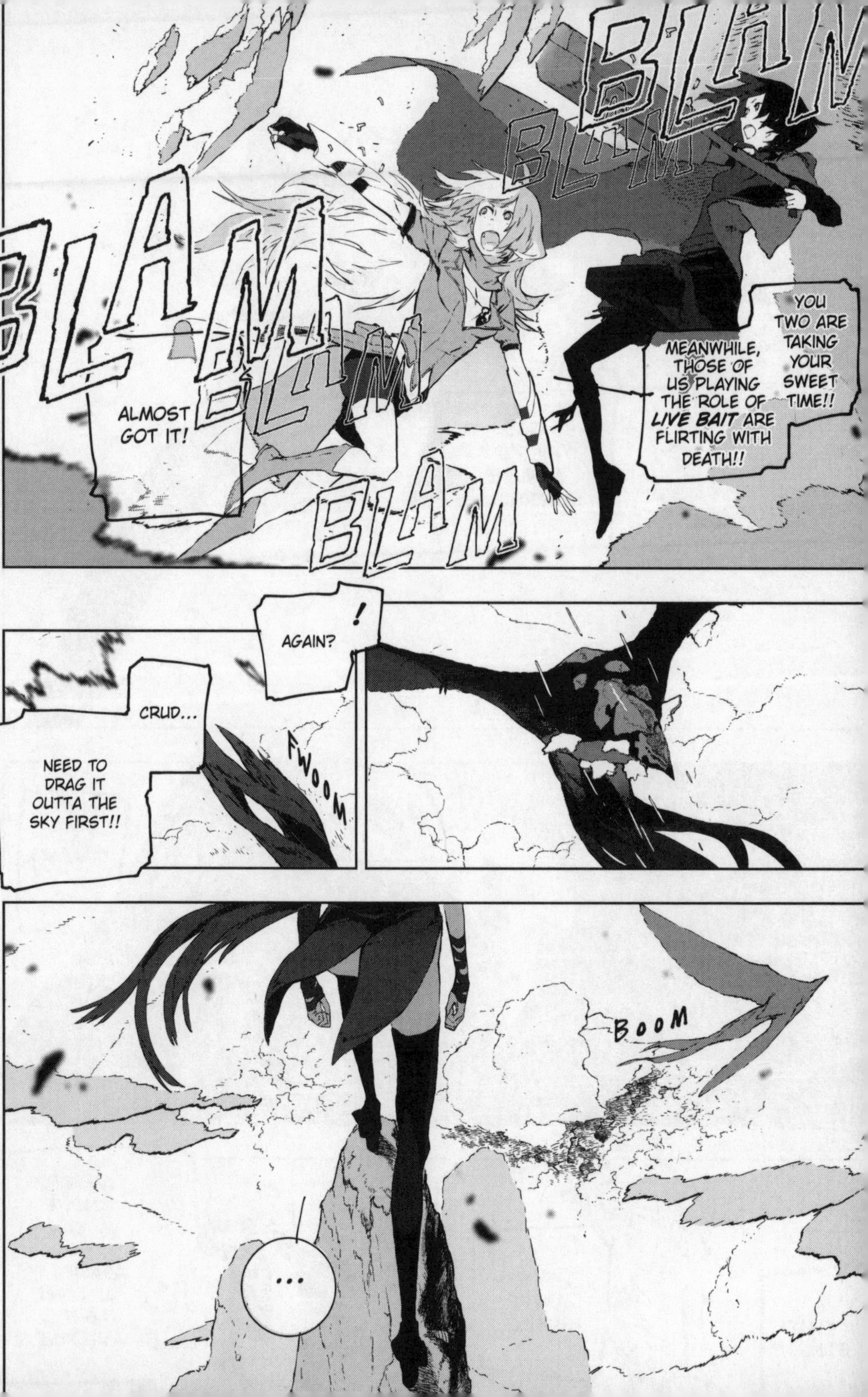
BLAM
BLAM
YOU TWO ARE TAKING YOUR SWEET TIME!!
MEANWHILE, THOSE OF US PLAYING THE ROLE OF *LIVE BAIT* ARE FLIRTING WITH DEATH!!
BLAM
BLAM
BLAM
BLAM
ALMOST GOT IT!
!
AGAIN?
CRUD...
NEED TO DRAG IT OUTTA THE SKY FIRST!!
FWOOOM
BOOM
...

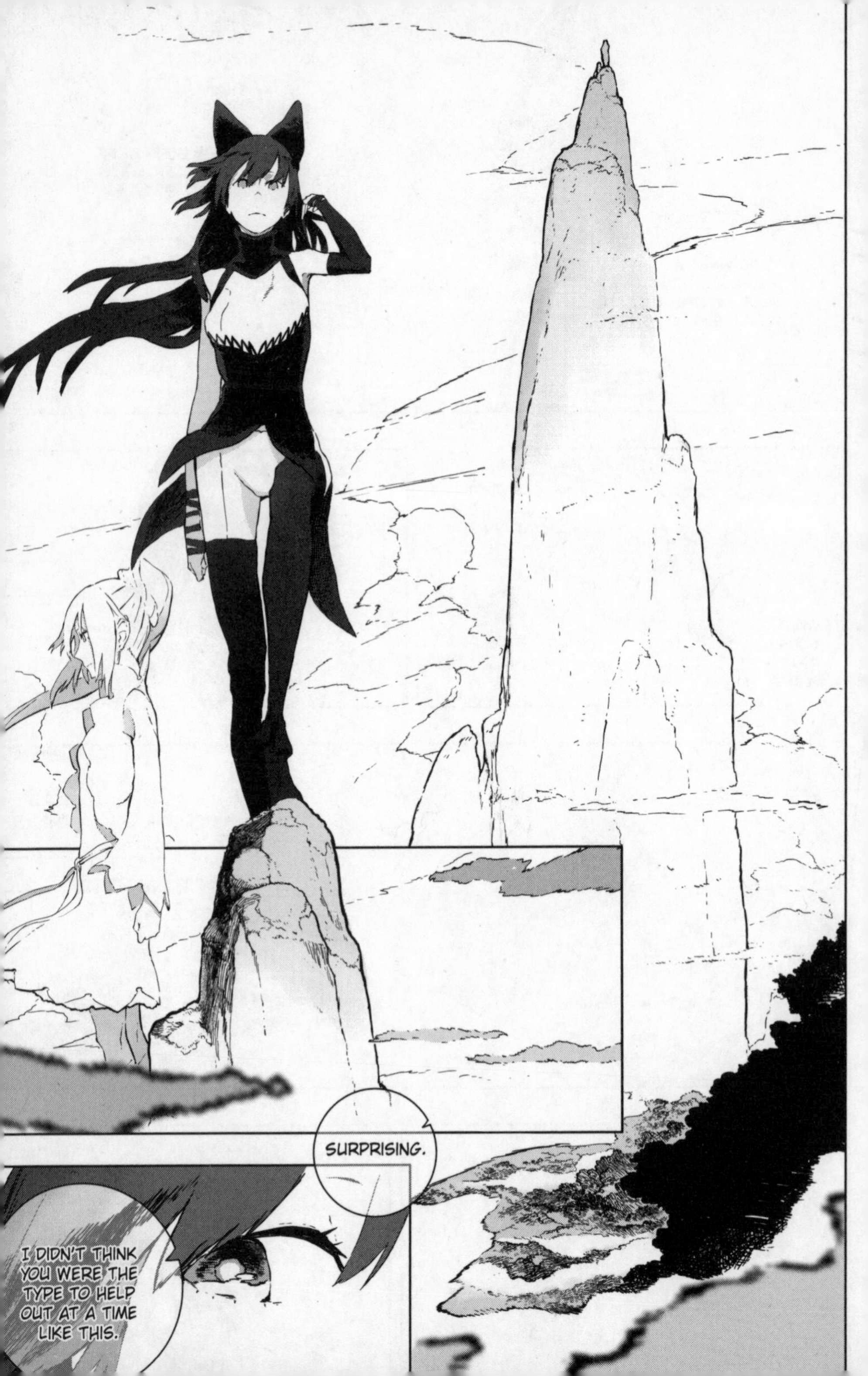
SURPRISING.
I DIDN'T THINK YOU WERE THE TYPE TO HELP OUT AT A TIME LIKE THIS.

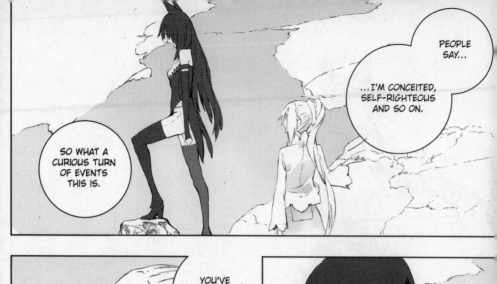

PEOPLE SAY...

...I'M CONCEITED, SELF-RIGHTEOUS AND SO ON.

SO WHAT A CURIOUS TURN OF EVENTS THIS IS.

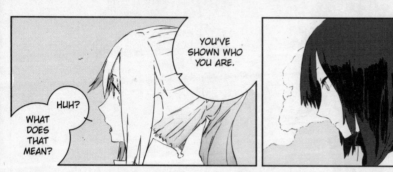

YOU'VE SHOWN WHO YOU ARE.

HUH?

WHAT DOES THAT MEAN?

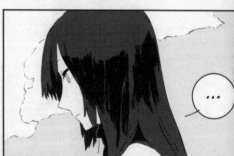

...

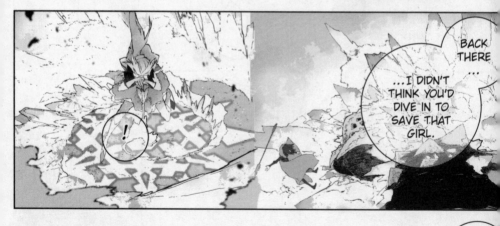

BACK THERE...

...I DIDN'T THINK YOU'D DIVE IN TO SAVE THAT GIRL.

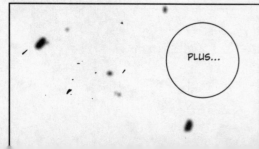

PLUS...

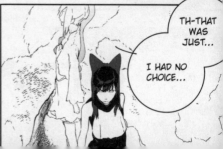

TH-THAT WAS JUST...

I HAD NO CHOICE...

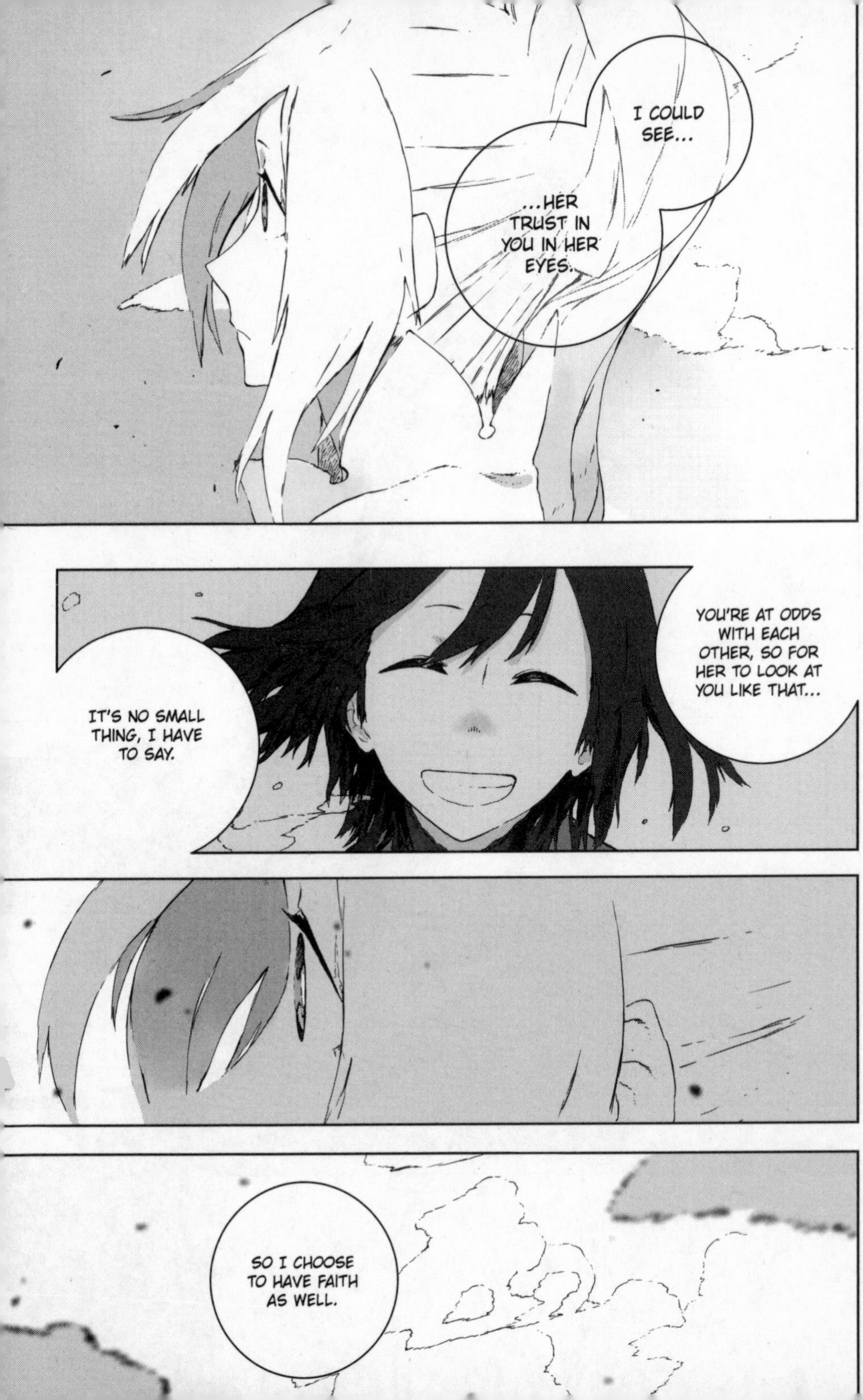
I COULD SEE...
...HER TRUST IN YOU IN HER EYES.
YOU'RE AT ODDS WITH EACH OTHER, SO FOR HER TO LOOK AT YOU LIKE THAT...
IT'S NO SMALL THING, I HAVE TO SAY.
SO I CHOOSE TO HAVE FAITH AS WELL.

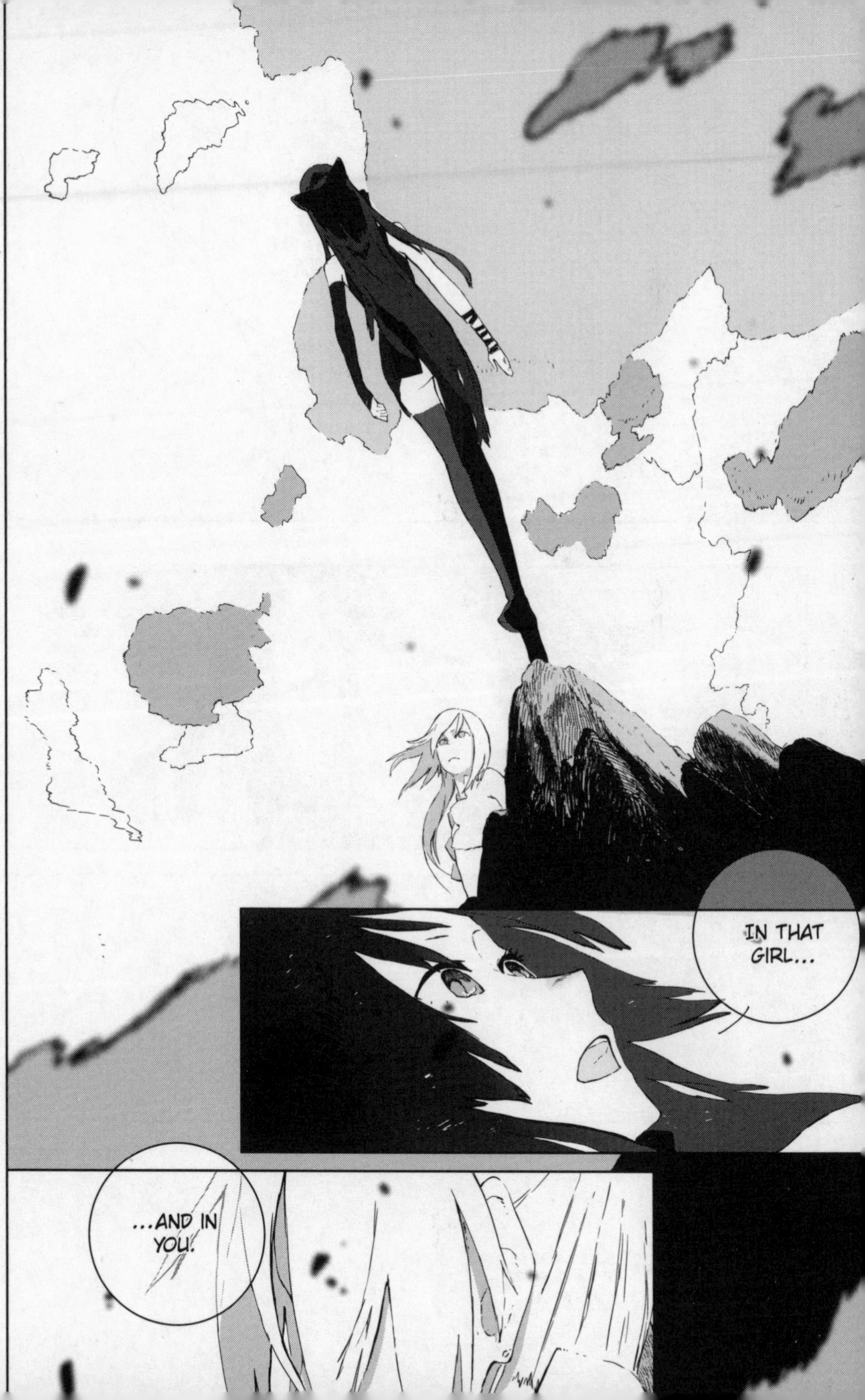
IN THAT GIRL...
...AND IN YOU.

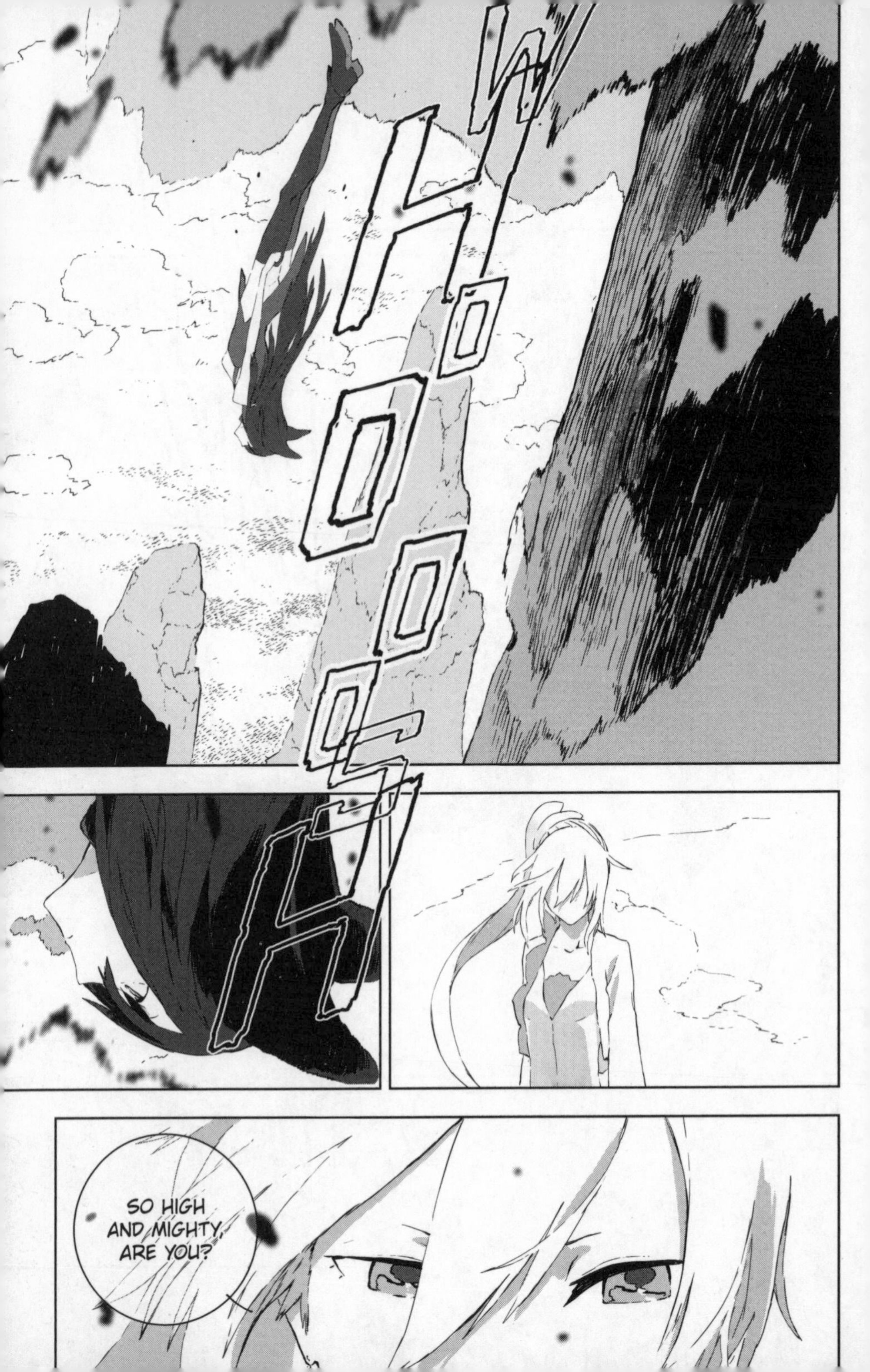
WHOOSH
SO HIGH AND MIGHTY, ARE YOU?

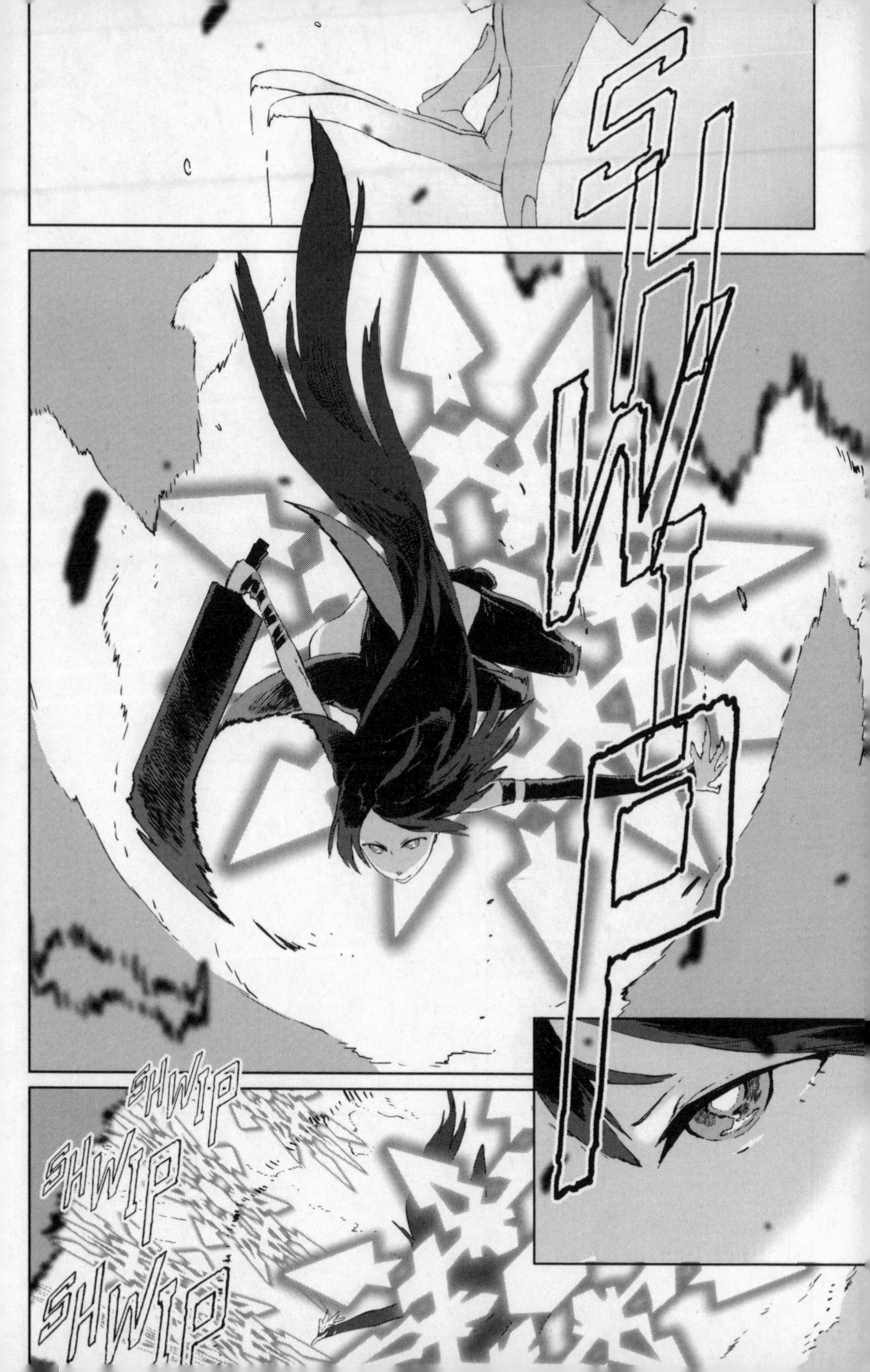
SHWIP
SHWIP
SHWIP
SHWIP

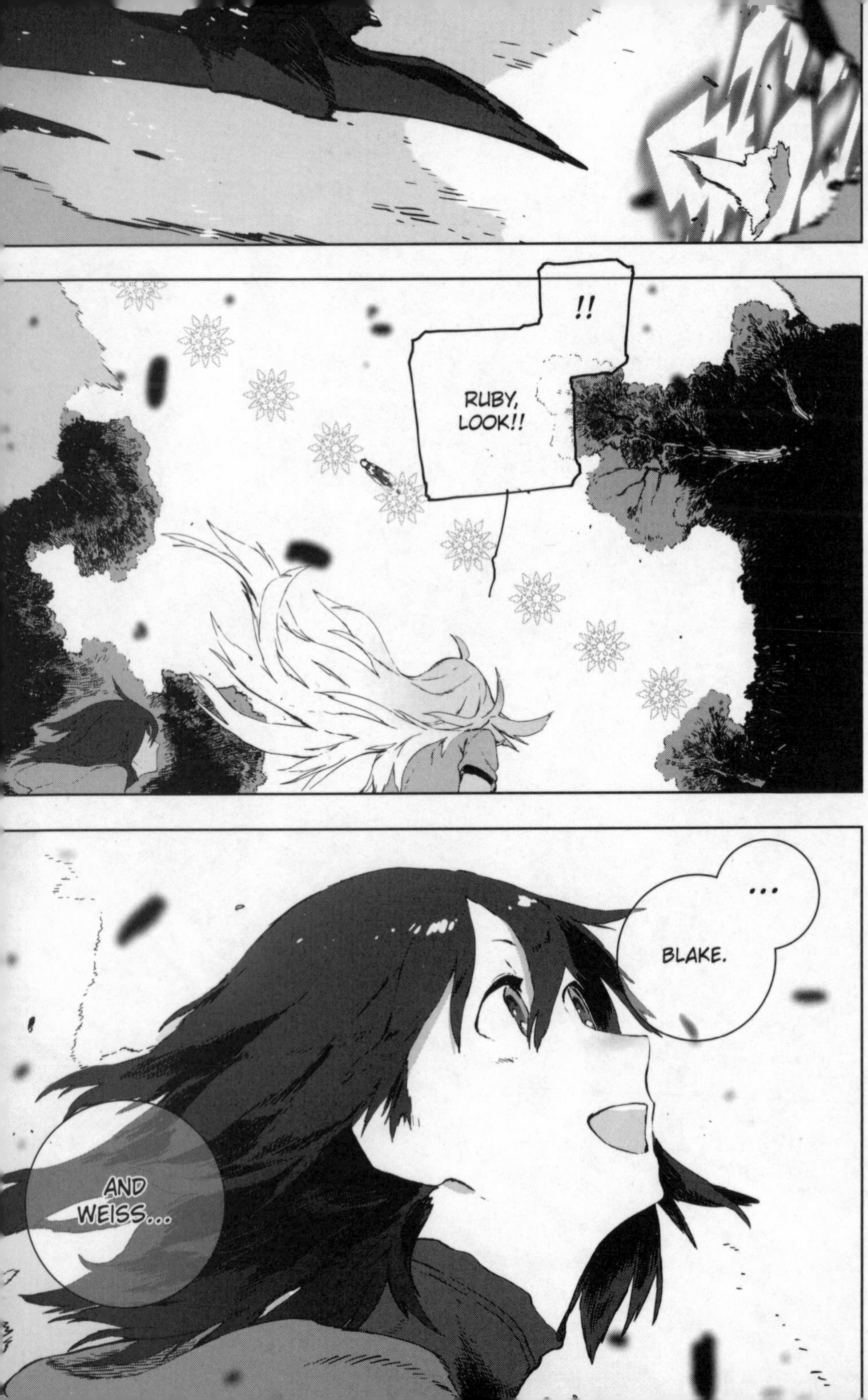
!!
RUBY, LOOK!!
...
BLAKE.
AND WEISS...

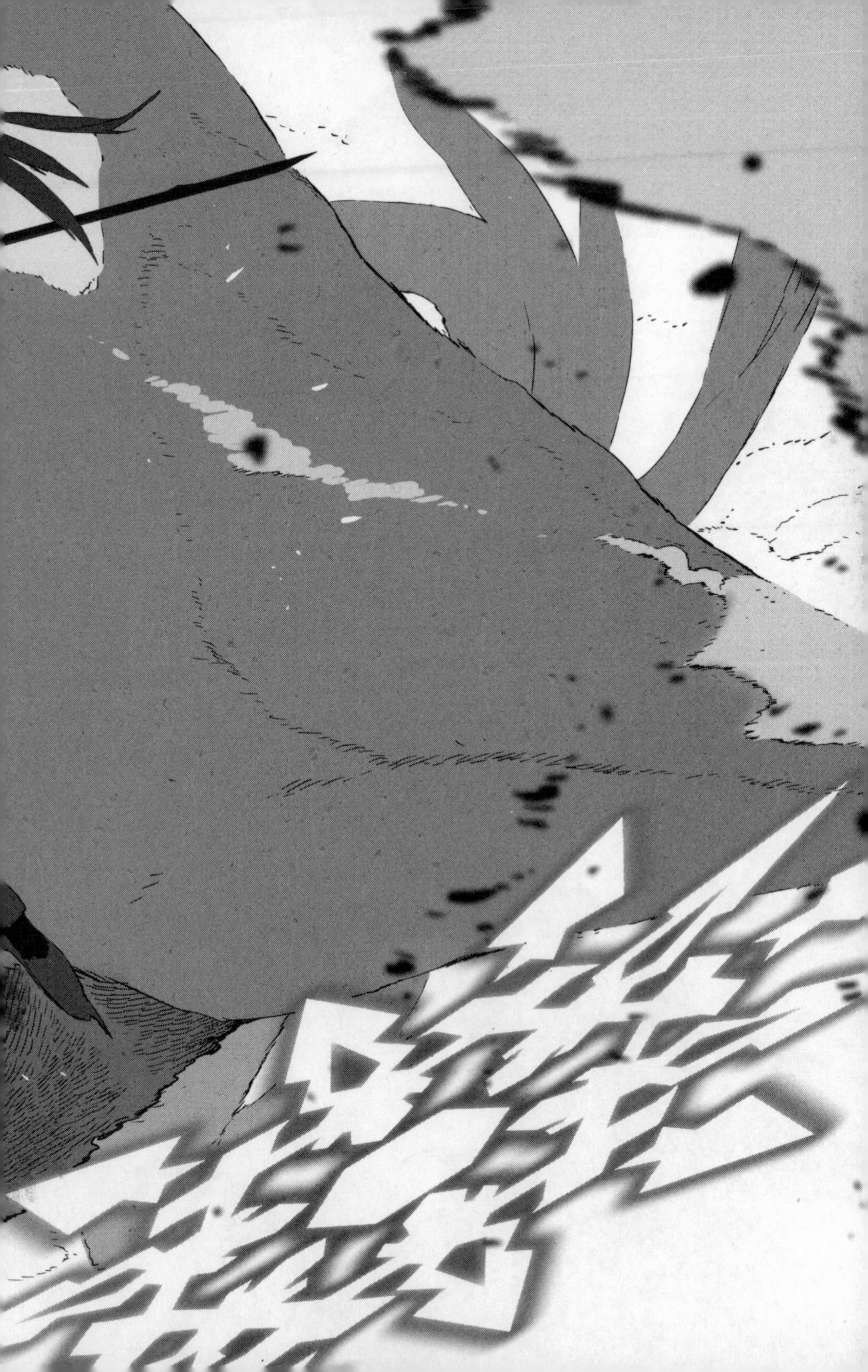

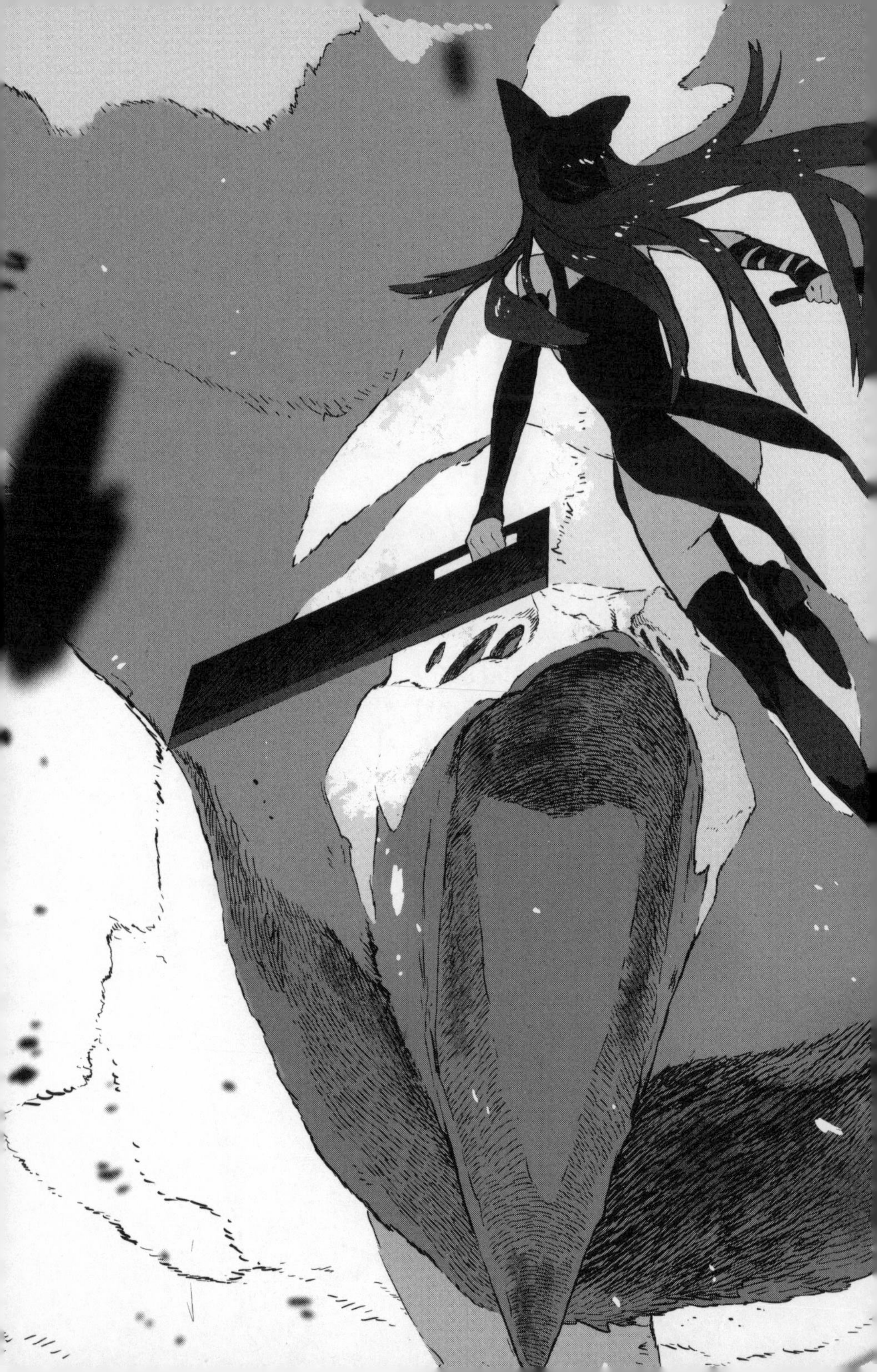

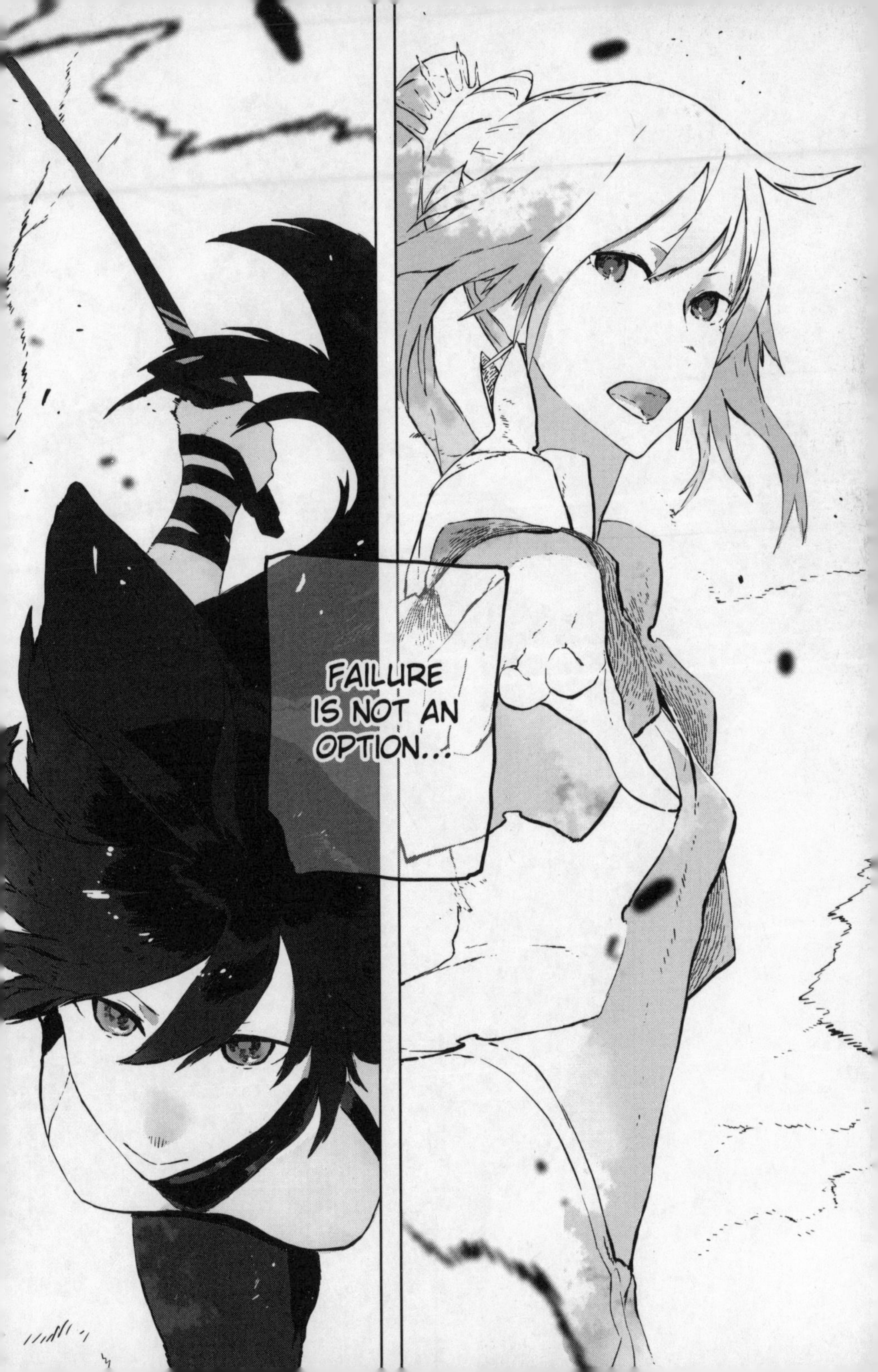
FAILURE IS NOT AN OPTION...

Episode 05

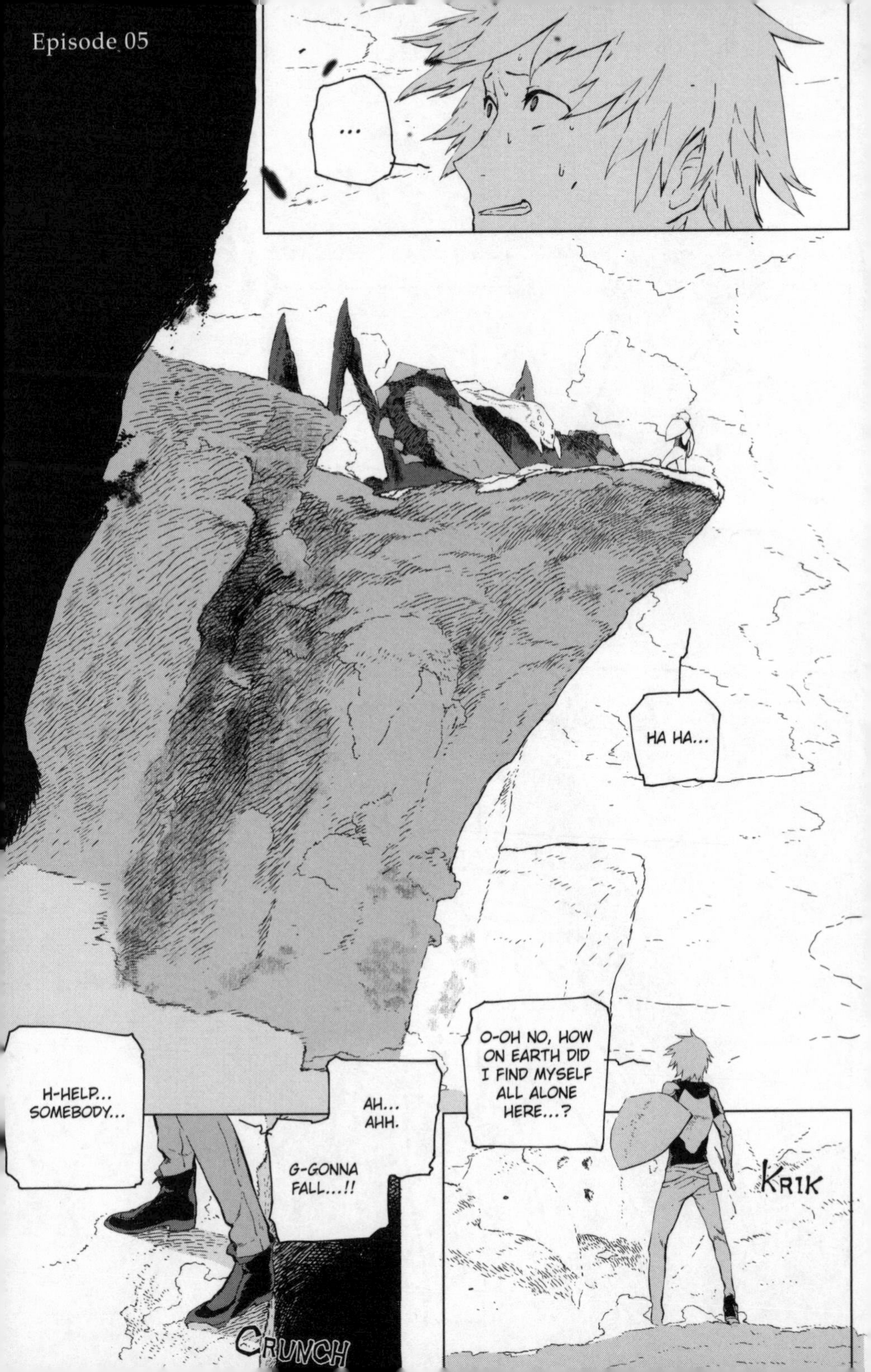
...
HA HA...
O-OH NO, HOW ON EARTH DID I FIND MYSELF ALL ALONE HERE...?
KRIK
AH... AHH.
G-GONNA FALL...!!
H-HELP... SOMEBODY...
CRUNCH

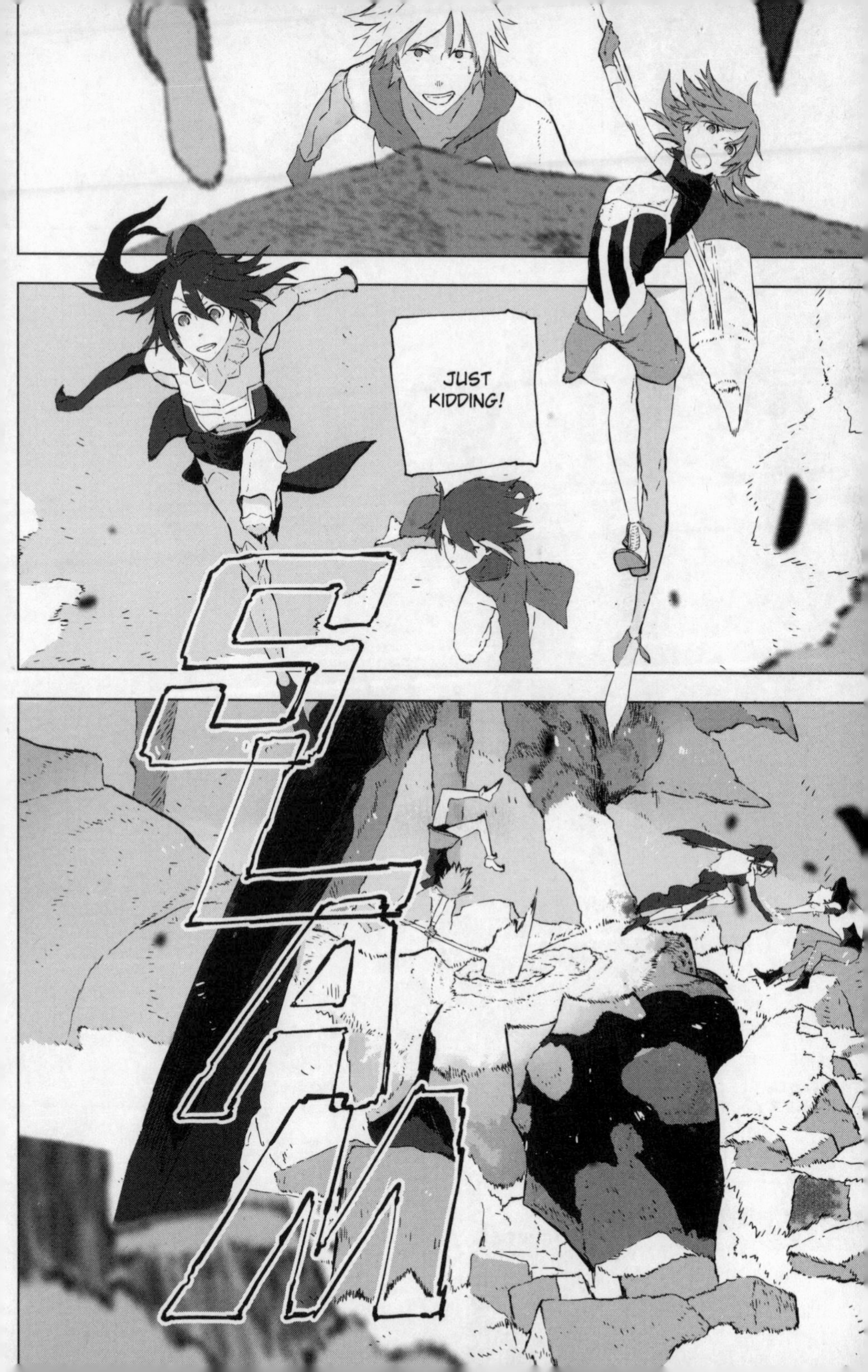
JUST KIDDING!
SLAM

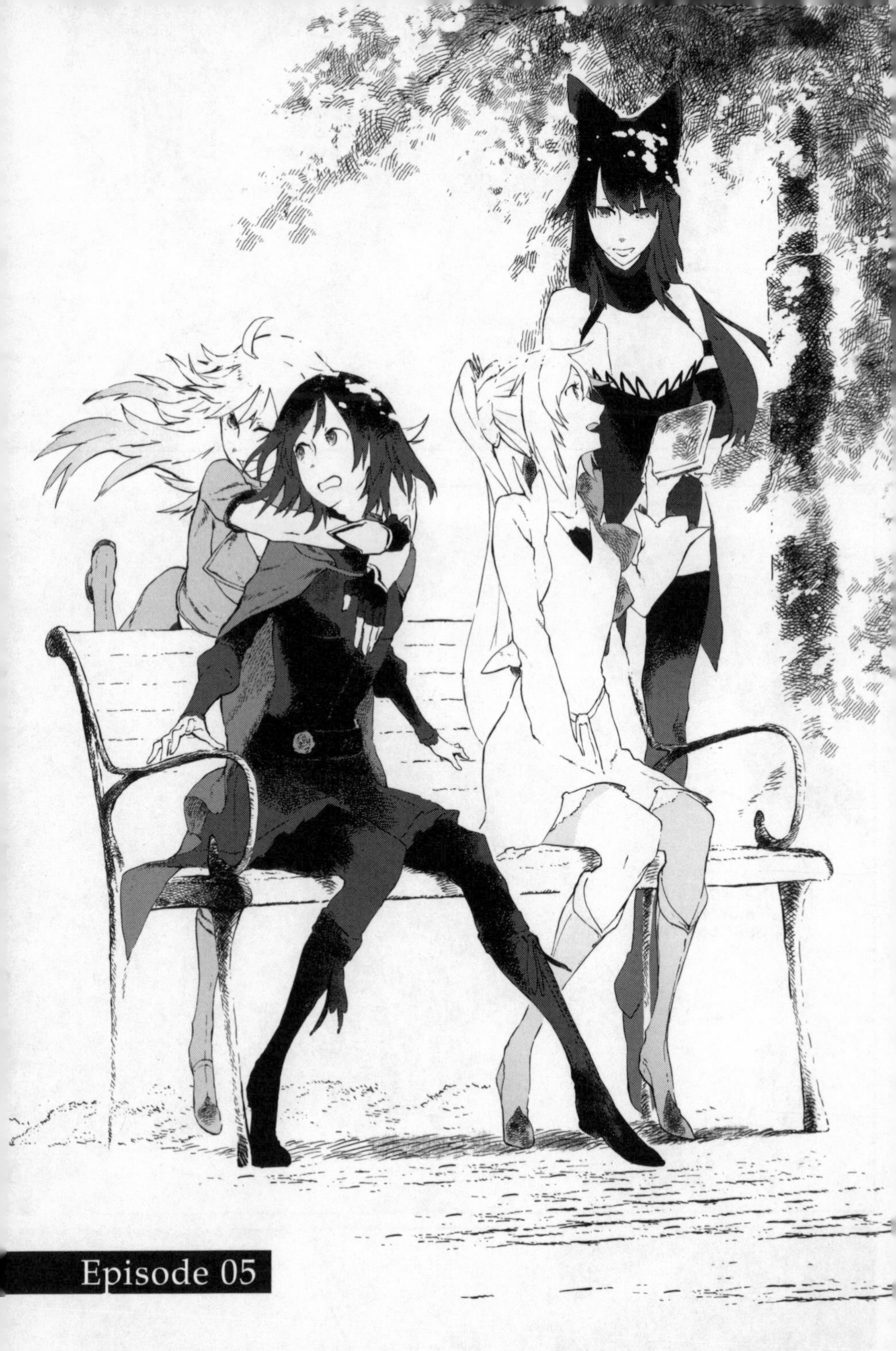

Episode 05

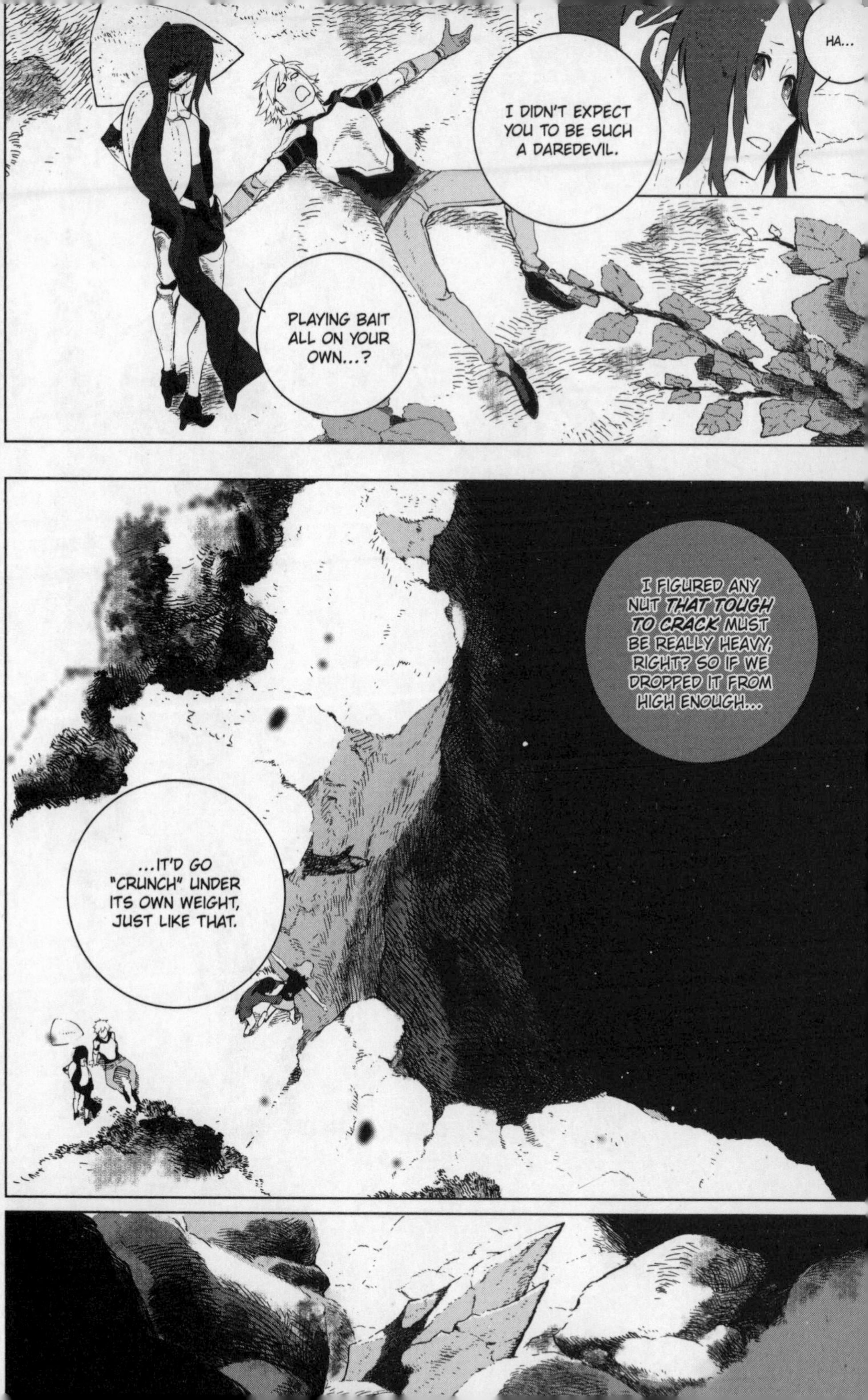
HA...
I DIDN'T EXPECT YOU TO BE SUCH A DAREDEVIL.
PLAYING BAIT ALL ON YOUR OWN...?
I FIGURED ANY NUT THAT TOUGH TO CRACK MUST BE REALLY HEAVY, RIGHT? SO IF WE DROPPED IT FROM HIGH ENOUGH...
...IT'D GO "CRUNCH" UNDER ITS OWN WEIGHT, JUST LIKE THAT.

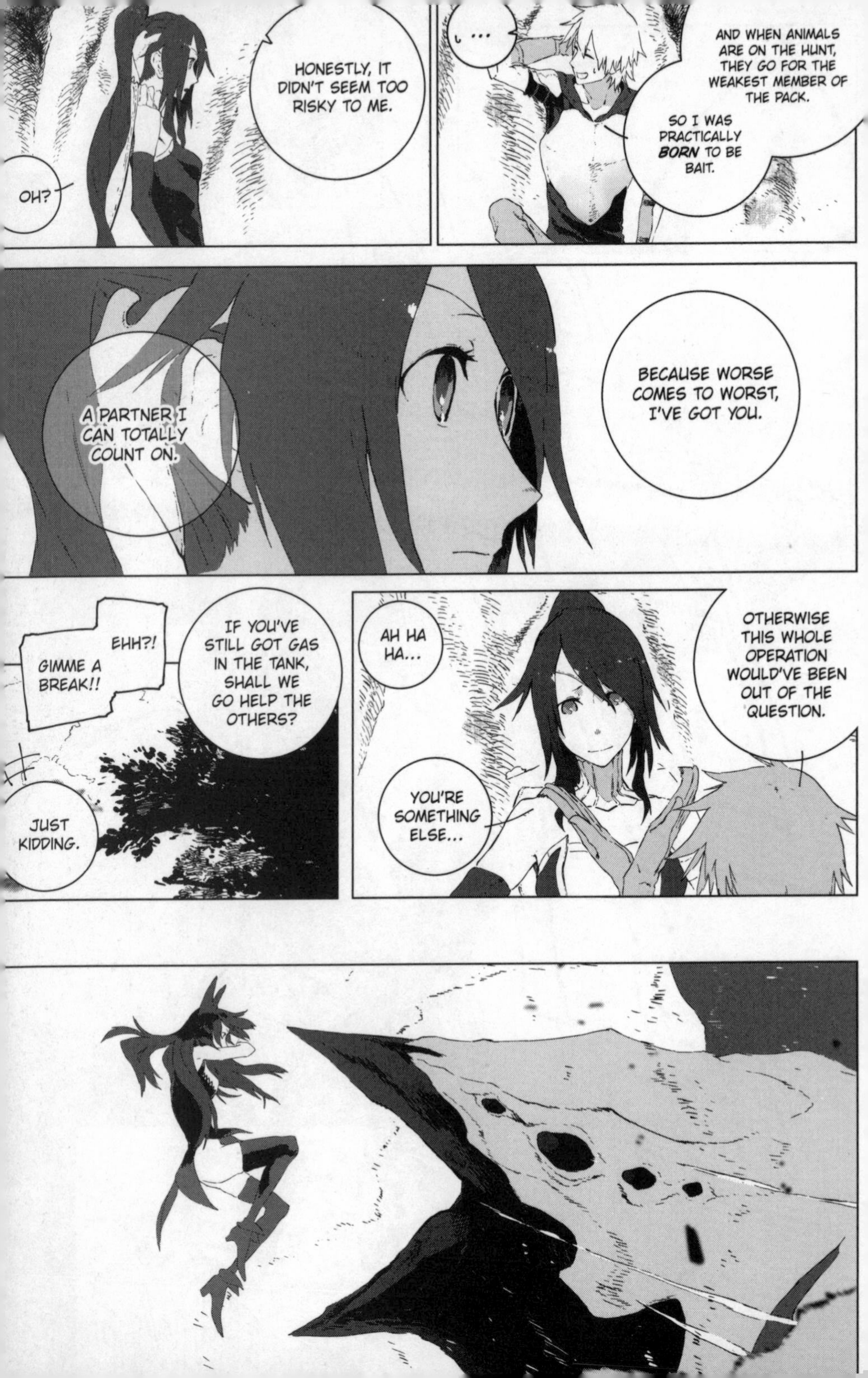
AND WHEN ANIMALS ARE ON THE HUNT, THEY GO FOR THE WEAKEST MEMBER OF THE PACK.
SO I WAS PRACTICALLY **BORN** TO BE BAIT.
...
HONESTLY, IT DIDN'T SEEM TOO RISKY TO ME.
OH?
BECAUSE WORSE COMES TO WORST, I'VE GOT YOU.
A PARTNER I CAN TOTALLY COUNT ON.
OTHERWISE THIS WHOLE OPERATION WOULD'VE BEEN OUT OF THE QUESTION.
AH HA HA...
YOU'RE SOMETHING ELSE...
IF YOU'VE STILL GOT GAS IN THE TANK, SHALL WE GO HELP THE OTHERS?
EHH?! GIMME A BREAK!!
JUST KIDDING.

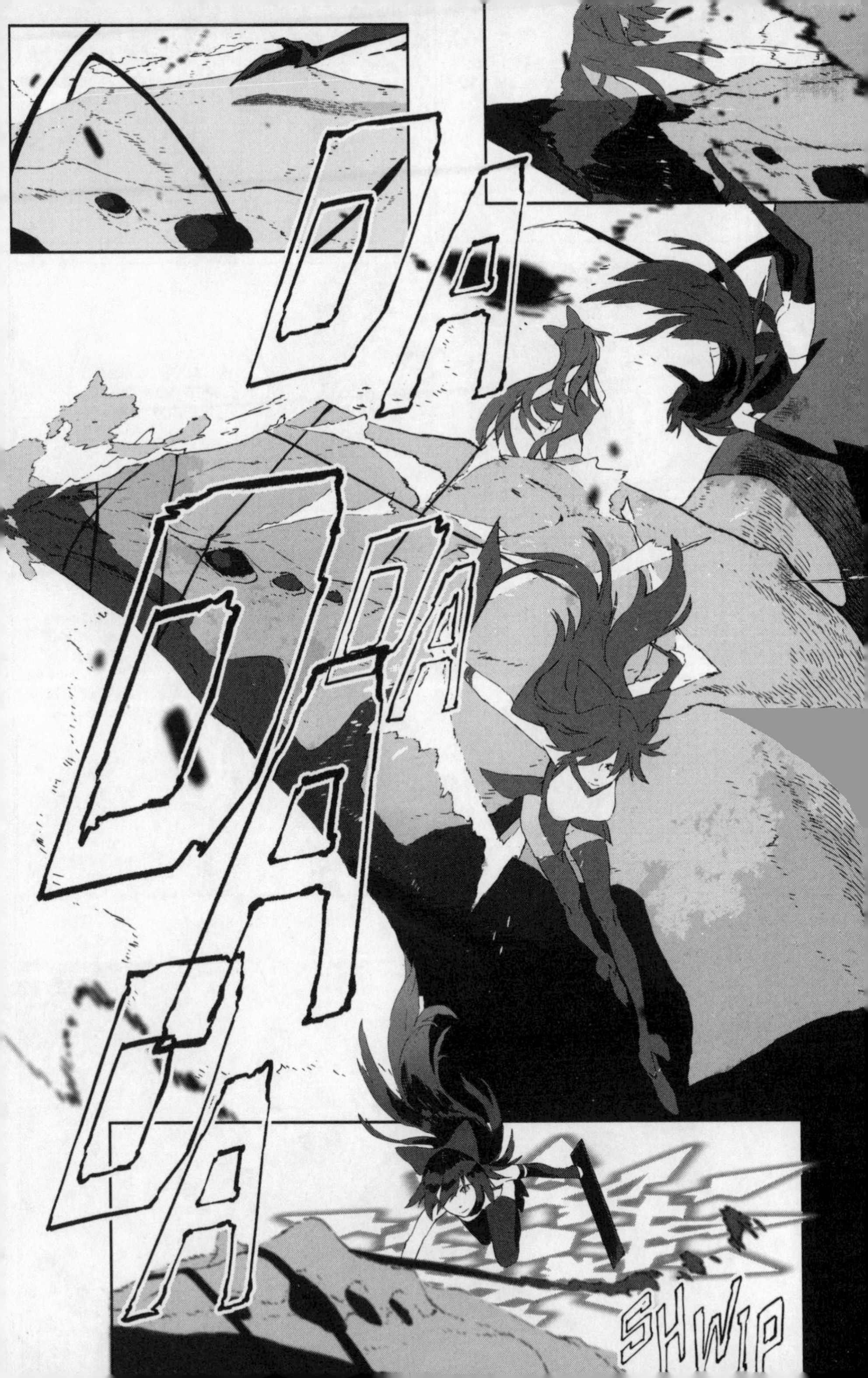
DA
DA
DA
DA
SHWIP

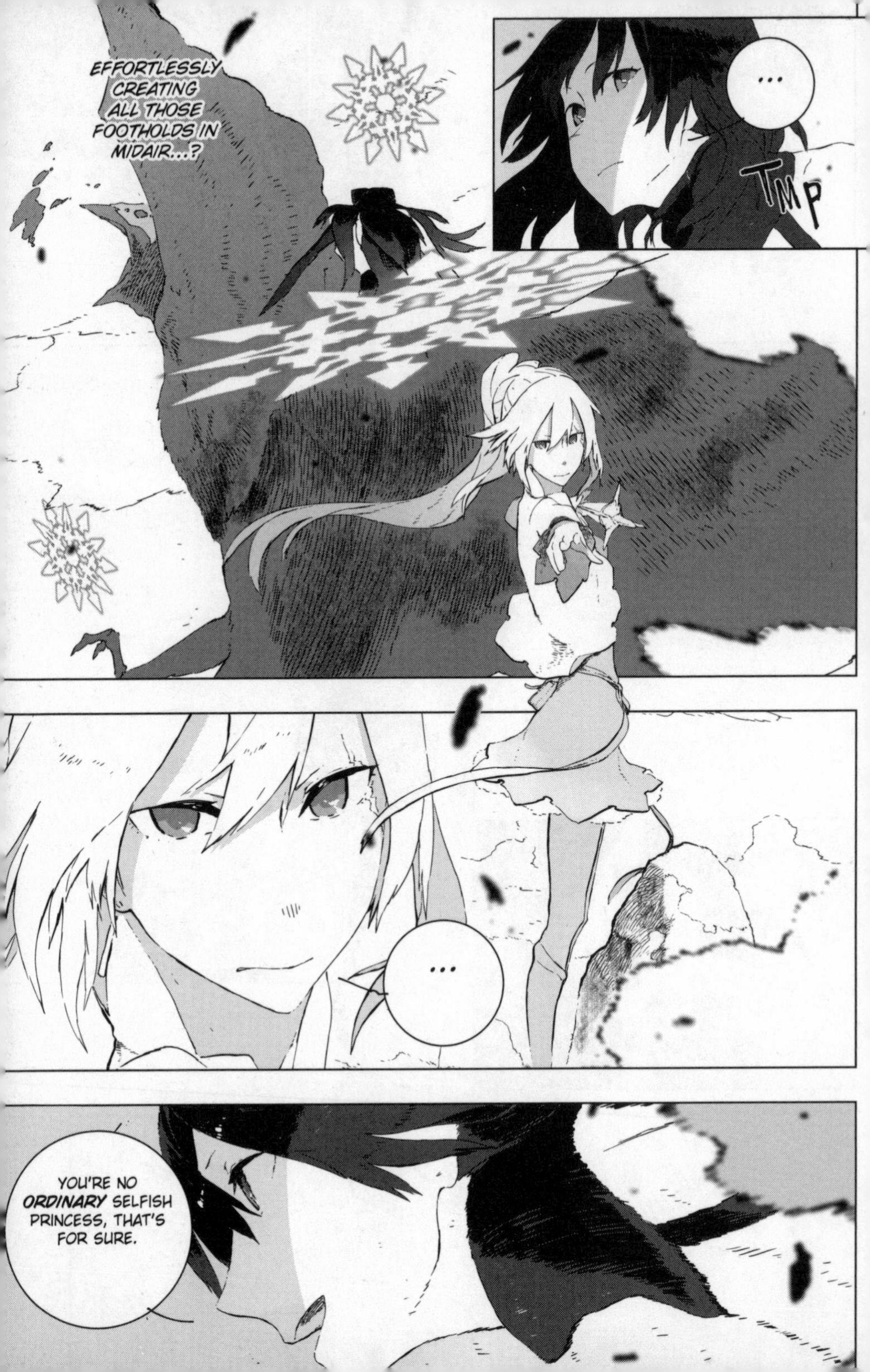
...
TMP
EFFORTLESSLY CREATING ALL THOSE FOOTHOLDS IN MIDAIR...?
...
YOU'RE NO ORDINARY SELFISH PRINCESS, THAT'S FOR SURE.

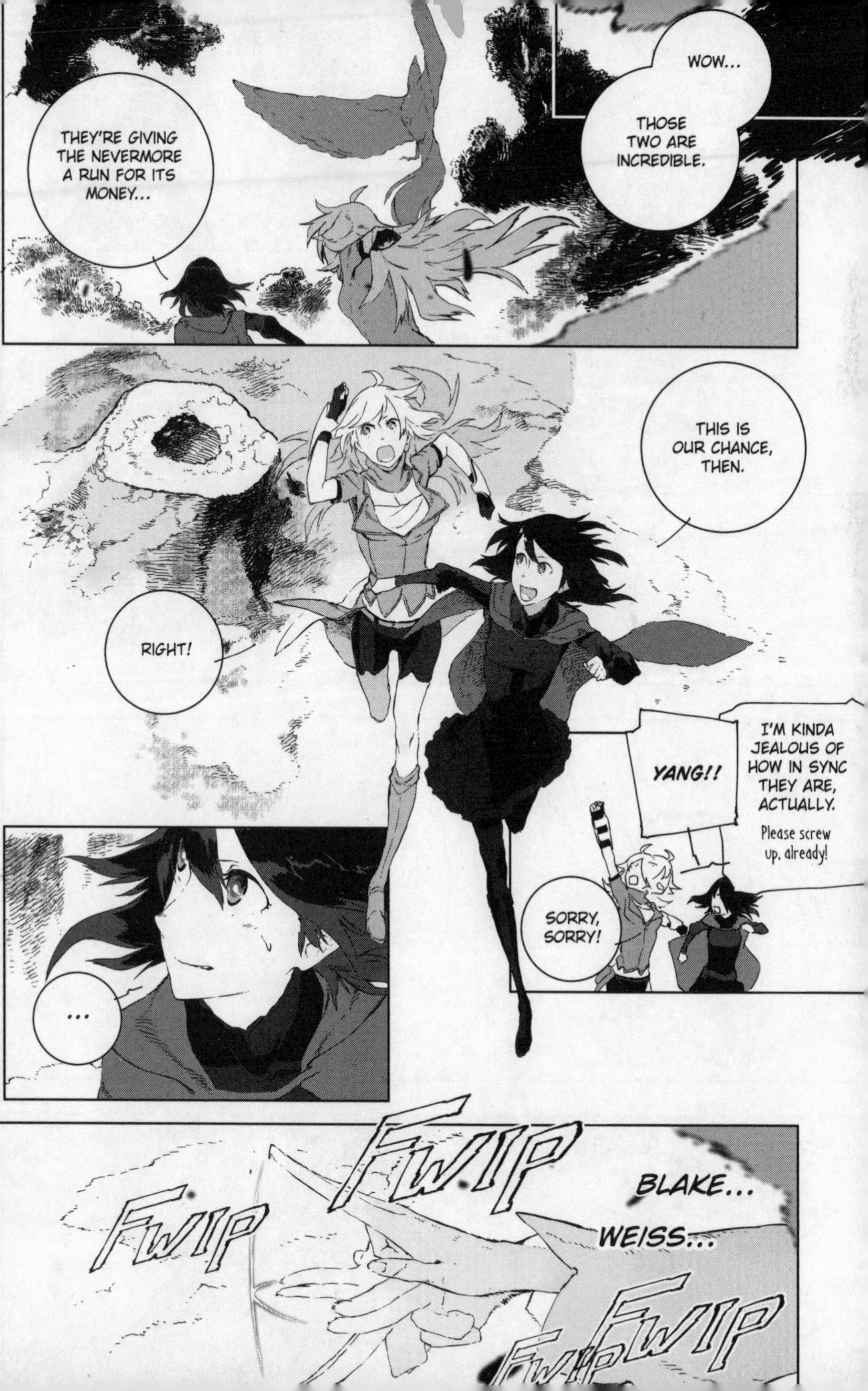
WOW...
THOSE TWO ARE INCREDIBLE.
THEY'RE GIVING THE NEVERMORE A RUN FOR ITS MONEY...
THIS IS OUR CHANCE, THEN.
RIGHT!
I'M KINDA JEALOUS OF HOW IN SYNC THEY ARE, ACTUALLY.
YANG!!
Please screw up, already!
SORRY, SORRY!
...
BLAKE...
WEISS...
FWIP
FWIP
FWIP
FWIP

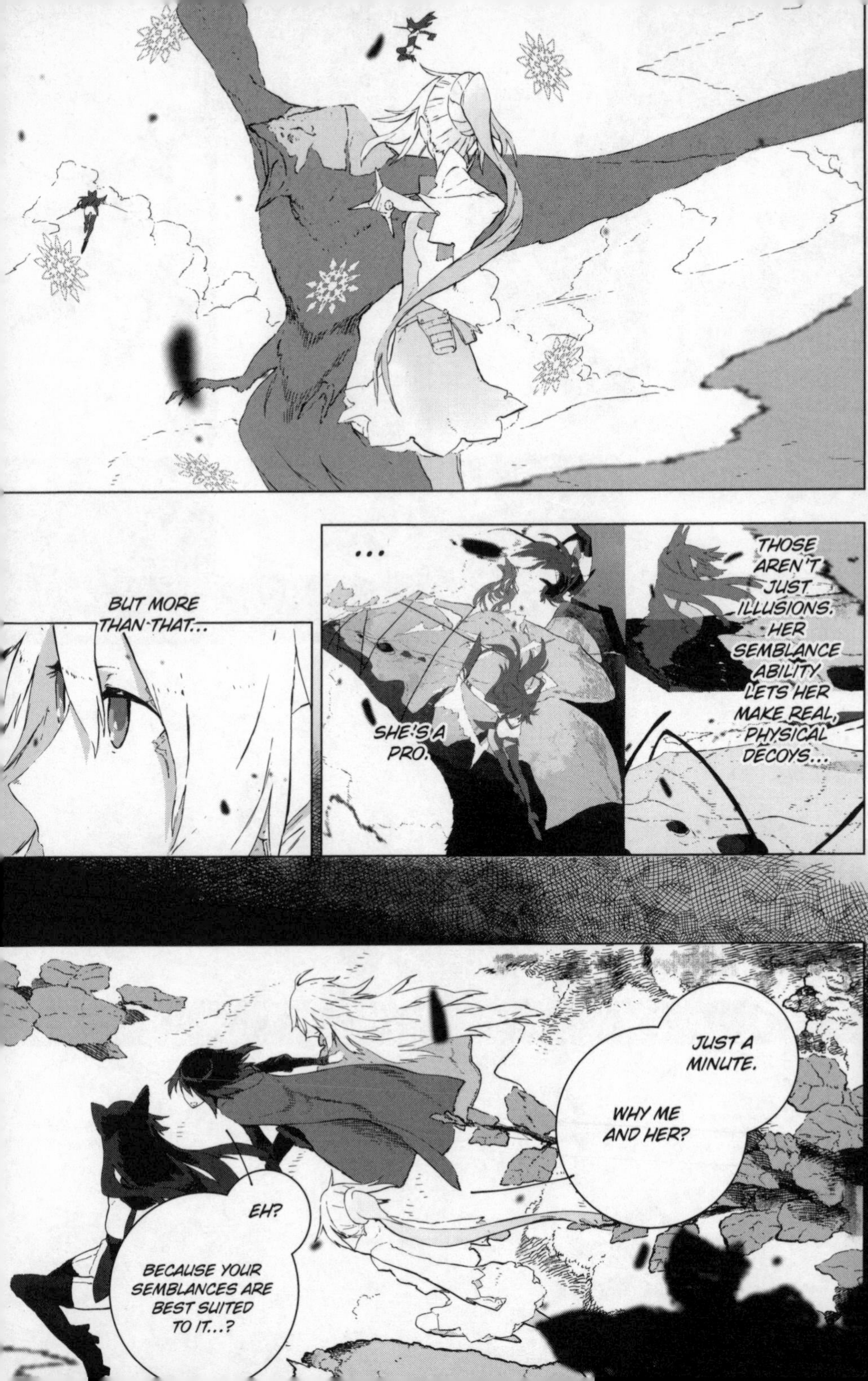
THOSE AREN'T JUST ILLUSIONS. HER SEMBLANCE ABILITY LETS HER MAKE REAL, PHYSICAL DECOYS...
...
SHE'S A PRO.
BUT MORE THAN THAT...
JUST A MINUTE.
WHY ME AND HER?
EH?
BECAUSE YOUR SEMBLANCES ARE BEST SUITED TO IT...?

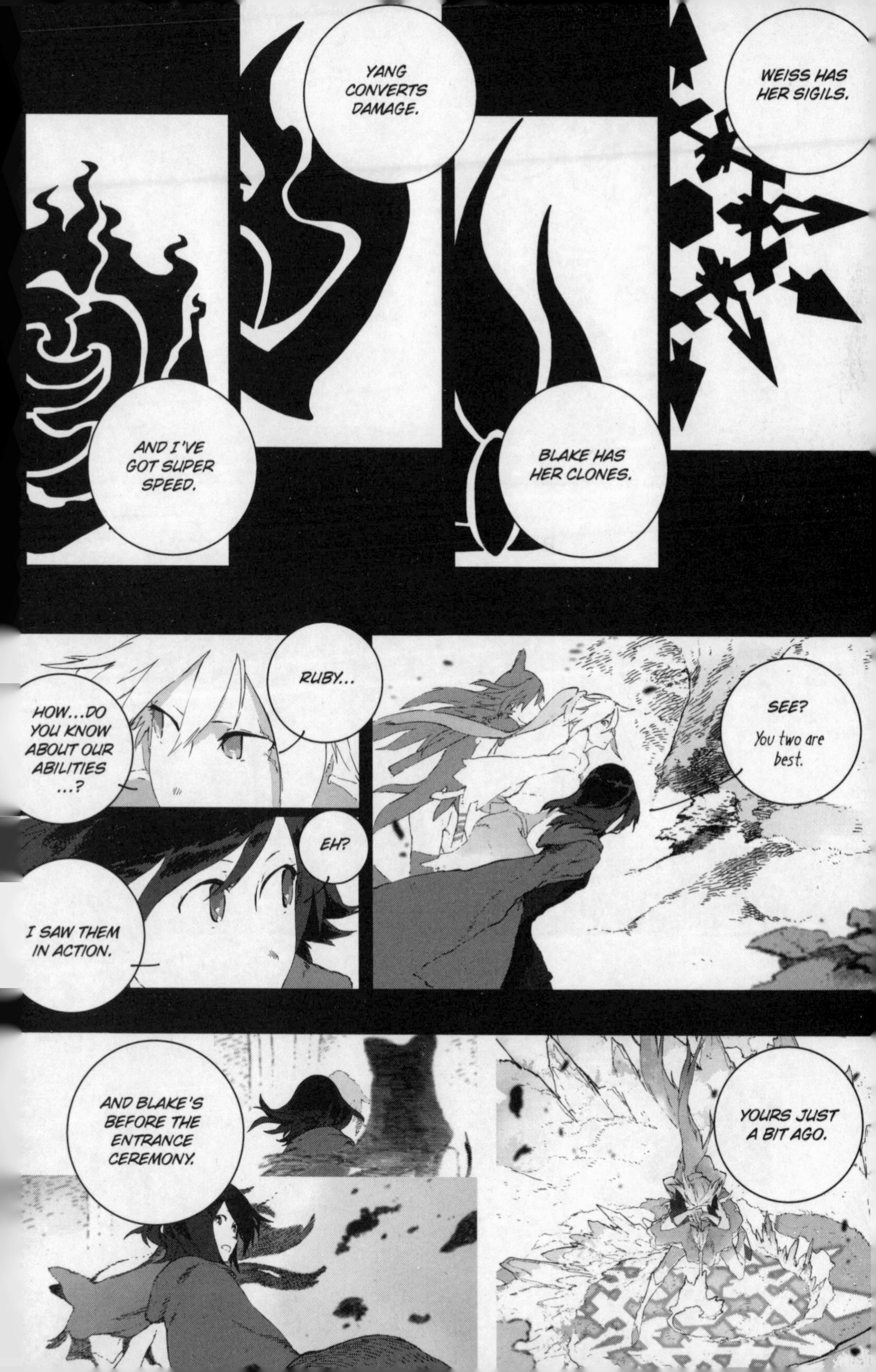
WEISS HAS HER SIGILS.
BLAKE HAS HER CLONES.
YANG CONVERTS DAMAGE.
AND I'VE GOT SUPER SPEED.
SEE? You two are best.
RUBY...
HOW...DO YOU KNOW ABOUT OUR ABILITIES ...?
EH?
I SAW THEM IN ACTION.
YOURS JUST A BIT AGO.
AND BLAKE'S BEFORE THE ENTRANCE CEREMONY.

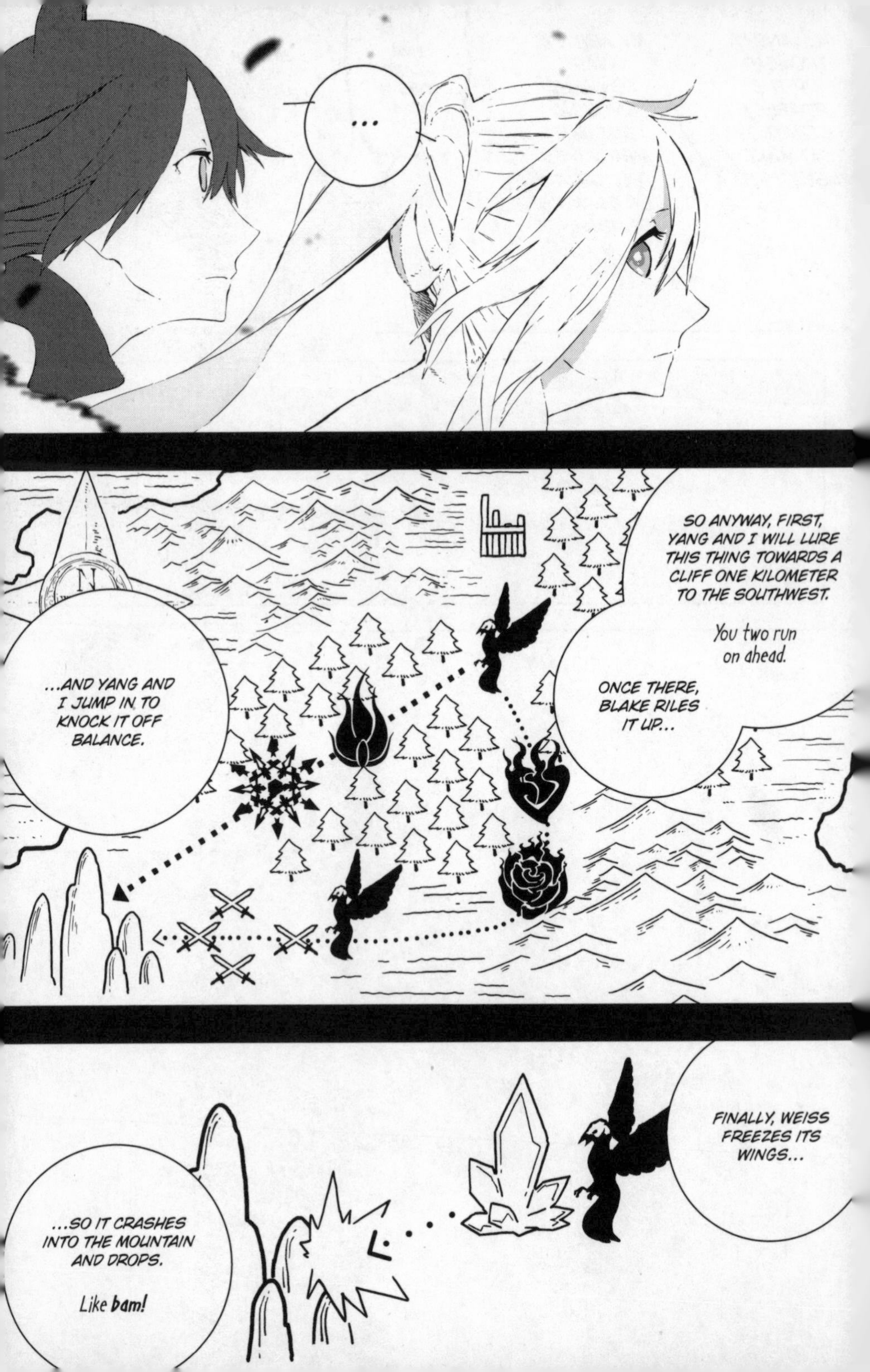
...
SO ANYWAY, FIRST, YANG AND I WILL LURE THIS THING TOWARDS A CLIFF ONE KILOMETER TO THE SOUTHWEST.
You two run on ahead.
ONCE THERE, BLAKE RILES IT UP...
...AND YANG AND I JUMP IN TO KNOCK IT OFF BALANCE.
FINALLY, WEISS FREEZES ITS WINGS...
...SO IT CRASHES INTO THE MOUNTAIN AND DROPS.
Like bam!
N

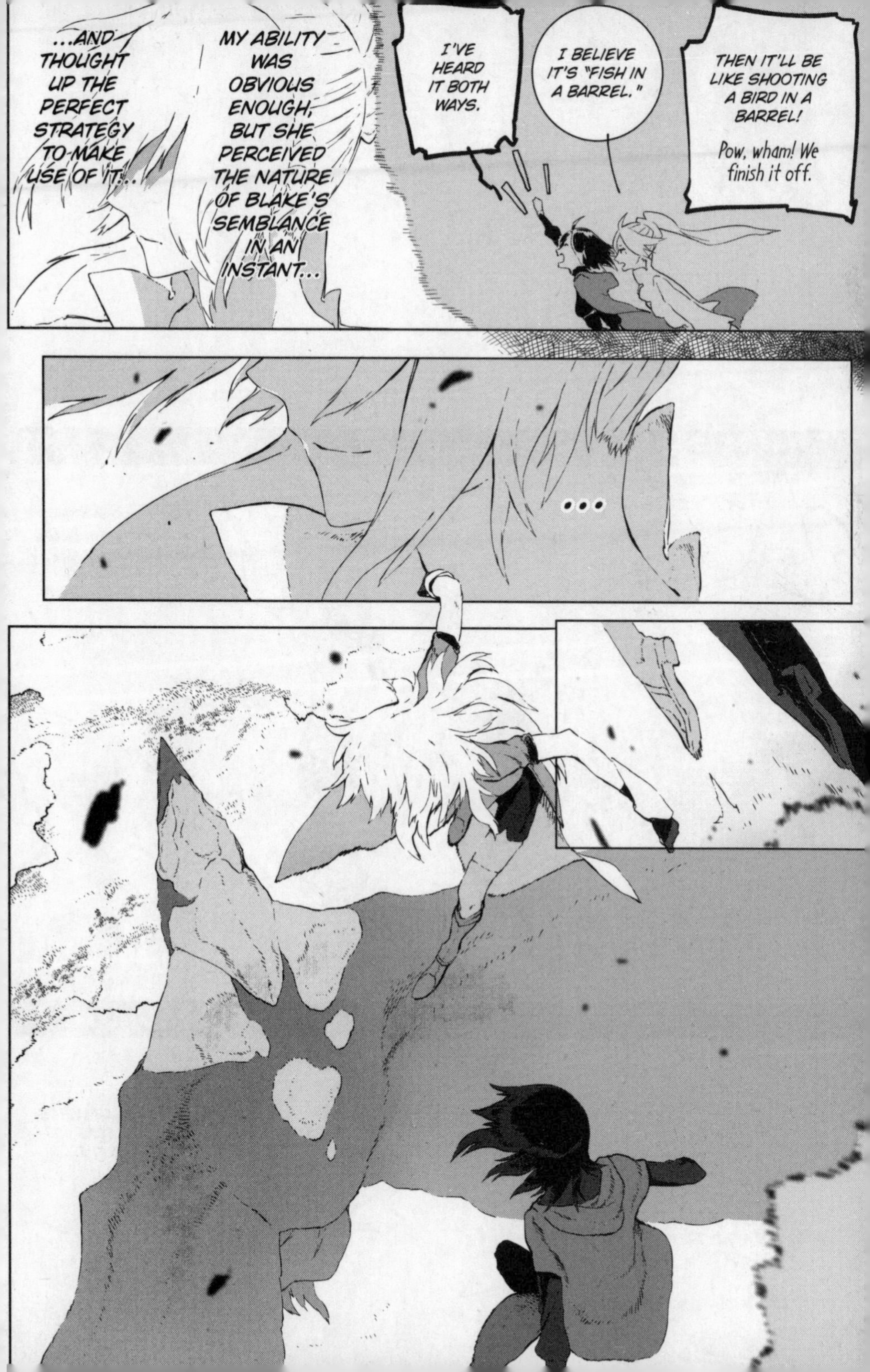
THEN IT'LL BE LIKE SHOOTING A BIRD IN A BARREL!
Pow, wham! We finish it off.
I BELIEVE IT'S "FISH IN A BARREL."
I'VE HEARD IT BOTH WAYS.
MY ABILITY WAS OBVIOUS ENOUGH, BUT SHE PERCEIVED THE NATURE OF BLAKE'S SEMBLANCE IN AN INSTANT...
...AND THOUGHT UP THE PERFECT STRATEGY TO MAKE USE OF IT...
...

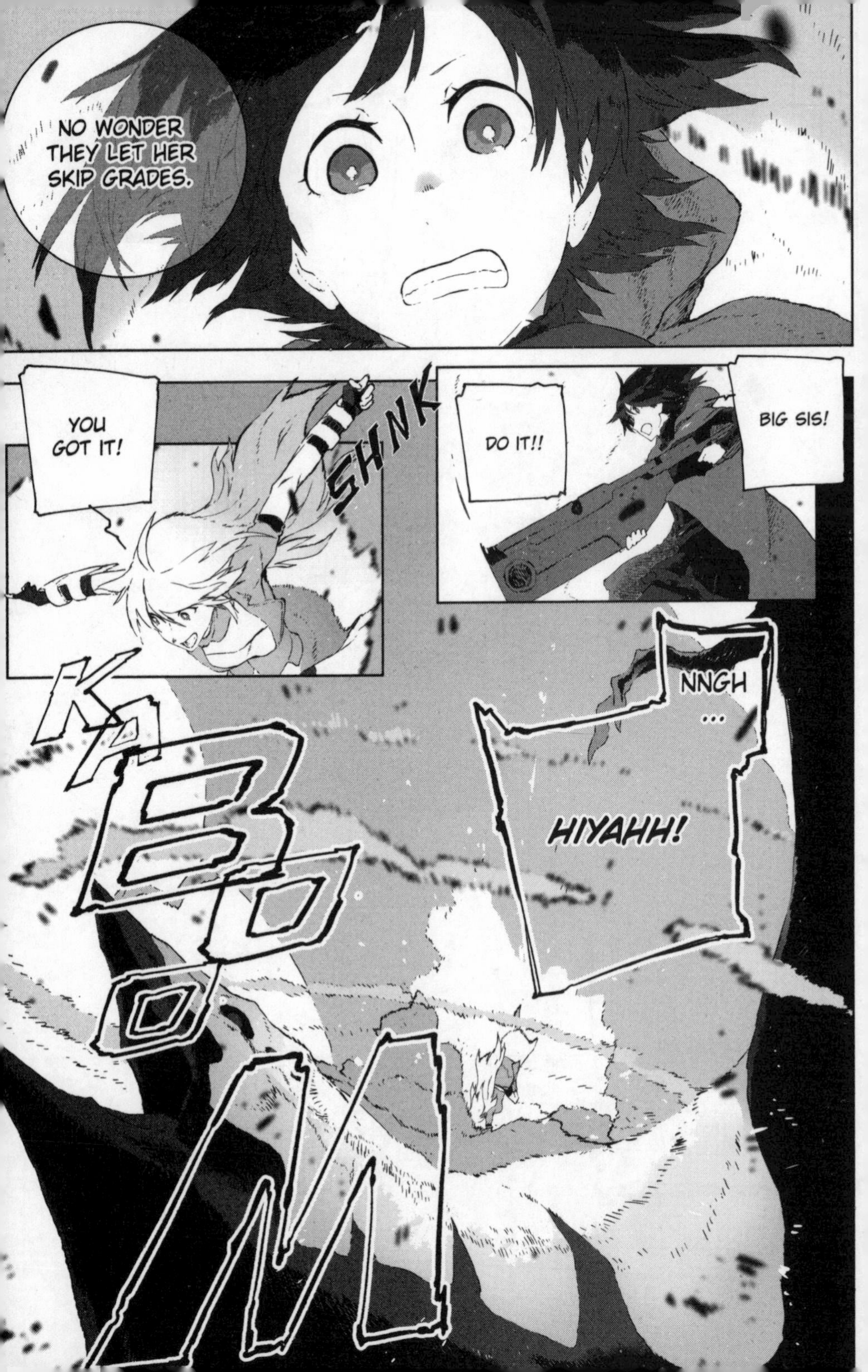
NO WONDER THEY LET HER SKIP GRADES.
BIG SIS!
DO IT!!
SHNK
YOU GOT IT!
NNGH ...
HIYAHH!
KABOOM

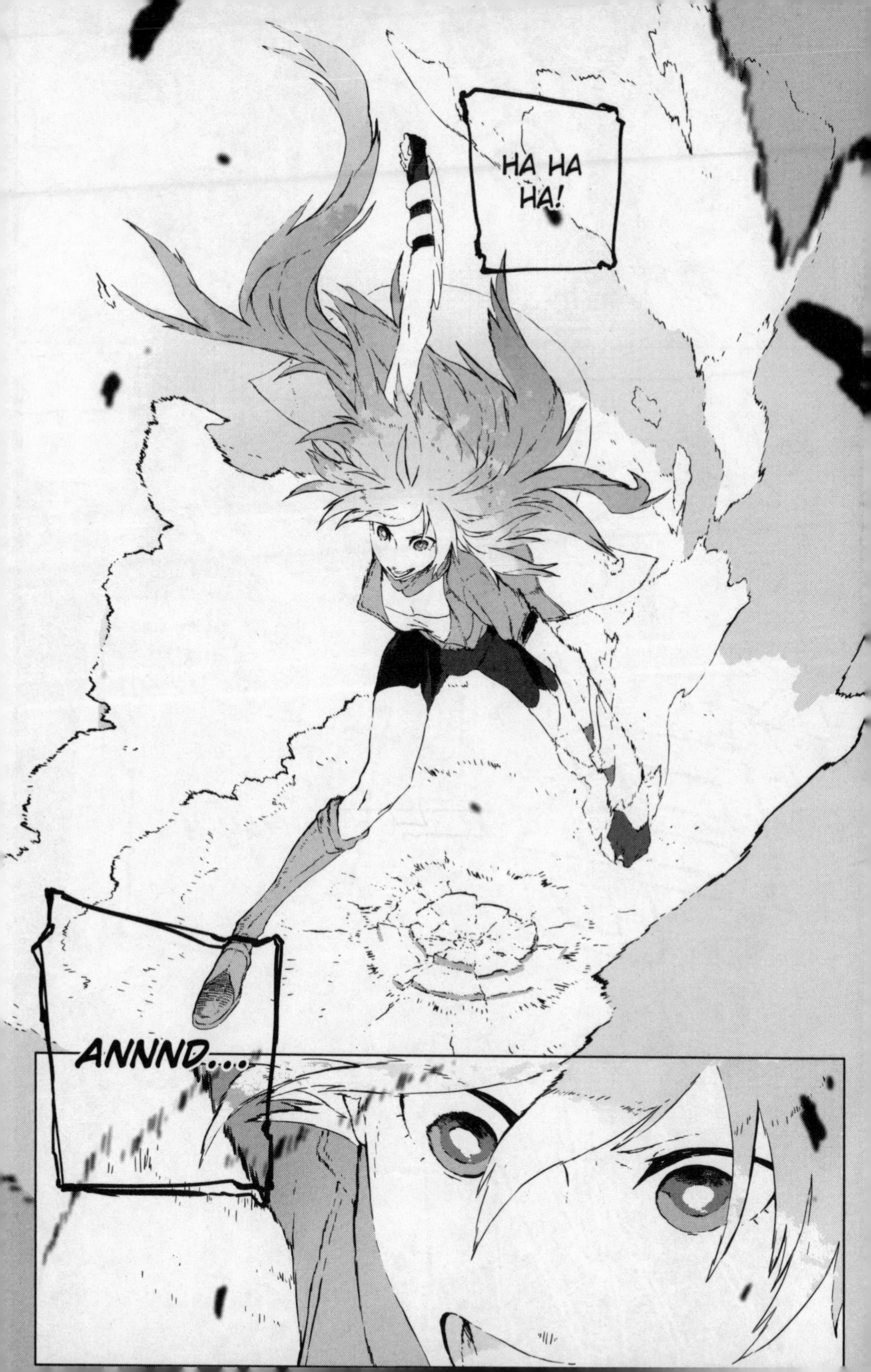
HA HA HA!
ANNND....

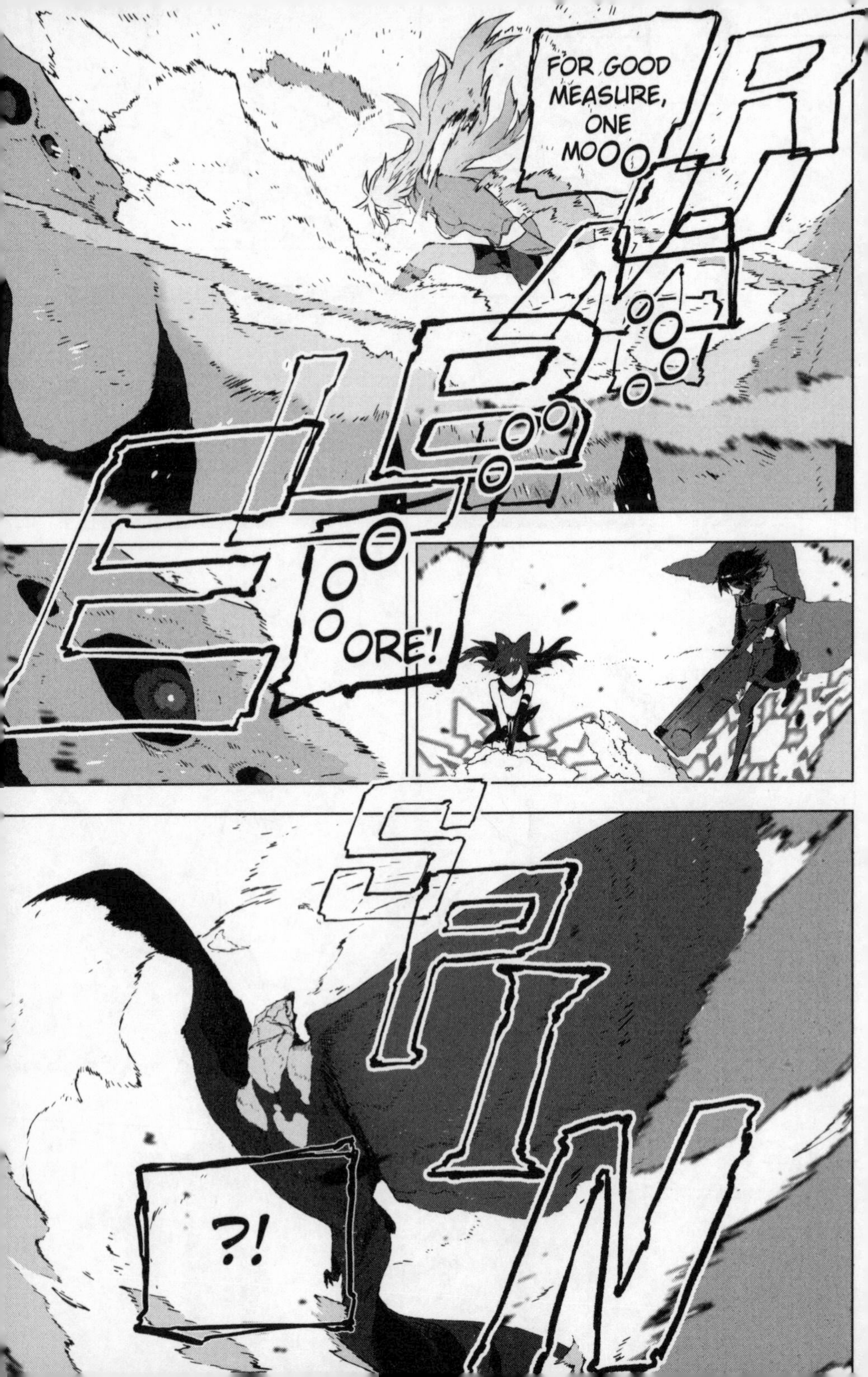
FOR GOOD MEASURE, ONE MOOOOOOOOOOOOOOORE!
?!

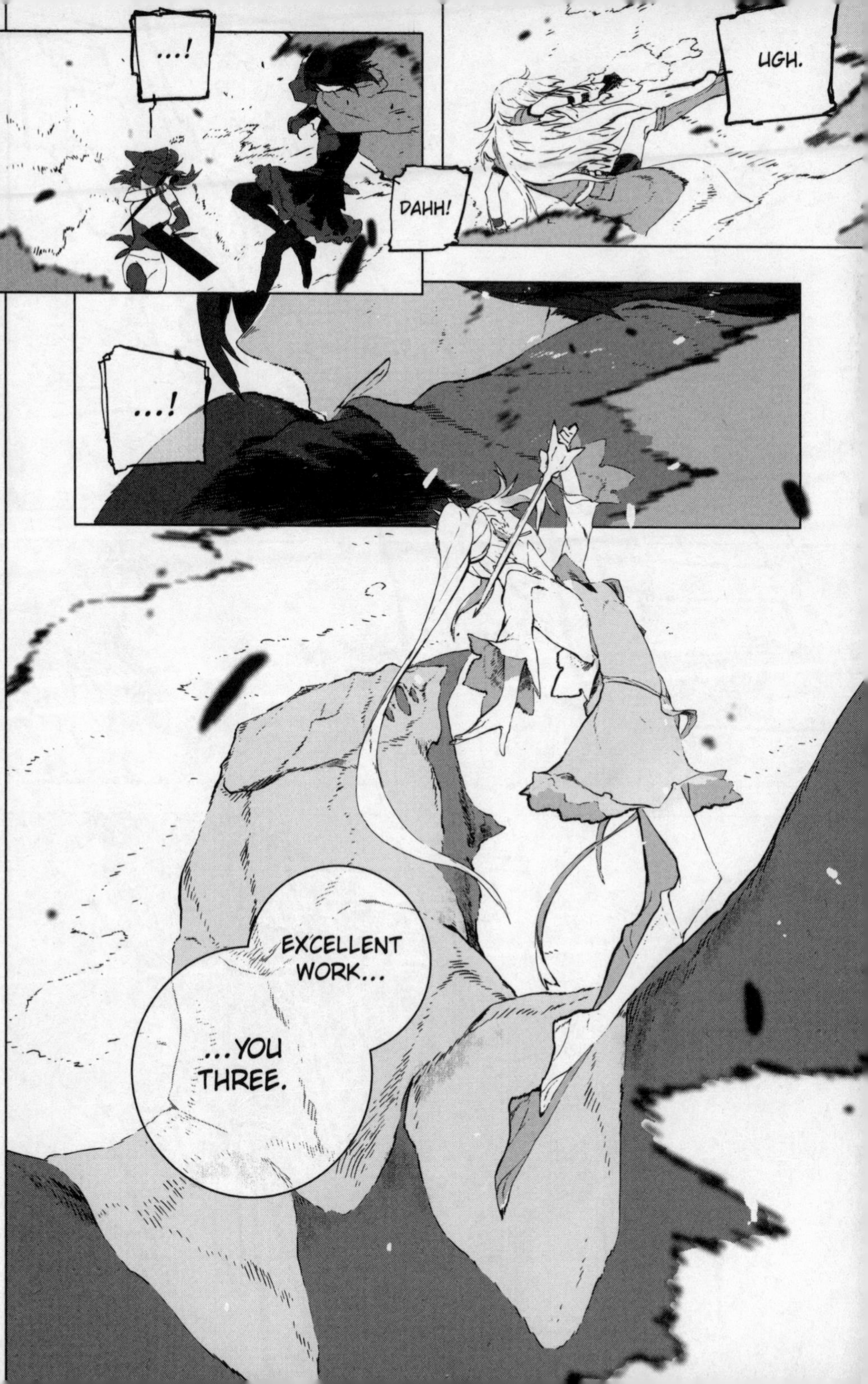
UGH.
DAHH!
...!
...!
EXCELLENT WORK...
...YOU THREE.

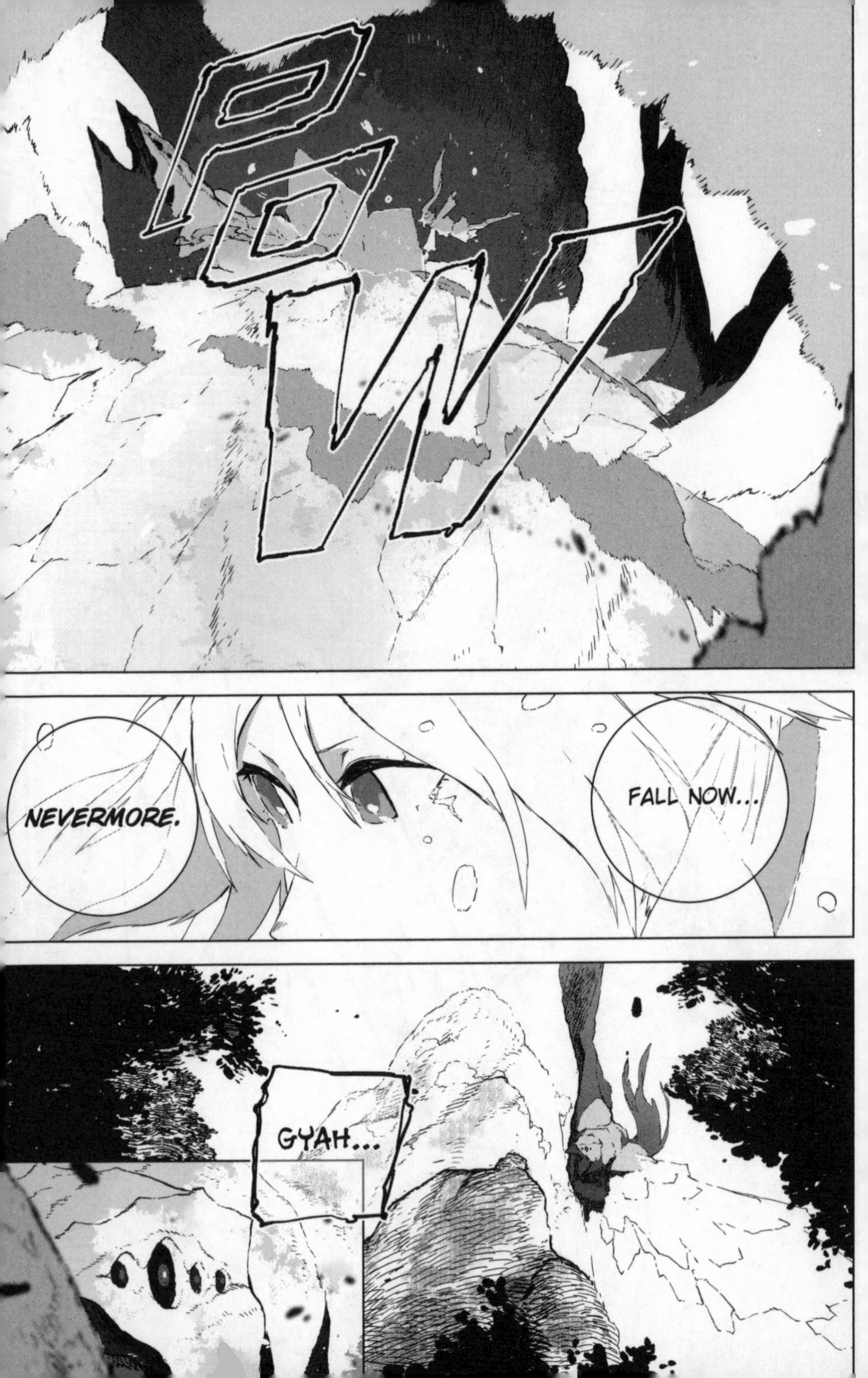
POW
FALL NOW...
NEVERMORE.
GYAH...

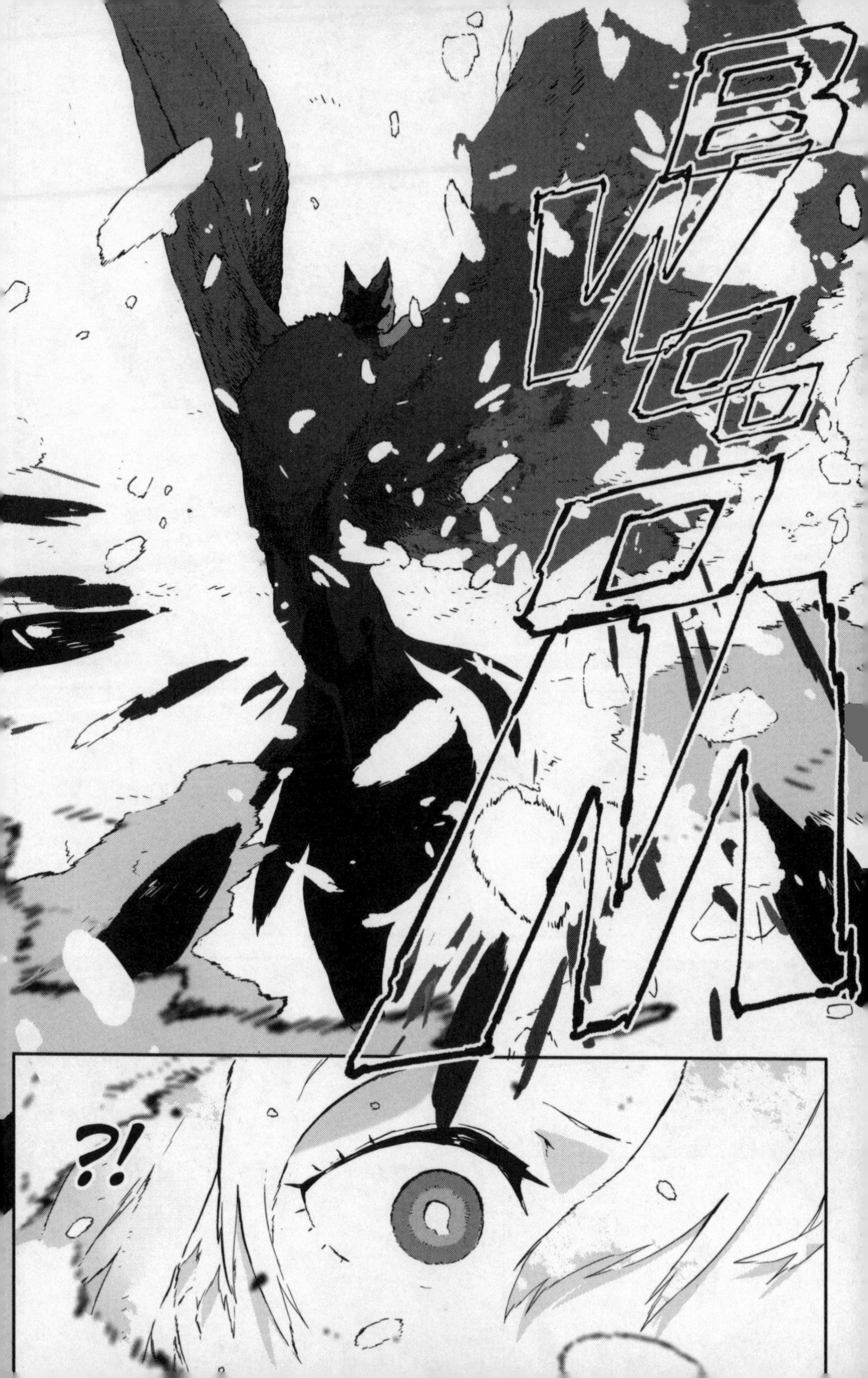
BWOOM
?!

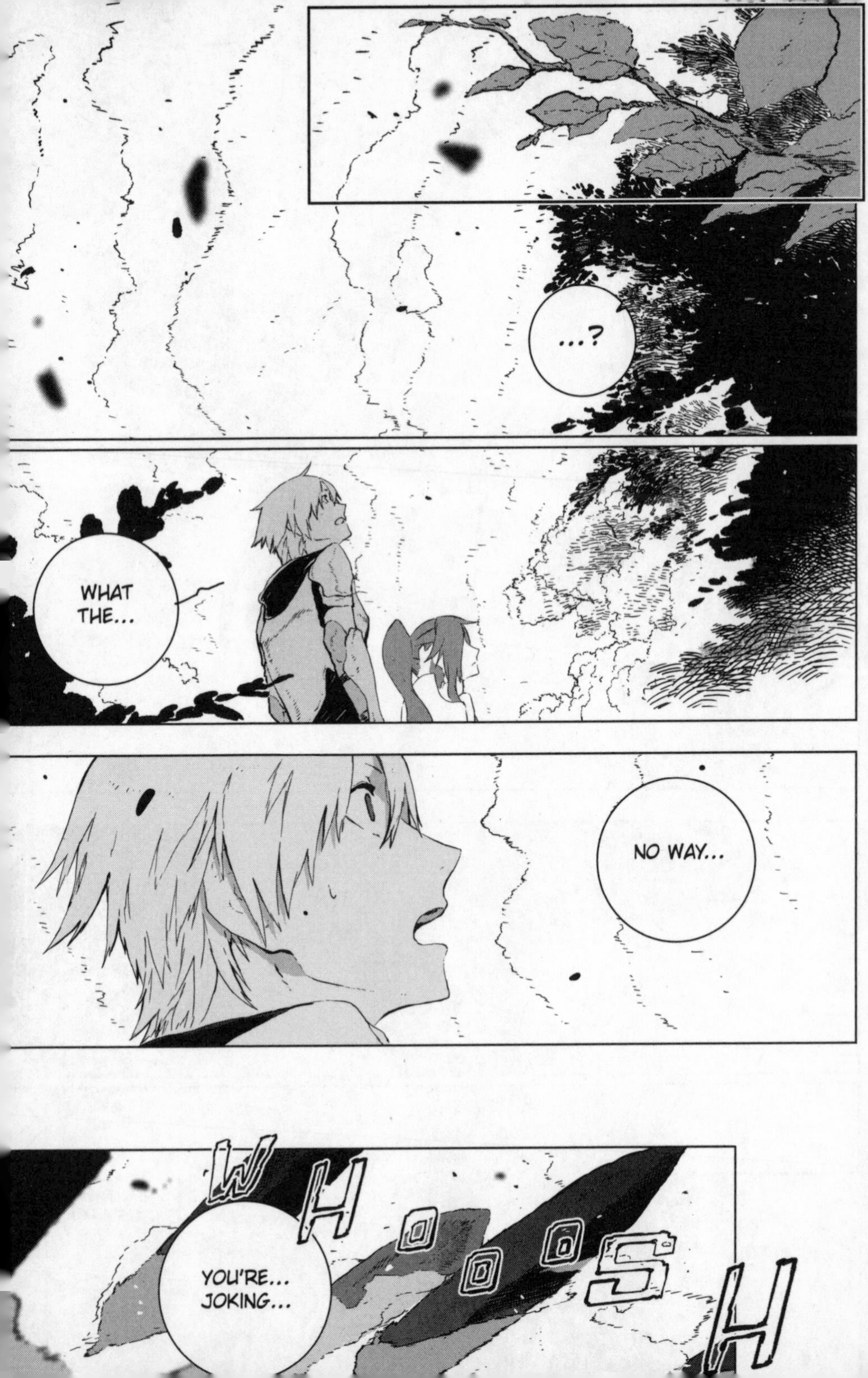
...?
WHAT THE...
NO WAY...
WHOOOSH
YOU'RE... JOKING...

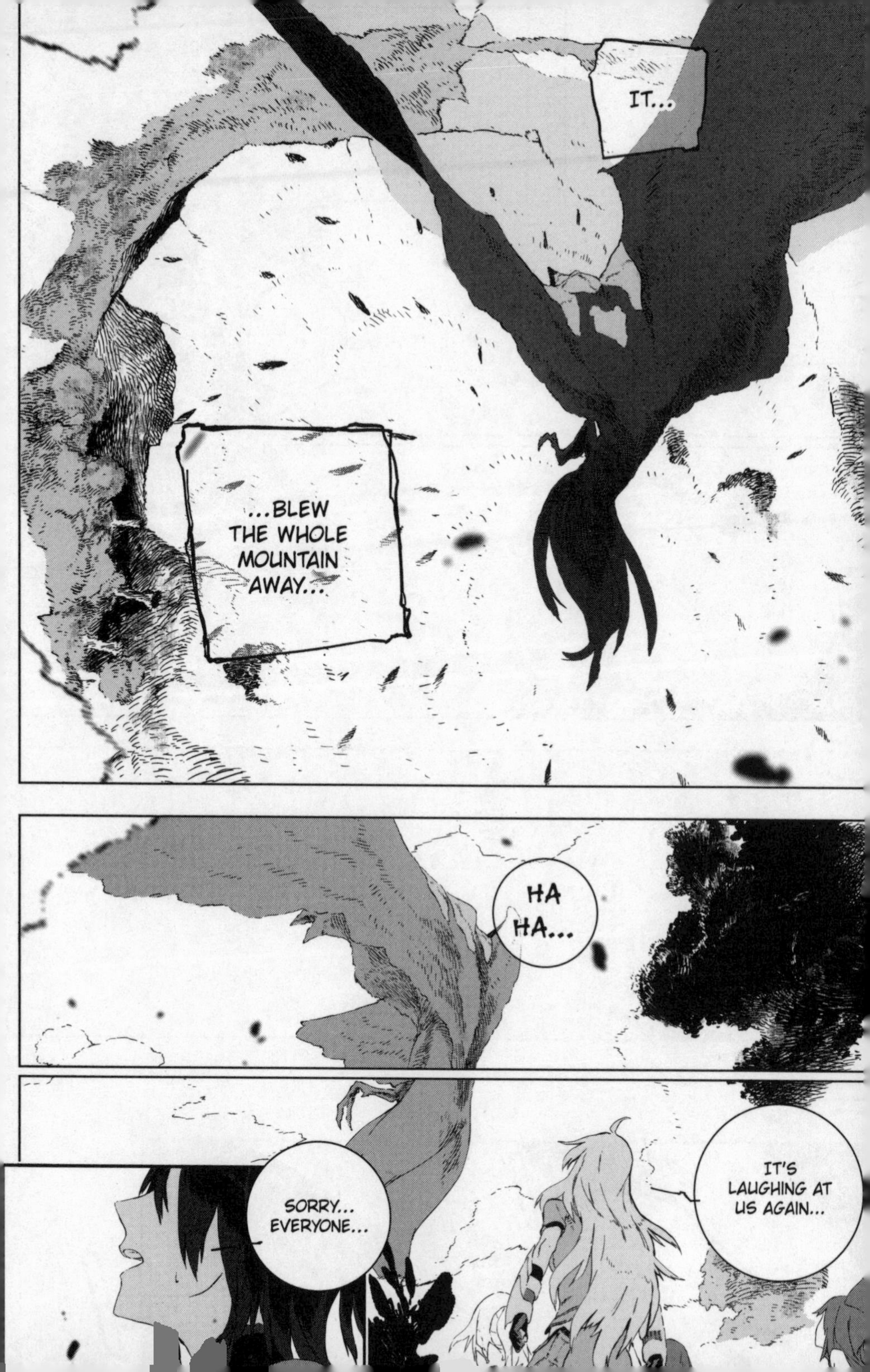
IT...
...BLEW THE WHOLE MOUNTAIN AWAY...
HA HA...
IT'S LAUGHING AT US AGAIN...
SORRY... EVERYONE...

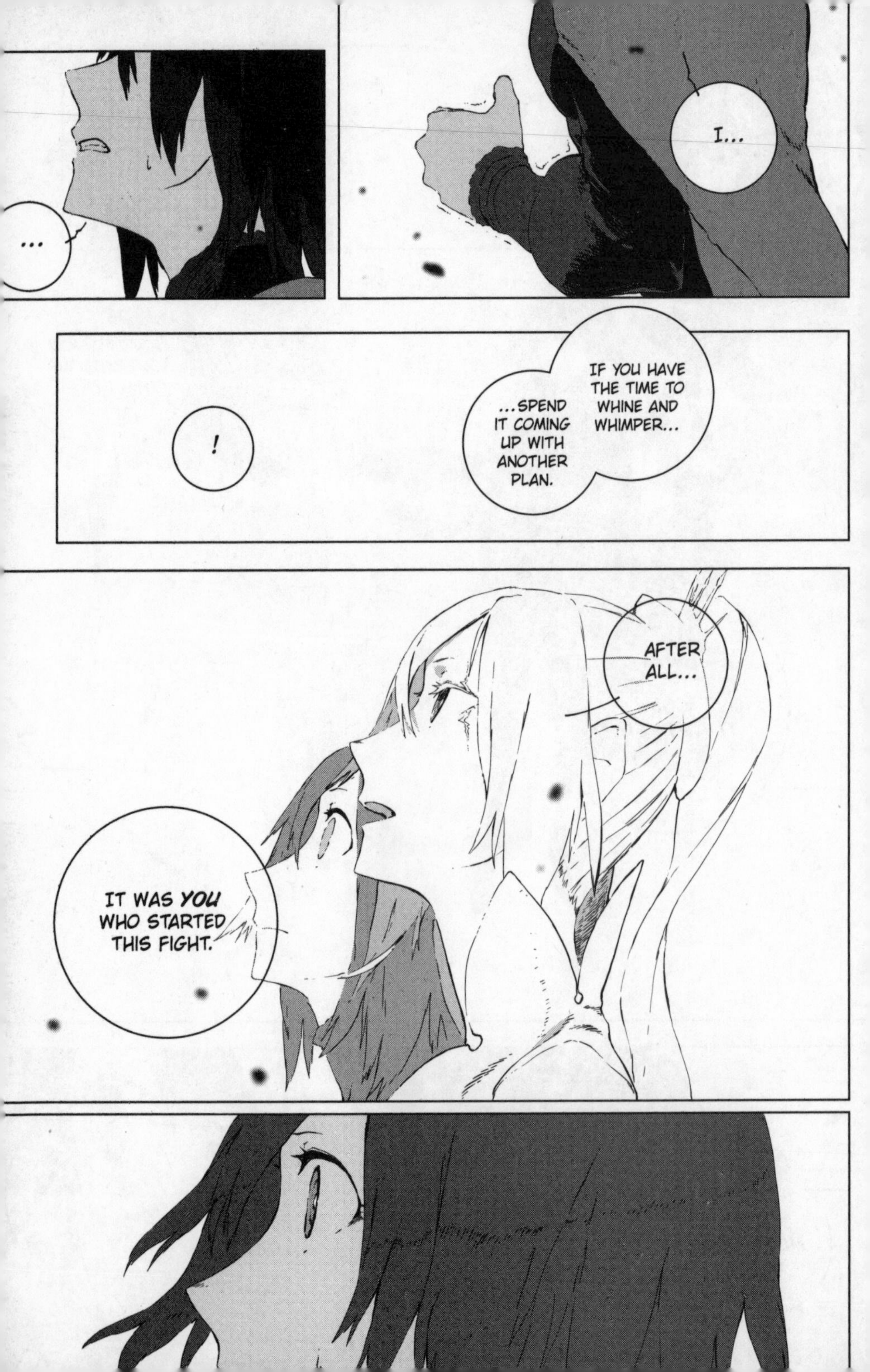
I...
...
IF YOU HAVE THE TIME TO WHINE AND WHIMPER...
...SPEND IT COMING UP WITH ANOTHER PLAN.
!
AFTER ALL...
IT WAS *YOU* WHO STARTED THIS FIGHT.

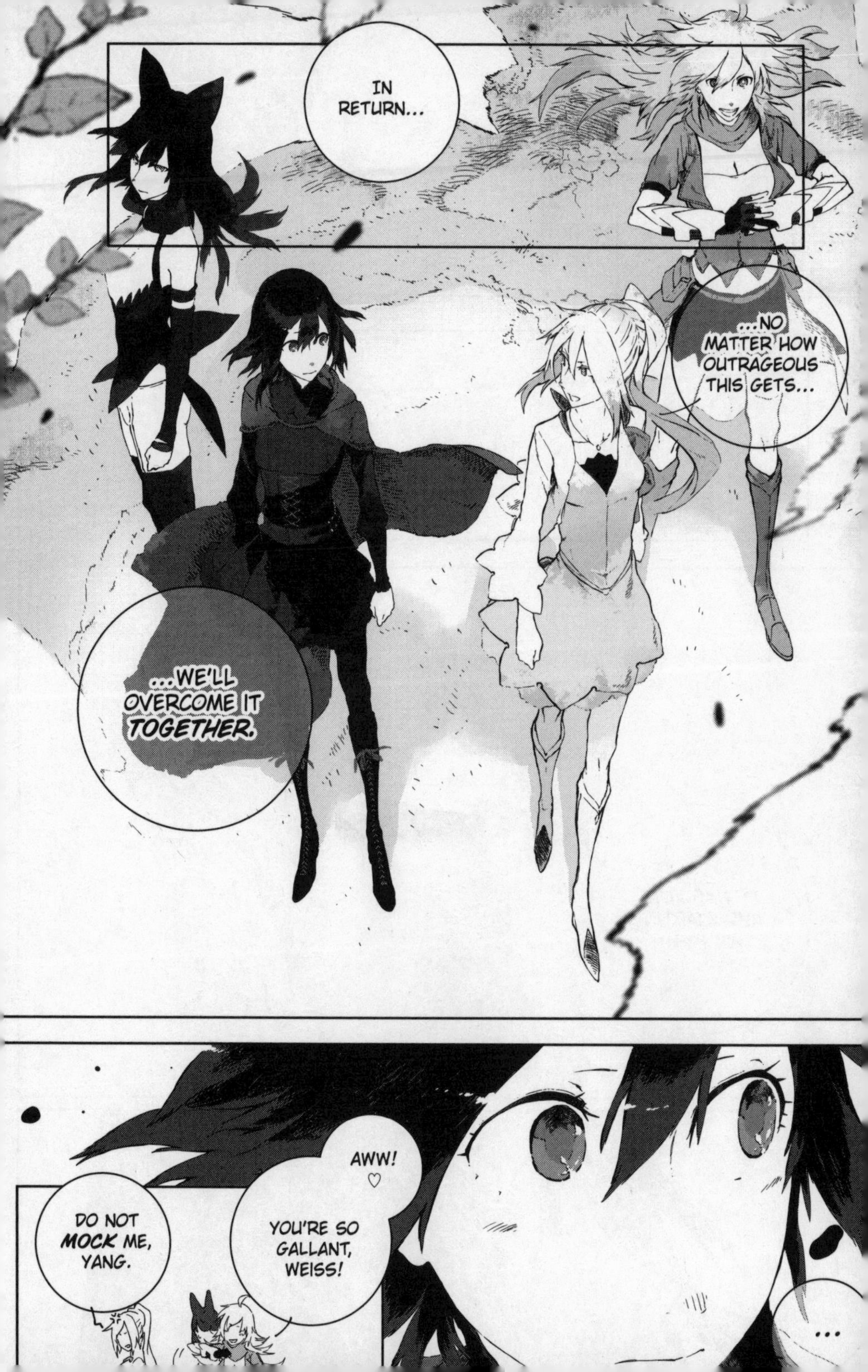
IN RETURN...
...NO MATTER HOW OUTRAGEOUS THIS GETS...
...WE'LL OVERCOME IT *TOGETHER.*
...
AWW! ♡
YOU'RE SO GALLANT, WEISS!
DO NOT **MOCK** ME, YANG.

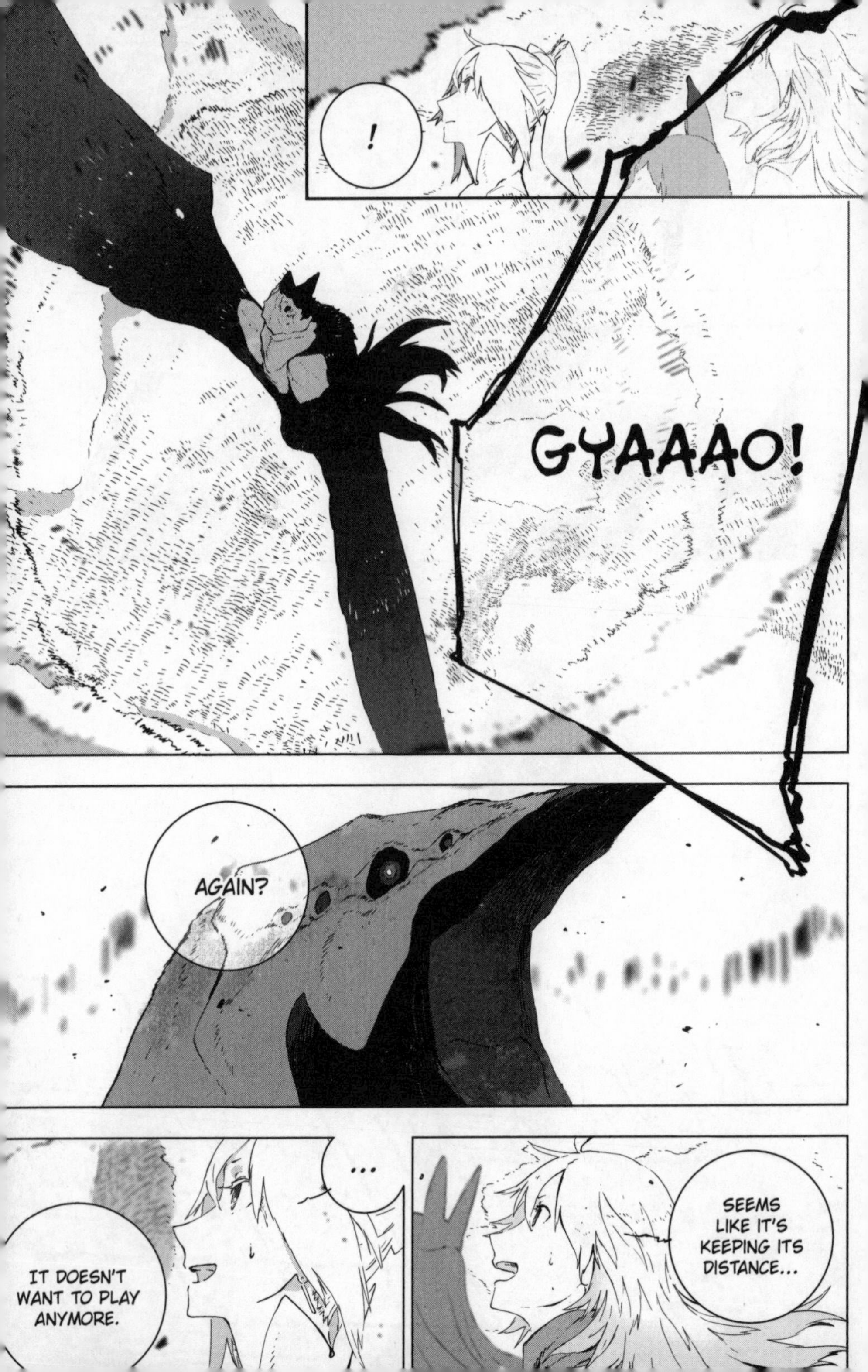
!
GYAAAO!
AGAIN?
SEEMS LIKE IT'S KEEPING ITS DISTANCE...
...
IT DOESN'T WANT TO PLAY ANYMORE.

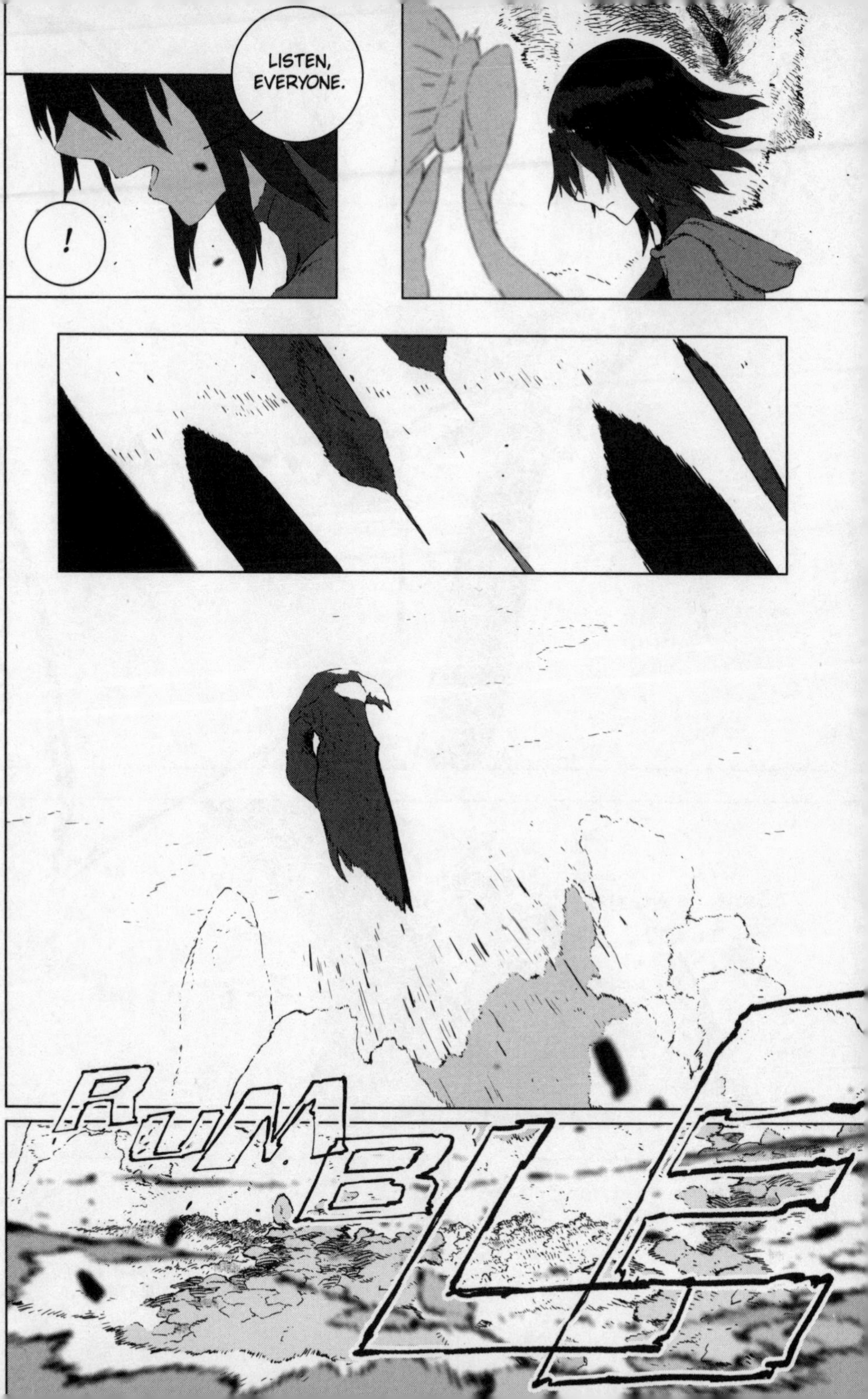
LISTEN, EVERYONE.
!
RUMBLE

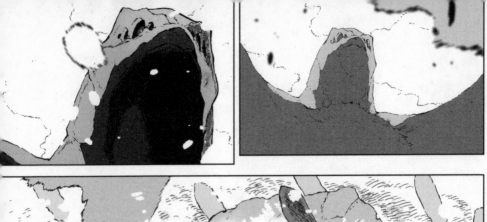

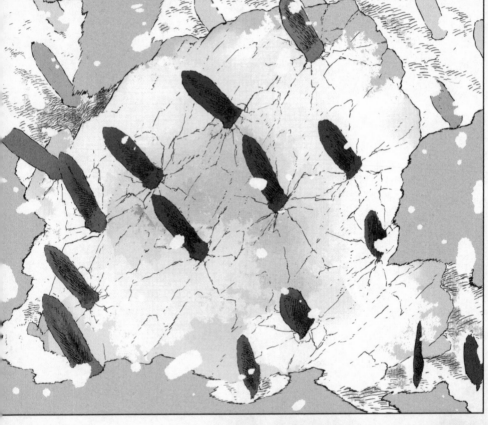

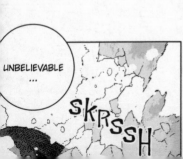

UNBELIEVABLE
...

SKRSSH

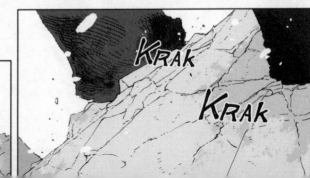

KRAK

KRAK

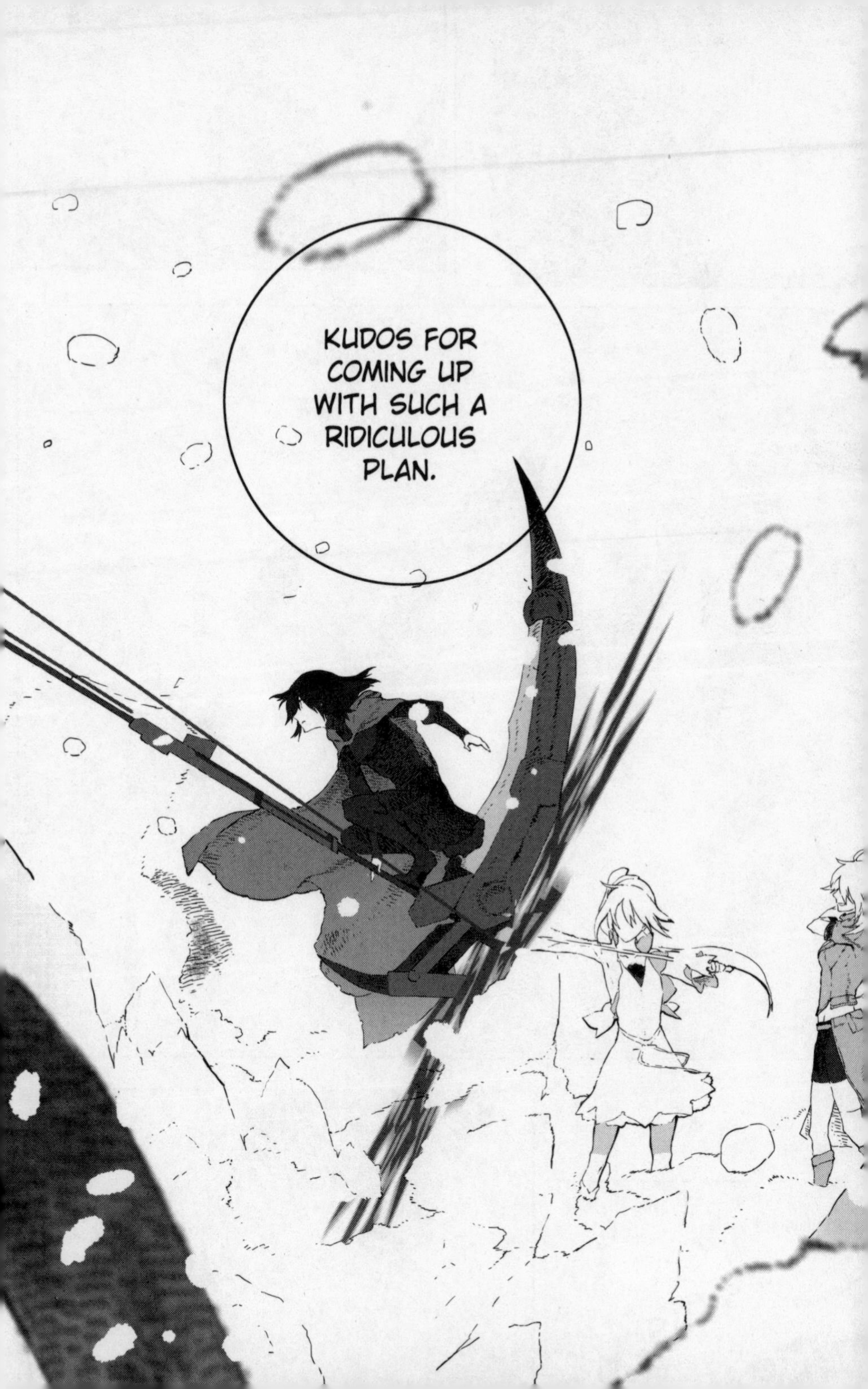
KUDOS FOR COMING UP WITH SUCH A RIDICULOUS PLAN.

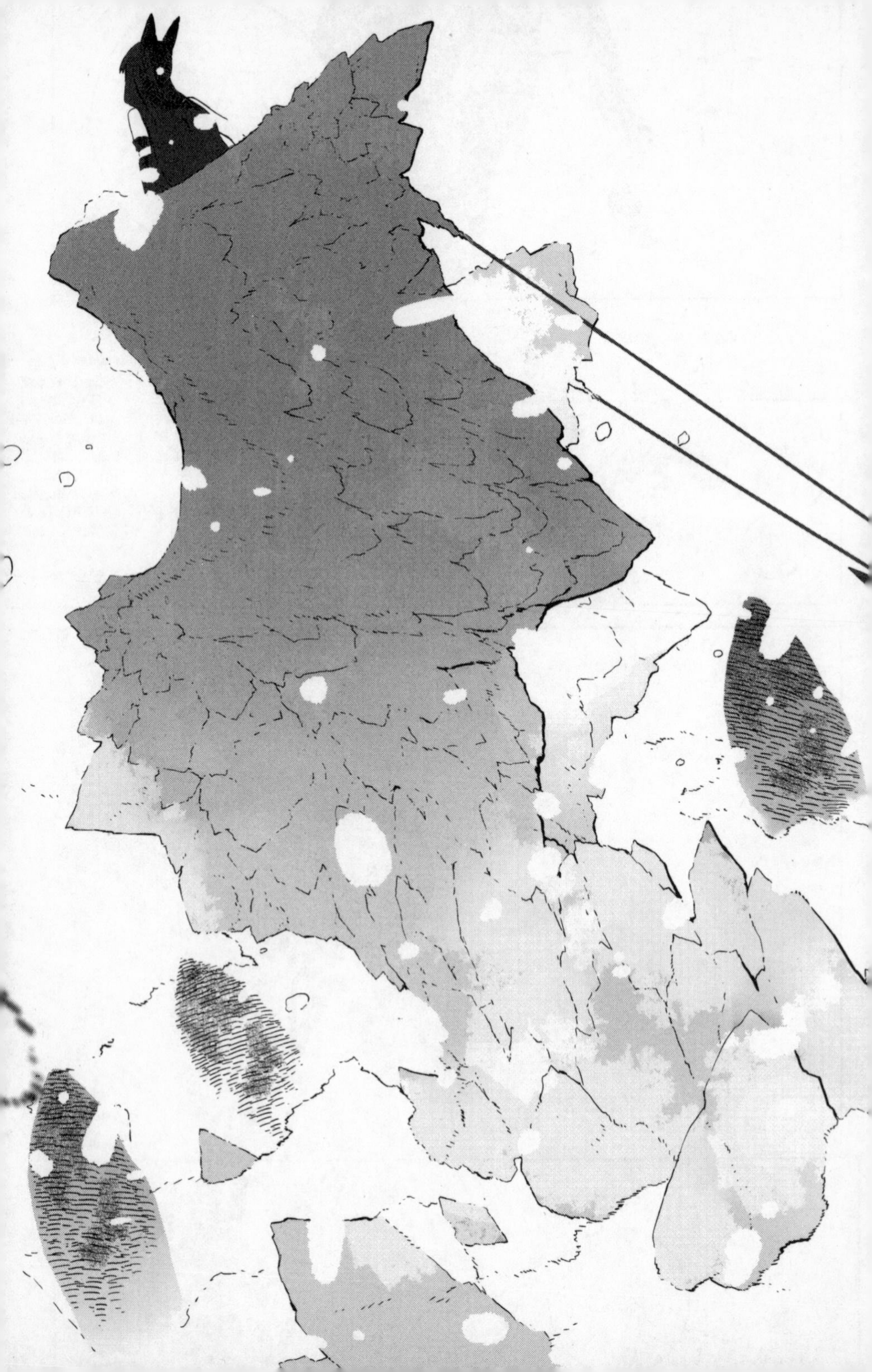

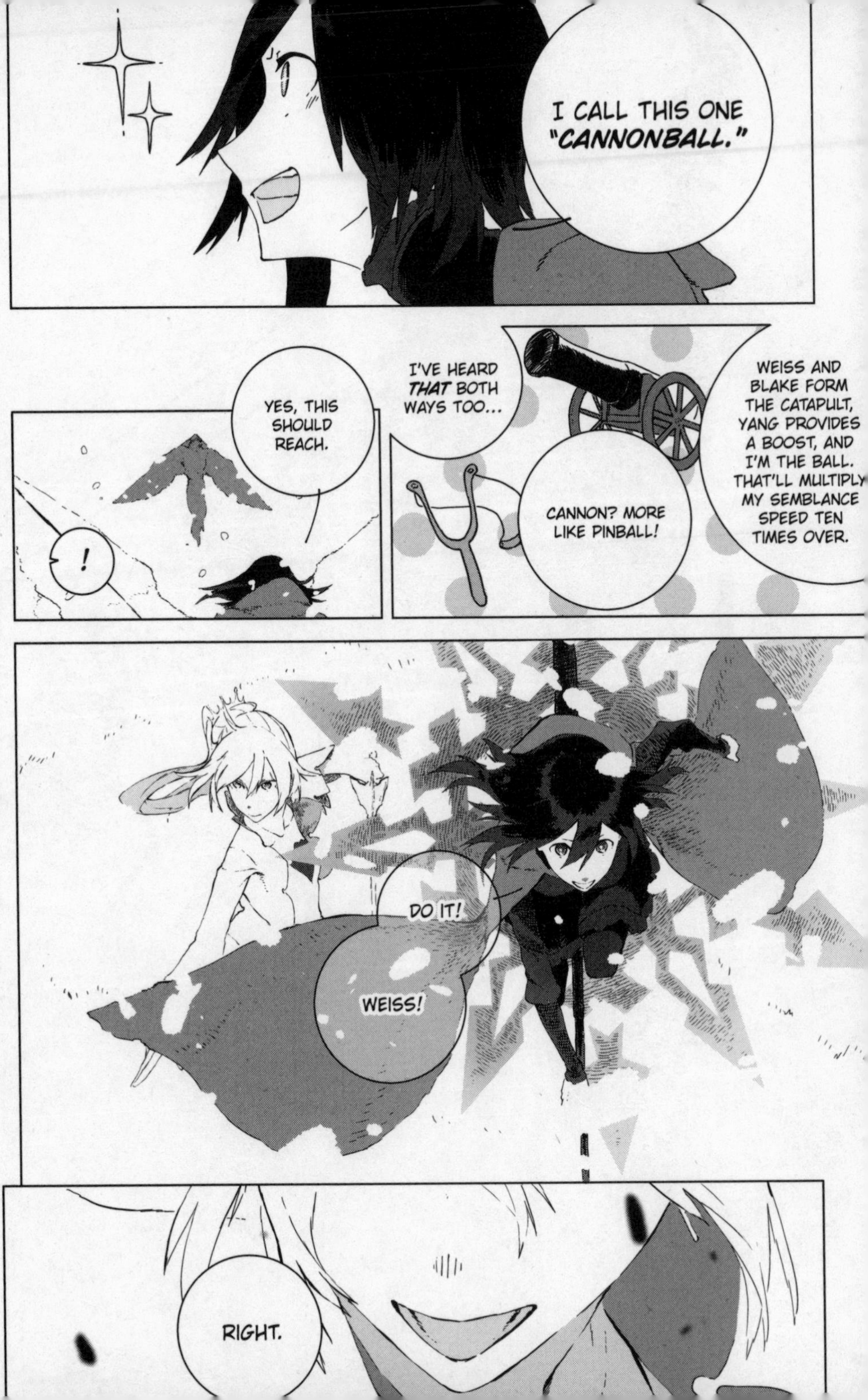
I CALL THIS ONE "CANNONBALL."
WEISS AND BLAKE FORM THE CATAPULT, YANG PROVIDES A BOOST, AND I'M THE BALL. THAT'LL MULTIPLY MY SEMBLANCE SPEED TEN TIMES OVER.
CANNON? MORE LIKE PINBALL!
I'VE HEARD THAT BOTH WAYS TOO...
YES, THIS SHOULD REACH.
!
DO IT!
WEISS!
RIGHT.

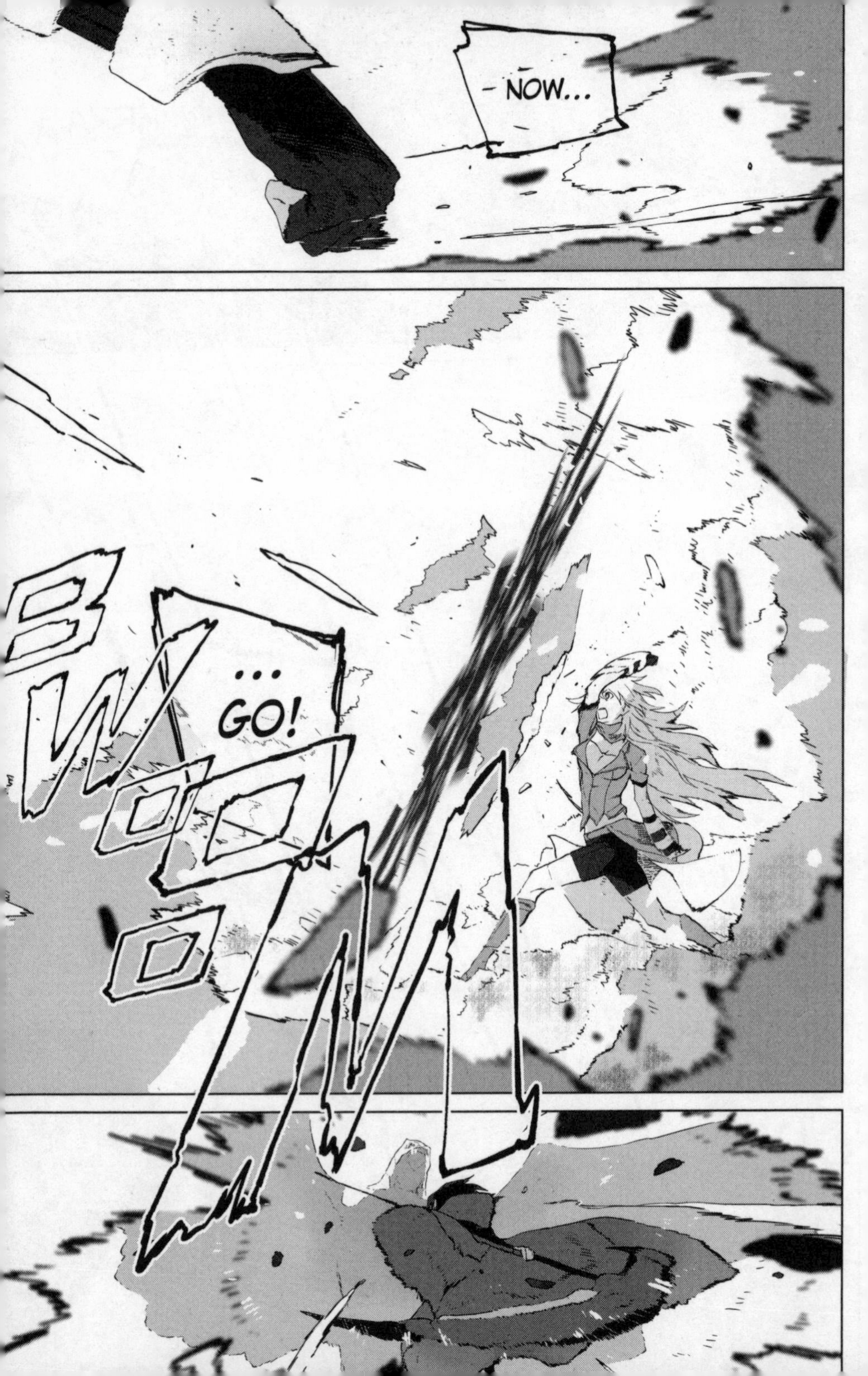
NOW...
...GO!
BWOOOM

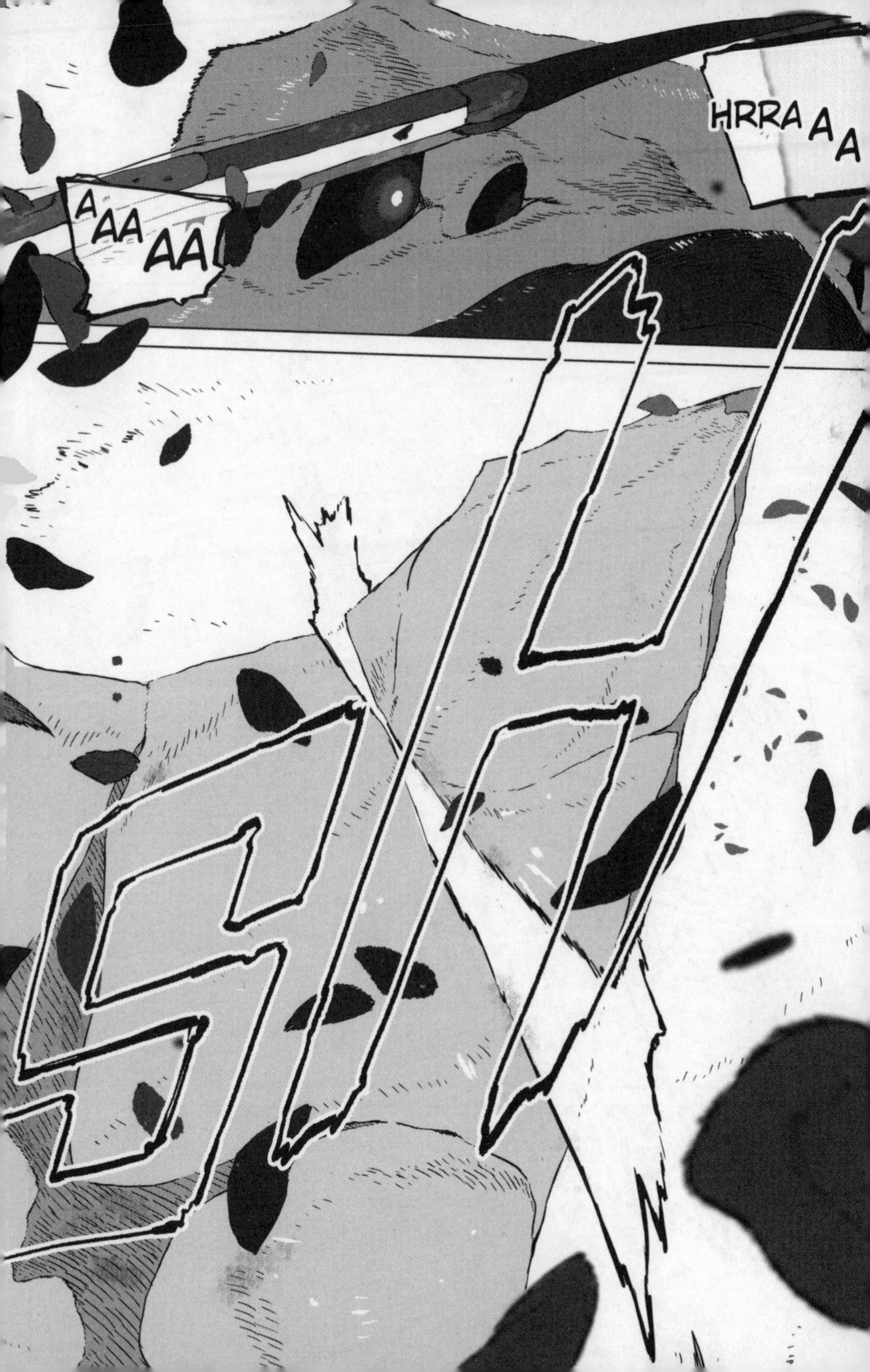
HRRAAAA
AAAAA

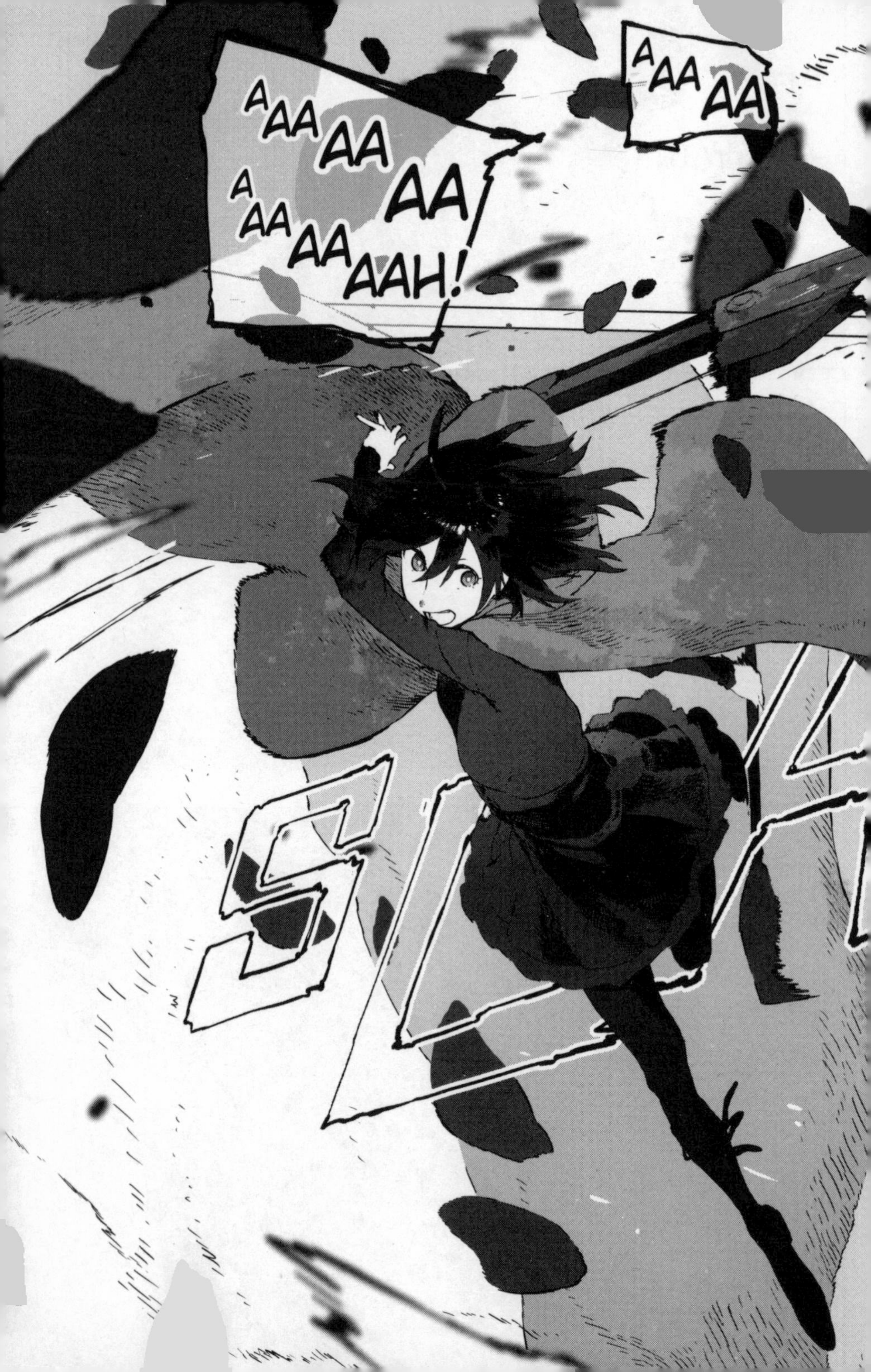
AAAAA
AAAAAAA AAAAAAAH!

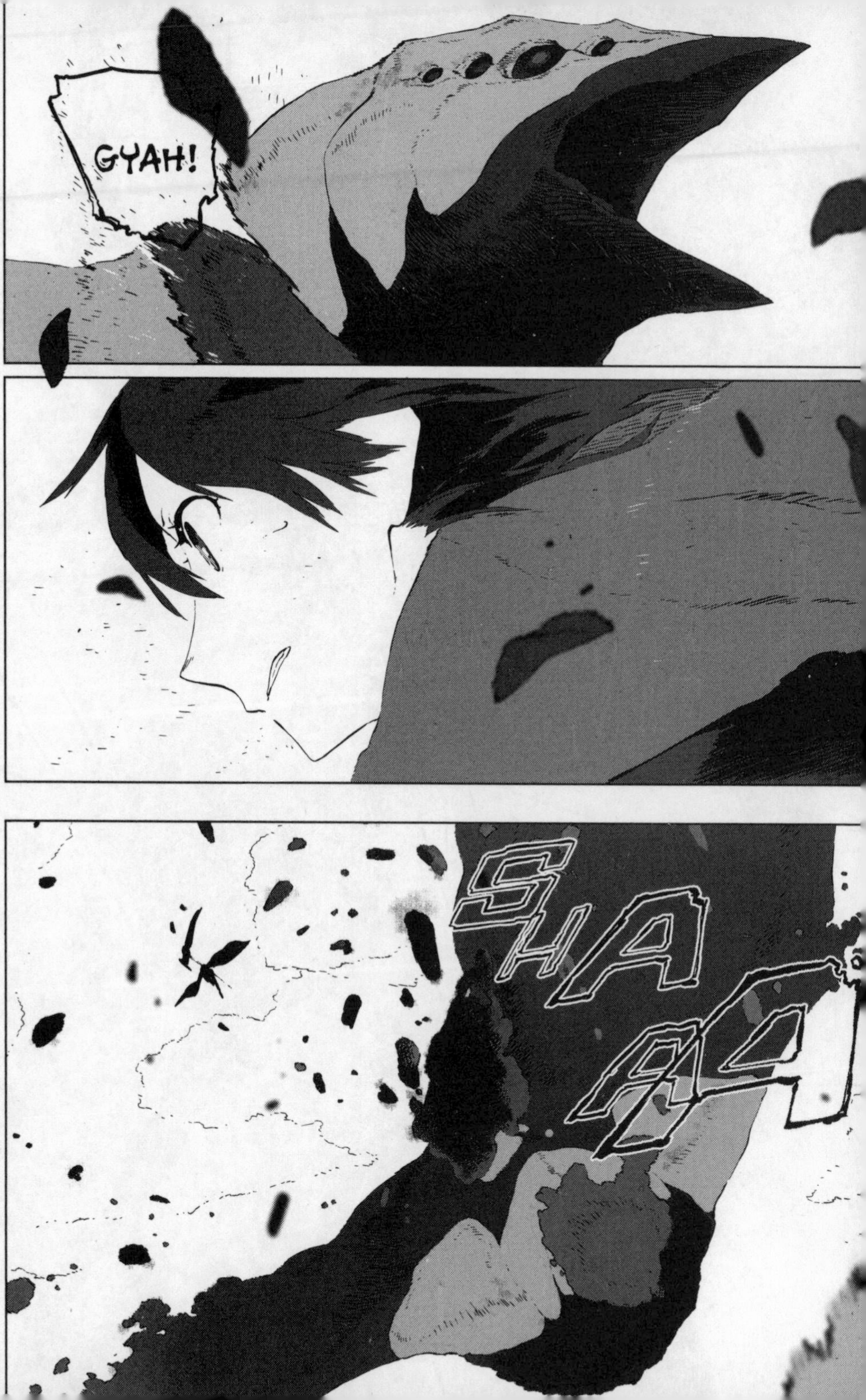
GYAH!
SHAAA

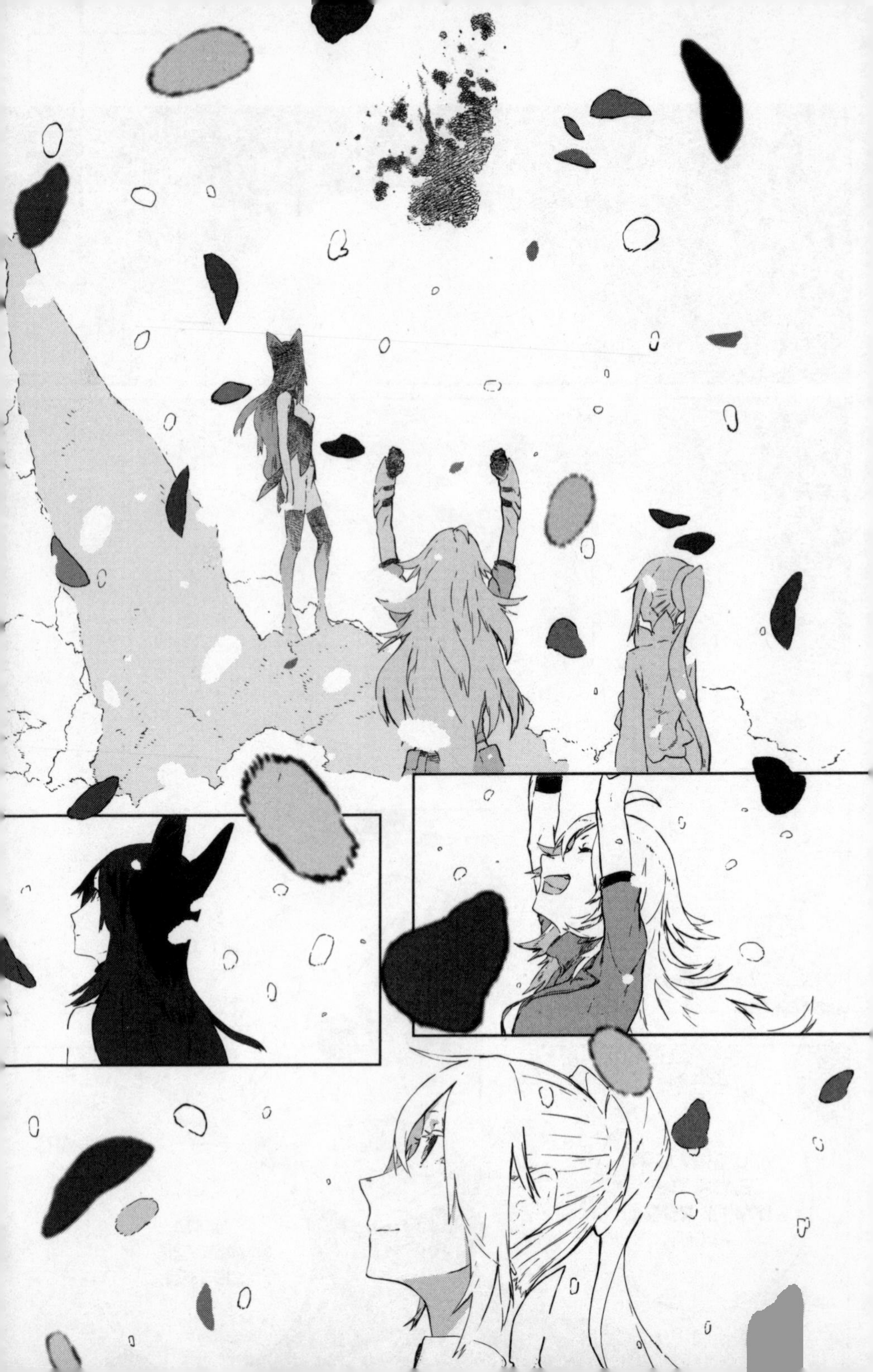

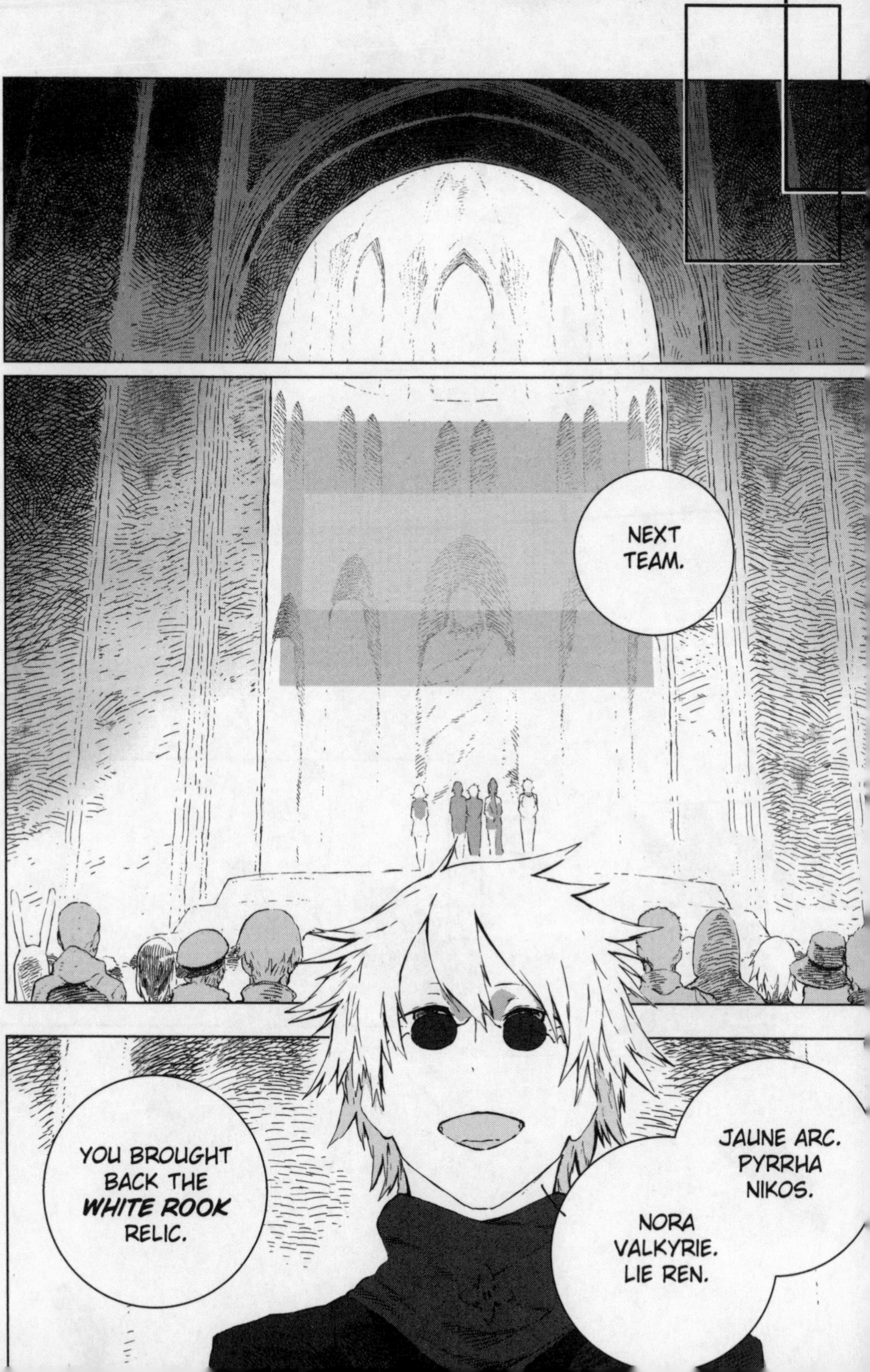
NEXT TEAM.
JAUNE ARC. PYRRHA NIKOS.
NORA VALKYRIE. LIE REN.
YOU BROUGHT BACK THE *WHITE ROOK* RELIC.

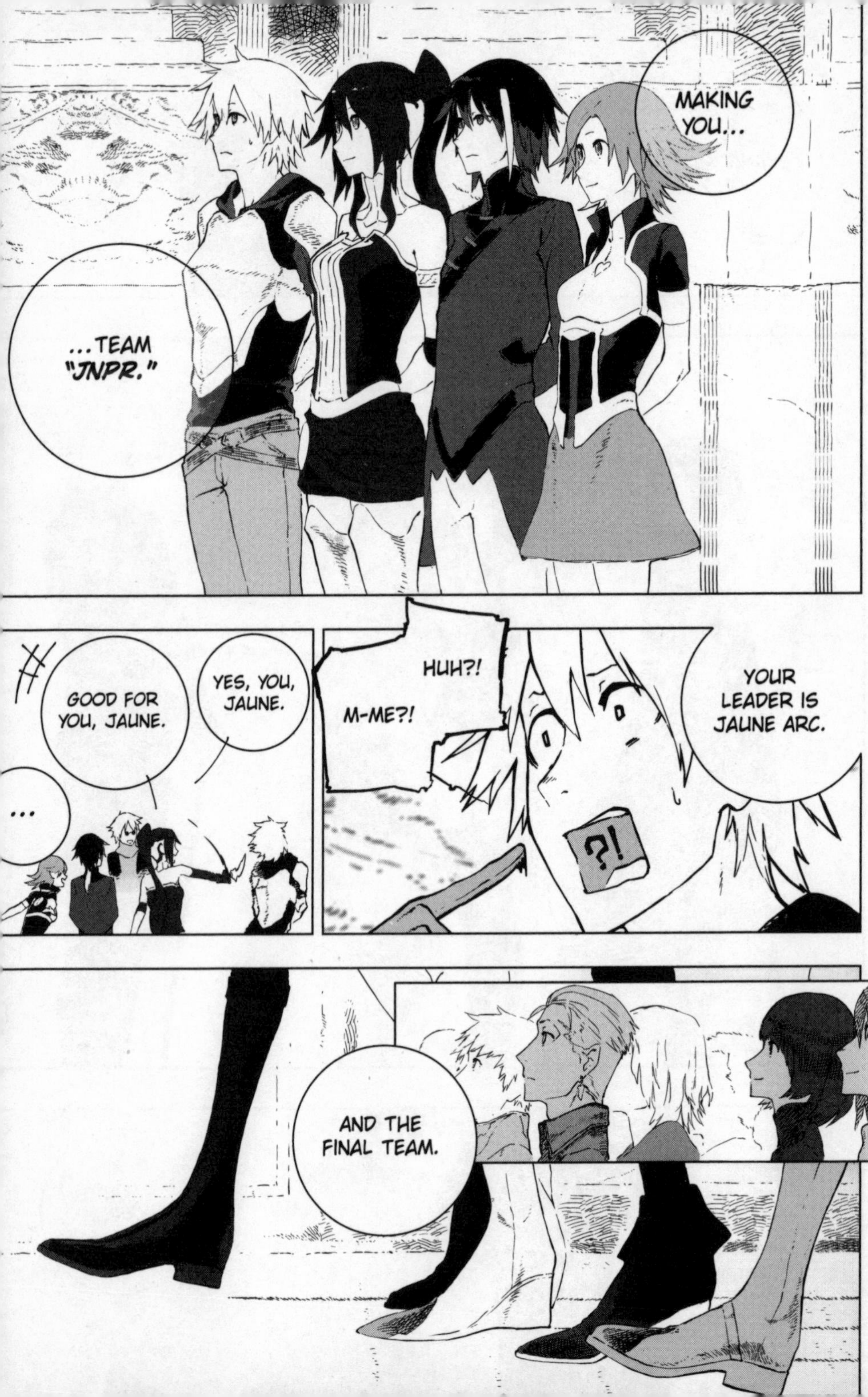
MAKING YOU...
...TEAM "JNPR."
YOUR LEADER IS JAUNE ARC.
HUH?!
M-ME?!
?!
YES, YOU, JAUNE.
GOOD FOR YOU, JAUNE.
...
AND THE FINAL TEAM.

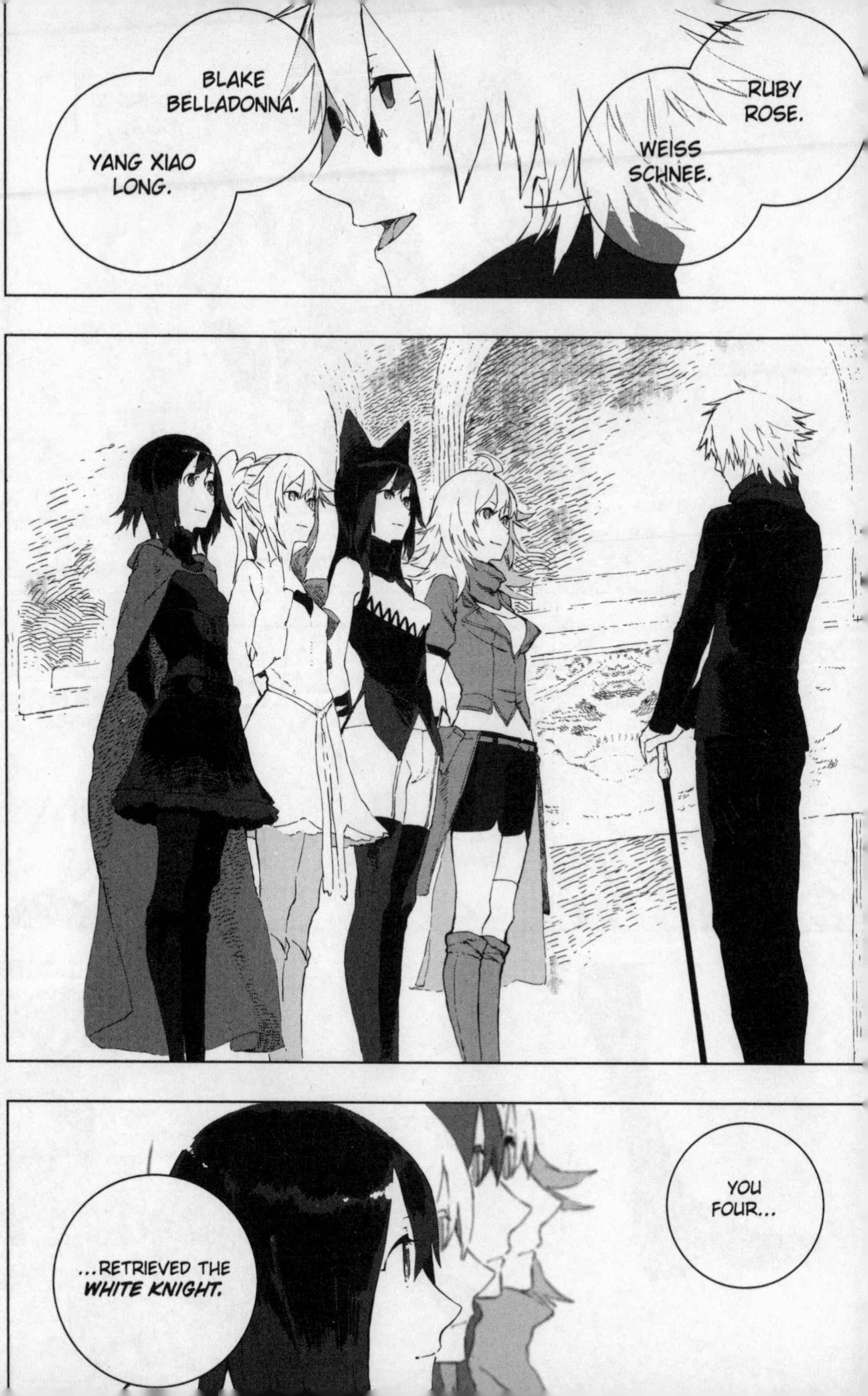
RUBY ROSE.
WEISS SCHNEE.
BLAKE BELLADONNA.
YANG XIAO LONG.
YOU FOUR...
...RETRIEVED THE *WHITE KNIGHT.*

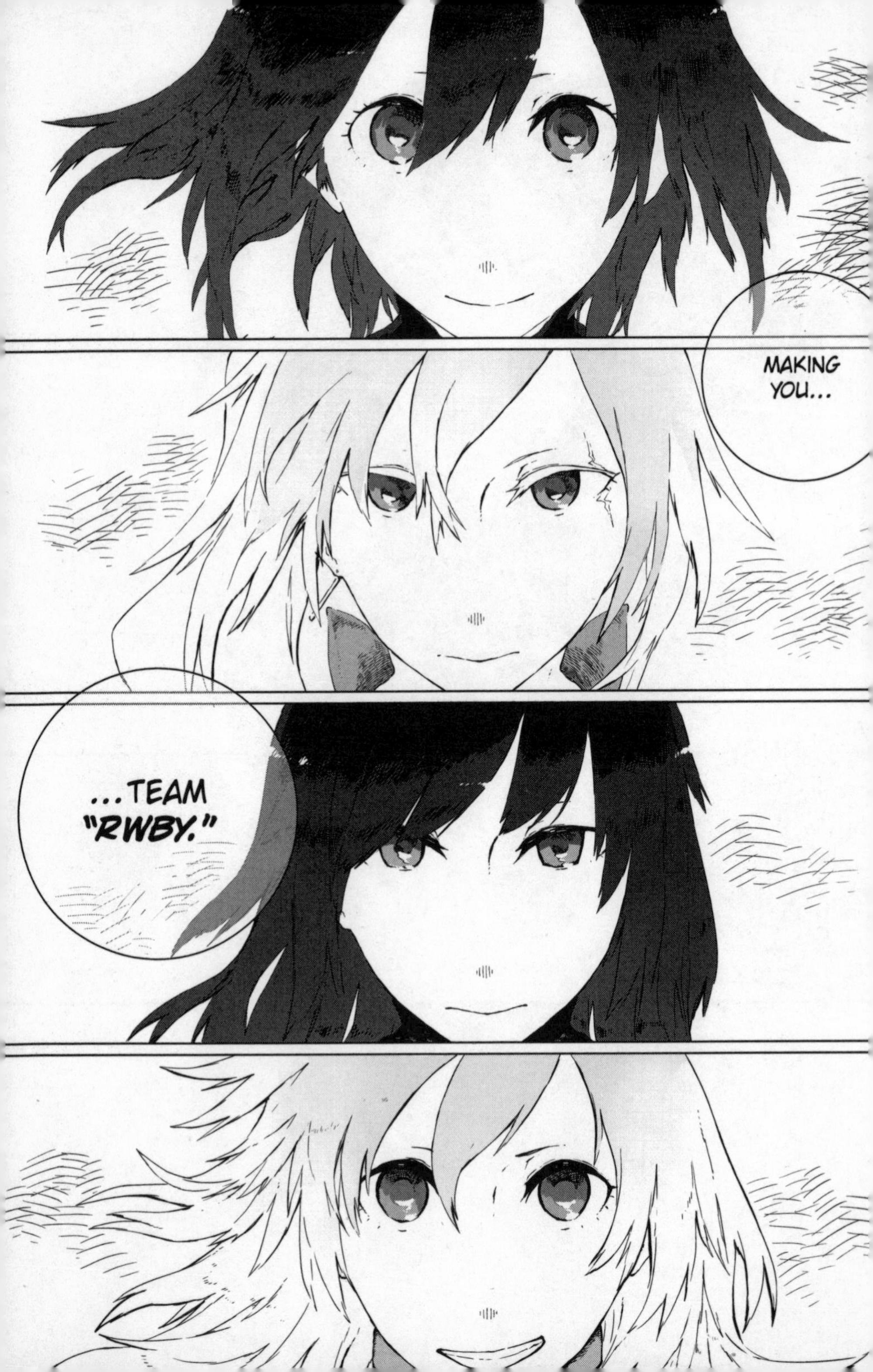
MAKING YOU...
...TEAM "RWBY."

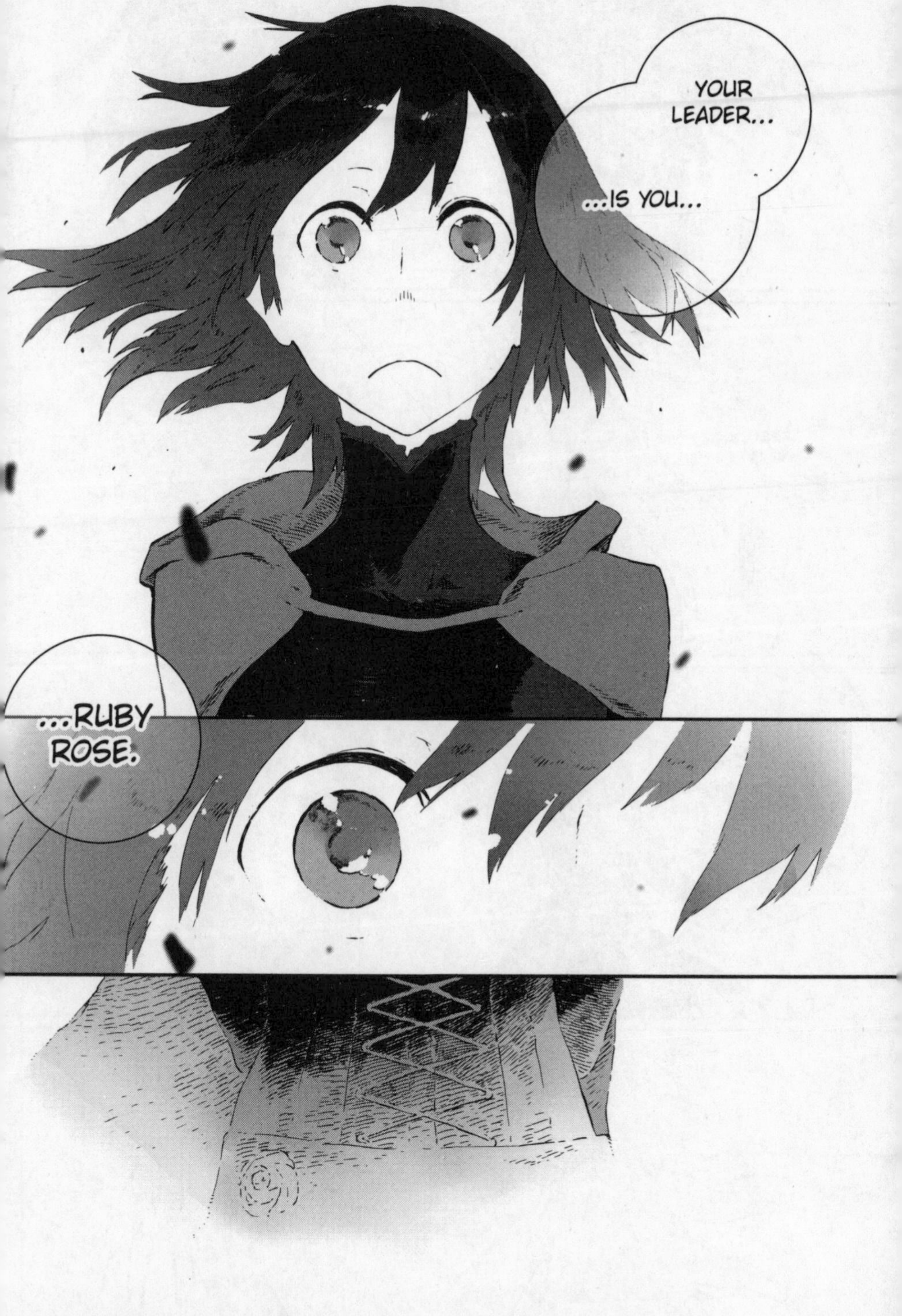
YOUR LEADER...
...IS YOU...
...RUBY ROSE.

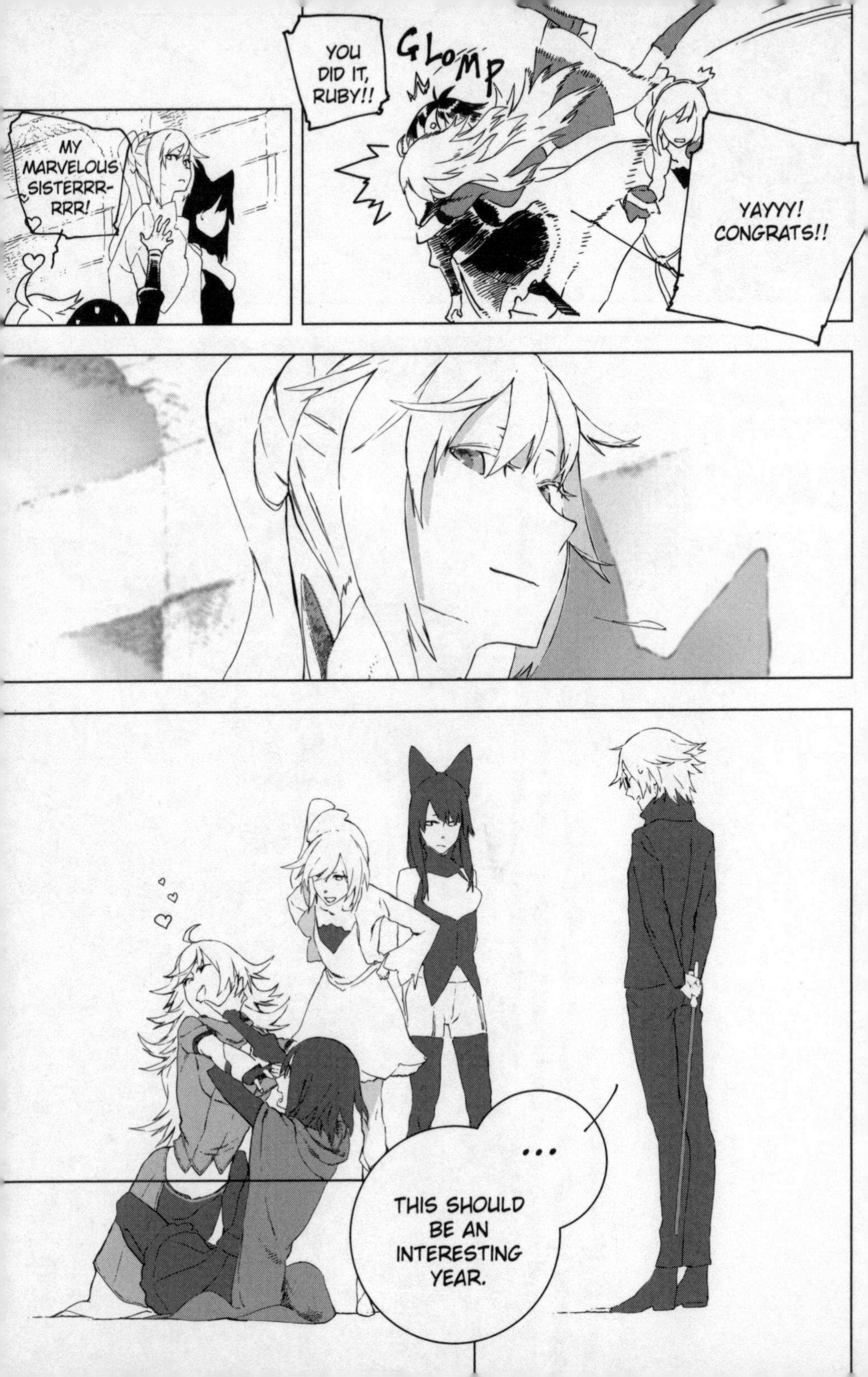
YOU DID IT, RUBY!!
GLOMP
YAYYY! CONGRATS!!
MY MARVELOUS SISTERRRR-RRR!
...
THIS SHOULD BE AN INTERESTING YEAR.

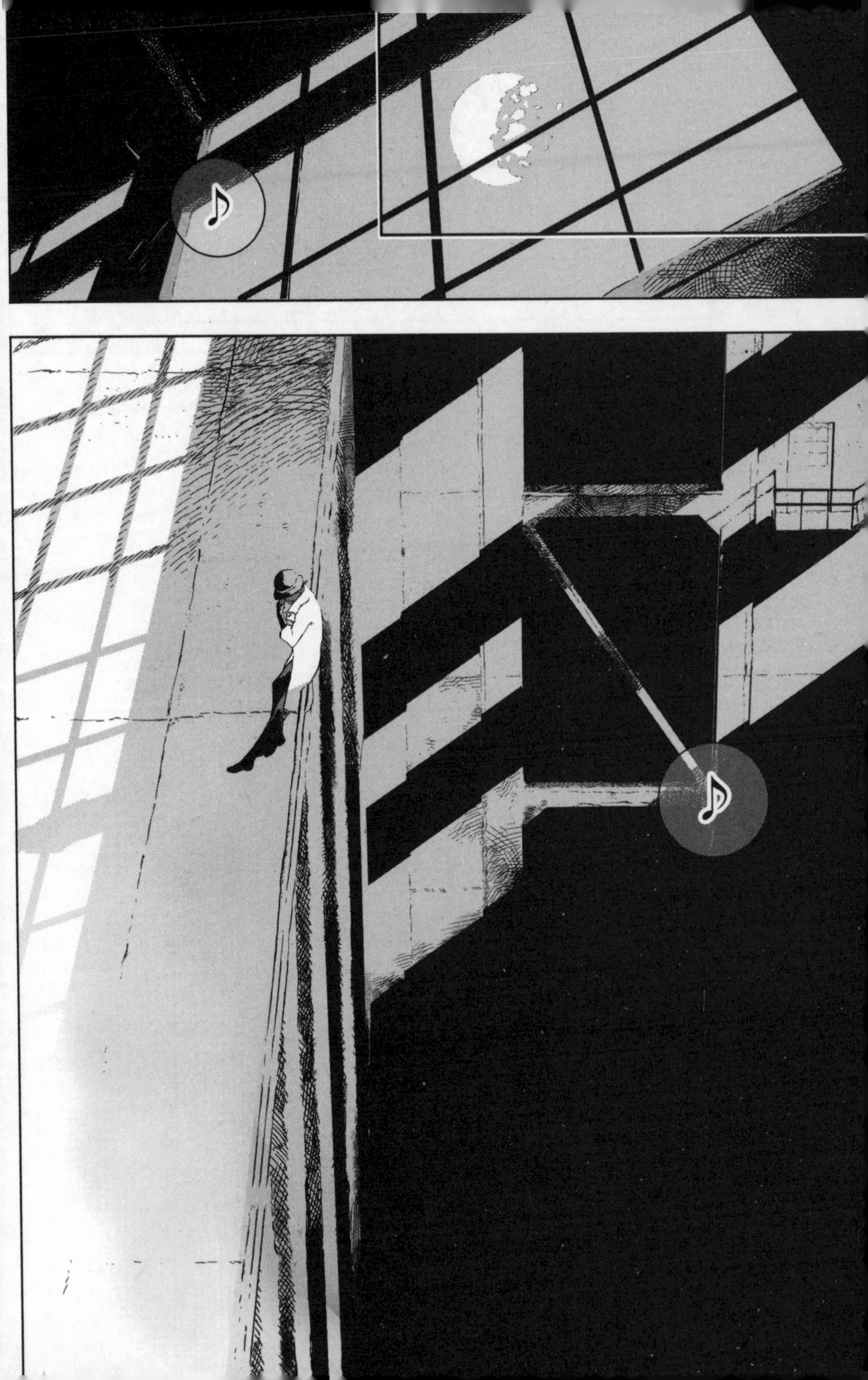

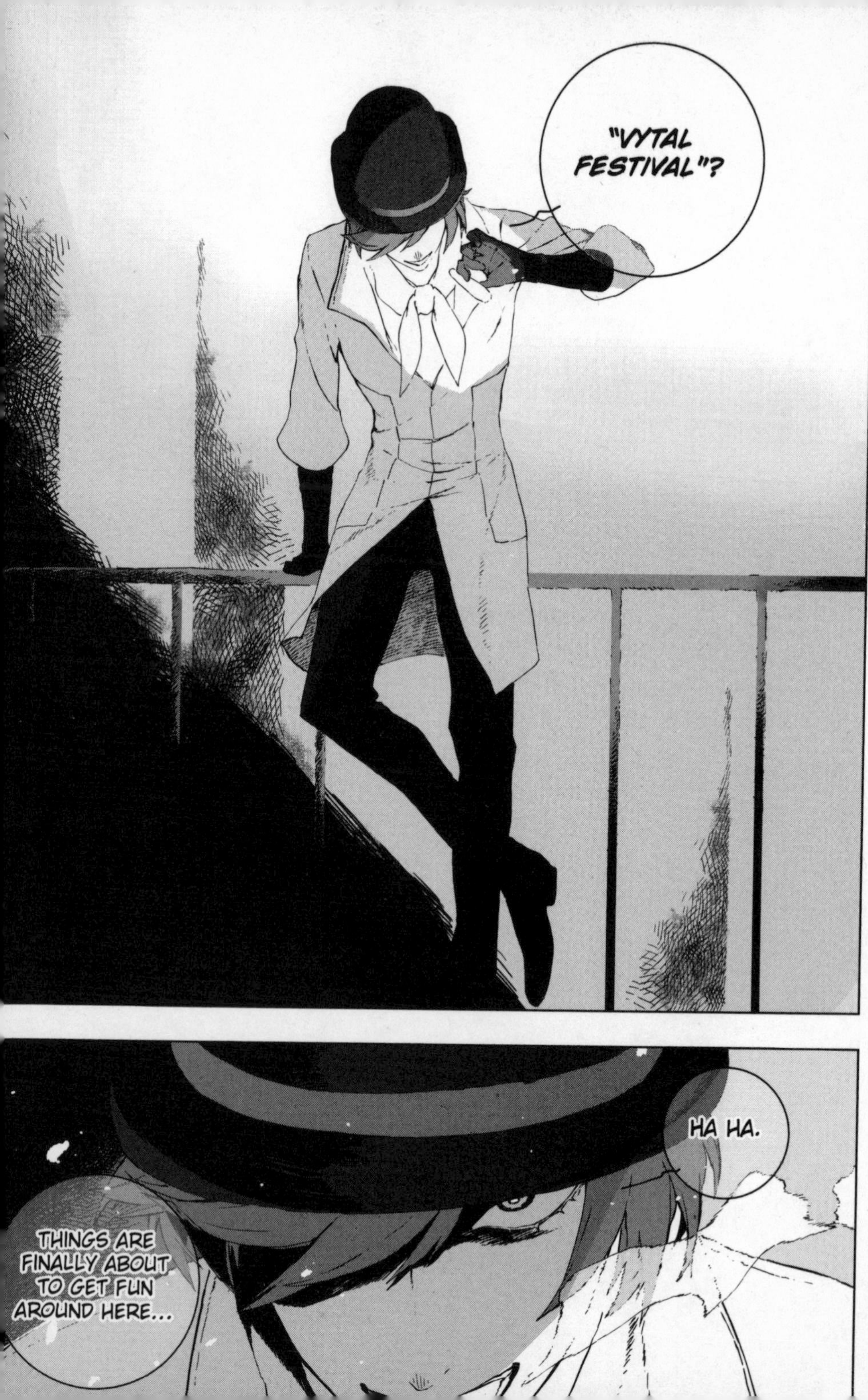
"VYTAL FESTIVAL"?
HA HA.
THINGS ARE FINALLY ABOUT TO GET FUN AROUND HERE...

BUNTA KINAMI was born in Ibaraki Prefecture in Japan, and started drawing manga after he noticed that his friends enjoyed drawing. His favorite series include *Dogs: Bullets & Carnage* by Shirow Miwa and *Nausicaä of the Valley of the Wind* by Hayao Miyazaki. He began his professional career with *RWBY: The Official Manga*.

RWBY THE OFFICIAL MANGA

VOLUME 1
VIZ SIGNATURE EDITION

STORY AND ART BY
BUNTA KINAMI

ORIGINAL STORY BY
MONTY OUM & ROOSTER TEETH PRODUCTIONS

TRANSLATION **Caleb Cook**
LETTERING **Evan Waldinger**
DESIGN **Shawn Carrico**
EDITOR **David Brothers**

First published in Japan in 2018 by SHUEISHA Inc., Tokyo.
English translation rights arranged by SHUEISHA Inc.

Printed in the U.S.A.

Published by VIZ Media, LLC
P.O. Box 77010
San Francisco, CA 94107

10 9 8 7 6 5 4 3 2 1
First Printing, July 2020

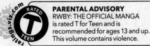

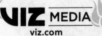

VIZ MEDIA
viz.com

VIZ SIGNATURE
vizsignature.com

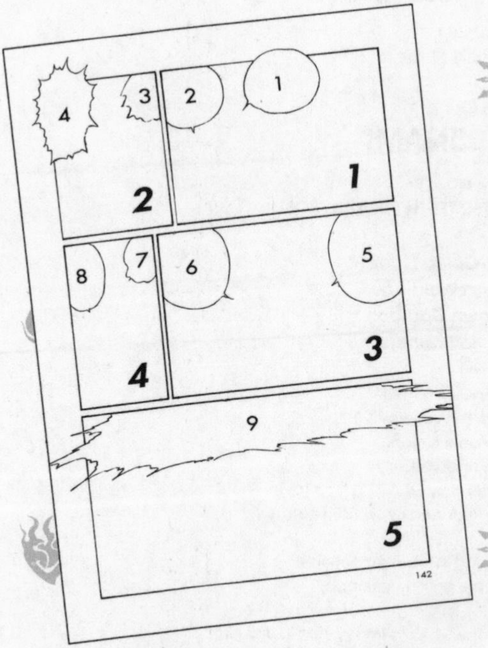

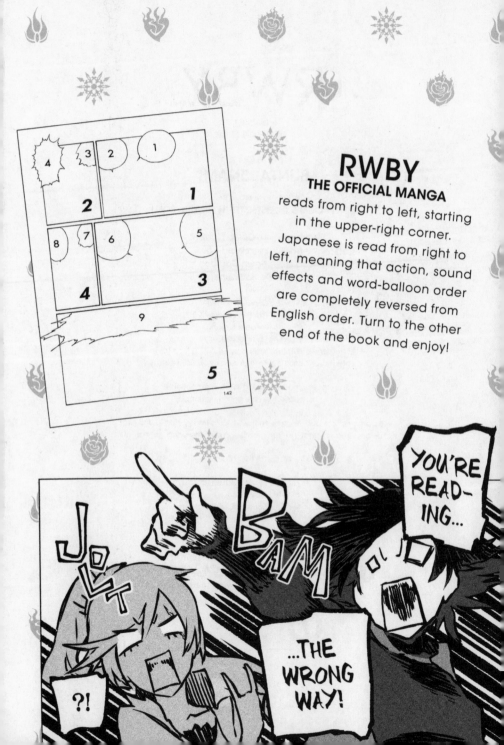

RWBY
THE OFFICIAL MANGA

reads from right to left, starting in the upper-right corner. Japanese is read from right to left, meaning that action, sound effects and word-balloon order are completely reversed from English order. Turn to the other end of the book and enjoy!

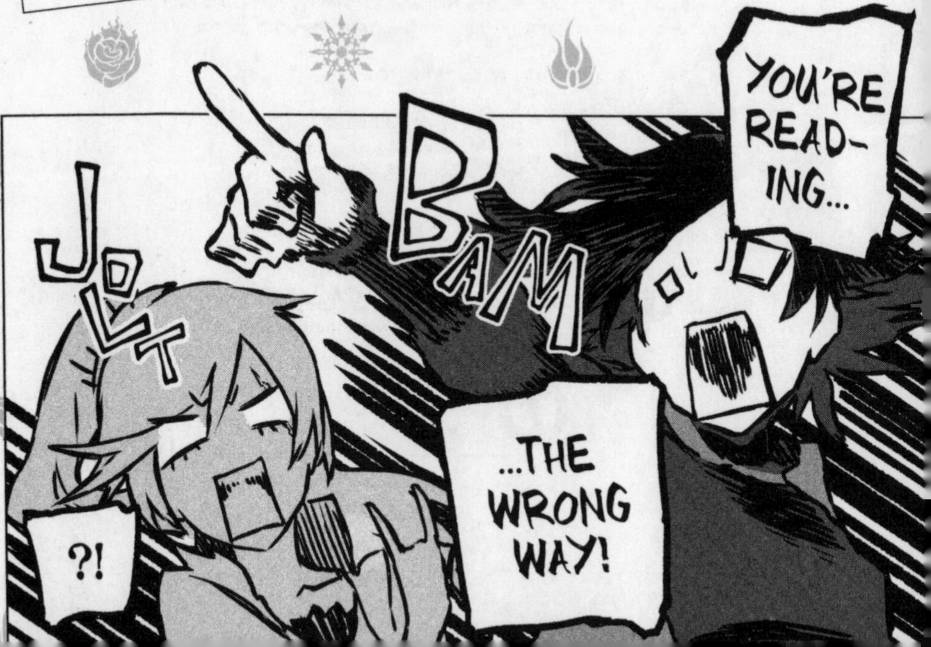
YOU'RE READING...
BAM
JOLT
...THE WRONG WAY!
?!